The Historical Books

The Biblical Seminar
40

The HISTORICAL BOOKS

edited by
J. Cheryl Exum

Sheffield
Academic Press

Copyright © 1997 Sheffield Academic Press

Published by
Sheffield Academic Press Ltd
Mansion House
19 Kingfield Road
Sheffield S11 9AS
England

Typeset by Sheffield Academic Press
and
Printed on acid-free paper in Great Britain
by Cromwell Press
Melksham, Wiltshire

British Library Cataloguing in Publication Data

A catalogue record for this book is available
from the British Library

ISBN 1-85075-786-0

CONTENTS

CHRONICLES, EZRA, NEHEMIAH

Contents

This Reader on *The Historical Books* belongs to a Series that aims to collect some of the best articles published on the books of the Hebrew Bible in the first seventy issues of the *Journal for the Study of the Old Testament* (1976–1996). Founded in 1976, with ten issues published between 1976 and 1978, *JSOT* has been published quarterly from 1979 to the present. *JSOT* has been especially influential within the discipline of biblical studies by publishing, from its earliest issues, avant-garde literary studies and articles employing the newer sociological and anthropological methods, both areas of investigation that have now become firmly established in the field. Complemented since its inaugural year by an important supplement series (Journal for the Study of the Old Testament Supplement Series), *JSOT* has become one of the leading publications in the field of biblical studies, and it continues to offer a forum for innovative and experimental scholarship, as well as for more traditionally oriented historical-critical studies.

The so-called historical books embrace a vast amount of biblical material, from Joshua to Nehemiah (following the order of the English Bible, which includes Ruth). This is a rather more diverse body of material than the Pentateuch, for example, or the Poetical Books. To select material for a single volume from the considerable number of excellent articles on the historical books published in the pages of *JSOT* was therefore a particularly difficult task. Selection was guided by various criteria. In the first instance, I was looking for breadth of coverage within each of the three divisions of this Reader: (1) Joshua, Judges, Ruth; (2) Samuel, Kings; and (3) Chronicles, Ezra, Nehemiah. Several outstanding articles dealing with specific passages or isolated topics were therefore passed over in favor of articles whose focus was at least a major segment of the book in question, if not the whole book, or investigations of a topic with larger implications for interpretation. The most comprehensive overview appears in the section dealing with Chronicles, Ezra, Nehemiah. If it is possible to extrapolate scholarly trends on the basis of publications in *JSOT*, then scholars have tended to treat the books of Chronicles, Ezra, and Nehemiah in their entirety, whereas the other books, except Ruth, are treated in a more fragmentary way. (Ruth was a special case: although a number of fine articles on Ruth have been published in *JSOT*, in the interest of space only one has been reprinted here.) The under-representation of 2 Kings in this collection reflects its under-representation in any extended way in *JSOT*.

Articles for this Reader were also selected to illustrate a range of methodological approaches, reflecting the variety of articles in *JSOT*. Literary and social-scientific investigations are represented, both in isolation and in dialogue with each other, along with overviews of scholarship and critical assessments of the state of the discipline. All the articles reprinted in this Reader were selected for their important contributions to the ongoing interpretation of the historical books. Many of the earlier articles reprinted here represent the cutting edge of scholarship for the time in which they were first published. They were selected not simply in view of their initial critical importance but because their insights are still important and because they illustrate emerging trends in the field.

It is hoped that the variety of both methodological approaches and critical issues brought together in this one volume will enable the reader to gain a sense of the kinds of critical questions currently being addressed to this extensive body of biblical material. The breadth of its scope combined with the depth of scholarship in the individual essays should make this Reader a useful resource as a supplementary text in undergraduate and graduate courses either on the historical books in general or on any of the three divisions represented here. For students embarking on intensive study of one or more of the historical books, and for researchers in the field interested in gaining an overview of developments outside their specialist areas, the Reader, both for the scholarly discussions it contains and for the further references to the scholarly literature in the footnotes and bibliographies, offers a valuable entry point into the current debate revolving around what have come to be known as the historical books.

J. Cheryl Exum
University of Sheffield

ABBREVIATIONS

AB	Anchor Bible
AnBib	Analecta biblica
AOAT	Alter Orient und Altes Testament
ATD	Das Alte Testament Deutsch
BA	*Biblical Archaeologist*
BASOR	*Bulletin of the American Schools of Oriental Research*
BHS	*Biblia hebraica stuttgartensia*
Bib	*Biblica*
BJS	Brown Judaic Studies
BKAT	Biblischer Kommentar: Altes Testament
BWANT	Beiträge zur Wissenschaft vom Alten und Neuen Testament
BZAW	Beihefte zur *ZAW*
CBQ	*Catholic Biblical Quarterly*
CBQMS	*Catholic Biblical Quarterly*, Monograph Series
CJT	*Canadian Journal of Theology*
ConBOT	Coniectanea biblica, Old Testament
EncJud	*Encyclopaedia Judaica*
EvT	*Evangelische Theologie*
FOTL	The Forms of the Old Testament Literature
FRLANT	Forschungen zur Religion und Literatur des Alten und Neuen Testaments
HAR	*Hebrew Annual Review*
HAT	Handbuch zum Alten Testament
HSM	Harvard Semitic Monographs
IB	*Interpreter's Bible*
IDBSup	*IDB*, Supplementary Volume
IEJ	*Israel Exploration Journal*
Int	*Interpretation*
JAAR	*Journal of the American Academy of Religion*
JBL	*Journal of Biblical Literature*
JAOS	*Journal of the American Oriental Society*
JNES	*Journal of Near Eastern Studies*
JSOT	*Journal for the Study of the Old Testament*
JSOTSup	*Journal for the Study of the Old Testament*, Supplement Series
JSS	*Journal of Semitic Studies*
JTS	*Journal of Theological Studies*
KAT	Kommentar zum Alten Testament
MVAG	Mitteilungen der Vorderasiatisch-ägyptischen Gesellschaft
NCB	New Century Bible

NICOT	New International Commentary on the Old Testament
OBT	Overtures to Biblical Theology
OTG	Old Testament Guides
OTL	Old Testament Library
OTS	*Oudtestamentische Studiën*
PEQ	*Palestine Exploration Quarterly*
PJ	*Palästina-Jahrbuch*
PMLA	Proceedings of the Modern Language Association
RB	*Revue biblique*
RTP	*Revue de théologie et de philosophie*
RTR	*Reformed Theological Review*
SBLDS	SBL Dissertation Series
SBLMS	SBL Monograph Series
SBT	Studies in Biblical Theology
SJOT	*Scandinavian Journal of the Old Testament*
SPB	Studia postbiblica
ST	*Studia theologica*
TDOT	G.J. Botterweck and H. Ringgren (eds.), *Theological Dictionary of the Old Testament*
ThWAT	G.J. Botterweck and H. Ringgren (eds.), *Theologisches Wörterbuch zum Alten Testament*
TLZ	*Theologische Literaturzeitung*
TRu	*Theologische Rundschau*
TTZ	*Trierer theologische Zeitschrift*
TynBul	*Tyndale Bulletin*
VT	*Vetus Testamentum*
VTSup	*Vetus Testamentum*, Supplements
WBC	Word Biblical Commentary
WMANT	Wissenschaftliche Monographien zum Alten und Neuen Testament
ZAW	*Zeitschrift für die alttestamentliche Wissenschaft*
ZDPV	*Zeitschrift des deutschen Palästina-Vereins*

LIST OF CONTRIBUTORS

Jon L. Berquist, Lawrenceburg, KY, USA

George W. Coats, Lexington, KY, USA

Richard Coggins, Lymington, UK

W.J. Dumbrell, New South Wales, Australia

Tamara C. Eskenazi, Los Angeles, CA, USA

Lyle Eslinger, Calgary, Alberta, Canada

James W. Flanagan, Cleveland, OH, USA

Sara Japhet, Jerusalem, Israel

Hans J.L. Jensen, Aarhus, Denmark

David Kraemer, New York, NY, USA

Stuart Lasine, Wichita, KS, USA

Donald Murray, Exeter, UK

K.I. Parker, St John's, Newfoundland, Canada

Leo G. Perdue, Fort Worth, TX, USA

Thomas R. Preston, Laramie, WY, USA

Hugh S. Pyper, Leeds, UK

Lori Rowlett, Newport News, VA, USA

Frank Anthony Spina, Seattle, WA, USA

Kenneth D. Tollefson, Seattle, WA, USA

Keith W. Whitelam, Stirling, UK

H.G.M. Williamson, Oxford, UK

JOSHUA, JUDGES, RUTH

JSOT 63 (1994), pp. 57-87

THE IDENTITY OF EARLY ISRAEL:
THE REALIGNMENT AND TRANSFORMATION
OF LATE BRONZE–IRON AGE PALESTINE*

Keith W. Whitelam

Introduction

The publication of research on the emergence of early Israel in Palestine, which reached a climax in the latter half of the 1980s, seems to have subsided into a new phase of assessment, critique and reformulation. The appearance of monographs by Halpern (1983), Lemche (1985), Ahlström (1986), Coote and Whitelam (1987), and Finkelstein (1988) marked the culmination of a period of intensive study arising out of growing dissatisfaction with the ability of the three major models of Israel's origins to cope with the increasing archaeological information or the growing impact of new literary studies on the Hebrew Bible. Trenchant criticisms of some of these views have been raised by Miller (1991a), Bimson (1989; 1991), M. and H. Weippert (1991), and Thompson (1992b), for example, which provoke important questions requiring further discussion and clarification. Coote (1990: viii), by contrast, goes so far as to say that 'recent research on early Israel has brought us to a new understanding', which he terms 'a new horizon', signalling a growing set of shared assumptions despite continuing important differences.[1] Just as we

---

* This paper contains some material or ideas that were originally presented in a joint paper with Robert Coote at the SBL/ASOR symposium in Boston, December 1987. I am grateful to Robert Coote for allowing me to include this material here and for his helpful criticisms of an earlier draft of this paper. I remain responsible for the final views expressed here.

1. There are, of course, numerous other specialist works that need to be taken into account in any review of current understandings. H. and M. Weippert (1991) provide an excellent and careful review of literature on the subject. Coote (1990) has

find recurrent patterns in the study of long-term trends in history, so we can trace interesting recurrent patterns in the history of scholarship. The present attempts at critique, reformulation, and synthesis at the beginning of the 1990s, following an intense period of research and publication in the 1980s, are not unlike the 1930s when the classic formulations of the infiltration and conquest models were produced by Alt and Albright, to be followed from the 1940s onwards by critique and debate.[2] The present essay is an attempt to explore some of the implications of questions raised by the recent debate on the emergence of early Israel for our understanding of ancient Palestine at the beginning of the early Iron Age and the broader issue of a Palestinian regional history.

It is now generally recognized that the convergence of so-called sociological approaches to the study of Israelite history and literary approaches to the study of the Hebrew Bible has resulted in a major paradigm shift in biblical studies.[3] However, this paradigm shift has largely been understood in terms of its implications for the study of the Hebrew Bible. It is now becoming clearer that such a shift has very profound implications for historical studies. There is now a recognition by a growing number of scholars of the emergence of Palestinian history as a subject in its own right. The study of the history of Israel and in particular the so-called emergence of Israel is a part of this larger regional history. Thompson

a very good up-to-date bibliography. He also summarizes the implications of recent research by stressing the areas of agreement rather than difference, thereby identifying what he calls a 'new horizon' in a synthesis of the most recent scholarship of the last decade or so. The various essays in *SJOT* 2 (1991), which were presented at the SBL/ASOR symposium in New Orleans, November 1990, also highlight areas of convergence as well as very significant differences and unanswered questions. See Thompson 1992b for a comprehensive review of scholarship which is particularly critical of the so-called 'sociological approach'. I provide a response (Whitelam 1995) to some of Thompson's representations and criticisms of this approach.

2.   It will be interesting to see if the trend is continued. The dynamism of the 1930s subsided into an impasse between the two competing models which was only broken by Mendenhall's innovative proposal (1962) and Gottwald's (1979) subsequent formulation of the revolt hypothesis. These in turn, of course, have become the subject of intense debate. It remains to be seen how far the new promise of a regional history of Palestine and its implications for understanding Israelite history will be fulfilled.

3.   Davies (1992) provides the most recent assessment of this paradigm shift and tries to draw out its implications for our understanding of the Hebrew Bible and the society that produced it. See also, now, Whitelam (1996).

(1992a: 2) talks in terms of a 'new historiographical paradigm'[4] and certainly the shift towards Palestinian history has been signalled most clearly by the recent publications of H. Weippert (1988), T.L. Thompson (1992b), and G.W. Ahlström (1993). Thompson (1992b: 107) sees a new and promising direction emerging from the studies of the mid-1980s away from biblical and archaeological syntheses towards what he terms an 'independent' history of Israel.[5] His study is a sustained argument for the development of a 'history of "Israel" within the context of a comprehensive regional and historical geography of *Palestine*' (Thompson 1992b: 401). It is the various successes, confusions and failures in the discussions of the mid to late 1980s of the 'emergence of Israel' that have led to a clearer conception of the need for the definition of a history of Palestine.

It is one of the ironies of scholarship that the works of Ahlström, Lemche, and Coote and Whitelam, in particular, which appeal so strongly to the interpretation of archaeological evidence in their reconstructions of the emergence of early Israel in Palestine, were all published before the appearance of Finkelstein's important work. The translation and publication of Finkelstein's monograph mark a significant point in the discussion, since it provides a quantity and quality of archaeological data on early Iron Age Palestine not available since the work of Albright and others in the 1930s. The promise of further publications of survey and site data will ensure that the debate will continue for some time. However, the paradoxical result of recent investigations, and particularly the accumulating archaeological data, appear to lead us even further from an understanding of the nature and organization of early Israel at the beginning of the early Iron Age. This expansion of archaeological data, ironically, just as it undermined Albright's conquest model, has led to many more questions than it has solved.

4. Thompson (1992a: 2-3) sees a strong connection with Chicago and Tübingen. However, it might be argued that the paradigm shift is inspired more by the crisis of the European nation-state and is associated particularly with European scholarship or scholars who have close connections with Europe.

5. Thompson's use of the term 'independent' is meant to signify a history of Israel independent of later biblical historiography, which he dates to the Persian and Hellenistic periods. The problem of an archaeologically-based history of Israel as distinct from a history of Palestine will be addressed below. Ahlström 1993 is an important work in terms of its conceptualization of a regional history of Palestine. Unfortunately, it was completed in 1986 and therefore does not include a detailed discussion of more recent developments.

It is testimony to the tenacity of particular ideas that they have managed to survive in a period in which so many of the basic assumptions that have underpinned biblical scholarship for much of this century have been brought into question or abandoned. Although there has been increasing acceptance in recent years that the emergence of early Israel in Palestine was largely the result of indigenous responses to significant external stimuli, as evidenced in the recent monographs, it remains a domain assumption within biblical studies that Israel in the pre-monarchic period was a unified tribal society. Yet how Israel is to be identified in the archaeological record of the Late Bronze–Iron Age transition or how it might have been organized are moot points. The implications of recent work on tribal organization seem to have had little effect on assumptions prevalent in biblical studies that derive from the work of Noth and others in the 1930s. Although the amphictyonic hypothesis was dramatically overturned two decades or more ago, there remains an underlying assumption of much research that Israel was organized as some form of supratribal *confederation* in the pre-monarchic period which was also an ethnic and religious unity.

Much of the current debate has focused upon the difficulties of differentiating Israelite material culture within the Late Bronze–Early Iron Age remains in Palestine. Even among those who argue that such a distinction is not possible on the basis of the archaeological evidence, the terms 'Israel' or 'Israelite' have been retained in their reconstructions of the period. Clearly a basic assumption of virtually all recent scholarship has been that the proliferation of highland villages during the early Iron Age is to be identified with 'Israel'. Thompson (1992b) has traced the development of this assumption from Alt and Albright through recent scholarship, illustrating how it has influenced almost all subsequent interpretations of the evidence. Equally as pervasive has been the notion that this entity was 'tribal'. Yet the most pressing question remains: How can we identify Israel and its organization? The usual appeal is to two important bodies of information: recent archaeological and survey data alongside the Merneptah stela, in conjunction with the biblical traditions. Although the increase in archaeological data has had a dramatic effect upon the discussion, it is questionable if the far-reaching consequences of this information have been fully recognized or admitted.

The Identity of Israel and Recent Archaeology

The publication of Finkelstein's monograph represents, to use his own words, 'a veritable revolution' in research (1988: 20). It is important to consider the implications of his publication of archaeological data, since it provides a body of data that will be at the centre of a continuing debate on the emergence of Israel for some time to come. This work, along with his numerous important reports in archaeological journals, is a model of clarity in the presentation of vital archaeological data, particularly from the Land of Israel Survey and his own important excavations, which will be the starting point for historians for the foreseeable future. One of the most noticeable trends in recent research, especially by some biblical specialists, has been the questioning of the reliability of the biblical narratives as sources for the history of early Israel in the pre-monarchic period and an appeal to archaeological evidence for an understanding of this period. Yet once again this debate and Finkelstein's interpretation of the data have demonstrated how difficult it is to free the debate from the constraints imposed by the Hebrew Bible.

Finkelstein's interpretation of the archaeological data and his overall reconstruction of what he terms 'Israelite Settlement' is heavily coloured by the picture presented in the Hebrew Bible. His working methodology (1988: 22), briefly set out in the opening chapter, is presented as being primarily concerned with archaeology and settlement, which

> will hardly touch upon the biblical evidence at all (except for site identifications etc.). Without in any way minimizing the singular importance of the Bible for the study of the history of Israel, attempts to reconstruct the process of Israelite Settlement by means of traditional biblical archaeology—by seeking direct correspondences between excavated finds and the biblical text—have been notoriously unsuccessful.

This would appear to be in line with the methodologies professed by Ahlström, Lemche, and Coote and Whitelam, among others. Finkelstein (1988: 22; see also 1991: 56) understands what he terms 'the primary biblical source', the book of Joshua, as being redacted centuries later and as reflecting the understanding of Israelite Settlement at the end of the period of the monarchy. Thus he too advocates trying to reconstruct the process on the basis of new archaeological research, after which it will be possible to return to the question of the implications of archaeological research for understanding the biblical narratives.

However, this strategy of investigating the archaeological evidence independently of the biblical text is not carried through in his attempt to identify 'Israel' and what constituted 'Israelite identity'. Finkelstein (1988: 27) believes that 'the formation of Israelite identity was a long, intricate and complex process which, in our opinion, was completed only at the beginning of the monarchy'. Yet, the presentation and interpretation of archaeological evidence is prefaced by a controlling assumption about Israelite identity which rests upon his understanding of biblical texts. He goes on to say (1988: 27),

> An important intermediate phase of this crystallization is connected with the establishment of supratribal sacral centers during the period of the Judges. The most important of these centers was the one at Shiloh, whose special role at the time is elucidated in 1 Samuel—*a historical work, as all agree...* (emphasis added).

The designation 'the period of the Judges' is, of course, derived from the categories and chronology of the Hebrew Bible rather than archaeological periodizations. Equally striking is his assumption that Shiloh was one of the 'supratribal sacral centers'.[6] This claim clearly embodies an explicit assumption that 'Israel' was some form of tribal organization and religious unity. It hardly needs to be pointed out that it is by no means the case that all agree on the categorization of 1 Samuel as a historical work reflecting the social reality of pre-monarchic and early monarchic Israel, as the proliferation of literary studies makes abundantly clear. Miller (1991a: 97-99) similarly draws attention to Finkelstein's use of biblical traditions such as the so-called Ark Narrative (1 Sam. 4–6; 2 Sam. 6) for controlling the interpretation of archaeological data (see also Dever 1991: 79).

The difficulties of trying to identify and define 'Israel' during the Iron I period are highlighted by Finkelstein's discussion. He admits (1988: 27)

---

6. The archaeological evidence presented in his preliminary report of the excavations at Shiloh (1988: 205-34) hardly supports such a claim. He describes (1988: 234) the terraced structures in area C as 'no ordinary houses', representing the only public buildings ever discovered at an 'Israelite' settlement site, 'which hint at the physical character of the sanctuary itself' (cf. also 1985: 168-70). This is rejected by Dever (1991: 82) as 'nothing but wishful thinking, hardly worthy of the hard-headed realism Finkelstein exhibits elsewhere'. Even if it were possible to interpret the archaeological data as evidence for some cultic installation at Shiloh, it goes far beyond the evidence to suggest that this was a 'supratribal sacral centre'.

that it is difficult because, he believes, distinctions between ethnic groups at that time were 'apparently still vague'. He goes on to say that it is doubtful whether a twelfth-century BCE inhabitant of Giloh would have described herself or himself as an 'Israelite'. However, despite these reservations, he is still prepared to refer to this site and its material culture with precisely this ethnic label on the justification that

> an Israelite during the Iron I period was anyone whose descendants—as early as the days of Shiloh (first half of the 11th century BCE) or as late as the beginning of the Monarchy—described themselves as Israelites (1988: 27).

This is a claim that can only be advanced on the basis of an acceptance of the essential historicity of the narratives in 1 Samuel, as Miller (1991a: 97-99) points out. In essence the term 'Israelite' is applied to anyone residing in what is thought to have been the territorial framework of the early monarchy, whether they considered themselves to be Israelite or not.

The weakness of this argument is highlighted by his own admission that Galilee poses a particular problem for this definition (1988: 28), especially since it was not part of the territorial jurisdiction of the early monarchy.[7] Furthermore, he illustrates (1988: 323-30) that Iron I settlement in the area was later than previously thought: settlement in Galilee belongs to a later or secondary phase rather than being part of the first phase of settlement as Aharoni believed. Even though it falls outside the territory of the monarchy, Finkelstein still insists, without giving precise reasons, that the population should be considered Israelite. He then offers a definition of 'Israelite' in the following terms:

> Israelites in the Iron I are those people who were in a process of sedentarization in those parts of the country that were part of Saul's monarchy, and in Galilee. The term 'Israelite' is used therefore in this book, when discussing the Iron I period, as no more than a *terminus technicus* for 'hill country people in the process of settling down' (1988: 28).

Essentially the term 'Israelite' is nothing more than a designation for those individuals and groups settling in the hill country during the Iron I period. In fact, Finkelstein (1991: 53) has stated more recently that he

---

7.   Thompson (1992b: 159-60, 239-50) also criticizes Finkelstein's understanding of the Galilee as being 'Israelite' while excluding the Jezreel valley. He argues that Finkelstein's assertion that these settlements are 'Israelite' is based on his reading of later biblical traditions.

might be willing to omit the term 'Israelite' from the discussion of Iron I settlement and refer instead to 'hill country settlers' until the period of the monarchy. As many have argued and, I believe, Finkelstein's own presentation of his archaeological findings makes clear, it is not possible to attach ethnic labels to the various sites at the end of the Late Bronze Age and beginning of the early Iron Age. Thus Finkelstein's adoption of the more neutral term 'hill country settlers' is much more prudent. If we cannot attach precise ethnic labels, then the settlement shift should be discussed in broader regional terms of the settlement distribution of the Palestinian highlands and margins in comparison with lowland and coastal areas. The terms 'Israelite' and 'Canaanite' are misleading and carry too many implications which the evidence at present does not support.[8]

It is important to note that a key element of Finkelstein's interpretation of what he terms 'Israelite Settlement' throughout his monograph is the priority of the biblical text for historical reconstruction. Thus he states,

> The starting point of a discussion about the characteristics of Israelite Settlement sites is the historical biblical text (*the only source available*), which specifies the location of the Israelite population at the end of the period of the Judges and at the beginning of the Monarchy. Israelite cultural traits must therefore be deduced from the Iron I sites in the central hill country, especially the southern sector, *where the identity of the population is not disputed* (1988: 28, emphasis added).

The view set out by Finkelstein here begs a whole series of questions. It is clear that his understanding of particular biblical texts has priority in the interpretative strategy which then acts as a controlling factor in understanding the archaeological evidence. The location of 'Israelite' sites depends upon an acceptance of the historical reliability of certain biblical texts that pertain to the so-called 'period of the Judges' immediately prior to the inauguration of an Israelite monarchy. The difficulty of identifying the inhabitants of Iron I villages on the basis of known archaeological data has been overcome by an appeal to these texts

---

8.   See Lemche 1991 for a study of the term 'Canaanite' and a late dating of biblical texts that use this term. Thompson (1992b: 311) also recognizes that 'the sharp boundaries, which the use of the terms "Canaanite" and "Israelite" make possible, are wholly unwarranted and inapplicable'. M. and H. Weippert (1991: 382) remark that Finkelstein's catalogue of criteria for distinguishing Israelite sites 'fällt freilich wie ein Kartenhaus in sich zusammen' when the evidence from Jordan is taken into consideration.

which are recognized as having priority. Once again, however, it is far from the case that the identity of the population of the central hill country sites of this period is undisputed. Equally questionable is his contention (1988: 29) that 'it is clear, then, that the Iron I sites in the southern and central sectors of the hill country can be defined as "Israelite" even if at that time certain older or foreign elements were present...' The question raised is what does such a term as 'Israelite' designate, and how are groups identified by this term understood in relation to 'older' or 'foreign' elements? The implication seems to be that Israelites are somehow 'younger' but 'not foreign'. Sites should not be labelled as Israelite solely on the basis that they were located in an area that became part of later monarchic Israel.[9] As we shall see, one of the most puzzling elements in the discussion is the precise relationship between the entity termed 'Israel' in the Merneptah stela, the highland settlements of the early Iron Age, and the later formation of an Israelite state.

The whole focus of our discussion of this period changes once it is accepted that a term such as 'Israelite identity' is much too restrictive when applied to the highland settlements of the Late Bronze–Iron I transition.[10] The ambiguities and lacunae in our current evidence demand that a much broader term has to be used to designate the inhabitants of Iron I villages, as Finkelstein (1991: 53) has now recognized. Thompson (1992b: 160) makes a similar point in relation to Finkelstein's earlier use of the term 'Israelite' when he asks, 'Is he not rather and

---

9.   Recent studies have raised serious questions about reconstructions of the monarchy or its extent. In particular, Jamieson-Duke (1991) has produced a very stimulating study of scribes and schools in monarchic Judah which raises doubts, on the basis of archaeological evidence, of standard interpretations of the formation of an Israelite state. He finds (1991: 138-39) little evidence that Judah functioned as a state prior to the eighth-century increase in population, building, production, centralization and specialization. Even then it was only a relatively small state. Garbini (1988: 21-32) questions the historicity of the traditions about the early monarchy from a different perspective. Wightman (1990) provides an interesting critique of attempts to identify 'Solomonic' structures in the archaeological record on the basis of the biblical records. See Miller 1991b for a brief discussion of some of the methodological problems in attempts to assess the historical reliability of the biblical traditions for reconstructing the reign of Solomon; this is a response to the more positive approach of Millard (1991).

10.   As long argued by Ahlström (1993) and Thompson (1992b) and made explicit in their recent major studies.

perhaps better dealing with the archaeology of the early Iron Age settlements of central *Palestine*, leaving for others the question of Israel's origin?'[11] This means that any attempt to explain this settlement shift can no longer be concerned solely with trying to identify or explain the origins or emergence of Israel. Rather the historian needs to try to identify and account for the *processes* involved in the settlement shift that took place in Palestine at the end of the Late Bronze Age and the beginning of the early Iron Age. The focus of concern becomes the transformation and realignment of Palestinian settlement. The concern with Israel has been a distraction which has obscured an understanding of the complex processes at work during this period. The socio-economic setting of Iron I sites, which Finkelstein does much to illuminate and confirm, is of considerably more relevance for our understanding than supposed ethnic labels.

This distraction is evident in the other works on the emergence of Israel which appeared in the mid to late 1980s. It has become a commonplace, following the work of Alt and Albright, to identify Israel with the growth in early Iron Age rural sites in the highlands and steppes of Palestine.[12] However, one of the major points that Ahlström, Lemche, and Coote and Whitelam emphasize, again in line with many other recent

11. It is puzzling therefore that Thompson (1992b: 161) goes on to argue that Finkelstein's book 'establishes a firm foundation for all of us to begin building an accurate, detailed, and methodologically sound history of Israel'. Thompson (1992b: 162) acknowledges the problems of archaeology, not least the problem of ethnicity, but asserts that 'this book has demonstrated that we must and can use primary historical evidence in writing a history of Israel'. It is difficult to see how this can be achieved without being able to attach ethnic labels to the material culture. The essential value of the data presented in Finkelstein's book, I would have thought, is that it provides primary data for exploring settlement patterns and societal changes in Palestine during the Late Bronze–Iron Age transition. What part 'Israel' plays in this is hidden from our view. The history we are writing, as Thompson argues elsewhere in his study, is a broad regional history of Palestine rather than a history of Israel. In fact he later makes this very point (Thompson 1992b: 311):

> If the distinction between Canaanite and Israelite cannot be made when we speak of the variant cultural traditions of Iron I, have we really sufficient grounds for seeing this period as uniquely the period of emergent Israel? Is the question of Israel's origin a question about events of the Late Bronze–Iron I transition, or is that transition rather only one among many factors relating to the prehistory of people some of whose descendants later formed part of Israel?

12. Thompson (1992b) is particularly critical of this scholarly trend.

studies, is that it is no longer possible to distinguish an 'Israelite' material culture from an indigenous material culture in terms of the archaeological data. The implication of this is that the term 'Israelite' becomes unusable in the context of the discussion once it is accepted that the biblical traditions do not bear upon the problem. Even though Coote and Whitelam, for the most part, concentrated on trying to understand and account for the processes that led to this switch in settlement during the Late Bronze–Iron Age transition, the term 'Israel' was retained throughout the discussion despite reservations (1987: 179 n. 3):

> We do not assume that by referring to the early Iron Age highland settlement as 'Israel' that anything qualitative has been said about 'early Israel'. We focus our history of 'Israel' on this highland settlement because it is the clearest archaeological datum that precedes the eventual emergence of the kingdoms of Israel and Judah.[13]

The analysis has not been carried through radically enough by those who discount the evidence of the biblical traditions for this period on methodological grounds.[14] However, in the absence of convincing

13. It is now apparent that there is a considerable assumption in the last sentence about our knowledge of the Israelite monarchy, its extent, and organization. See n. 5 above. Of more significance, however, is the question of the relationship between the emergence of Israel and the settlement of the highlands. Coote (1991: 45) has pointed out quite clearly that these are not the same issue. 'How and why Israel emerged and how and why village settlement extended in the highland are two different questions.' He acknowledges that this was not stated clearly enough in Coote and Whitelam 1987.

14. Miller (1991a: 95) has made this point in his forceful criticism of what he sees as 'a methodological confusion' in recent studies:

> Any time historians, archaeologists, sociologists, or whoever speak of Israelite tribes in the central Palestinian hill country at the beginning of the Iron Age I, or about the Davidic–Solomonic monarchy, or about two contemporary kingdoms emerging from this early monarchy, they are presupposing information that comes from, and only from, the Hebrew Bible.

Miller (1991a: 95) is particularly critical of Coote and Whitelam 1987 and Whitelam 1986 for claiming to write a history of Israel without recourse to the Hebrew Bible while in effect assuming the basic outline of the biblical account. Although Miller highlights an important and difficult methodological problem, the major concern is with trying to free research from the constraints of the picture presented in the Hebrew Bible. The construction of the past presented in the Hebrew Bible has to be understood in the context of its social construction: it is important evidence for the historian in relation to the time at which it was composed. Clearly there are major disagreements on how to date or utilize the narratives and the information they

evidence, either from the archaeological record or corroborative literary materials, it is better to leave aside the distraction of the supposed ethnic labels and to concentrate on trying to explain the settlement shift in broader regional terms. Or, as Thompson (1992b: 310) puts it, 'It has become exceedingly misleading to speak of the term "Israelite" in an archaeological context of Iron I *Palestine*'. Thus an irony of the increase in archaeological data, such as that provided by Finkelstein, is that it has resulted in a situation where, far from placing discussions of Israel's emergence in Palestine on surer ground, it has led to a position in which it is possible to say very little about 'Israel' at all during the Late Bronze–Iron Age transition. The preoccupation with Israel has drawn attention away from the most immediate task facing the historian: the task of trying to explain the shifts in regional settlement and society during the Late Bronze–Iron Age transition.

The Identity and Organization of Israel in the Merneptah Stela

The most obvious objection to the above argument is that such an entity is referred to in the Merneptah stela toward the end of the thirteenth century BCE. It is well known that the Merneptah stela represents the earliest reference to Israel outside of the biblical texts. Yet despite the fact that this information has been available since 1896, when the stela was discovered, there is still considerable debate as to its meaning or significance.[15] The mention of 'Israel' in the stela raises three major questions which are important for the present investigation: what was the entity called 'Israel', how was it organized, and what was its relationship to the settlement shift at the end of the Late Bronze Age and beginning of the Iron Age?

contain. However, it is misleading to speak in terms of trying to write a history of Israel without recourse to the Hebrew Bible. It is a primary source for the period and groups that produced it. It is an entirely different matter whether or not the construction of the past in terms of the history of early Israel corresponds to historical reality. See Davies 1992 for an exploration of the implications of such an approach.

15. Serious questions have been raised about the historical reliability of the stela as representing a Palestinian campaign by Merneptah (see Redford 1986: 196-99). However, even if the description of the campaign is not authentic, it is still the case that the scribes of Merneptah knew of some entity which they termed 'Israel'. Finkelstein's (1991: 56) insistence that 'there was no political entity named Israel before the late-11th century' is puzzling in the light of the reference to Israel in the stela.

The first question as to the identity of 'Israel' in the stela has received considerable attention. It is not necessary to review recent theories in detail, but only to mention the salient points which bear upon the present discussion.[16] The significance and meaning of the determinative attached to Israel in comparison with the determinative used for Ashkelon, Gezer and Yano'am and the other entities mentioned in the stela is the most tantalizing feature. Obviously such a contrast invites speculation, but it has to be admitted that we are hardly in a position to solve the puzzle. Evidently there appears to be some differentiation in the minds of the Egyptian scribes but the reference is so ambiguous and tantalizing that the historian can only proceed with the utmost caution. It seems reasonable to conclude that this entity must have been a *relatively* significant political force in the region for it to be mentioned by the Egyptian scribes. But again caution is required here since we are dealing with a political and ideological presentation of the achievements of the pharaoh. The scribes are hardly likely to imply that the pharaoh's victory was insignificant, hence it is proclaimed in such categorical terms: 'Israel is laid waste, his seed is not'.

Moreover, the stela offers us precious little information on the precise location or organization of this entity and certainly tells us nothing of its origins. The northern location of Israel in the stela has been asserted on the basis of a supposed south–north arrangement within the text.

16.   Yurco's (1986) understanding of the stela in comparison with his reinterpretation of the battle reliefs at Karnak as coming from the reign of Merneptah rather than Rameses II suggests that 'Israel' is indigenous to Palestine. He asserts (1986: 210) that 'one thing is clear, *the Israelites* (Scene 4) *were not depicted as Shasu, but as Canaanites*' (his italics). Here he cites Stager's view (1985: 60) that the Shasu are pictorially and textually Shasu, whereas the Israelites in Scene 4 are pictorially Canaanites, and also textually by inference in the Israel stela where it is linked with Ashkelon, Gezer and Yano'am. This, he claims, refutes suggestions that Israel emerged out of a Shasu milieu (*contra* Giveon 1971 and Weippert). Redford (1986: 199-200) rejects this claim and states that

> All the names in the poem appear in the relief sequence except for Israel. Thus the ethnic group depicted and named 'Shasu' by the scribes of Seti I and Ramesses II at the beginning of the thirteenth century BCE was known to the poet of Merneptah two generations later as 'Israel'.

See further Redford 1992: 257-80. Interestingly, the assumption always seems to be that each of the terms designates an ethnic distinction rather than a sociopolitical differentiation. As Coote (1990: 178 n. 5) points out, Israelites could have been both *Shasu* and non-*Shasu*.

However, once again the evidence is ambiguous. The location of Yano'am is unknown, undermining attempts to correlate the literary arrangement with precise geographical information. Taking into account the dispute over whether or not Canaan is referred to before Ashkelon or whether this ought to be translated as Gaza, the existence of a south–north orientation rests upon the citation of two (or possibly three) towns and a third (or fourth) unidentified site. The few place names cited, even assuming a positive identification for Yano'am, are too small a statistical sample to confirm or deny their perceived geographical arrangement. If Gaza is not mentioned, but is a reference to Canaan as a whole, as some argue, then the attempt to find a south–north orientation is even more questionable. By contrast, Ahlström (1991: 32; 1986; see also Ahlström and Edelman 1985) believes that a perceived literary structure of the text in terms of a ring structure equates Israel with Canaan as making up Hurru: Canaan represents the well-populated lowlands while Israel refers to the central highlands. Emerton (1988: 372-73) illustrates the problems of such an approach in his critique of Ahlström's attempts to discover a ring structure in the text.[17] Even if it is possible to demonstrate that the stela, or, more accurately, this brief reference at the end of a victory hymn over Libya, has a recognizable literary structure, it is still a major shift in argumentation to conclude that it provides precise geographical information for the location of Israel on the basis of such an arrangement.

Bimson (1991) has drawn some significant conclusions from the stela in his critique of recent discussions of the emergence of early Israel. An important assumption embodied in the work of Bimson is that there is a clear relationship between Israel of the Merneptah stela and the inhabitants of the highland villages at the beginning of the Iron Age. He subscribes to the general scholarly assumption that the inhabitants of these villages were 'Israelites': he refers (1991: 6) to an 'Israelite occupation' at Shiloh separated from a Late Bronze stratum, but he does not spell out the reasons for such an assertion. The existence of some entity called 'Israel' as early as the end of the thirteenth century BCE is considered to be of prime importance in the discussion of this settlement shift. However, in the absence of more precise information, it is difficult to know

---

17. Emerton (1988) also makes the telling point that there is no explanation as to why the last few lines of the text are omitted from the proposed ring structure. Bimson (1991: 21-22) argues for a different understanding of the ring structure which does take into account the following lines except the list of royal titles that completes the inscription.

how this entity referred to by Egyptian scribes relates to the settlement shift at the beginning of the Iron Age. Bimson (1991: 14) is certain that 'there is no reason at all to doubt that the Israel of the stela is biblical Israel of the pre-monarchic period' and that 'it is quite unreasonable to deny that the Merenptah's inscription refers to biblical Israel'. He admits that we cannot be sure what form Israel took in Merenptah's day. Nevertheless, he is 'reasonably sure that Merenptah's Israel was a tribal confederation, such as we find reflected in the Song of Deborah' (1991: 14). Such a view begs a host of questions: what is 'biblical Israel', what is our evidence for 'premonarchic Israel', what is the relationship with Mernepath's Israel, and how do we know that it was organized tribally? Does 'biblical Israel' refer to Israel as pictured in biblical texts? If so, which texts are being considered and why? The question remains whether the representation of Israel in Joshua, Judges and Samuel conforms to historical reality or portrays an important ideological and political presentation of the past from the perspective of the later monarchy or Second Temple period.[18] However, Bimson draws a further important conclusion from the Merneptah stela: 'We may conclude that in Merenptah's reign Israel was a geographically extensive tribal coalition with considerable significance in Egyptian eyes' (1991: 22-23). It has been pointed out above that although it is a reasonable conclusion that Israel is being cited as a relatively significant political entity in the region, it is difficult to see how it can be concluded on the basis of the evidence of the inscription that it was 'geographically extensive' or that it was necessarily tribal. The view that Israel of the stela was a 'tribal coalition' can only be maintained on the basis of biblical and extrabiblical evidence and parallels, since the stela itself provides no direct evidence for such a conclusion.[19]

18. See Davies 1992 for a devastating critique of attempts to equate 'biblical Israel' with historical reality.

19. Lemche (1985: 430-31), whom Bimson cites in support, also refers to 'a fully developed tribal organization' on the basis of the reference to Israel in the Merneptah stela. Ahlström (1991: 33-34) is categorical in his denial that such information can be deduced from the stela:

> There is no way of knowing the social organization of the people who lived in the territory of Israel; one cannot deduce from the Merneptah stele that Israel was a tribe, a tribal league or confederation, as J.J. Bimson, A. Mazar, and L.E. Stager do, even if this could have been the case. The Egyptian text does not give any clue about the social structure of the people of Israel. To draw the conclusion that Israel refers to a tribal league is an inference from another kind of material.

The notion of the existence of a pan-Israelite tribal structure prior to the period of the monarchy is still influential in much biblical scholarship despite the demise of Noth's amphictyonic hypothesis.[20] This notion is evident in Finkelstein's discussion of the results of his archaeological investigation of Shiloh, as we have seen, when he concludes that this site was one of the 'supratribal sacral centers'. As noted above, this is a conclusion based upon an understanding of the biblical traditions and their applicability to historical reconstruction for this period, rather than an analysis of the archaeological data alone. Similarly, Bimson states (1991: 25) that there were 'cultic centres which seem to have served non-sedentary groups, e.g. at Shechem and Shiloh, places that feature as important centres for Israel in biblical traditions concerning the settlement and judges periods (Josh. 24; Judg. 21; etc.)'. In his discussion of the work of Finkelstein, he states that 'since Merenptah's inscription predates the sedentarization process, the Israel to which it refers was presumably nomadic' (1991: 19). In his conclusion, he states that 'before the beginning of the Iron Age, Israel must have been chiefly a semi-nomadic people' (1991: 24) and then adds that 'archaeological evidence for the existence of a semi-nomadic population in the highlands during LBA (Finkelstein 1988: 343-45) is probably of relevance to Israel's presedentary stage'. It is not entirely clear from this discussion whether or not he is drawing a clear distinction between nomadism and sedentarization that entails a view of nomadism as some kind of evolutionary stage that is prior to sedentarization.[21]

By contrast, we might compare the recent discussion of the nature of Israel in the Merneptah stela by Coote (1990: 72-83), which superficially

Redford (1992: 260) holds a similar view—all that can be known for certain is that Egyptian scribes knew of some entity called Israel somewhere in Palestine. Coote (1991: 39-42) understands Merneptah's Israel to be tribal in a political sense as part of 'a complex network of relations of power'.

20. The idea that early Israel was tribal or a tribal confederation has been challenged by Rogerson (1986), who is particularly concerned with the notion of segmentary organization. See Martin 1989 for a recent summary of some of the problems involved in this discussion. Lemche (1985: 84-163, 202-44) provides a detailed treatment of the complexities of nomadic organization and structure and the problems involved in using particular models or parallels to describe the organization of early Israel.

21. Bimson (1991: 24 n. 1) does refer in a footnote to the work of Lemche in making the point that some wealthy individuals in nomadic societies make the transition to a settled existence.

seems to be very much in line with Bimson's reading. Although Coote concludes that 'Israel' of the stela was a major political and military power in the region in the thirteenth century BCE and that it was a 'tribe or tribal confederation', his understanding is significantly different from that of Bimson. Coote (1990: 71) concludes that Israel was not a 'single religious group, family, nation, race, nor ethnic group' but as a tribe or tribal confederation during the New Kingdom period 'it was a name for power'. His view is that the biblical texts do not describe the origin of Israel but what some later court writers thought was the origin of Israel on the basis of ideas and experiences of their own time and place.[22] His understanding of the nature of tribal Israel is based upon a wide body of evidence including parallels drawn from similar periods in the history of Palestine. Coote recognizes that the reference to Israel in the Merneptah stela predates the highland settlement by 'at least one generation, and probably several' (1990: 72). However, he also draws a direct link between this entity and the inhabitants of the highland settlements: 'In the twelfth and eleventh centuries, people named Israel inhabited recently founded villages in the highland' (1990: 72). Yet it is difficult to see what archaeological evidence or information on the stela would justify such a link. The root of the problem again appears to be the distraction of the term 'Israel' and the search for the identity of the inhabitants of Iron I highland settlements.

Coote's discussion (1990: 75-93) of the nature of tribal organization in Palestine, on the basis of better-known parallels, and his concentration upon the *political* conditions of highland settlement in the early Iron Age are particularly valuable. He points out that such organization was essentially a concept of political identity and relationship among individuals and families, and between their chiefs and the state. The shifting nature of tribal structures and membership, invariably in response to political and economic conditions, is an important factor that needs to be borne in mind in the discussion of Palestinian history and settlement. It is misleading to think of tribal organizations as necessarily expressions of ethnic or religious unity. It is well known that genealogies in traditional societies constantly change to reflect political and social relationships rather than biological descent. As Coote (1990: 78) notes, 'It continues to beg the question of the nature of Israel, particularly its

---

22. Coote places the biblical traditions of Israel's origins at the court of David. See Coote and Ord 1989 and Coote and Coote 1990.

variability, by implying a singularity and continuity with later Israel, which are commonly presumed but improbable and misleading'.

The historical study of this period is a prime example of the way in which the concerns and categories of the Hebrew Bible have dominated the discussion. The overriding concern with the origins or emergence of Israel has obscured the need to understand and account for the political and economic conditions that influenced the highland settlement shift during the Late Bronze–Iron Age transition. If we think of a realignment of Palestinian society in broad regional terms in response to the disruption of local and regional economies rather than trying to identify highland settlements with 'Israel', then Coote's discussion has a great deal to contribute to our understanding of this settlement shift. Nomadism, with its heavy emphasis on the pastoral element, is a form of specialization that many in the indigenous population adopt under particular political and economic conditions. It forms part of the social continuum rather than being a discrete system (cf. Cribb 1991: 16). The political and economic conditions provide the stimulus for an amalgamation of diverse groups, ethnically and tribally, which is then presented in terms of a lineage system. As Cribb (1991: 53) points out, notions of a perceived lineage system are often products of conscious rationalizations by provincial administrators or tribal leaders. He notes (1991: 54) that many tribal groupings in the Near East involve nomadism only marginally, if at all, ranging from sedentary Kurdish mountain villagers, Berber citrus cultivators, to Marsh Arabs. Importantly, the common denominator appears to be a fluid territorial system and intense competition for scarce land or water resources: 'The inherent instability of the pastoral mode of subsistence, accompanied by constant changes of residence and fluctuations in the size and composition of co-resident groups, both demands and facilitates a territorial system of great complexity and maximum flexibility'. His emphasis (1991: 54) on the notion of the tribe as the sociopolitical structure that is able to secure access to scarce resources is relevant to the sociopolitical situation in Palestine during the Late Bronze–Iron Age transition when the social and political upheavals caused by the disruption of urban-based trade required flexibility of response in order to secure resources for survival.[23]

23. Cribb offers some instructive examples of the importance of the pastoral element of Middle Eastern society in his dismissal of long-held assumptions that population change is the result of nomadic invasions, particularly during periods of weak state control, and the replacement of the indigenous population. He points out that

It is these aspects of tribal organization that undermine the easy assumption that there is a direct and demonstrable link between the 'Israel' of the Merneptah stela, the inhabitants of the highland settlements, or the later Israelite monarchy.[24] The problems inherent in this assumption were referred to by Coote and Whitelam (1987: 179 n. 3). In the light of the above discussion, it needs to be made clearer that the identification of 'Israel' with the highland settlements is even more questionable on the basis of available evidence. The term 'Israel' in this context is misleading and diverts attention away from an important discussion about the sociopolitical conditions that accompany this marked settlement shift. This was not made clear enough in Coote and Whitelam (1987), despite the important proviso that was added to the earlier cited statement (1987: 179 n. 3):[25] 'The reference to "Israel" in the Merneptah stela may not refer to the settlement of the highland or to any social group directly ancestral to monarchic Israel'. Bimson objects to this on the ground that such a view is not justified by the evidence (1991: 17). He suspects that the suggestion derives from a realization that 'even

> This is not what happened on the Syrian steppe in the last century, nor in western Iran during World War II and only a few years ago after the fall of the Shah. What would a migrationist make of the dozens of abandoned and burned villages? What of the nomad camps that replaced them? Yet in both cases—certainly in the latter—the departed villagers and the newly arrived nomads were in fact the same people! The collapse of state authority, instead of opening the way for a nomad 'invasion', simply permitted large numbers of people to resume a preferred migratory lifestyle more consistent with their unstable mode of subsistence (1991: 153).

He goes on to add that the widespread desolation of northern Mesopotamia recorded by nineteenth-century travellers, with numerous deserted villages interspersed or overlapping with tent camps, is consistent with weak Ottoman rule and mounting disorder. But the nomads themselves may well have been the former inhabitants of the villages who had become too mobile to maintain a permanent village base. He notes that

> It is curious that the period during which major nomad invasions are known to have occured throughout the Near East—the eleventh and twelfth century—was one of general prosperity and flourishing trade with little hint in the historical or archaeological settlement record of major upheavals or depopulation... Prior to the Seljuk Empire most of this area was Greek- or Persian-speaking, and afterwards mostly Turkish-speaking, showing how complex are the interwoven strands of nomad migration, ethnic affiliation and regional economy (1991: 153-54).

24. Similarly, Thompson (1992b: 311) argues for a difference between 'Israel' of the stela and the referent of the same name in the Assyrian period.

25. However, see n. 6 above.

with the traditional dating of the Iron I settlements, there may not have been time for Israel to emerge through the process which they envisage before Merneptah's fifth year' (1991: 17-18). However, this is not the reason for the qualification. The problem arises out of an understanding of the complex and variable nature of tribal organization. Far from ignoring the evidence of the Merneptah stela, its evidence is seen to be significant. If 'Israel' of the stela was organized tribally, as Bimson accepts, but which is not evident from the stela itself, then the very nature of tribal organization calls into question the precise relationship between this entity, the highland settlements, and any later Israelite monarchy. However, once again the major distraction for virtually all proponents in the recent debate has been the concentration upon Israel and the assumption that there is a close fit between 'Israel' and the spread of highland settlement in early Iron Age Palestine.

The Transformation and Realignment
of Late Bronze–Iron Age Palestine

The search for early Israel has proven to be a serious distraction which, in the absence of further unambiguous evidence, ought to be abandoned for the time being, while we concentrate on historical judgments, which need to be constantly revised and improved, regarding the probabilities of the history of Palestine in the thirteenth to eleventh centuries BCE. In particular, the historian needs to explain the processes at work in the settlement shift that took place during the Late Bronze–Iron Age transition. Hitherto the discussion of early Israel and its emergence has advanced primarily through the juxtaposition of archaeological data and biblical texts. From now on the discussion of peoples, societies and cultures—including whatever may be designated 'Israel'—will need to advance largely without the biblical text, for this period at least. The traditions of Israel's origins are more important as sources of information for the nature of later monarchic, exilic and Second Temple Israel. Those who have said that the history of early Israel cannot be written in any conventional sense of a text-based reconstruction are correct, at least until major bodies of historical texts from the period are discovered—and even then such texts would have to find their place within the constellation of other categories of evidence. Research strategies need to break free from the constraints of traditional text-based reconstructions by pursuing insights gained through the juxtaposition of archaeological data and historical parallels generated by such broad comparative disciplines as anthropology, historical geography, macro-sociology and historical demography. Furthermore, Braudel's conception of *la longue durée* offers a perspective from which to view familiar problems and encourages the search for patterns in history that are often obscured or overlooked by intense concentration on limited periods of time or geographical area.

Any study of the history of Palestine has to take into account the complex arrangement of micro-environments which have ensured that the region as a whole has seldom been unified and which have conferred a large degree of autonomy on the different sub-regions and their inhabitants, thereby contributing to the diversity of Palestine. Thompson's (1992b) study rightly emphasizes the importance of Palestinian regional variation in trying to understand its history. However, it is also important that such an emphasis does not lose sight of world history. Palestine has been and remains a part of world history; its strategic location on the trade and military routes by land and sea at the hub of three continents has meant that its history is intricately linked to global history. The ways in which the micro-environments have been exploited has often been determined by outside factors such as imperial investment of finance, labour and technology. Once the history of this area and its populations are set in the context of 'world history' then it is possible to ask important comparative questions about the nature of cultural, social, political, economic and religious interrelationships and changes.

The settlement variation which occurred in Palestine during the Late Bronze–Iron Age transition cannot usefully be studied as though it arose in a temporal and spatial vacuum. The disruptions that occurred throughout the eastern Mediterranean towards the end of the Late Bronze Age appear familiar enough for us to talk in terms of a collapse or even dramatic collapse on an interregional scale. The use of such terminology, however, raises expectations and assumptions that such a collapse was immediate and gave rise to a radical break in material culture in different regions. It is important to be continually reminded of the imprecision of our terminology and chronology in which distinctions between centuries, for instance, for purposes of classification, are arbitrary and particularly dangerous when they lead to assumptions that something dramatic happened in 1200 BCE that distinguishes what had gone on immediately before from what followed. Such distinctions encourage the study of history as a series of discrete events in which sociopolitical changes are neatly categorized (Bloch 1954: 183-84). In what sense do the destructions of Late Bronze Age urban sites in Palestine represent a collapse? The dating of the destruction layers of Late Bronze Age urban centres in Palestine is controversial and constantly being revised (Fritz 1987: 86-89), but it is to be doubted that this was a 'sudden' occurrence. Present estimates at dating point to the fact that this was part of a protracted process that lasted at least half a century, if not more, and can only be understood as part of longer-term trends in the history of the region.

The historian needs to explain the restructuring of the social system expressed in the changes of settlement patterns which are so evident at the end of the Late Bronze and the beginning of the Iron Ages. It might be a better reflection of the situation if we adopted the terms transformation and realignment of Late Bronze–Iron Age Palestine rather than collapse. Sabloff (1986: 114) has recently argued for a similar reappraisal of the so-called Mayan collapse (800–1200 CE) in terms of a demographic, political and economic realignment. Such terms overcome expectations of a radical break at a particular point in time—a radical break that fits well with assumptions about external invasion, conquest or infiltration by different ethnic groups. It also challenges our perspective on basic data by encouraging appreciation of continuities rather than an undue emphasis on differences and discontinuities in material culture. The historian is dealing with complex and protracted processes that cannot easily be reduced to or analysed simply in terms of particular moments in time but must be understood in the widest geographical and temporal context. H. Weippert (1988: 26-27) has drawn attention to the problem of the different rates of development between different sub-regions of Palestine and to the fact that the dates for periods of transition can only be approximations.[26] Similarly, T. Dothan (1989: 1-14) in a

26. Finkelstein pointed out in an oral response at the Boston symposium that it is extremely difficult to date early Iron I sites within a margin of error of fifty years. This is obviously a critical problem for the historian who needs such information in order to produce an understanding of the relative chronology of settlement shift but who is dependent upon the judgments of specialists. Finkelstein states the case well:

> It has been practically impossible to make fine chronological distinctions in the pottery from Settlement sites. The problem will naturally crop up at various points in this work, since it is crucial for understanding the processes of occupation and the development of material culture at early Israelite Settlement sites . . . In some instances, we will thus try to make the distinction between early and late pottery of the Iron I period, despite the risks inherent in this attempt; to refrain from doing so would obviously impede our attempts to advance the analysis of the process of Settlement.

recent reassessment of the initial appearance and settlement of the Philistines and other Sea Peoples in Palestine illustrates that cultural change during the transition period from Late Bronze–Iron I Age was not uniform or simultaneous throughout the country. It was characterized by a complex process in which indigenous, Egyptian and Philistine cultures overlapped for certain periods.

The realignment and transformation of Late Bronze–Iron I society was clearly a very complex process, as we would expect, and it is in the discussion of the processes at work that the greatest differences are likely to occur. Thompson (1992b: 180) doubts that the breakdown of international trade at the end of the Early Bronze and Late Bronze Ages could have such an effect upon the Palestinian economy as to result in 'wholesale dislocations throughout the region, and especially in so many sub-regions (such as the hill country and the Northern Negev)', since such regions were only marginally affected by trade routes. He believes (1992b: 215) that the evidence points to major climatic change resulting in widespread drought and famine from c. 1200–1000 BCE.[27] Climate is obviously an important factor, given the marginal nature of the sub-regions of Palestine, where dramatic variations in rainfall over two or more years can have devastating effects. Famine, however, is not always a direct result of periods of drought but is frequently the result of sociopolitical factors, as the tragic events in parts of modern-day Africa all too vividly illustrate (cf. Thompson 1992b: 219-20). It is also the case that Palestine has witnessed important shifts in settlement during more modern periods when the climate in the region has remained stable.

Dever (1991: 83) notes that Finkelstein's analysis of Iron I pottery is pivotal but only 'for the few specialists capable of judging Finkelstein's arguments. (They *are* few; so hereafter generalists, biblical scholars, and historians must defer to experts, rather than continuing to offer historical-cultural conclusions based on their own ceramic evaluations, which are invalid and misleading).'

27. Thompson (1992b: 204) goes so far as to claim that the change in climate was 'a primary cause of the changes in economy and settlement patterns in Palestine during the Middle Bronze period'. This is surprising in the light of the fact that he criticizes (1992b: 150) Coote and Whitelam for imposing a mono-causal explanation—the disruption of international trade—on settlement shift, when in fact they only refer to correlations between such settlement shifts and trade cycles, leaving open the question of causal priority (Coote and Whitelam 1987: 79). However, Thompson has reintroduced an important topic into the discussion which needs careful consideration.

Thompson (1992b: 261) points out that the Phoenician cities survived the drought without widespread collapse, attributing their political and economic autonomy to their relative geographical isolation. This would suggest that it is sociopolitical factors that are of greater importance in understanding the settlement shifts rather than climatic change. Geographical isolation is no protection against catastrophic climatic change.

The complex of trade networks which in antiquity linked the Mediterranean, Red Sea, Persian Gulf and Indian Ocean means that Palestine has long been part of a 'world economy' in which the urban elite benefited from interregional trade. Palestine has occupied a strategic place in the world trade axis throughout history, and the urban and bedouin elite have often benefited from their participation in or control of transit trade through the area. But their position on the transit routes to and from core areas has meant that their roles and opportunities were particularly sensitive to any disruption or decline in the core. The existence of such a closely integrated world economy, in particular in the eastern Mediterranean during the Late Bronze Age, also meant that any disruption to part of the trade network influenced other areas. Palestine invariably played a dependent role in trade, since it provided the land bridge, and a hub of the waterways, to the infrastructurally more important economies of the major continents. Palestinian urban centres were therefore sensitive and vulnerable to trade cycles and suffered severely from the disruption of the Mycenaean world, whatever the causes may have been.[28] Societies are not monolithic entities but overlapping networks of different power structures and groups (Mann 1986: 1). Since the eastern Mediterranean was a closely interlocking network of different power groups and spatial entities, any structural alterations on such a widespread scale were bound to influence Palestinian society. It is not possible then simply to concentrate our attention on settlement shifts in the highlands of Palestine at the beginning of the Iron I period without taking adequate account of the structural changes brought about by changes in the wider network. The decline of trade and economy along with the many circumstances that attended it were integral to the transformation of economic, political and social relations in Palestine.[29]

28. Liverani (1987) provides a good account of the interconnections throughout the eastern Mediterranean during this period.

29. There is no adequate account of the factors that contributed to the decline of interregional trade in the eastern Mediterranean. Renfrew's comparative study (1979) of general systems collapse offers an introduction to an important area of future

The most evident result of this realignment in Palestine is an increase in highland rural settlements as part of similar settlement shifts in other areas of the eastern Mediterranean. Desborough (1972: 19-20, 82, 88) notes that the decline of the Mycenaean palace centres was accompanied by a shift in settlement to highland or more remote areas. Interestingly he notes that Sub-Mycenaean pottery represents a clear cultural continuum, even though there was a sharp deterioration in material terms (Desborough 1972: 29, 41; Snodgrass 1971: 34, 40). This is in striking contrast to earlier assumptions that the destruction of the Mycenaean world was caused by external invasion and represented a radical cultural break (see also Lemche 1985). Such settlement shifts as a response to urban decline can be observed in many areas of the world. For example, Iron Age Zealand in Denmark experienced a similar urban decline and corresponding increase in autonomous settlements in remote, often virgin, areas (Kristiansen 1987). The mountains have long been a place of refuge for peasant communities from the periodic political instability of the exposed lowlands throughout the history of the Mediterranean (Braudel 1972: 34, 53). The settlement of the Palestinian highlands and steppes during the Iron I period is not a unique event, but part of the centuries-long cycle of growth, stagnation, decline and regeneration in the history of Palestine (Coote and Whitelam 1987: 27-28).

The importance of the various material features is not that they confirm or deny the ethnicity of populations at different sites, but that they provide evidence of important continuities in material culture from the Late Bronze Age to Iron I that need to be recognized and given sufficient weight. Regional variations need to be acknowledged and accounted for not on the basis of ethnicity, itself the subject of continuing anthropological research, but rather on the basis of the socioeconomic and sociopolitical environment. The continuities in material

research, but clearly much more needs to done in order to understand the transformation of the eastern Mediterranean in general. It should be noted that the disruption of trade and economy is not considered as some mono-causal explanation of settlement change. The significance of fluctuations in the Palestinian economy is the way in which they often correlate with major settlement change. Coote and Whitelam (1987: 49-50) stated that 'although it is appropriate for us to give thorough attention to interregional economic exchange, it is not our purpose to prove its causal priority. Its relative explanatory significance in any particular instance will and should always be a matter for assessment.' Trade here is understood in the widest possible terms as an indicator of regional and interregional economy.

culture add to the case that we are dealing with the realignment of Palestinian society rather than the collapse and destruction of Late Bronze Age culture and its replacement by new ethnic groups emerging from the desert fringes, the far north, Egypt, or anywhere else. The identification of aspects of the material culture or of particular sites as 'Israelite' is not based upon positive evidence in the archaeological record but rather upon assumptions about the existence or location of Israelite sites in particular areas on the basis of traditions within the Hebrew Bible. The various aspects of the material culture of Iron I need to be understood as functions of socio-environmental and political conditions rather than distinctive ethnic innovations or markers for the national ethnic entities posited by the religious traditions of the Hebrew Bible.[30]

The evidence that Finkelstein puts forward, once the distraction of the label 'Israelite' is removed, adds further weight to this view. As he states (1988: 338), 'Human material culture is influenced first and foremost by the socioeconomic situation and by the environmental conditions'. The appearance and use of pillared buildings, silos, cisterns, terracing, and pottery forms such as collared-rim ware are explicable in terms of the topographical and environmental conditions facing the inhabitants of highland and marginal settlements in the context of the disruption of local and regional economies (see also Dever 1991: 83-84). The technological solutions and expertise displayed in the use of cisterns, terracing, or the construction of pillared buildings militate against the view that the population of these sites were nomads in the process of sedentarization (Coote and Whitelam 1987: 123-34). The evidence put forward by Finkelstein, when stripped of the distractions of putative ethnic labels, provides further support for the view that the settlement shift at the end

---

30. It is not possible on the basis of the archaeological record to assume that the Iron I sites indicate common ethnic identity. Alternatively, the regional interactions or environmental conditions that contributed to material similarities among the rural groups may have led eventually to the recognition or imposition and acceptance of ethnic identity in these areas of Palestine. In a sense, the tendency has been to pose the question the wrong way round by identifying similarities and then asking what ethnic group was responsible. There may be little or no ethnic identity at first, but such identity may result from the common solution to problems of subsistence among interacting polities over a period of time. In this sense ethnic identity would be more relevant to a discussion of the processes involved in the formation of an Israelite state or later.

of the Late Bronze Age and beginning of the Iron I period was a reaction to economic disruption which had an impact on all aspects and levels of Palestinian society rather than being the direct result of social conflict brought about by class struggle or external invasion or infiltration.

Historians must await the results of further archaeological research, particularly comprehensive surveys of the lowlands and coastal areas, along with comparative excavations of sites of differing sizes in these areas, in order to produce a more complete regional picture of the settlement patterns. The lack of comprehensive surveys of all regions of Palestine, and particularly of the lowlands, is a major obstacle in trying to understand the processes at work in the Late Bronze–Iron Age transition. London (1989: 42) makes the point that 'until now archaeologists have been comparing rural sites in the hill country with urban sites in the lowlands and then attributing the differences to Israelite versus Canaanite communities. The differences may be more indicative of rural versus urban lifestyles.'[31] The existence of villages on the exposed edge of the highlands, or other villages with or without outer defences, indicates that social conflict was only part of the processes that explain the shift in settlement. Progress in this field is now even more dependent upon the continued publication and judgments of archaeologists, so that historians can interpret the material in a comparative interdisciplinary context.

The power of the Hebrew Bible over historians, even those who profess to try to free themselves of its hold, is clearly demonstrated in

---

31. Finkelstein (1991: 51), in replying to the criticisms of London that he had compared the rural site of 'Izbet Ṣarṭah with urban sites such as Aphek, Qasile and Gezer, responds by pointing out that Aphek and Qasile were apparently no larger than 'Izbet Ṣarṭah. However, Dever (1991: 78) similarly believes that the proliferation of collared-rim ware in Iron I hill country sites, compared with its absence at large sites such as Gezer, is evidence for differences in urban–rural distribution rather than an ethnic dichotomy.

It is interesting to note that Finkelstein has revised his original and restrictive view of the applicability of archaeological data from 'Canaanite' sites. He was previously of the opinion (1988: 22-23) that evidence from 'large Canaanite mounds' may contribute to our understanding of the Late Bronze Age but is of little value for understanding the processes at work in 'Israelite Settlement'. More recently, he has recognized (1991: 48-49) that comprehensive surveys in the lowlands to match the work already carried out in the hill country need to be completed along with the excavation of single period Iron I sites in different parts of Palestine.

recent discussions of the emergence of early Israel, as Miller (1991a) has shown. The Merneptah stela illustrates that some entity called 'Israel' was in existence, and possibly as a relatively significant political force, in the thirteenth century BCE. Even though many historians and archaeologists suspect that some entity called Israel was involved in the settlement of the Palestinian highlands in the Late Bronze–Iron Age transition, this cannot be stated with any degree of certainty on the basis of the evidence currently available. Furthermore, it is distracting and misleading to retain references to Israel, however much they may be qualified or however much we may try and encode our uncertainties with quotation marks ('Israel').[32] It is distracting because the use of the term Israel also brings with it the inevitable assumptions of tribal organization and ethnic or religious unity. Once we are able to relinquish our attachment to the label it allows us to concentrate on the critical issues of the processes involved in the transformation and realignment of Palestinian society. It means that historians are freed to ask crucial questions about the processes at work unencumbered by the theological baggage and agenda of the Hebrew Bible which has had such a profound hold on the study of the region and the presentation of its history.

32. This is also true of Dever's (1991: 88 n.7) reference to 'Proto-Israel'.

BIBLIOGRAPHY

Ahlström, G.W.
    1986   *Who Were the Israelites?* (Winona Lake, IN: Eisenbrauns).
    1991   'The Origin of Israel in Palestine', *SJOT* 2: 19-34.
    1993   *The History of Ancient Palestine from the Palaeolithic to Alexander's Conquest* (JSOTSup, 146; Sheffield: JSOT Press).
Ahlström, G.W., and D. Edelman
    1985   'Merneptah's Israel', *JNES* 44: 59-61.
Bimson, J.
    1989   'The Origins of Israel in Canaan: An Examination of Recent Theories', *Themelios* 15: 4-15.
    1991   'Merenptah's Israel and Recent Theories of Israelite Origins', *JSOT* 49: 3-29.
Bloch, M.
    1954   *The Historian's Craft* (Manchester: Manchester University Press).
Braudel, F.
    1972   *The Mediterranean and the Mediterranean World in the Age of Philip II* (2 vols.; London: Collins).
Coote, R.B.
    1990   *Early Israel: A New Horizon* (Minneapolis: Fortress Press).
    1991   'Early Israel', *SJOT* 2: 35-46.
Coote, R.B., and M. Coote
    1990   *Power, Politics, and the Making of the Bible* (Minneapolis: Fortress Press).
Coote, R.B., and D.R. Ord
    1989   *The Bible's First History* (Philadelphia: Fortress Press).
Coote, R.B., and K.W. Whitelam
    1987   *The Emergence of Early Israel in Historical Perspective* (Sheffield: Almond Press).
Cribb, R.
    1991   *Nomads in Archaeology* (Cambridge: Cambridge University Press).
Davies, P.R.
    1992   *In Search of 'Ancient Israel'* (JSOTSup, 148; Sheffield: JSOT Press).
Desborough, V.R.
    1972   *The Greek Dark Ages* (London: Benn).
Dever, W.G.
    1991   'Archaeological Data on the Israelite Settlement: A Review of Two Recent Works', *BASOR* 284: 77-90.
Dothan, T.
    1989   'The Arrival of the Sea Peoples: Cultural Diversity in Early Iron Age Canaan', in S. Gitin and W.G. Dever (eds.), *Recent Excavations in Israel: Studies in Iron Age Archaeology* (Winona Lake, IN: ASOR/ Eisenbrauns): 1-14.
Emerton, J.A.
    1988   Review of G.W. Ahlström, *Who Were the Israelites?*, *VT* 38: 372-73.

Finkelstein, I.
    1985   'Excavations at Shiloh 1981–1984: Preliminary Report', *Tel Aviv* 12:
                123-80.
    1988   *The Archaeology of the Israelite Settlement* (Jerusalem: Israel
                Exploration Society).
    1991   'The Emergence of Israel in Canaan: Consensus, Mainstream and
                Dispute', *SJOT* 2: 47-59.
Fritz, V.
    1987   'Conquest or Settlement? The Early Iron Age in Palestine', *BA* 50:
                84-100.
Garbini, G.
    1988   *History and Ideology in Ancient Israel* (London: SCM Press).
Giveon, R.
    1971   *Les bédouins Shosou des documents égyptiens* (Leiden: Brill).
Gottwald, N.K.
    1979   *The Tribes of Yahweh: A Sociology of Liberated Israel, 1250–1050
                BCE* (London: SCM Press).
Halpern, B.
    1983   *The Emergence of Israel in Canaan* (Chico, CA: Scholars Press).
Jamieson-Duke, D.W.
    1991   *Scribes and Schools in Monarchic Judah: A Socio-Archaeologial
                Approach* (Sheffield: Almond Press).
Kristiansen, K.
    1987   'Center and Periphery in Bronze Age Scandinavia', in M. Rowlands,
                M. Larsen and K. Kristiansen (eds.), *Centre and Periphery in the
                Ancient World* (Cambridge: Cambridge University Press): 74-85.
Lemche, N.P.
    1985   *Early Israel: Anthropological and Historical Studies in the Israelite
                Society before the Monarchy* (Leiden: Brill).
    1991   *The Canaanites and their Land: The Tradition of the Canaanites*
                (JSOTSup, 110; Sheffield: JSOT Press).
Liverani, M.
    1987   'The Collapse of the Near Eastern Regional System at the End of the
                Bronze Age: The Case of Syria', in M. Rowlands, M. Larsen and K.
                Kristiansen (eds.), *Centre and Periphery in the Ancient World*
                (Cambridge: Cambridge University Press): 66-73.
London, G.
    1989   'A Comparison of Two Contemporaneous Lifestyles of the Late
                Second Millennium BC', *BASOR* 273: 37-55.
Mann, M.
    1986   *The Sources of Social Power*. I. *A History of Power from the
                Beginning to AD 1760* (Cambridge: Cambridge University Press).
Martin, J.D.
    1989   'Israel as a Tribal Society', in R.E. Clements (ed.), *The World of
                Ancient Israel: Sociological, Anthropological and Political
                Perspectives* (Cambridge: Cambridge University Press): 95-117.
Mendenhall, G.E.
    1962   'The Hebrew Conquest of Palestine', *BA* 25: 66-87.

Millard, A.R.
  1991   'Texts and Archaeology: Weighing the Evidence. The Case for King Solomon', *PEQ* (Jan–Dec): 19-27.

Miller, J.M.
  1991a   'Is It Possible to Write a History of Israel without Relying on the Hebrew Bible?', in D. Edelman (ed.), *The Fabric of History: Text, Artifact and Israel's Past* (JSOTSup, 127; Sheffield: JSOT Press): 93-102.
  1991b   'Solomon: International Potentate or Local King?', *PEQ* (Jan–Dec): 28-31.

Redford, D.B.
  1986   'The Ashkelon Relief at Karnak and the Israel Stela', *IEJ* 36: 188-200.
  1992   *Egypt, Canaan, and Israel in Ancient Times* (Princeton: Princeton University Press).

Renfrew, C.
  1979   'Systems Collapse as Social Transformation: Catastrophe and Anastrophe in Early State Societies', in C. Renfrew and K.L. Cooke (eds.), *Transformations: Mathematical Changes to Culture Change* (New York: Academic Press): 481-506.

Rogerson, J.W.
  1986   'Was Early Israel a Segmentary Society?', *JSOT* 36: 17-26.

Sabloff, J.A.
  1986   'Interaction among Classic Maya Polities: A Preliminary Examination', in C. Renfrew and J.F. Cherry (eds.), *Peer Polity Interaction and Socio-Political Change* (Cambridge: Cambridge University Press): 109-16.

Snodgrass, A.
  1971   *The Dark Ages of Greece: An Archaeological Survey of the Eleventh to the Eighth Century BC* (Edinburgh: Edinburgh University Press).

Stager, L.E.
  1985   'Merneptah, Israel and the Sea Peoples: New Light on an Old Relief', *Eretz Israel* 18: 56*-64*.

Thompson, T.L.
  1992a   'Palestinian Pastoralism and Israel's Origins', *SJOT* 6: 1-13.
  1992b   *Early History of the Israelite People: From the Written and Archaeological Sources* (Leiden: Brill).

Weippert, H.
  1988   *Palästina in vorhellenistischer Zeit* (Handbuch der Archäologie, 2.1; Munich: Beck).

Weippert, M.
  1971   *The Settlement of the Israelite Tribes in Palestine: A Critical Survey of Recent Scholarly Debate* (London: SCM Press).

Weippert, M. and H. Weippert
  1991   'Die Vorgeschichte Israels in neuem Licht', *TRu* 56: 341-90.

Whitelam, K.W.
  1986   'Recreating the History of Israel', *JSOT* 35: 45-70.

1995   'New Deuteronomistic Heroes and Villains: A Response to T.L. Thompson', *SJOT* 9: 97-118.

1996   *The Invention of Ancient Israel: The Silencing of Palestinian History* (London: Routledge).

Wightman, G.J.

1990   'The Myth of Solomon', *BASOR* 228: 5-22.

Yurco, F.J.

1986   'Merenptah's Canaanite Campaign', *Journal of the American Research Center in Egypt* 23: 189–215.

JSOT 38 (1987), pp. 15-32

THE BOOK OF JOSHUA:
HEROIC SAGA OR CONQUEST THEME?

George W. Coats

What is the book of Joshua? The most obvious answer to the question lies in the structure of the Old Testament canon. The book of Joshua is the first segment in the Former Prophets, distinct from the five books of the Torah commonly called the Pentateuch. Indeed, the literary character of the book appears to have more in common with the following series of books, identified by Old Testament scholars as the Deuteronomistic History,[1] than with the preceding books of the Torah. While some scholars find evidence of one or more of the Pentateuch four in Joshua,[2] the tendency at the moment is to deny that J, E, or P can be recovered from its narratives. Yet the character of the Joshua material suggests something more than simply a single piece of literary construction. The complexity has led recent work on Joshua to identify at least two literary sources: Dtr 1 and Dtr 2.[3]

Despite the history of the canon that attaches Joshua to the Former Prophets and leaves the Pentateuch as the Torah, a distinct unit of the Old Testament as Scripture, there is nonetheless a sense of unity between the narratives of the Pentateuch and Joshua. In Genesis, God promises

1. M. Noth, The *Deuteronomistic History* (JSOTSup, 15; Sheffield: JSOT Press, 1981).

2. For example, S. Mowinckel, *Tetrateuch–Pentateuch–Hexateuch: Die Berichte über die Landnahme in den drei altisraelitischen Geschichtswerken* (BZAW, 90; Berlin: Töpelmann, 1964).

3. F.M. Cross, 'The Themes of the Book of Kings and the Structure of the Deuteronomistic History', in *Canaanite Myth and Hebrew Epic* (Cambridge, MA: Harvard University Press, 1973), pp. 274-89. See, more recently, R.D. Nelson, *The Double Redaction of the Deuteronomistic History* (JSOTSup, 18; Sheffield: JSOT Press, 1981).

the patriarchal ancestors of Israel that a great land would belong to their great posterity. In some sense, the promise anticipates immediate fulfillment. Abraham purchases a cave as a burial spot for his wife and, in the process, establishes possession of land in the land.[4] But, at best, the possession is only a prolepsis. The patriarchs remain strangers on the land until the third generation, the family of Jacob, is forced by famine to leave. Slavery in Egypt leads to an exodus under the power of the Lord and the leadership of Moses. Crises in the wilderness set the stage for both rebellion against Moses and the Lord, and a display of the Lord's power to aid his people in the face of those wilderness crises. Indeed, the Lord extends his aid to those rebellious people even to the point of giving them the law. With that gift of grace, the people would not need to struggle in confusion to know how to obey divine leadership.

But the Pentateuch ends with the death of Moses at the edge of the promised land. The story falls short of an obvious climax. In the Pentateuch, the Lord promised Israel a great land for a great posterity. The great posterity now rests on the edge of the promise, without a leader. Joshua has the mark of the heir apparent (cf. Num. 27.12-23). And there the Pentateuch ends. Does the tradition not demand that the story continue to the anticipated climax? Is Joshua not attached by the history of the traditions more directly to the Pentateuch than to the following Former Prophets? Must we not consider the suggestion that for the shape of the story, if not for the history of the canon, the primary unit for the tradition about Israel's early history is the Hexateuch?[5]

Source criticism does not support this prospect. If the Pentateuch four found any home in the narrative of Joshua, a possibility that has been defended, perhaps most notably by Mowinckel,[6] the evidence for that possibility seems now completely submerged under the style of Dtr. But the point does not undercut the hypothesis that the primary unit is the Hexateuch since, according to the analysis, Dtr begins in Deuteronomy. What evidence does the book of Joshua itself offer for establishing its

4.   G. von Rad, *Genesis, a Commentary* (trans. J.H. Marks; OTL; Philadelphia: Westminster Press, 1972), p. 250.

5.   G. von Rad, 'The Form-Critical Problem of the Hexateuch', in *The Problem of the Hexateuch and Other Essays* (trans. E.W. Trueman Dicken; London: Oliver & Boyd, 1965), pp. 1-78; 'The Promised Land and Yahweh's Land in the Hexateuch', in *The Problem of the Hexateuch*, pp. 79-93.

6.   Mowinckel, *Tetrateuch–Pentateuch–Hexateuch*, pp. 51-76.

position in the structure of the Old Testament narrative?

I do not intend at this point to explore evidence for identifying the literary sources in Joshua as a means for addressing the question. If Joshua does in fact belong with the narratives of the Pentateuch, one might expect to find some sign of that fact by uncovering elements of the Yahwist, the priestly source, or perhaps even the elusive Elohist in the patterns of the narrative. But before that question can be addressed adequately, the form-critical character of the narrative must be clarified.[7] What does the form or structure of the book reveal about its character as a pericope? Does that question uncover anything about the unity of the narrative that might be relevant for the issue of sources? What is the genre of the book?[8] Does the genre suggest contact with the preceding or the following narratives? Would it be possible to draw conclusions from these observations about structure and genre that would clarify the setting of the piece? If so, would the setting suggest union with Genesis–Deuteronomy or Judges–Kings? And finally, what is the intention of the pericope? Does the goal of the unit place the narrative in context with Genesis–Deuteronomy more harmoniously than with Judges–Kings?

I

Gerhard von Rad suggested that the structure of the Hexateuch could be clarified by reference to a series of texts representing a 'little historical credo'.[9] These texts, represented in Joshua by 24.2-13, recite the history of God's mighty acts on behalf of Israel ranging from the patriarchs to the conquest. Four distinct themes emerge from these events as stereotypical elements of structure: (1) the patriarchs, 24.2-4; (2) the exodus, 24.5; (3) the wilderness, 24.6-7; (4) the conquest, 24.8-13. In comparison with the expanded narrative represented by the Hexateuch,

---

7.   On the issue of the relationship between source criticism and form criticism, see G.W. Coats, *From Canaan to Egypt: Structural and Theological Context for the Joseph Story* (CBQMS, 4; Washington, DC: Catholic Biblical Association, 1976), pp. 55-79.

8.   The question implies that a single genre definition for the whole is possible. One must hold open the possibility that Joshua is simply a collection of various units that maintain independence. In that case, Joshua would be simply a collection of pieces, each reflecting its own genre. The argument of this essay, however, defends a conclusion that the book is unified, a distinct pericope, and this represents one genre category.

9.   Von Rad, 'Form-Critical Problem', pp. 79-93.

the problem is, of course, that no reference to the Sinai traditions or the primeval period appears in the credo, at least until a late form of the credo emerges. But the four themes, or at least three of the four, appear in the credos with regularity. At times, the wilderness theme drops out of a credo. In Deut. 6.21-23 and 26.5-11, no allusion to the wilderness appears. But the patriarchs, the exodus, and the conquest are stable elements of structure.

Martin Noth built his analysis of the Pentateuch around the foundation established by von Rad's analysis of the credo.[10] Noth insisted, however, that the themes of tradition represented by the elements of structure in the credo were originally independent, distinct items of cultic tradition that grew together as the distinct elements of population in the wilderness or in the land grew together to form one people. The analysis of the credo according to von Rad's pattern seems to me to be correct. Indeed, von Rad observed that the structure of the credo is in fact the structure of the Hexateuch. The Hexateuch is a baroque elaboration in narrative of the articles of faith confessed by the worshipping community by means of the credo.[11] Noth's procedure would highlight the disunity of that narrative. Each theme would reveal a separate and independent origin and history. But von Rad's analytical pattern does not necessarily require such disjunction. In fact, it suggests an impressive and recurring structure that accounts for unity in the whole.

This sense of unity for the structure of the Hexateuch as a whole receives support from the distinctive elements of structure for each theme. Each unit in the Hexateuch can be identified by reference to a clear beginning and an explicit ending. Particularly, each theme begins with an introduction, an exposition that discloses principles for the narrative, a point of crisis that constitutes control for an arc of tension in the narration that moves to an ending, and typically a leitmotif that characterizes the theme. Thus, the theme about the patriarchs begins with Gen. 12.1-3, an exposition that emphasizes *blessing* as a key leitmotif for the narration.[12] The exodus begins with Exod. 1.1-14, an exposition that highlights *oppression* from the Egyptians as the controlling motif for the following story.[13] The wilderness exposition, Exod. 13.17-22, focuses on

---

10. M. Noth, *A History of Pentateuchal Traditions* (trans. B.W. Anderson; Englewood Cliffs: Prentice-Hall, 1972).

11. Von Rad, 'Form-Critical Problem', pp. 1-3.

12. H.W. Wolff, 'The Kerygma of the Yahwist', *Int* 20 (1966), pp. 131-58.

13. G.W. Coats, 'A Structural Transition in Exodus', *VT* 22 (1972), pp. 129-42.

leadership from God as the key for constructing the relevant narratives.[14] And the conquest exposition appears in Joshua 1–5, with special emphasis on the fear of the Canaanites who succumb to Israel and its God when they enter the land.[15] The similarity in structure, each theme introduced by an explicit exposition with an explicit leitmotif as the controlling point of the narrative, suggests unity in the narrative that ranges from Genesis 12 through Joshua 24.[16] Could one not conclude, then, on the basis of the larger whole, that the book of Joshua, introduced by an exposition in Joshua 1–5, is the conquest theme that completes the narrative display of the credo traditions? Would it not stand as a complement to the patriarchal theme in Genesis 12–50, the exodus theme in Exod. 1.1–13.16, and the wilderness theme in Exod. 13.17–Deut. 34.12?

Key elements of structure in the book of Joshua support this judgment. If the judgment about this narrative as the conquest theme is sound, however, the structure of the book should reveal a clear definition of the ending of the conquest theme. Does Joshua 24 function adequately as the conclusion for the theme? Or does the theme, now resident in Dtr, continue into the book of Judges?

1. The exposition of the theme is composite. Yet the character of the whole unit as a unified pericope about the conquest emerges with distinctive lines:

a. 1.1a establishes an effective transition from the Moses saga by relating the events it introduces as items that occurred after the death of Moses (cf. Judg. 1.1). The piece functions as a disjunction. But even the disjunction implies some kind of relationship. It marks a new beginning for the material it introduces. But the beginning stands in explicit contrast and thus in relationship to the preceding tradition represented by the allusion to the death of Moses.

b. 5.1 then introduces the conquest The verse refers to an event described in Joshua 3–4. Indeed, the description suggests a ritual process that establishes the beginning of the conquest by effective participation

---

14. G.W. Coats, 'An Exposition for the Wilderness Theme', *VT* 22 (1972), pp. 288-95.

15. G.W. Coats, 'An Exposition for the Conquest Theme', *CBQ* 47 (1985), pp. 47-54.

16. The relationship between Joshua and Judges remains an open question. Judg. 1.1 assumes some relationship with the preceding narrative but functions essentially as a disjunctive element. Yet Exod. 1.1-8 appears with the same kind of disjunction. The important point is that the tradition in Judges is not represented in the credo. But the issue cannot be explored in detail here.

in the ritual. It is an event that occurs *ex opere operato*. 5.1 then reflects
the results of the ritual: 'their heart melted, and there was no longer any
spirit in them, because of the Israelites'. The fear of the Canaanites
marks their response to Israel's move into the land. And that motif
functions as the structural leitmotif for the conquest theme.[17]

c. An etiology for circumcision at Gilgal appears in 5.2-9. The element
is not obviously a part of the transition from wilderness to conquest. It
appears on the surface to be simply an etiology for the place name. Yet
in its present position, it functions as a part of the transition. And the
function is explicit. In the wilderness, no circumcision had occurred.
Now, in anticipation of a new life, that facet of wilderness experience
stands corrected. The ritual act is renewed.

d. 5.10-12 returns to the function of transition. Verse 10 reports celebration of the Passover at Gilgal, an element that relates to the preceding
etiology not only on the basis of the common place, Gilgal, but also on
the basis of ritual process. Circumcision as an act of commitment is
complemented by the renewal of the ritual for the Passover. Indeed, circumcision functions as effective preparation for the Passover celebration
(Exod. 12.43-49). Then, the transition marks the end of the wilderness
manna, v. 12aαא and v. 12aβ, and the beginning of a new era symbolized by eating the fruit of the land, vv. 11, 12aαב and 12b. The pattern
of structure in this section may be illustrated by the following formula: a
b a b a. The pattern, suggesting a self-conscious construction, sets the
tone for narrating Israel's move into the land by observing that the land
can support the people, an allusion to coming events in contrast to the
end of support from the wilderness, an allusion to the past events. This
twofold character typifies the structure of transition pieces.[18] But it also
sets a tone for recognizing another self-conscious construction, a chiasm
for the larger exposition:

A   Commission to Joshua, 1.1-18
B   Entry into the land, 3.1–4.24
C   Exposition for the conquest, 5.1
C′   Circumcision etiology, 5.2-9
B′   Transition to the conquest, 5.10-12
A′   Commission to Joshua, 5.13-15.

17. Coats, 'Exposition for the Conquest'.
18. Coats, 'Transition in Exodus'.

If this description of structure for the exposition of a conquest theme in Joshua is adequate, it highlights at least two problems in defining the whole as a conquest theme:

i. Elements B and B′ along with C and C′ have obvious roles to fill in setting the stage for a conquest theme. But the pattern seems to offer no position for the tale about Rahab in 2.1-24. To the contrary, the tale anticipates the account of the ritual that effects *ex opere operato* the fall of Jericho in 6.1-27. Does that point mean that the tight structure of the chiasm has been broken by insertion of an element of tradition that did not originally belong in that position? Is this piece evidence for combination of two literary sources, Dtr 1 and Dtr 2? Or does some other factor explain the position of the tale and its corresponding ritual for effecting the fall of Jericho? It is significant that at the end of the Jericho account, an account that might have placed great emphasis on the Lord as the one who gives Israel the land, and thus an account that would have created an effective complement for the theme of the conquest, the tradition reports that 'the Lord was with Joshua; and his fame was in all the land'. The antecedent for the possessive suffix, *šom'ô*, must be Joshua.

ii. Elements A and A′ feature the divine commission of Joshua. The emphasis at this point is only secondarily on the Lord's act in giving Israel the land. The primary point of intention in both of these elements is to account for the authority of Joshua to lead the people. Indeed, in both sections, the commission shows an explicit goal for depicting Joshua, the man whose authority now receives validation, as a new Moses. Thus, in 1.5, Joshua's position as commissioned leader of the people parallels Moses' position. The assistance formula, the promise for divine presence with Joshua for the effective execution of the commission, is compared explicitly to the assistance formula in the Moses traditions. 'As I was with Moses, so I will be with you.' And the theophany that completes the commission in 5.13-15 describes Joshua's response in an image that recalls Moses' response to the theophany at the burning bush (so, Exod. 3.6). But an even more direct parallel appears in the address from the commander of the Lord's army: 'Put off your shoes from your feet. For the place where you stand is holy.' The Lord's address to Moses requires the same act. Indeed, the texts are, with orthographic exceptions, identical.

I suggest, therefore, that the exposition to the narrative in the book of Joshua plays a double role. It not only introduces the narratives about the conquest of the land as an element of Israel's confessions about God's mighty acts. It also introduces narratives about Joshua, the leader of the people in the move that established the people on the land. Indeed, on the basis of the analogy with Moses, an analogy that is an explicit part of the Joshua narration, I suggest that the book of Joshua appears as both the conquest theme with its emphasis on God's mighty act and a heroic saga with its emphasis on the mighty acts of Joshua.[19] The exposition in Joshua 1–5 would function effectively for both.

2. Josh. 6.1-27 contains the account of the ritual that effects the fall of Jericho. As noted above, the obvious intention of this pericope is to affirm God's act in giving the Canaanites into the hand of the Israelites. And indeed, the Rahab tale in Joshua 2 anticipates this account. Yet the conclusion to the Jericho ritual affirms Joshua's stature in all the land. The double character of the tradition thus appears in this pericope with forceful effect, just as in the exposition.

3. Joshua 7 reports a violation of stipulations for dispensing spoil from the victory at Jericho. One Achan took items for his own use from the spoil dedicated to God. And as a consequence, the army of Israel suffered defeat at the hands of the citizens of Ai. The handicap blocking Israel's success in battle could be removed only by removing the guilty from the people. Once the culprit had been executed, the process of conquest could continue without blockage. The narrative shows no particular emphasis on Joshua's leadership. Joshua simply represents the Lord in the trial and passes the sentence of death on the victim with an admonition that, at this moment in his life, Achan should praise the Lord. The focus here spotlights the Lord as the offended party and, by inference, the one who would give Israel victory over the enemy once the offense had been removed.

The same point can be made for the battle report in Joshua 8. With the offense purged, the people launch a second attack on Ai. Verse 7b makes the point for the battle report clear. 'For the Lord your God will give it into your hand.' But the victory over Ai occurs (vv. 18-23) when, in obedience to the Lord's command, Joshua held his javelin which was in his hand over the city. The image recalls the heroic legend about Moses who held the rod of God over the Amalekites in order to

---

19. G.W. Coats, *Moses: Heroic Man, Man of God* (JSOTSup, 57; Sheffield: JSOT Press, 1988). The double character of the tradition is present in the Moses saga. But it does not suggest two independent literary sources.

achieve a military victory (Exod. 17.8-13).[20] Thus, even though the victory in such a military encounter as this one belongs to the Lord, the hero complements that affirmation by effecting the Lord's act on the field of human conflict. So, in Josh. 8.26, Joshua's role is clear: 'So Joshua did not draw back his hand which he raised with the javelin, until he [singular] had utterly destroyed all the inhabitants of Ai'.

On this occasion, the point of the tradition is clear: God gives Israel victory over the enemy. But God does not do that as an act of divine intervention imposed on the plane of human events. God's deed succeeds only because Joshua acts in accord with the divine purpose. There is no act of God apart from the creative initiative displayed by Joshua. Joshua is the man of God, the servant whose leadership God uses to accomplish his goals. The little unit in 8.30-35 changes the pace of the narrative. In an act that constitutes a cultic renewal of the covenant, anticipating 24.1-28, Joshua builds an altar, reads the law at Gerizim and Ebal, and establishes the holy community. Joshua's initiative is clear. He does what he does as the leader of the people. But precisely here, the heroic leader emerges as the servant of God, for in this act Joshua renews the order for community established by Moses, the servant of the Lord (cf. v. 33). Joshua becomes the lawgiver.

4. Joshua 9 recounts the misguided events that led to a covenant with the Gibeonites. Had the Israelites consulted the Lord about the process, they would not have fallen into the Gibeonite trap. Again, the position of the piece supports the theme about God's act in giving Israel the land by setting out a contrast. Yet even in the contrast, Joshua's position is distinctive. Joshua was himself involved in the diplomacy that produced a treaty covenant with the Gibeonites (so, 9.6, 8, 15). Yet, the confrontation scene following discovery of the deception pits the 'leaders of the congregation' (*nᵉśî'ê hā'ēdâ*) against the Gibeonites. Joshua subsequently takes charge of the interview, reducing the Gibeonites to slavery. Joshua's position thus appears to be exculpated. Indeed, Joshua's stature, even in this pericope with its shadows for Joshua's role, is nevertheless great. The chapter opens with an observation that the Canaanite coalition assembled in order to fight *Joshua* and Israel (9.2). And the Gibeonite ploy developed because they had heard of *Joshua's* victory at Jericho and Ai. Thus, even in a tradition that implicates Joshua in failure to consult the Lord, Joshua remains the principal figure. Indeed, Joshua

---

20. G.W. Coats, 'Moses versus Amalek: Aetiology and Legend in Exodus xvii 8-16', in *Congress Volume Edinburgh* (VTSup, 28; Leiden: Brill, 1975), pp. 29-41.

stands in some sense for all of Israel (v. 2). Is the involvement with the Gibeonite contract the heroic flaw for the Joshua saga (cf. Num. 20.2-13)?

The same double tradition appears in the elements of the battle itinerary in Joshua 10–11. In 10.1, the list reports that Adonizedek heard of *Joshua's* victory at Ai. Verse 6 notes that Gibeon sent men to *Joshua* in order to petition for aid. The ancient poem in vv. 12-13 has been placed in the mouth of Joshua. Indeed, v. 14 must have Joshua in view when it observes: 'There was nothing like that day before it or after it, when the Lord hearkened to the voice of a man'. But the double character remains nonetheless: 'The Lord fought for Israel'. The same refrain appears *mutatis mutandis* in 10.18-19, 25, 28, 29, 31-33, 34-35, 36-37, 38-39. The summary in vv. 40-42 makes the point effectively: 'Joshua captured all of these kings and their lands at one time because the Lord, the God of Israel, fought for Israel'. And the summary in 11.21-23 accomplishes the same point: 'Joshua came at that time and wiped out the Anakim... Joshua utterly destroyed them with their cities... Joshua took the whole land, according to all that the Lord had spoken to Moses. And Joshua gave it for an inheritance to Israel...' The victory comes from the Lord. It even comes through Moses. But it is effected by Joshua.

The king list in Joshua 12 carries the conquest theme. The Lord gives victory over the Canaanites. However, the vehicle for the victory is again Joshua (v. 7) or, in Transjordan, Moses (v. 6). The character of the Joshua tradition thus again parallels Moses. Joshua 13 introduces the death topos for the hero (cf. Num. 27.12-33). Yet the focus of the pericope still highlights conquest and distribution of the land. And the facet parallels the Moses tradition again (so Josh. 13.8-33; 14.1-15). The parallel is apparent in the appeal to Moses' act (vv. 6-12), and the blessing for the act from Joshua (vv. 13-15).

The tradition about allocation of land involves Joshua as the agent of the divine, appointed to effect the allocation by sacred lot (Josh. 15–19), and for designation of the cities of refuge and the Levitical cities. The tradition about civil war over an altar in Transjordan reflects the same role for Joshua as the leader of the people and representative for God. Joshua 23 is the next text of importance for the thesis. Joshua's farewell address, at the point of his death, rehearses the events of the conquest, then offers a final admonition from the leader. He reminds the people of the faithful commitment from the Lord for all of his promises; then he calls for obedience to the law in the covenant. The hero admonishes his own people to maintain the community even in his absence.

Joshua 24 identifies Joshua as the convener for the great assembly that effects the covenant (renewal?) for all who now belong to Israel. The appeal for the convention of the assembly may suggest that the constitution of Israel is now inclusive. Even if some had not experienced the exodus and the wilderness with its Sinai covenant, now, by embracing those traditions in the new covenant, they may become a part of Israel. The repetition of the appeal (v. 19) placed emphasis on the serious quality of this relationship with the Lord. Indeed, for the people to assume a legal position as witness against themselves makes the weight of punishment for failure or reward for obedience rest on their own decisions (cf. Deut. 30.19). The covenant community closes ranks therefore in its commitment to the Lord. And thus the act of God in giving the land comes to an end. Significantly, the conquest theme begins with a leitmotif that emphasizes the fear of the Canaanites for invading Israel. It ends with the same motif (v. 14). But now the motif has been transformed. Joshua again appeals to Israel: 'Now fear the Lord and serve him in sincerity and faithfulness...' The verb, *wayyîr$^{e'}$û*, appears in the field of diction for the conquest theme leitmotif (Josh. 10.2). In fact, the verb functions in an admonition from Joshua to the people regarding their response to the Canaanites (Josh. 10.8, 25). But in 24.14, the verb describes a positive relationship for Israel with the Lord, a relationship effected by the covenant ceremony with its sacramental participation in the credo, perhaps also in the ritual crossing of the Jordan. With the new fear, the conquest theme comes to an end. And the sign of the end is the stone of witness (v. 27). The stone is on the land (contrast 22.11). Joshua responds in v. 28 with an act that concludes the theme: 'Joshua sent the people away, each to his own *inheritance*'.

It is significant that the central figure in the process is Joshua. Joshua was the convener for the assembly. Joshua sent the people away. Moreover, v. 29 contains the Joshua death notice. At this point, Joshua is named as the servant of the Lord. That title had been reserved before this point for Moses. Further, the summary statement of Joshua's life illustrates the double character of the tradition: 'Israel served the Lord all the days of Joshua'.

It seems to be clear, then, that the book of Joshua reveals a double structure. It is both the conquest theme, depicting in narrative form the story of God's mighty act, the gift of the land to Israel effected by the hand of Joshua's leadership, and a heroic saga about the mighty acts of Joshua. The double form sets the book of Joshua alongside the longer tradition about Moses as heroic man and man of God. Joshua acts as the representative of God's word. He effects God's act in the gift of the land. And in that role, he is the servant of God (Josh. 24.29). But he also initiates action on behalf of Israel. And in that role, he is the heroic man whose reputation depicts his contribution (Josh. 10.1).

Robert Boling refers to the double elements of the tradition about Joshua:

> There are two views on this subject clearly reflected in the Book of Joshua. The first view focused on Joshua as bearer of the sicklesword on behalf of his commander in chief Yahweh and who, like Moses of old, had produced an 'effective victory-sign' in the second battle for the Ruin... The latter, expressing yet another vision, told the story of the Ruin as ironic preview of Gibeah's defeat in the costly civil war with Benjamin...[21]

But Boling's conclusion relates these two views to literary sources. 'In these two views we may surely recognize the historians we have been calling Dtr 1 and Dtr 2 respectively.'[22] The argument is the same as the conclusions typically advanced to explain the dual character of the Moses tradition. The one facet belongs to the Yahwist and the other to the Elohist.[23] But the problem in the text is not the result of combining two literary sources in order to produce a composite. The problem reflects a particular stage in the history of the tradition.[24]

---

21. R.G. Boling, *Joshua, a New Translation with Notes and Commentary* (AB, 6; Garden City, NY: Doubleday, 1982), p. 244.

22. Boling, *Joshua*, p. 244.

23. M. Noth, *Exodus, a Commentary* (OTL; Philadelphia: Westminster Press, 1962), p. 41.

24. See my comments about the problem in the Moses traditions (*Moses*). The argument does not attack the general hypothesis about the dual nature of Dtr. It does deny the value of the argument from the dual nature of the role of Joshua as evidence for Dtr 1 and Dtr 2. The point of this observation is that the dual nature does not derive, so it seems to me, from a redaction of the story that combines two literary sources, originally independent of each other, into one whole. Rather, the dual nature of the narrative, still preserved in literary form by the text of Joshua, derives from a combination of traditions at a level in the tradition's history before the tradition became a written source. Indeed, it is conceivable that the dual character was a very early part of the tradition, that the character of the narrative as conquest never existed as a distinct and independent story apart from the Joshua saga, that the compound

The Joshua volume in the Anchor Bible series develops another, related argument for understanding the Joshua tradition. In the introduction, G. Ernest Wright comments about the articles of faith in the credo tradition. 'There is one hero, and only one. It is God himself, and to him Israel must give all praise and credit.'[25] Boling supports this general position with a comment about the conquest traditions.

> Yet the honor of the great victories does not fall to Joshua. He is merely an instrument of God's power. The victories are God's alone. Israel can claim no credit. The book does not enable one to fashion hero stories... the victories and the credit belong to God alone.[26]

The argument is identical to von Rad's definition of the role of Moses in the Pentateuch.

> Not a single one of all these stories, in which Moses is the central figure, was really written about Moses. Great as was the veneration of the writers for this man to whom God had been pleased to reveal Himself, in all these stories it is not Moses himself, Moses the man, but God who is the central figure. *God's* words and *God's* deeds, these are the things that the writers intend to set forth.[27]

For both Moses and Joshua, it is a distortion of the tradition to elevate the role of God in the narrative to the exclusion of the role for the hero. The two stand together as complements. To deny the creative role of the one in elevating the creative role of the other misses the significant insight of the tradition. To be sure, God is the Lord of the hero for these traditions. But the creative role of the hero nonetheless emerges from the Moses and Joshua stories with clarity. The tradition itself does not miss the character of heroic leadership in Israel's common life.

The issue turns here on the character of the Joshua tradition as heroic. It is relatively clear that the Joshua image has been modelled on the basis of the Moses image. The Moses image is, in my opinion, fully heroic.[28] Even at the point where Moses is presented as the man of God, thus dependent on God and not at that point technically heroic, the quality of the tradition generally as heroic is not compromised. One might suggest

nature of the story was a part of the tradition from the beginning, not the result of secondary redaction.

25. G.E. Wright, 'Introduction', in Boling, *Joshua*, p. 13.

26. Boling, *Joshua*, p. 51.

27. G. von Rad, *Moses* (World Christian Books, 32; London: Lutterworth Press, 1960), pp. 8-9.

28. Coats, *Moses*.

that heroic and non-heroic images come together.[29] Perhaps the combination most adequately depicts the union of heroic man and man of God, of heroic saga and exodus theme or wilderness theme. For Joshua, the same point would be clear. Conquest theme emphasizes God's mighty act. And Joshua's role in it is non-heroic. But the non-heroic does not cancel the heroic. The two exist side by side. The human leader of the people has two natures. Moreover, the non-heroic does not underwrite a theological position that demotes Joshua to second billing, much less to a position of sinful unworthiness. The priestly tradition in the Pentateuch depicts Moses as unworthy sinner, denied access to the land.[30] But the Yahwist knows Moses only as hero, the man of God. And the Deuteronomist knows Joshua only as hero, the man of God. Even Joshua's involvement in the covenant with the Gibeonites does not detract from his role as the hero for the people, the one who defends the people and enables God's gift of the land to be realized.

The impact of this insight for understanding not only the character of Joshua in the tradition, but also the character of a theology about human beings who function as leaders for the people, must be clear. The leader in the Joshua tradition is not an automaton. He is not a meek and mild little man who folds his hands and 'waits on the Lord'. He is an aggressive leader. Moreover, the tradition does not condemn him for his aggressive leadership. Like Moses, Joshua shows no reluctance to act. Like Moses, this man demonstrates his integrity as a leader not by functioning as a mere instrument for the power of God, as a conduit that transports the spirit of God to the people and then in embarrassed humility denies his value in the process. This man demonstrates his integrity as a leader by taking charge, in the name of the Lord, of the crisis situations confronting Israel. He acts as a responsible agent of God's word, not as a passive puppet with no responsibility beyond an automatic response to the pull on the string. For the tradition about Joshua, as for the tradition about Moses, responsible servanthood to God requires responsible leadership for the people, vigorous heroic leadership that will set the hero into the middle of the life of the people.

29. H.M. Chadwick and N.K. Chadwick, *The Growth of Literature* (Cambridge: Cambridge University Press, 1936), II, pp. 645-65.

30. T.C. Butler, 'An Anti-Moses Tradition', *JSOT* 12 (1979), pp. 9-15; S. West, 'Moses—Man of Indecision', *Dor le Dor* 9 (1980), pp. 33-43.

II

On the basis of the preceding analysis, the following conclusions seem to be in order:

1. The form of the book of Joshua still reflects the patterns of the heroic saga. From the commission of Joshua to stand in the place of Moses to the death report, the structure of the whole shows its similarity to the Moses heroic saga. To be sure, that structure has been more heavily laden with tradition that belongs to the theme of Israel's confession about God's mighty act in giving the Israelites the land. In that theme, Joshua appears not as the hero who saves his people, but as the man of God who effects the gift of the land as Israel's inheritance. The combination of the two traditions gives the Joshua story a double character. Indeed, it influences the form of the unit. That combination is the result of shaping in the history of tradition, not the combination of distinct literary sources. It affects the characterization of Joshua. The figure does not appear in the narrative with as much force as the Moses figure. In fact, one must consider the possibility that the tradition is now non-heroic. But the combination does not finally obscure the character of the whole as heroic saga.

2. The generic character of the Joshua story suggests a point of cohesion with the Moses heroic saga.[31] Indeed, the point is an explicit element in the narrative. Joshua appears clearly as a New Moses. This element is in contrast to the relationship in genre between the book of Joshua and the book of Judges. The stories in Judges may be defined also as heroic, perhaps even as heroic saga. In fact, the structure of the book may suggest unity in tradition with the conquest theme (so, Judg. 1.2-4). The unity between Joshua and Judges remains an open question. However, the internal structure of Joshua points to both exposition and conclusion for the theme. And the generic character of that unit, both implicitly and explicitly, has more in common with the Moses saga than it does with the heroic sagas in Judges.

3. The structure of Joshua does in fact reveal a double nature. But that fact derives from the combination of the heroic saga with the conquest theme.[32] It is a product of the tradition's history at a level of growth in

31. Coats, *Moses*.
32. D.J. McCarthy, 'The Theology of Leadership in Joshua 1–9', *Bib* 52 (1971), p. 175. McCarthy pinpoints the dual nature of the Joshua tradition: 'This gives us

the tradition rather than at the level of a combination of literary sources. The argument for Dtr 1 and Dtr 2 in this narrative is not defeated by this conclusion. The conclusion affects only one point in the argument. But it does suggest that the dual nature of the Joshua narrative is not evidence for distinguishing Dtr 1 from Dtr 2, just as the dual nature of the Moses narrative is not evidence for distinguishing E from J.

4. The setting for the Joshua saga appears to be influenced by the cult. The ritual for crossing the Jordan or for effecting the fall of Jericho comes from the cult. Yet one cannot conclude that the setting for Joshua generally is cult because two pericopae reflect a cultic ritual. One must in fact show caution even in concluding that the setting for Joshua 3–4 is the cult simply on the basis of the ritual character of the event. It would seem correct to suggest that the setting for the Joshua saga is the world of the storyteller. To be sure, stories can be told in the cult. But they can in fact be told anywhere. The point is that the setting for the storyteller is popular. The storyteller tells stories wherever the people are.

If, in fact, the setting for Joshua is popular, that fact would place the tradition in context both with the Moses saga and with the stories that follow in Judges. The question of setting thus does not clarify the issues represented by Pentateuch/Hexateuch.

5. When one asks about the intention of the book of Joshua, the issues emerge with sharper lines. The Moses saga affirms the initiative of the hero on behalf of his people by showing how he effected the exodus and the wilderness with its Sinai, law-giving station. The Joshua saga affirms the initiative of the hero on behalf of his people by showing how he effected the conquest. At this point, the unity of Joshua with the Pentateuch is clear. Moreover, that unity is supported by the generic qualities of the Moses/Joshua narratives. The Pentateuch can claim distinction as a complete unit by recognizing that the Moses saga plus the patriarchal sagas account for its compass. But when one considers that

two intertwined unifying themes in the first chapters of the Book of Joshua: the Jericho operation which inaugurates and virtually accomplishes the taking of the land, and the figure of Joshua who as Yahweh's chosen leader is the means by which this is done'. But McCarthy does not relate the dual nature of these chapters to literary sources. The two belong together in a single statement of a theology about legitimate leadership. Indeed, McCarthy sees this tradition as pre-deuteronomistic (p. 174). I am suggesting that this same dual character is constitutive for the entire book, that it does not provide evidence for distinguishing between Dtr 1 and Dtr 2, but rather it adds by its dual nature to the picture of similarities between the Joshua traditions and the Moses traditions.

unit of tradition represented by the credos, then the issue of unity must move beyond patriarchs and Moses to embrace Joshua. And that unity is not violated by the questions of structure or genre.

The structure of Joshua, with its exposition marking the beginning of the conquest theme and a conclusion in a covenant act marking the end, suggests that while conquest traditions may appear in the book of Judges, the conquest theme is in the book of Joshua. The book of Judges has a quite different structure and is not a part of the conquest theme as a structural unit parallel to the exodus theme or the wilderness theme. The character of these narratives suggests, therefore, that the primary unit, from the perspective of the traditions, is Hexateuch. The term 'Pentateuch' refers to that section of the Old Testament canon commonly called the Torah. The term 'Hexateuch' refers to that section of tradition in the Old Testament canon that moves beyond the Torah to Joshua, yet that reveals a distinct unity in structure and content binding Joshua with the preceding narration. 'Pentateuch' derives from the history of the canon. 'Hexateuch' derives from an analysis of the history of the tradition in the Pentateuch plus Joshua, a history that suggests that the story does not end with Deuteronomy but moves into Joshua in order to account for the possession of the land.

JSOT 55 (1992), pp. 15-23

INCLUSION, EXCLUSION AND MARGINALITY
IN THE BOOK OF JOSHUA

Lori Rowlett

Times of turmoil tend to produce narratives of identity, requiring a set of axiomatic principles, usually unspoken, but inscribed in the text, which differentiate between 'us' and 'them' (the Other). The conquest narrative of the book of Joshua is such a narrative of identity. On one level, the story appears to be a simple national epic, a narrative of warfare, in which 'all Israel' marches into the land of Canaan by miraculously crossing the Jordan, which functions as a boundary to the promised land.[1] At first glance the division between Israel and the Others appears to be ethnic. The Canaanites are to be destroyed by military action with divine assistance so that 'all Israel' can possess the land. However, most of the episodes in Joshua are not simple battle stories. The focus throughout most of the book of Joshua is on the marginal cases, exploring the questions: who is included, who is excluded, what are the criteria for inclusion, and most importantly, why?

As 'New Historicist' literary critic Stephen Greenblatt has pointed out, a work of art will not only reflect the negotiations and exchanges of power taking place in the society which produced it, but will also be a part of the process.[2] Therefore, any text has an ideological function as an assertion of power. My interest is in the way that the text of Joshua interacts with its socio-political context, since the threat inherent in the tales of violence functions as an instrument of coercion, or at least encouragement, to submission. The message is that the punishment of

1. D. Jobling, 'The Jordan a Boundary', in *The Sense of Biblical Narrative*, II (JSOTSup, 39; Sheffield: JSOT Press, 1986), pp. 88-132.
2. S. Greenblatt, *Shakespearean Negotiations: The Circulation of Social Energy in Renaissance England* (Los Angeles: University of California Press, 1988).

Otherness is death, and that insiders can easily become outsiders (Others) by failure to submit to the central government asserting its authority.

Most scholars of Hebrew Bible agree that the conquest narrative in Joshua, as part of the Deuteronomistic History, was composed in the wake of Assyrian domination, and subsequently re-edited by an exilic redactor or redactors. M. Fishbane,[3] M. Weinfeld,[4] B. Halpern,[5] F.M. Cross[6] and R.D. Nelson[7] see evidence of at least two layers of redaction (one Josianic, one exilic or post-exilic), on the basis of stylistic distinctions and of divergences in theological attitudes. Several German scholars, most notably W. Dietrich[8] and R. Smend,[9] have put forth the hypothesis that the exilic additions were made by two different hands: a nomistic redactor with legal interests, and a prophetic redactor. However, the number of later (exilic or post-exilic) editors (whether one or more) is irrelevant to my central point that the main body of the text took shape during the time of King Josiah, when the monarchy's control was far from secure, as the Assyrian Empire was crumbling and the Neo-Babylonian Empire had not yet risen to power. The values promulgated through the book of Joshua are the values being asserted in Josiah's attempt to consolidate his kingdom.

On the surface level, the book of Joshua tells the story of the people Israel and how they conquered the land of Canaan. The story of their battles is gruesome but apparently simple. The deity Yahweh is giving Israel the land and enabling them to defeat the various groups of Canaanites who are living there. Israel is 'us', the people with whom the

3.   M. Fishbane, *Biblical Interpretation in Ancient Israel* (Oxford: Clarendon Press, 1985).

4.   M. Weinfeld, *Deuteronomy and the Deuteronomic School* (Oxford: Clarendon Press, 1972).

5.   B. Halpern, *The First Historians: The Hebrew Bible and History* (San Francisco: Harper & Row, 1988).

6.   F.M. Cross, *Canaanite Myth and Hebrew Epic* (Cambridge, MA: Harvard University Press, 1973).

7.   R.D. Nelson, *The Double Redaction of the Deuteronomistic History* (JSOTSup, 18; Sheffield: JSOT Press, 1981).

8.   W. Dietrich, *Prophetie und Geschichte* (Göttingen: Vandenhoeck & Ruprecht, 1972).

9.   R. Smend, 'Das Gesetz und die Völker: Ein Beitrag zur deuteronomistischen Redaktionsgeschichte', in H.W. Wolff (ed.), *Probleme Biblischer Theologie: Gerhard von Rad zum 70. Geburtstag* (Munich: Chr. Kaiser Verlag, 1971), pp. 494-509.

reader is to identify. The Canaanites are the opponents, the 'Others'. The emphasis in the battle narratives is on *total* destruction:

> Joshua captured Makkedah...he utterly destroyed it and every person in it. He left no survivor (Josh. 10.28).

> And Yahweh gave it (Libnah) with its king into the hands of Israel, and he struck it and every person who was in it with the edge of the sword. He left no survivor (Josh. 10.30).

> And Joshua and all Israel with him passed on from Lachish to Eglon, and they camped by it and fought against it. And on that day they captured it and struck it with the edge of the sword, and utterly destroyed every person who was in it...(Josh. 10.34-35).

Time after time the same words are repeated: 'he utterly destroyed every person who was in it; he left no survivor'. The text makes its point absolutely clear: the punishment for Otherness is death.

However, the distinction between Israel and the Others based primarily on ethnic, cultural and religious difference begins to break down almost immediately. The surface ideology, in which the cohesive group 'all Israel' is to take complete control of the land inside the boundary of the Jordan and institute pure Yahweh worship there, is already undermined by the problem of the Transjordanian tribes in the first chapter. Therefore, the first set of negotiations and exchanges in the text has to do with the question of a marginal case. The Transjordanians have the right ethnicity, the right patriarchal lineage, but they receive their inheritance outside the symbolic boundary of purity, the Jordan—right ethnicity (qualified for insider status), but wrong geographical location (outside). They make an interesting case when compared with another group, the Gibeonites, who are exactly the obverse: wrong ethnicity, but inside the boundary of the 'pure' geographical location. In both marginal cases, the standard of demarcation turns out to be voluntary submission to the authority structure represented by Joshua and his military men; the alternative is the standard punishment for otherness: death.

The book of Joshua begins with a clear delineation of the lines of authority. Yahweh, as the national deity, is to be supreme commander of military affairs. Since Moses the servant of Yahweh is dead, Joshua the servant of Moses is elevated to second-in-command, representing Yahweh on earth. The people are represented as a cohesive entity under the central authority of Joshua. Although they are arranged hierarchically under tribal authority, the text continually reinforces the idea that the people are to find their primary identity as parts of the unified whole, 'all Israel'; tribal identity is to be secondary.

The military hierarchy continues to receive emphasis after Yahweh puts Joshua in charge. The first thing Joshua does, when the deity has finished giving him his orders to cross the Jordan and conquer the terri- tory, is to command the officers of the people, telling them to pass through the camp, commanding (in turn) the people, with exactly the same orders:

> Pass through the midst of the camp and command the people, saying, 'Prepare provisions for yourselves. Within three days you are to cross this Jordan to go in and take possession of this land, which Yahweh your god is giving you to possess' (Josh. 1.11).

The repetitiousness underscores the hierarchical military values of the text.

Once the lines of authority have been established and commands given, Joshua turns to his first marginal case, the tribes of Reuben, Gad and the half-tribe of Manasseh. His words include them as part of the whole. He tells them to cross over with the rest and help them to take possession; afterwards, they may return to their own possessions on the other side of the Jordan. They willingly place themselves under Joshua's authority: 'all that you have commanded us we will do, and wherever you send us we will go' (Josh. 1.16). The lines of military hierarchy are once again reinforced when they promise to obey Joshua, just as they obeyed Moses 'in all things' (v. 17). The most telling part of their sub- mission to authority, however, is their elaboration on their willingness both to obey and to enforce obedience in their own internal ranks (v. 18): 'Anyone who rebels against your command and does not obey your words in everything which you command us, he shall be put to death'. Anyone who steps outside the lines of authority incurs the same fate as the Others, the enemy troops: death.

The Gibeonites in ch. 9 also voluntarily submit to Joshua's central authority and take a place in the hierarchy. 'We are your servants', they announce to Joshua in v. 8. With elaborate trickery, they get Israel to make a covenant by presenting themselves as inhabitants of a land far away when they are actually ethnic outsiders living in the promised land. So their problem is the obverse of that of the Transjordanians: the Transjordanians were the right people on the wrong land, whereas the Gibeonites are the wrong people on the right land. Their motive for submitting to Joshua is their fear of his, and Yahweh's, military prowess.

They have heard of what Yahweh and Joshua did to destroy other opponents. Joshua makes a covenant with them, backed up by an oath sworn by the leaders of the congregation (v. 15): 'Joshua made peace with them and made a covenant with them, to let them live...' Then when their trickery is discovered, the congregation becomes annoyed because of the deception, but the leaders say,

> We have sworn by Yahweh, God of Israel, so we cannot touch them. This will we do for them: let them live, lest wrath be upon us for the oath which we swore to them. The leaders said, 'Let them live' (vv. 19-21).

In return for their deception, the Gibeonites are made into permanent slaves, to hew wood and draw water for Israel, which does not seem like a very appealing covenant from the Gibeonite point of view. The Gibeonites, however, seem to accept their lowly status with gratitude for their lives:

> ...we greatly feared for our lives because of you, and we have done this thing [meaning the deception]. Now, behold, we are in your hand. As it seems good and right in your eyes to do unto us, do it. So he did unto them. He delivered them out of the hand of the sons of Israel, so that they did not slay them (vv. 24-26).

Thus they are spared the usual punishment for otherness, which is death, because of their voluntary submission to Joshua's and Yahweh's authority. They are allowed to live, and even to stay within the geographical boundaries of the promised land, but they have to take a lowly place in the hierarchy and remain in it forever.

Another pair of marginal cases which can be used to test the theory that voluntary submission to the central authority is the line of demarcation for otherness is Achan and Rahab. Rahab seeks the protection of Joshua's men when she says to the spies,

> I know that Yahweh has given you the land, and the terror of you has fallen on us...(Josh. 2.9). For we have heard how Yahweh dried up the water of the Red Sea before you...and what you did to the two kings of the Amorites who were beyond the Jordan, Sihon and Og, whom you utterly destroyed (Josh. 2.10).

The men under Yahweh's military command receive homage from Rahab precisely because of their ability to destroy others (like Sihon and Og) in battle.

A key incident in the Joshua story, one which reveals who the real target of the threatened violence in the text is, can be found in the story

of Achan. Achan (Josh. 7) is the obverse of Rahab (Josh. 2 and 6).
Rahab, a woman and a prostitute as well as a Canaanite, was the ultimate 'Other' who became an insider by voluntarily submitting and
pledging her allegiance to Yahweh's hierarchy, represented by Joshua's
military machine. Achan was the exemplary insider (with the right lineage) who made himself 'Other' by his lack of submission to the hierarchical authority headed by Yahweh. In his confession to Joshua, Achan
acknowledges the deity Yahweh as the one against whom he has ultimately committed his act of insubordination (Josh. 7.20). The hierarchy
under Yahweh is further delineated by the repetition of Joshua's name in
both the posing of the question and Achan's answer:

> Then *Joshua* said to Achan, 'My son I implore you, give glory to
> Yahweh the god of Israel, and give praise to him; and tell *me* now what
> you have done. Do not hide it from me.' So Achan answered *Joshua* and
> said, 'Truly I have sinned against Yahweh, the god of Israel, and this is
> what I did...' (Josh. 7.19-20, italics mine).

In the space of just a few lines, the text has told us not once, but twice,
that Yahweh is the 'god of Israel' and that Joshua is his human representative to whom Achan is answerable. Central to M. Foucault's analysis of power relations is the issue of who has the right (power) to pose
questions, and who is obligated to answer them.[10] The text here is highlighting Joshua's authority, second only to Yahweh's in the hierarchy.

Achan's initial insider status is emphasized in the text by the double
citation of his parentage and affiliation in precise, patrilineal terms. Again
a hierarchical order is given twice (forward and backward) within the
space of a few lines:

> Joshua arose early in the morning and brought Israel near by tribes, and
> the tribe of Judah was taken. And he brought the families of Judah near
> and the family of the Zerahites was taken; and he brought the family of
> the Zerahites near, man by man, and Zabdi was taken. And he brought
> his household near, man by man, and Achan, son of Carmi, son of Zabdi,
> son of Zerah, from the tribe of Judah, was taken (Josh. 7.16-18).

The strong overcoding of the lines of authority in the text makes the
power assertion inherent within it perfectly clear: individuals belong to
households, which belong to families; the families are subordinate to the
patriarchal heads of the tribes, who, in turn, are to find their identity
primarily as components of the entity 'Israel', whose god is Yahweh.

10. M. Foucault, *Surveiller et Punir* (Paris: Gallimard, 1975).

The deity's chosen representative on earth, to whom Yahweh gives commands and to whom the people are answerable, is Joshua. Everyone has a particular place in the centralized system, and everyone ('all Israel') belongs firmly under Joshua's control. Achan, the individual who has tried to step out from under the lines of authority, is therefore subject to punishment not only by Joshua but by 'all Israel', the cohesive yet stratified entity:

> Joshua and all Israel with him took Achan the son of Zerah, the silver, the mantle, the bar of gold, his sons, his daughters, his oxen, his donkeys, his sheep, his tent and all that belonged to him; and they brought them up to the Valley of Achor. And Joshua said, 'Why have you troubled us? Yahweh will trouble you this day.' And all Israel stoned them with stones, and they burned them with fire after they had stoned them with stones (Josh. 7.24-25).

Everything which falls underneath Achan's control in the patriarchal system, namely his offspring and possessions, is destroyed along with him, which serves to emphasize further the hierarchical aspect of the political arrangement. The total destruction of Achan and everything under him is also reminiscent of the ban, which Achan had violated in his insubordination. By hoarding the booty from Jericho, he had infected the entire community with its presence among them. In order to restore purity, the source of the pollution—Achan himself, possessor of the banned items, and everyone in close proximity to him—had to be removed from the community. (The purity–impurity aspect of the ban is emphasized also in Deut. 7.22-26 and 13.13-17.) Impurity is usually projected onto the opponents in literature of violence in an attempt to justify the action taken against them.

Rahab's function as an obverse image of Achan is reinforced by her reappearance in the text (Josh. 6.22-25) immediately before the Achan incident of Joshua 7. According to the basic structure of the conquest narrative in Joshua, Israelites are insiders and Canaanites are outsiders (Others) to be utterly destroyed in battle. In the battle reports and war oracles, the lines are starkly drawn in ethnic terms. However, most of the book of Joshua consists of a series of what Greenblatt would call 'negotiations and exchanges',[11] which determine who will be accepted and who will be categorized as the unacceptable Other. The pairing of the Rahab and Achan episodes back-to-back in chs. 6 and 7 undermines

---

11. *Shakespearean Negotiations*, p. 12.

the initial impression, given by the battle sequences in the text, that ethnicity is paramount. The two stories illustrate the process of negotiations
and exchanges by which insiders may become outsiders and outsiders
may become insiders. Comparison of Rahab's behavior and fate with
Achan's reveals that the true organizing principle of the narrative is not
ethnic identity, but voluntary submission to authority structures, including the patriarchal political arrangement as well as the central ruling
establishment represented by Joshua. The usual punishment for Otherness is death and destruction, as demonstrated by the many incidents in
which all the Canaanites of a city or territory were 'slain with a great
slaughter' or 'struck with the edge of the sword', leaving 'no survivor'.
Yet the Canaanite Rahab is spared, along with everyone and everything
under her (possessions and relatives), while Achan, along with his possessions and relatives, is violently destroyed. Although Rahab is a woman,
she is described as a head of household in patriarchal language, almost as
though she were a man:

> So the young men who were spies went in and brought out Rahab and her
> father and her mother and her brothers and all she had; they also brought
> out all her relatives and placed them outside the camp of Israel
> (Josh. 6.23).

While she remains in a transitional situation 'outside the camp of Israel',
her femaleness is temporarily ignored in the text, and so is her low status
as a prostitute; for once she is simply 'Rahab', rather than 'Rahab the
harlot', her usual appellation. Then in v. 25 she is put into her hierarchical 'place' (in accordance with the patriarchal values of the text), with
her father designated as head of the household, as she and her relatives
settle permanently in the midst of Israel:

> However, Rahab the harlot and *her father's household* and all that she
> had, Joshua spared; and she has lived in the midst of Israel to this day
> (Josh. 6.25, italics mine).

Thus Rahab and her family were 'spared' the usual punishment for
Otherness (death). The contrasting fate of the rest of the inhabitants of
Jericho is graphically spelled out:

> And they (Joshua's men) utterly destroyed all in the city, both man and
> woman, young and old, and ox and sheep and donkey, with the edge of
> the sword (Josh. 6.21).

As in the battle reports of chs. 10 and 11 (cited earlier), the emphasis is
on total destruction. By her voluntary submission to Joshua's authority

and her acknowledgment of Yahweh (Josh. 2.11), Rahab was transformed from the quintessential Other into an insider deemed worthy of protection (and life). She accepted the structures of control and was allowed a place within the hierarchy of insiders. Achan, on the other hand, forfeited his place within the hierarchical system, although he was a born insider, by his attempt to circumvent the structures of control. His lack of submission to the lines of authority placed him (along with his offspring, because of the patriarchal nature of the system) outside the boundaries of control, thereby earning him (and them) the standard punishment for Otherness: a violent death.

The primary ideological purpose of the conquest narrative is to send a message to internal rivals, potential Achans, that they can make themselves into outsiders very easily. The text is more concerned with demonstrating to the internal populace the extent of the governing authorities' strength than with sending to external groups (real ethnic 'others') a statement about their military capabilities. The in-group, headed by King Josiah, was motivated by the need to constitute itself as a power structure in the wake of imperial domination.

JSOT 25 (1983), pp. 23-33

'IN THOSE DAYS THERE WAS NO KING IN ISRAEL;
EVERY MAN DID WHAT WAS RIGHT IN HIS OWN EYES':
THE PURPOSE OF THE BOOK OF JUDGES RECONSIDERED

W.J. Dumbrell

There would seem to be absolutely no room for doubt that the period to which the writer refers in this concluding comment to the book of Judges (21.25) is being negatively assessed. 'In those days' when every man did what was right in his own eyes, Israel had faced an extremely anarchic situation with which is certainly being contrasted the regulated, firmly authoritarian position in which Israelite government found itself under the later monarchy. On the face of it, therefore, this editorial comment which ends the Judges period and which ushers in the age of the monarchy seems to locate the specific problem treated by the book of Judges, namely the absence of a definitive authority. Whatever the shortcomings of the Israelite monarchy, there was no uncertainty in Israel during that period as to the sphere from which leadership was expected.

The design of this paper, however, is to call into question the traditional interpretation of Judg. 21.25 as an introduction to the monarchical books which follow. This will demand a reassessment of the function of the verse in its immediate and wider contexts; we will begin by noting the transitional character of the formula itself.

The Editorial Unity of the Book of Judges and its Connections with 1 and 2 Samuel

The concluding comment of 21.25 forms an 'inclusion' with an identical remark introduced at Judg. 17.6 and serving there to sum up the bizarre narrative in which a household shrine presided over by one Micah came into being in the hill country of Ephraim. It may thus seem that

Judg. 21.25 does not refer to the Judges period as a whole, but serves merely to conclude the series of inter-tribal degenerations described in the last five chapters of the book, and all the more so since virtually the same phrase is found at Judg. 18.1 and 19.1. Yet it has been suggested that the unity between chs. 17–21 is redactional only, betraying earlier independent complexes of 17–18 and 19–21. So Martin Noth,[1] while agreeing that Judges 17–21 was a redactional unit, argued that the editorial comments at Judg. 19.1a and 21.25 had been taken over from Judges 17–18 when the complexes of 17–18 and 19–21 were joined, since Judg. 17.6 and 18.1 appeared to be seamed into the narratives whereas 19.1a and 21.25 were obviously an introduction and conclusion. Judg. 21.25 in particular seemed a little superfluous. But, *contra* Noth, F. Crüsemann has observed[2] that Judg. 19.1a is also built into the continuing structure of the narrative, having been assimilated to the formula with which Judges 19 had been introduced, and it functions there to begin a new phase of the narrative. Clearly Judg. 18.1 provides a similar transition from Judges 17 and thus serves as introduction to the Danite migration of Judges 18, for it does more than merely conclude the thematic remark of Judg. 17.6 of which it is a compression. Equally, Judg. 17.6, while concluding the account of Micah's cultic aberration (17.1-5), provides a transition to the following account of the embellishment of the shrine with Levitical service and the attraction which it therefore held for the migratory Danites. Thus, in all four cases (17.6; 18.1; 19.1a; 21.25) the sentence does not operate merely as introduction or conclusion, but rather as a junction between narratives which stand in close relationship. So we may suspect that the concluding statement of the book (21.25) closes comment upon the dubious social character of Shiloh and yet serves to introduce further material which follows in 1 Samuel 1–3. In 1 Samuel, however, the standpoint is pan-Israelite, not tribal as in Judges.

The Editorial Unity of the Book of Judges

It might be reasonable to suppose, therefore, that pan-Israelite concerns similar to those which appear in the early chapters of 1 Samuel have

---

1. In 'The Background of Judges 17–18', in B.W. Anderson and W. Harrelson (eds.), *Israel's Prophetic Heritage* (London: SCM Press, 1962), p. 79.
2. F. Crüsemann, *Der Widerstand gegen das Königtum* (Neukirchen–Vluyn: Neukirchener Verlag, 1978), pp. 156-57.

engaged the editor of the book of Judges. This is demonstrable in the
Shiloh episodes of Judges 21 and clear from the interconnections established between the material of Judges 17–21. In passing it may be noted
that Abraham Malamat has seen in Judges 19–21 a description of a well-
knit Israelite tribal structure in operation. He notes that Bethel operated
as a confederate sanctuary (Judg. 20.18, 26-27), but also that elements of
an older political constitution seem to be attested by other features of the
narrative, notably the general assembly of all Israel (cf. the use of *'ēdāh*,
Judg. 20.1).[3] We may plausibly argue, therefore, that Judges 17–21 as a
whole exhibits pan-Israelite concerns. In regard, however, to the relationship of this material to the remainder of the book, R.G. Boling has
demonstrated that the presentation of the holy war material of Judges
19–21 has brought us full circle from the introductory war chapter of
Judges 1, indicating the redactional (and the theological) unity of the
entire book.[4]

To be sure, Judges is very much an *editorial* unity with a pan-Israelite
ideal in mind. Much of the book is schematic in its presentation; note the
way in which encounters with foreign aggressors have been handled.
The narratives have been arranged geographically by tribes, ranging
from Judah in the south (3.9) to Benjamin (3.15), to Ephraim in the
centre (4.5), to Manasseh (6.15), to Gilead (and thus Gad?—in 11.1), and
to Dan in the north (13.2). Yet the crises are never merely local.[5] While
the Othniel account is nothing but a bare paradigm for the later deliverance narratives,[6] Ehud, on the other hand, enlists support from the north
(3.27), and there are at least ten identifiable groups in the song of
Deborah. In the song of Deborah the tribal list has been so skillfully
interwoven as to make it a unit with the poem as a whole, so that it
is stylistically improbable that the substance of this poem should be
reduced to a basic deposit which may have involved originally only few

3.   Cf. A. Malamat, 'The Period of the Judges', in B. Mazar (ed.), *The World History of the Jewish People*, III (London: W.H. Allen, 1971), p. 162.
4.   So R.G. Boling, *Judges* (AB, 6A; Garden City, NY: Doubleday, 1975), pp. 36-38.
5.   A. Malamat, 'Charismatic Leadership in the Book of Judges', in F.M. Cross *et al.* (eds.), *Magnalia Dei: The Mighty Acts of God: Essays on the Bible and Archeology in Memory of G. Ernest Wright* (Garden City, NY: Doubleday, 1976), pp. 153-68, has convincingly demonstrated the geographical scheme underlying the Judges 'hero' presentations.
6.   Cf. W. Richter, *Die Bearbeitungen des 'Retterbuches' in der deuterono-mischen Epoch* (Bonn: Peter Hanstein, 1964), pp. 90-91.

tribes.[7] Though the poetic rhetoric makes historical reconstruction risky, the poem clearly envisages an assault upon most of the centre and north. In the case of the Midianite assault, the picture given us is of attack on most of the Palestinian area, since many of the central and northern tribes are involved (Manasseh, Asher, Zebulon, Naphthali), and, according to Judg. 6.4, the Midianite thrust reached as far south and east as Gaza. Jephthah's Gilead deliverance is presented as a pan-Israelite defence of territory which had been held by the confederation for over three hundred years and, moreover, Ephraimites present themselves as concerned, though uninvolved parties (12.1). In the Samson narratives Judah as well as Dan is threatened. In short, in every detailed hero narrative the action is portrayed as neither local nor limited.

As an editorial unity, the main thrust of the book is to present the concept of a united Israelite confederacy. In these circumstances the concluding comment of Judg. 21.25 which allows that the period ended with 'Israel' intact needs careful evaluation. Many, of course, would hold that such a reference to an Israel is an anachronism. In this paper, however, it is the theological purpose of the book rather than its historical precision that is under examination. Our question concerns the nature of the Israel of that period which the author seeks to convey, and whether his closing comment is a disparaging rejection of that anarchic period.

Israel and its Leadership in the Judges Period

If the Israel in view is presented as a political as well as a religious entity, we must ask what sort of political structure was envisaged. We may point to the continuity with the Samuel narrative where 'Israel' is a confederation of tribes led by successive 'hero' figures; the roles of both Samuel and Saul are virtually identical with the hero roles of the Judges period. In regard to the figure of Samuel, while the birth narratives had insisted that his major role would be that of a prophet (cf. 1 Sam. 3.20), he was the successor to Eli and thus also acted as Judge (cf. 1 Sam. 4.18 for Eli's role). This we actually see him doing at 1 Samuel 7, a significant chapter which follows hard upon the loss of the ark and the twenty-year-long domination by the Philistines, a subjugation which is acknowledged to have been caused (1 Sam. 7.3) by Israel's apostasy.

---

7. M.D. Coogan has very plausibly demonstrated the stylistic unity of Judg. 5; cf. 'A Structural and Literary Analysis of the Song of Deborah', *CBQ* 40 (1978), pp. 143-66.

Accordingly, in the style of a typical Judge, Samuel promises deliverance
to Israel if it will remove foreign deities and return wholeheartedly to
Yahweh. This release from external Philistine pressure is then described
in 1 Sam. 7.5-14, being declared to have been orchestrated by Samuel
as Judge (1 Sam. 7.6). The concluding comment of 1 Sam. 7.15-17 deals
with the wise internal administration of Samuel and his general super-
intendence of all Israel—just as had been the practice of victorious
Judges. As for the figure of Saul, the continuance of the office of Judge
in his truncated kingship is clear from the narrative of 1 Samuel 11.
Such a narrative well illustrates a belief in the tenacity of charismatic rule
and the reluctance of Israel to depart from it. The replacement of the
office of Judge by kingship and the struggle which ensued for political
control between Samuel and Saul displays the view that judgeship and
kingship were incompatible, and that, at least in Samuel's view, kingship
was a political degeneration from earlier ideals.

We now may look more closely in the book of Judges at the style of
leadership of which Samuel's was the last real expression. Convention-
ally, since the somewhat infelicitous application of the term by Max
Weber earlier this century, the term 'charismatic' has been applied to
Israel's leadership in the Judges era. If we accept this term, however, we
must divest it of the connotations with which Weber had endowed it.
For him it depicted the career of an extraordinarily and brilliantly gifted
individual for whose talents historical circumstances had provided opportunity. 'Charismatic' as applied to the role of the Judges, however, must
refer to their Spirit-directed, non-repeatable leadership: they had been
directly raised by Yahweh to meet successive crises in Israel's affairs.
This form of leadership is regarded as having been acceptable to and
understood by the community, who presumably viewed it as a continuation of the functions exercised by Moses and Joshua.[8]

If the leadership of the Judges period appears to have been held to
continue the style of leadership to which Israel had been accustomed
from Sinai onwards then we may expect the presentation to suggest that
the institution of kingship would have been at odds with that entrenched
office. For example, the concept of 'holy war' firmly associated with the

8.   Here the breadth of the office contained in the concept of *šōpēṭ* is noted. The
West Semitic verb *šapāṭum* clearly bears the original meaning of 'govern',
'administer' or the like; cf. T. Ishida, 'The Leaders of the Tribal League "Israel" in
the Pre-Monarchic Period', *RB* 80 (1973), p. 516. In this sense the 'Judges' of the
Judges period were supreme authority figures.

Sinai, Conquest and Judges period regarded Yahweh as the architect and achiever of Israel's victories; but this view is seriously undermined by the advent of the standing army at the beginning of the early monarchy. It is not surprising that the historian of the monarchy presents the institution of kingship as hedged about with a series of prophetic checks and balances whereby the temporalities only were left to the king; the spiritualities and hence the real substance of continuity, to the prophet.

The Evaluation of Kingship in the Judges Period

Given the continuity between the book of Judges and 1 and 2 Samuel for which I have argued, is it likely that we have a positive appraisal of kingship in the concluding verse of Judges (21.25)?[9] If so, we are faced with the problem that Judg. 21.25 exhibits a different attitude to kingship than that evinced by earlier sections of the book of Judges, especially the Gideon narrative. We pass over the view of Martin Buber, who posited two types of material concerning kingship in the book of Judges without any attempt having been made to reconcile them,[10] for R.G. Boling has ruled this out by his demonstration of the redactional unity of the entire book.[11]

Read in this way, Judg. 21.25 sets before us a dilemma. If it endorses kingship with enthusiasm, then it contradicts earlier accounts which damn the institution. Gideon (Judg. 8.23) is offered kingship after the Midianite defeat and dynastic kingship to boot! But with an affirmation that not he but Yahweh will reign over Israel, Gideon declines. The

9. Not a great deal more specificity can be introduced into the phrase 'every man did what was right in his own eyes'. In the sense of doing what is personally convenient, the phrase occurs at 2 Sam. 19.7; Jer. 40.5. At Prov. 12.15; 21.2 a contrast is drawn by the use of the statement between a human morality displayed and a divine imperative which is required. Deut. 12.8 provides an even more suggestive context by which Judg. 17.6 and 21.25 might be compared, namely with the use of the phrase in connection with a call for the avoidance of pagan worship in order that divine rest in the land, which is the aim of the settlement (Deut. 12.9), might be realized. But in Judges it is to the disorders of the period that reference is being made and not to the many acts of apostasy by which it was characterized; we should therefore take the phrase at Judg. 21.25 as referring to the extreme individualism which stamped the times.

10. As M. Buber, *The Kingship of God* (London: Allen & Unwin, 3rd edn, 1967), pp. 77-78, does.

11. Boling, *Judges*, pp. 29-38.

narratives of Judges 8 and 9 then go on to vindicate his decision by pointing to his later personal aberrations. These would, the narrative implies, have made even him a very unhappy choice and a totally unsuitable recipient of such absolute power as kingship conferred. In the Abimelech narrative that follows, the narrator is clearly depicting what the granting of dynastic monarchy to Gideon's family would have meant in the long term for Israel. He is thus underscoring the narrow escape at that period which Israel had had. Abimelech is presented, as Malamat has shown,[12] as the one person who did actually exercise kingship during the period, but who was the very antithesis of all that the Judge of Israel should have been. His rise to power by personal astuteness and his use of mercenaries to establish his position deny any element of spontaneity to this office. The total effect of Judges 9 is to present kingship to us as a humanistic alternative to the great series of divine initiatives which maintained Israel's position through the activity of the successive hero figures.[13]

The interesting Jotham fable of Judges 9 betrays, under the image of protection offered by the shadow that kingship will cast (9.15), a knowledge of the pretentious claims that contemporary dynastic monarchies made.[14] It also advances the view that kingship of the Abimelech type (and thus kingship generally, for Abimelech's is that form of Canaanite city-state kingship with which Israel at that time would have been most familiar; cf. 1 Sam. 8) would have been inimical to the best interests of Israel. Kingship, says the fable, is only aimed at by those who are unworthy of the office, by political adventurers and social misfits such as Abimelech. It is not that the kingship must be endorsed and that if the best men do not take it up the charlatans will,[15] but that the office of kingship is an unprofitable one, which is not only unproductive, but

12. Malamat, 'Charismatic Leadership', pp. 163-64.

13. It has been suggested, e.g. by G.H. Davies, 'Judges VIII 22-23', *VT* 13 (1963), pp. 151-57, that the kingship was accepted and established by Gideon and that Judg. 8.23 which reads like a refusal must be considered to be a polite oriental acceptance of office. Certainly, however, the editor of the book of Judges did not view Gideon's answer in that light, since the typical editorial framework which follows the death of Gideon (Judg. 8.33-35) shows no hint of the existence of monarchy.

14. Crüsemann, *Der Widerstand*, pp. 21-22.

15. As E. Maly, 'The Jotham Fable—Anti-Monarchical?', *CBQ* 22 (1960), pp. 299-304, has argued.

incapable of offering any real protection to the community.[16]

This other assessment of kingship in the earlier half of the book requires us to ask once again what is meant by the comment of Judg. 21.25. Clearly the author is drawing from the experiences of the Judges period important lessons which have relevance for the community of his own age. Would the probable establishment of the date of the redaction of the book help us in the more appropriate evaluation of Judg. 21.25?

The Vantage Point of the Author

Some dating clues are contained in 18.30-31. It is there noted that the Danite priesthood continued 'until the day of the captivity of the land', and that the Danite shrine with its graven image endured as long as the house of God was at Shiloh. The latter note is of little help in dating the redaction of the book, for it may mean no more than that Shiloh was never regarded by the Danites as the replacement for their own sanctuary; it is not implied that the destruction of Dan was co-incident with the fall of Shiloh.

The previous chronological note is more helpful: 'the day of the captivity of the land'. Most naturally the 'captivity' would refer to the exile of the North in 722 BCE, all the more so since the removal of the northern priesthood seems to have been part of the Assyrian deportation policy (2 Kgs 17.27) and we know that the Danite sanctuary was still flourishing in Amos's day (Amos 8.14). If the comment of 18.30 does refer to 722 BCE, it was doubtless made at a very much later remove and thus quite possibly after the fall of Jerusalem. Equally well, a reference to a 'captivity' could, as a comment by a southern redactor, refer absolutely to 586 BCE, rather than 722. In either case the notation would seem to stem from an 'exilic' period, a time when a theological stamp was being put upon the history of the entire monarchical period.

If this is so, then Judg. 21.25 is not a comment which arises from within the golden age of the monarchy, as some have supposed. Further, if the theological perspective of the book of Judges is prophetic in stance, it would be surprising if kingship were commended in such a work. A prophetic bent characterizes the 'Deuteronomistic' corpus as a whole, and that work can hardly be said to take a favourable stance to kingship as such. The subject of that corpus is the rise and fall of the

---

16. Cf. Crüsemann, *Der Widerstand*, p. 29.

Davidic monarchy,[17] its closing verses (2 Kgs 25.27-30) holding little hope for the continuance of the Davidic line (*contra* G. von Rad[18]). Martin Noth is no doubt right in declaring that the release of Jehoiachin is a slim thread upon which to hang a theology of hope, and he is certainly correct in emphasizing the sombre note upon which the second book of Kings ends.[19]

It is probable that the book of Judges was redacted within the exile. That period's view of the possibilities which the kingship held out on the eve of its introduction is consistent then with the reality which kingship proved to be. It is against the background of the failures and excesses of that office that the writer in exile narrates the chequered history of his people.

Judges 21.25—A Recommendation for Post-Exilic Israel

I would conclude therefore that the book of Judges can hardly have been an apology for the monarchy, as is usually thought.[20] What then is its function? And how does its final sentence serve that function? What Judg. 21.25 underscores (as Boling notes) is the persistence—in a most improbable and dubious fashion, in a state of absolute disorder—of the notion of Israel. As the writer surveys the period of the Judges he is clearly appalled by the social and religious disintegration he sees. No political system, no platform of tribal co-operation could have produced the survival of the Israel of that period. Judg. 21.25, as Boling says, meant that 'the time had arrived once again for every man to do what was right before Yahweh without any sacral political apparatus to get in the way'.[21] The exile constituted a time when Israel could again be

17. As I have argued in 'Kingship and Temple in the Post-Exilic Period', *RTR* 37 (1978), pp. 41-42.

18. G. von Rad, 'The Deuteronomic Theology of History in 1 and 2 Kings', in *The Problem of the Hexateuch and Other Essays* (London: Oliver & Boyd, 1966), pp. 205-21.

19. Cf. M. Noth, 'The Jerusalem Catastrophe of 587 BC', in *The Laws in the Pentateuch and Other Essays* (London: Oliver & Boyd, 1967), pp. 271-80. Similarly F.M. Cross who evaluates the merits of the von Rad/Noth debate in his 'The Themes of the Book of Kings and the Structure of the Deuteronomistic History', in *Canaanite Myth and Hebrew Epic* (Cambridge, MA: Harvard University Press, 1973), p. 277.

20. Cf. A. Cundall, 'Judges—An Apology for the Monarchy?', *EvT* 81 (1970), pp. 178-81.

21. Boling, *Judges*, p. 293.

united in peace. Again there was no king in Israel. Out of the chaos of the older Judges period (Boling suggests), there had come the bizarre and, indeed, comic resolution of Israel's problems which Judges 19–21 demonstrates. Who knows whether out of the disillusion of exile a new beginning for Israel, in somewhat parallel circumstances of the collapse of the state, would not be possible? The Israel of the Judges period had been too preoccupied with its own internal affairs to do more than have merely a random thought for Yahweh. Now Israel in exile, having been deflected from Yahweh by a long period of monarchy, is called upon to heed the lessons of its past. It is to recognize that Israel as a concept— and an entity—has survived the exile, again within the intention of Yahweh, and, analogously to the Judges period, is thus being called upon to begin again.

Boling's tragi-comical interpretation of the closing chapters of the book (and indeed of the book as a whole), though stimulating, does not come to terms with the purpose of the book of Judges within the sequence of the historical literature in which it stands. The book had commenced with Israel united in the task of consolidating the conquest. After a period in which Israel had sown the seeds of its own demise the ideal of a united Israel meets us again at the end of the book and expands further in 1 and 2 Samuel. The point which the author has made is a simple one. The ideal of Israel had been preserved throughout this period *in spite of* Israel. Its preservation has not depended upon social or governmental forms of any type, let alone upon the existence of such a bureaucratic institution as a monarchy. What had preserved Israel had been the constant interventions of Israel's deity. Israel had constantly resiled from its covenantal obligations but there was a commitment to Israel which Yahweh would not break. Whether there was a future for political Israel at the end of the Judges period depended entirely upon the willingness of Yahweh to maintain such a structure. At that time he had been willing to do so, and it had been this willingness which had accounted for the continuance of Israel. In the summary verse to the book (Judg. 21.25) there is no denial by the writer of the disordered political condition of the period and the blatant individualism which characterized it. But in spite of the tremendous social upheavals of the age, in spite of the fact that there was a lack of a strong authoritarian administration such as that which the later monarchy produced, something of value remained at the end of this period of total debacle. After the glaring apostasy which the accounts present, what remained, surprisingly (from a human point of view), was the ideal which was Israel. Despite the absence of the sort of human support which might have preserved a human religious or political ideal, in spite of the fact that every man did what was right in his own eyes, Yahweh has preserved the reality of a united Israel with which the book had commenced. Probably also the author is offering a recommendation to his fellow-exiles by means of such a comment. He is suggesting that the pattern of direct divine intervention, with theocratic leadership, upon which Israel's well-being had always hung, had been never so really demonstrated as it had been in the age of the Judges. It is the revival of this manner of leadership which alone would hold the key to Israel's future.

Perhaps that is the absolute message that the redactor of the book of Judges is seeking to convey to his constituency. Yahweh has been pleased to preserve Israel through the exile in spite of Israel itself. What would happen now when Israel had run out of political alternatives? What future can exist in exile when temple, kingship, priesthood, cult, even the land itself have been surrendered by progressive and alarming acts of apostasy? The response of the writer is to point back to a time when the political accoutrements with which Israel became identified were in process of being acquired, when not even the land had been totally secured, when Israel was principally a tenuous theological ideal rather than a firm political reality. God alone had preserved the concept of Israel then, God alone in exile would do it again. One could not assume that pre-exilic political forms would not re-emerge. But God would not violate his covenant arrangement. Whatever the transmutations the exile would effect, the covenant relationship which had guaranteed the continuance of divine promises to an unlikely people in such an unruly age as that of the Judges would stand. Ultimately the book of Judges addressed the exiles from the perspective of Israel's election. The concept of Israel, located in an elective ideal to which Sinai had given expression, was indefectibly associated with divine purposes and would be the result of divine intervention alone.

JSOT 57 (1993), pp. 23-37

ROLE DEDIFFERENTIATION IN THE BOOK OF RUTH

Jon L. Berquist

The simple story of Ruth often proves a difficult ground for precise exegesis. In recent years, many studies have utilized literary methods to understand the narrative structure of the book and its plot and characterization.[1] It is common to view the book of Ruth as an artistic short story, a literary fiction with no precise historical setting, although there is a consensus that Ruth is post-exilic. In these studies, sociological analysis has been conspicuously absent.

The potential of sociological methods for the interpretation of the book of Ruth is great. In order to be understandable to their readers, stories must possess a degree of conformity with familiar elements of the readers' social world. Specifically, the interaction between characters within a narrative must correlate to observable social processes, and these processes create possible foci for sociological investigation. This does not imply that the story's characterization depicts historical persons; rather, with appropriate suspension of belief, the reader must imagine these literary characters to be persons who behave in recognizable ways.

1. E.F. Campbell, *Ruth* (AB, 7; Garden City, NY: Doubleday, 1975); P. Trible, *God and the Rhetoric of Sexuality* (OBT; Philadelphia: Fortress Press, 1978), pp. 166-99; J.M. Sasson, *Ruth: A New Translation with a Philological Commentary and a Formalist-Folklorist Interpretation* (Sheffield: JSOT Press, 1979); R.E. Murphy, *Wisdom Literature: Job, Proverbs, Ruth, Canticles, Ecclesiastes, and Esther* (FOTL; Grand Rapids: Eerdmans, 1981), pp. 83-96; A. Berlin, 'Ruth', in J.L. Mays (ed.), *Harper's Bible Commentary* (San Francisco: Harper & Row, 1988), pp. 262-67; and D.N. Fewell and D.M. Gunn, *Compromising Redemption: Relating Characters in the Book of Ruth* (Literary Currents in Biblical Interpretation; Louisville, KY: Westminster/John Knox Press, 1990).

Sociological approaches, therefore, can be helpful in the study of the book of Ruth through a nuanced understanding of human social behavior. Of course, the interpreter must be careful not to assume that the literary depictions are historically 'accurate', that is, that the depictions can be used as sociological evidence. This use of sociological methodology does not deny the literary nature of texts, but instead finds ways in which literary and sociological approaches can cooperate in exegesis.[2]

In the book of Ruth, the social roles of the main characters (Naomi, Ruth and Boaz) undergo observable changes involving the addition of various roles. This process of characterization corresponds to the sociological theory of role dedifferentiation, by which persons respond to crisis through adding roles, including roles that would be socially inappropriate in normal times. This theory can assist the literary interpretation of the book of Ruth.

Role Dedifferentiation

Many sociological theories depend on notions of increasing distinctions between elements of a system, which is termed differentiation.[3] Through structural differentiation, social systems become increasingly complex. At the microsociological level, individuals' roles become more distinct from others. Modern bureaucracies evince the results of differentiation, both as a system and as a set of roles, since the system tends toward complexity and the roles of individuals toward specialization.

Recently, certain sociologists have focused their attention on the complementary process of dedifferentiation. Edward Tiryakian defined dedifferentiation as the undoing of prior patterns and role definitions, resulting in a condition of less structure.[4] He has argued that this process is not necessarily negative, but that societies undergo dedifferentiation in order to release additional energy and to remobilize themselves for greater efficiency under new situations.

---

2.   I develop more fully the social context of the book of Ruth in J.L. Berquist, *Judaism in Persia's Shadow: A Social and Historical Approach* (Minneapolis: Fortress Press, 1995), pp. 221-32.

3.   For a classic discussion of differentiation, see T. Parsons, *Structure and Process in Modern Societies* (New York: Free Press, 1960).

4.   E.A. Tiryakian, 'On the Significance of De-Differentiation', in S.N. Eisenstadt and H.J. Helle (eds.), *Macro-Sociological Theory: Perspectives on Sociological Theory*, I (London: Sage, 1985), pp. 118-34.

Jean Lipman-Blumen noticed a connection between dedifferentiation and times of social turmoil and uncertainty. During crises, roles merge, as each person assumes additional roles.[5] Her chief example concerned women in the United States during the Second World War. As a systemic response to crisis, there was a sharp increase in the number of women employed in jobs such as manufacturing. These positions, which had previously been male gender-specific, were suddenly dedifferentiated by the removal of the gender distinctions. Both men and women could attain these positions. This redefined job roles and gender roles, but after the crisis the roles partially redifferentiated. This temporary dedifferentiation responded to a crisis, during which the redefinition of social and sexual roles resulted in society's greater ability to adjust.[6]

Ruth's Dedifferentiation of Roles

Setting the Stage: Crisis and Role Death

In Lipman-Blumen's understanding of role dedifferentiation, crisis catalyzes role shifts. In the book of Ruth, famine represents the crisis that triggers dedifferentiation (1.1). As the characters react to the famine, roles lose their stability.

The first role shift involves Naomi, the Ephrathite matriarch of the small family that migrates from Judah to Moab in search of food. Famine motivates the move, but once there, Naomi's husband and sons die (1.1-5). For Naomi, this transition from 'wife' to 'bereft woman' (1.5) is not a case of dedifferentiation, because she loses her major roles.

5. J. Lipman-Blumen, 'Role De-Differentiation as a System Response to Crisis: Occupational and Political Roles of Women', *Sociological Inquiry* 43 (1973), pp. 105-29. For a general discussion of role theory, see R. Dahrendorf, '*Homo Sociologicus*: On the History, Significance, and Limits of the Category of Social Role', in *idem* (ed.), *Essays in the Theory of Society* (Stanford, CA: Stanford University Press, 1968), pp. 19-87; and T.R. Sarbin and V.L. Allen, 'Role Theory', in G. Lindzey and E. Aronson (eds.), *The Handbook of Social Psychology*, I (Reading, MA: Addison–Wesley, 2nd edn, 1968), pp. 488-567. A recent revisioning of role theory and social structure is J.S. Coleman, *The Asymmetric Society* (Syracuse, NY: Syracuse University Press, 1982).

6. For recent work on the theory of sex roles and gender in society, see A.H. Eagly, *Sex Differences in Social Behavior: A Social-Role Interpretation* (Hillsdale, NJ: Lawrence Erlbaum, 1987); and J.M.C. Nielsen, *Sex and Gender in Society: Perspectives on Stratification* (Prospect Heights, IL: Waveland, 2nd edn, 1990).

She is left without affiliation and with little connection to the larger
institutions of society (1.21). She severs her remaining connections to
her adopted country (1.6-7) and to her daughters-in-law (1.8-9, 11-12).
The beginning crisis, then, is threefold: a famine of national or international scale, the death of three men and virtual role death for Naomi.[7]
This crisis signals the possibility for the response of role dedifferentiation.

Ruth's Clinging
Ruth enters the story in 1.4, where she is named; she does not act until
1.14, when she and Orpah provide different responses to Naomi's role
death. For ten verses, Ruth watches the crisis grow to overwhelming
proportions. Whereas family relations define Ruth's role in 1.4, the death
of the family gives birth to Ruth as actor. The crises of famine and death
lead directly to her dedifferentiation.

Orpah accepts her role as bereaved daughter-in-law and obeys her
mother-in-law, in accord with the norms of her stratified society. By
returning to her previous family, Orpah fulfills her role expectations.
Ruth, however, deviates from her mother-in-law's command and from
standard expectations for young widows: she clings (דבקה) to Naomi
(1.14). The Hebrew word 'cling, cleave' (דבק) is a moderately common
term, occurring 40 times in the G stem. The most frequent Hebrew
Bible use of this term is in the phrase 'to cling to God'.[8] However, there
are only eight references to clinging between humans, and four of these
appear in Ruth. Of the other references, perhaps the best known is
Gen. 2.24: 'a man leaves his father and his mother and clings to his wife,
and they become one flesh'. This clinging between a man and a woman
relates to love, to marriage, and/or to intimate sexual relations.[9]

---

7.   The end of 1.13 should be translated, 'it is more bitter for me [Naomi] than
for you [Ruth and Orpah]'. See Fewell and Gunn, *Compromising Redemption*,
p. 28 n. 12.

8.   M. Weinfeld also notices the use of דבק in a Deuteronomistic phrase of religious disloyalty, 'cling to the nations' (Josh. 23.12; 1 Kgs 11.2), but he miscon-
strues this phrase, which refers more particularly to the practices of marrying women
of other nations (*Deuteronomy and the Deuteronomic School* [Oxford: Clarendon
Press, 1972], pp. 83, 333, 341).

9.   Against Campbell, *Ruth*, p. 81, who sees דבק as covenant language. But the
three other non-Ruth uses of דבק for intrahuman relationships also carry a sexual
meaning. Shechem's infatuation with Dinah results in kidnapping and rape, but then
his soul 'clings' to Dinah (the parallel verb is אהב, 'to love'); Shechem then desires
marriage (Gen. 34.3). Josh. 23.12 explains 'clinging to the nations' as a reference to

Furthermore, דבק refers to the male role in initiating marriage. Outside of Ruth, the term 'cling' never describes a woman's act. This makes Ruth 1.14 all the more striking. When Ruth clings to Naomi, Ruth takes the male role in initiating a relationship of formal commitment, similar to marriage.[10]

Ruth responds to crisis with dedifferentiation by adding roles. She remains in the female role of daughter-in-law even though there is no longer any basis for that role, and she adds the male role of 'clinging' to Naomi as a husband. Ruth maintains both roles; she is still daughter-in-law (1.22) even *after* she clings (1.14). This is not role replacement, but role addition. Facing a crisis in which there are not enough men to fulfill typical male roles, Ruth adds a specifically non-female role, 'clinging'. This is an instance of role dedifferentiation.

Family Roles

Ruth's second chapter begins with a notice that Naomi has a relative (2.1). By the end of ch. 2, Naomi exclaims, 'The man is close to us; he is one of our redeemers (מגאלנו)!' (2.20). Thus, family connections provide an important set of roles, including the role of redeemer that would provide a possible solution to the crisis. Whereas the narrator unswervingly reports the precise familial relationship of mother-in-law and daughter-in-law (1.6, 7, 8, 14, 15, 22; 2.18, 19, 20, 22, 23), Naomi calls Ruth 'daughter' or 'my daughter' (2.2, 22).

Within this network of family relations, the reader finds an essential clue about the nature of the problem to be solved. Naomi attributes her initial role death to her lack of sons (1.11-14), agreeing with the narrator's definition of the problem (1.5). The issue is not the lack of children or fertility *per se*, but specifically the lack of *sons*. Once Naomi sees Ruth taking the husband role of clinging, Naomi accepts Ruth as kin, in the form of a son. This restores a familial relationship, albeit a strange

---

marrying (חתן) foreign women. Similarly, 1 Kgs 11.2 condemns Solomon for 'clinging' in love to foreign women, preceding an enumeration of Solomon's wives and concubines.

10. Fewell and Gunn (*Compromising Redemption*, pp. 97, 103) notice Ruth's caretaking of Naomi as represented in this term and they understand this as a husband image, but they do not further develop Ruth's taking of a specifically male role. As discussed below, the other uses of this term in Ruth carry different connotations, but the reader familiar with other texts would have likely used the standard marriage meaning to interpret Ruth's first use of the term in 1.14.

one, and Ruth begins to provide for Naomi, offering a short-term solution to the problem of bereavement.

A Plan for Role Development: Gleaner and Seducer
Ruth's dedifferentiation does not stop with these family roles of husband and son. In the larger society, Ruth adds non-family roles, beginning with the role of gleaner, in order to provide Naomi with food (2.2).[11] Levitical regulation specified that all landowners must allow the poor and the foreigner to enter the fields after the harvesting, in order to gather up whatever was missed or dropped by the field laborers (Lev. 19.9-10). The gleaners could keep what they gathered. The law required landowners and laborers to cooperate, but reluctance could well be expected. Gleaning provided subsistence for those lowest in social status. In Ruth's case, with two persons eating one's gleanings, even survival would be questionable. Ruth must find another solution to hunger and poverty.

The narrative immediately indicates another, more permanent solution. Ruth suggests more than gleaning when she says, 'I intend to go to the field, so that I may glean among the grain after anyone in whose eyes I find favor' (2.2). Since the law insists that all landowners allow gleaning, Ruth's intention seems more than finding kindness. The expression 'to find favor in one's eyes' (מצא חן בעיניו) typically refers to petitioning, but in Ruth 2.2 the phrase is a sexual innuendo.[12] Here finding favor cannot refer to a petition, since gleaning would not require permission from the landowner (Lev. 19.9-10), and since Ruth does not seek permission from anyone before she gleans (2.3).[13]

Ruth intends to use gleaning to attract a husband who would take the role of provider. Thus, her statement announces both a short-term solution to hunger (gleaning) and a plan for a long-term solution (marriage).

11. Fewell and Gunn (*Compromising Redemption*, pp. 76, 98) refer aptly to Ruth as a breadwinner.

12. The expression occurs 48 times, of which 14 refer to a man's petitioning of God and 23 to a man's petitioning of a higher-status male. In fact, relative status is often a crucial point (Gen. 39.4, 21; 47.25, 29; 50.4). Of the 11 cases of women's use of the phrase, 7 are petitions, but 4 cases (Deut. 24.1; Ruth 2.2; Est. 2.15, 17) suggest the context of sexual attraction.

13. Campbell (*Ruth*, p. 94) argues that Ruth asks for permission in 2.7, but the text is missing.

For the proposed long-term solution, Ruth adds another role: seducer.[14] Ruth's intention of sexual attraction allows a clearer understanding of her actions in the field (2.3-16).

> [3]So she walked and came and gleaned in the countryside after the field-workers, and happened across the portion of the countryside that belonged to Boaz, who was from the family of Elimelech.
> [4]Then Boaz came from Bethlehem, and he said to the fieldworkers, 'YHWH be with you'. They said to him, 'May YHWH bless you'. [5]Boaz said to his boy, who was in charge of the fieldworkers, 'Who is this girl?' [6]The boy who was in charge of the fieldworkers answered and said, 'She is the Moabite girl who returned with Naomi from the country of Moab. [7]She said, "I wish to glean and to gather among the ears of grain after the fieldworkers", and she came and stood from then in the morning until now. She stayed in the house only a little.'[15]

Ruth 2.3 tells of Ruth gleaning in fields and happening across Boaz's field, but the scene shifts in 2.4 to focus upon Boaz's entry into the field. In this new scene, Ruth's location remains unannounced. In fact, though the setting for the first part of this scene (2.3) is clearly the field, the setting of the rest (2.4-7) is ambiguous. Though the reader may presume the field, the last line (2.7b) forces a re-reading, especially as the next scene starts (2.8-13). Suddenly, Boaz's house seems the location! The narrative brings the scene into shocking clarity. Boaz entered his property and passed by the fieldworkers on the way to his house, where a surprise awaited him: his field supervisor with a foreign girl. With apt suspicion, Boaz challenged the supervisor, 'Who is this girl?' The supervisor's infelicitous speech betrayed the nervousness of his defense, insisting that Ruth intended gleaning and had hardly been inside long enough to do anything improper. In the context of Ruth's announced intentions to seduce some man (2.2), this scene seems clearly to be evoked: during a morning's gleaning, Ruth located the ranking man present and began her seduction.[16] Now an even higher-ranking man catches her and uncovers her plot. Immediately, the supervisor exits from the narrative, and Ruth's designs focus solely on Boaz.

14. In this role, Ruth parallels Tamar's actions toward Judah (Gen. 38), as recognized by Fewell and Gunn, *Compromising Redemption*, pp. 46-48.

15. This reading has the advantage of requiring no emendation of the MT.

16. Echoes of Potiphar's wife (Gen. 39) resound here: a woman's seduction leads a young man into trouble with his superior. In that story as well, the house (and the master's possession of all therein) is a key point.

Boaz's references to Ruth are oddly ambiguous. He uses the term 'cling' (דבק), as discussed above, to describe Ruth's relationship to Boaz's female servants in the harvest, and he encourages her to stay away from the men in the field, suggesting a protected status (2.9). Not only should Ruth follow behind these women, but she should identify with them and become part of their association.[17]

This passage portrays the relationship between Boaz and Ruth. He forbids her contact with other males and gives her freedom to glean, which the law already granted. Ruth had worked to seduce the supervisor; Boaz counters that and sends Ruth back out into the field. Since Boaz understands this as an act of protection, Ruth capitalizes on his action and interprets it as 'finding favor' (2.10), referring to the beginnings of sexual attraction.[18] His pious blessings appear ironic: Ruth does not seek refuge in God, but in a man. Despite his protestations, Boaz now appears to be that man (2.12), and she seeks her reward under Boaz's 'wings' or skirt (3.9).[19]

At this point in the narrative, Ruth has attempted to take the role of Boaz's seductress, but Boaz has not accepted her advances. However, Ruth's role dedifferentiation continues to expand. At this point, the narrative breaks down. Boaz has blocked Ruth's seduction, while encouraging her role as gleaner. As gleaner, Ruth attains a short-term solution, but without her seduction she finds no role that leads to a permanent amelioration of the incipient crisis. Thus, the narrative must find another opportunity for the seduction to continue.

17. Note the rejection of parents in Ruth 2.11 and Gen. 2.24, both of which appear with clinging language. This strengthens the impression of a close relationship, similar to marriage. In another reference to the early narratives, Boaz credits Ruth with going to a previously unknown land, as Abram left Ur (Gen. 12.1).

18. Also, the phrase 'speak to the heart' has sexual connotations, according to Fewell and Gunn (*Compromising Redemption*, p. 102).

19. As fitting for someone in the process of role dedifferentiation, Ruth concerns herself with role labels. She rejects Boaz's title of female servant (2.13), but she accepts the title 'girl' (2.6), which parallels the title of the supervisor. She takes egalitarian role labels while rejecting subservient ones. Eventually, she receives the role label that she prefers: 'woman of strength' (3.11), parallel to Boaz, who is a 'man, a hero of strength' (2.1).

The Spreading of Dedifferentiation

Naomi as Matchmaker

The second chapter ends with a desperate situation. Ruth's short-term solution of gleaning would soon fail, since the harvest was approaching its end, and Boaz's rejection of Ruth's seduction blocked the marriage that would have provided the permanent solution. In the narrative's time frame, months pass in a single verse until the need for action is once again crucial (2.23).

Naomi then undertakes her second active role.[20] In 3.1-4, Naomi prods Ruth to act toward the permanent solution. Naomi assumes the role of the matchmaker who seeks rest for Ruth (3.1, אבקש־לך מנוח). The term for rest (מנוח) usually refers to a place in which one can rest, and thus some translations render the word as 'home'.[21] Along with this meaning can also reside the sense that Ruth should find a way to rest from the daily labor that has provided survival for her and her mother-in-law. Thus, Naomi directs the active search for a long-term solution, which is profitable marriage.

The addition of the matchmaker role is role dedifferentiation. In ancient Israel, fathers arranged marriages for their children.[22] Naomi's matchmaking is a male role. Once more, dedifferentiation sets the narrative into motion. When Naomi oversteps the roles acceptable for women, work toward the permanent solution restarts.

Boaz as Suitor

Boaz adopts the role of suitor when he acknowledges Ruth as seducer (3.8, 10). Boaz's response facilitates the solutions to the story's problems, since his wealth can save Ruth and Naomi from hunger and social isolation. Ruth's attempts at the seduction of a provider (2.2) and Naomi's prodding toward these ends (3.1-4) both advance the plot in anticipation of Boaz's reply. The plot's success requires not only that Boaz accept the sexual seduction, but also that he undertake the proper courting of Ruth. Appropriately, his response to Ruth's unexpected

20. See J.W.H. Bos, 'Out of the Shadows: Genesis 38; Judges 4.17-22; Ruth 3', *Semeia* 42 (1988), pp. 58-64.

21. Trible, *God and the Rhetoric of Sexuality*, p. 182.

22. See R. de Vaux, *Ancient Israel*. I. *Social Institutions* (New York: McGraw–Hill, 1961), p. 29. Rebekah initiates the search for a wife for Jacob (Gen. 27.46), but Isaac makes the arrangements (Gen. 28.1-5), and she has no further role.

presence on the threshing floor moves from acceptance of her loyalty
(3.10, חסדך) to a proclamation of action (3.11). Thus, Boaz allows Ruth
to perform her role of seducer successfully, and he responds with the
appropriate parallel role of suitor.

Boaz as Redeemer
As Boaz acknowledges his added role as suitor, he also accepts the role
label of redeemer (3.9, 12, גאל) that Ruth attributes to him.[23] Boaz's
acquisition of this role violates social expectation, since he is *not* the
closest of Elimelech's relatives. The sexual liaison could be fleeting, but
the role of redeemer grounds their relationship in the wider network of
social and familial obligations. When Boaz accepts this role of redeemer,
he obligates himself to the purchase of the land once owned by
Elimelech (4.3). The law requires a close relative to buy back real property sold because of debt (Lev. 25, 27).[24] Naomi does not currently own
this land; Elimelech sold it to pay off debts, probably forcing the family's
move away from Judah.

Boaz's pending redemption of the land would entail the purchase of
the land from whomever currently owned it and the ensuing transfer of
that land from Boaz to Naomi, as the representative of Elimelech, at no
charge.[25] This would provide a one-time infusion of funds to Naomi and
Ruth. Though such an action would discharge Boaz's responsibility, it
does not solve the women's long-term problem. Two women could not
farm to feed themselves, since they had no means to invest in seed or to

23. The view of redemption presented herein is similar to that developed by
R. Gordis, 'Love, Marriage, and Business in the Book of Ruth: A Chapter in Hebrew
Customary Law', in H.N. Bream, R.D. Heim and C.A. Moore (eds.), *A Light unto
My Path: Old Testament Studies in Honor of Jacob M. Myers* (Philadelphia: Temple
University Press, 1974), pp. 241-64.

24. Cf. Exod. 6.6 and 15.13, where God redeems the enslaved people by buying
them from their owners.

25. Ruth 4.3 indicates that Naomi owned the land outright, causing interpretive
difficulties because there has been no mention of this property earlier in the story.
But this problem can be solved through a close investigation of the redemption law.
The redeemer would buy the land from the stranger and then give it to Naomi, who
would sell it back to the redeemer. The redeemer would gain land (at twice its value,
one presumes) and Naomi would gain some funds with which to live for a while. In
4.6, the closest relative refuses purchase because he could not afford to buy the land
and the slave, Ruth, from Naomi, since that would be his second purchase of the
property. For a more standard view, see E.W. Davies, 'Inheritance Rights and the
Hebrew Levirate Marriage', *VT* 31 (1981), pp. 138-44, 257-68.

survive the off-season. The role of redeemer did not obligate Boaz to long-term care, and ch. 3 does not refer to Boaz as potential husband, a role that does not necessarily follow upon that of redeemer.

Boaz does not lose his previous roles as he gains new ones. He maintains his role as provider (3.15, cf. 2.16) and as man of worth, as seen in his attribution of a parallel role label to Ruth (3.11). This gain without complementary role loss presents role dedifferentiation.

Boaz reluctantly agrees to function as redeemer in ch. 3, and then seeks the closest relative to be Naomi's redeemer.[26] The nameless relative accepts the challenge to buy back the land, but then Boaz springs a trap: there is also a slave to be repurchased with the land (4.5). Boaz, however, gives the other relative a chance to renege on the family duty by offering to serve as redeemer himself (4.4). Though the relative agrees to buy the land, he does not accept the idea of repurchasing the slave. The expense of purchasing and/or maintaining the slave would be too great, and such a purchase would deplete his funds that were available for inheritance (4.6).[27] Through the legal machinations in the gate, Boaz assumes the role of legal redeemer for Naomi and Ruth. He locates someone else to take responsibility, but then he uses trickery to bind himself with the enormous costs of redemption.

Boaz as Husband

Surprisingly, Boaz volunteers for the role of Ruth's husband (4.5, 10). This is a permanent legal role; Boaz the husband must provide for Ruth and Naomi for the rest of their lives, unless divorce should sever the relationship. Were Boaz only redeemer, then the one-time transfer of funds would have continued the marginal existence and social isolation of Naomi and Ruth. However, the new role of husband creates a long-term relationship between Boaz and the women that grants them society's greatest guarantees of economic and social security.[28]

---

26. Campbell (*Ruth*, pp. 109-10) emphasizes Boaz's willingness to help, but Fewell and Gunn (*Compromising Redemption*, pp. 87-92) realize his reluctance.

27. Though there would have been a need to pass Elimelech's redeemed wealth to Elimelech's son through Ruth, there is no evidence that redemption law required the child of a redeemed woman to receive *all* of a man's inheritance. Thus, the traditional argument that the relative fears his own sons receiving nothing with all of the family wealth going to Ruth's son is erroneous. The depletion of funds due to the expense of the repurchase seems a simpler explanation.

28. Sasson (*Ruth*, p. 91) also argues that redemption and marriage are separate acts.

Marriage provides an elegant solution to the economic interplay of the
redemption process. By bringing his distant relatives into his own family,
Boaz acquires Elimelech's property at cost. His machinations in the gate
work to his own economic benefit, and so he becomes a fitting trickster
hero within the traditions of the Hebrew Bible. Once Boaz considers
marrying Ruth, he has a perfect plan to maximize his own wealth, if
only he can trick his relative out of his rights to redeem the property.
Apparently, the plan succeeds only because Boaz's opponent cannot
envision marriage to a foreign woman. For Boaz, the entire narrative
takes on a different character. He searches for ways to maximize his
own advantage while maintaining his proper family honor; his solution
bends the social rules about marriage while adhering to and exceeding
the redemption law. Thus, the story ends in success for him because of
his willingness to go beyond the role of redeemer and into the role of
husband.[29]

The narrative emphasizes Boaz's final role dedifferentiation by depicting it in two stages. In ch. 3, Boaz functions only as potential redeemer,
with no indication of the husband role. In 4.5, Boaz asserts the necessity
of providing a child to Ruth to perpetuate Elimelech's legacy, but marriage *per se* does not yet appear; Ruth is 'the wife of the dead one' (4.5),
not Boaz's future wife. Only in Boaz's concluding speech of the book
does he state that he will take Ruth as wife (4.10); the narrator echoes
this in 4.13. With this last action of role dedifferentiation, Boaz falls
silent; his story has ended.

Role Restoration

At the end of the story, Ruth acquires her last role as she becomes
mother (4.13), which leads to the popular proclamation that she is more
than seven sons to Naomi (4.15). Naomi, whose bereavement begins the
narrative, now ends the tale with a final role dedifferentiation. She
becomes the mother of the child, Obed, even to the point of nursing him
(4.16). The women's chorus agrees, asserting that this son has been born
to Naomi (4.17). The barren (1.11) receives a child. The cycle of the
story finds its completion with Naomi's assumption of the role of
mother.[30]

29. For the trickery involved here, see Sasson, *Ruth*, pp. 168-69.
30. Bos ('Out of the Shadows', p. 58) clearly articulates the 'radical reversal'
implied here, as does Trible (*God and the Rhetoric of Sexuality*, p. 196).

Social Deconstruction of Gender in the Book of Ruth

Though the social processes of the characters within the book of Ruth do not necessarily correspond to any social roles within historical Israel, the narrator presents characters who perform their roles in ways that ancient readers would comprehend. This social sensibility allows socio-logical analysis to join with literary study in the exegesis of this story. Attention to role dedifferentiation demonstrates that the plot depends upon Ruth's addition of roles and upon this tendency's spread to Naomi and Boaz. Once all of the characters are adding non-standard roles, the narrative's problems attain solutions.

From the start of the story, women deconstruct their gender by dedif-ferentiating their roles. Specifically, the women take a number of roles that, in their society, were exclusively or predominantly male roles. Naomi dedifferentiates her roles in ways that catalyze; Ruth's dediffer-entiation is more active, leading directly to the solution of the story's problems. In terms of gender boundaries, Ruth operates as a man in a man's world, and thus she can affect the changes needed to assure her own survival in a male-dominated culture.

The crucial point in the narrative comes when Boaz adds the roles of suitor, redeemer and husband, thus undergoing role dedifferentiation. When the most prominent male in the story redefines his own roles in response to the story's dedifferentiating women, solutions to the story's problems become available. Boaz accepts the role reversals, including those of gender, even to the point of rescinding his right to the naming of his child.

In this way, the book of Ruth deconstructs gender. Problems attain solutions only when people transgress social conventions and take roles that society limits to the other gender. In the process, the actors reinvent their own social roles and perhaps even their own selves.[31] Certainly, the actions of the story's characters change the social reality of their narra-tive world, so that gender no longer defines and limits potential and possibilities. The deconstructing of gender empowers and enables, even-tually resulting in the solution of the story's original problems.

If one recognizes the book of Ruth as a deconstruction of gender, then

---

31. L.A. Zurcher, *Social Roles: Conformity, Conflict, and Creativity* (Beverly Hills, CA: Sage, 1983), pp. 211-37; and B.R. Schlenker (ed.), *The Self and Social Life* (New York: McGraw–Hill, 1985).

the book may well have functioned as a rationale for social change.[32] Though the motives of its characters make sense within a framework of patriarchy,[33] their modes of action are explicitly nonsensical because they violate the norms that socially construct reality. This text moves to deconstruct the social sexual reality of its narrative world, thereby offering a critique of the social-sexual role expectations of its implied audience.

Through a depiction of crisis-initiated dedifferentiation, the narrative deconstructs the gender boundaries of the narrative world in lasting ways. Even after marriage and birth re-establish the story's original state, the women continue to add men's roles, as the women of the community name the new child. The surprising end demonstrates the power of the story, in which people permanently destroy gender role boundaries in mutually profitable ways. Though this process began as a response to crisis, its continuation marks a permanent change within the narrative world. In that context, the story is subversive, focusing not on a redeemer's salvation of the needy through established social rules, but on a disadvantaged foreigner's deconstruction of gender boundaries in order to save herself and her woman.

32. A. LaCocque (*The Feminine Unconventional: Four Subversive Figures in Israel's Tradition* [OBT; Minneapolis: Fortress Press, 1990]) argues that Ruth protests the Ezra–Nehemiah marriage reforms.

33. For a recent discussion of the patriarchy implicit in biblical texts, see K.M. Craig and M.A. Kristjansson, 'Women Reading as Men/Women Reading as Women: A Structural Analysis for the Historical Project', *Semeia* 51 (1990), pp. 119-36.

SAMUEL, KINGS

JSOT 62 (1994), pp. 67-75

ELI'S SEAT:
THE TRANSITION FROM PRIEST TO PROPHET IN 1 SAMUEL 1–4

Frank Anthony Spina

I

In the final canonical form of 1 Samuel *the seat* (*hakkissē'*) on which Eli
the priest sat is mentioned three times. He was sitting on *the seat* by the
sanctuary doorposts when Hannah came to pray for a child (1.10), while
awaiting word about the fate of the ark which Israel had taken into
battle against the Philistines (4.13), and when he fell upon hearing the
terrible news about the ark's having been captured (4.18).

To my knowledge, only Robert Polzin has treated these references as
more than incidental. He suggests that the description of Eli sitting on
hakkissē', in tandem with other clues (e.g. mention of the *hêkāl*, which
connotes temple and palace), presents Eli as a royal figure. This characterization of Eli functions as a metaphor for Israel's kingship, an institution which from the Deuteronomist's viewpoint was doomed to fail
from the outset. When the aged priest fell from *hakkissē'*, this 'foreshadows and embodies the Deuteronomist's graphic evaluation of the
institution [i.e. kingship] that Israel at first thought would bring good
news and glad tidings; the news results mostly in death and destruction'.[1] Thus, instead of being superfluous, the occurrence of *hakkissē'*
and other suggestive terms is an important clue for ascertaining how
these early chapters of 1 Samuel should be viewed, namely, as a paradigm for Israel's disastrous experiment with monarchy.

1. R. Polzin, *Samuel and the Deuteronomist* (San Francisco: Harper & Row,
1989), pp. 23, 61, 64. D.W. Caspari also regards these references as more than
incidental, but he does not elaborate. See *Die Samuelbücher* (Leipzig: Deichart,
1926), pp. 35, 71.

Given the way *kissē'* is used in the Hebrew Bible, Polzin is probably correct to think that its appearance in this pericope should be given more attention than has been customary.[2] As the following chart illustrates, usually *kissē'* refers to a divine or human royal throne; it rarely if ever is used of ordinary furniture.

kissē' *in the Hebrew Bible*

1 *kissē' as Human Royal Throne in DH*	2 *kissē' as Human Royal Throne in Rest of the Hebrew Bible*	3 *kissē' as Divine Royal Throne in the Hebrew Bible*	4 *Other Uses of kissē'*
Deut. 17.18; Judg. 3.20; 1 Sam. 2.8; 2 Sam. 3.10; 7.13, 16; 14.9; 1 Kgs 1.13, 17, 20, 24, 27, 30, 35, 37, 46, 47, 48; 2.4, 12, 19, 24, 33, 45; 3.6; 5.19; 7.7(?); 8.20, 25; 9.5; 10.9, 18, 19; 16.11; 22.10; 2 Kgs 10.3, 30; 11.19; 13.13; 15.12	Gen. 41.40; Exod. 11.5; 12.29; 17.16(?); Isa. 9.6; 14.9, 13; 22.23; 47.1; Jer. 1.15; 13.13; 17.25; 22.2, 4, 30; 29.16; 33.17, 21; 36.30; 43.10; Ezek. 26.16; Hag. 2.22; Jon. 3.6; Pss. 89.5, 30, 45; 122.5; 132.11, 12; Job 36.7; Est. 1.2; 5.1; Prov. 16.12; 20.8, 28; 25.5; 29.14; 1 Chron. 17.12, 14; 22.10; 28.5; 29.23; 2 Chron. 6.10, 16; 7.18; 9.8, 17, 18; 18.9; 23.20	1 Kgs 22.19; Isa. 6.1; 16.5(?); 66.1; Jer. 3.17; 14.21; Ezek. 1.26; 10.1; 43.7; 49.38(?); Pss. 9.5, 8; 11.4; 45.7; 47.9; 89.15, 37; 93.2; 94.20; 97.2; 103.19; 122.5; Job 26.9; Lam. 5.19; 2 Chron. 18.18	1 Sam. 1.9; 4.13, 18; 1 Kgs 2.19; 2 Kgs 4.10; 25.28; Jer. 52.32; Zech. 6.13; Prov. 9.14; Neh. 3.7; Est. 3.1

2. J.T. Willis opines that the reference to Eli's seat is a 'matter-of-fact statement' ('Samuel Versus Eli', *TZ* 35.4 [1979], p. 207). The following scholars take Eli's seat to be an ordinary piece of furniture: H.J. Fabry, 'אסכ, *kissē*'', *ThWAT*, IV, pp. 7, 36-37; R.W. Klein, *1 Samuel* (WBC, 10; Waco, TX: Word Books, 1983), pp. 1, 37; K. Budde, *Die Bücher Samuel* (KHAT; Tübingen: Mohr, 1902), p. 7; A. Schulz, *Die Bücher Samuel* (Münster: Aschendorff, 1919), pp. 1, 13; H.J. Stoebe, *Das erste Buch Samuelis* (Gütersloh: Gerd Mohn, 1973), p. 88; P.K. McCarter, *I Samuel* (AB, 8; Garden City, NY: Doubleday, 1980), pp. 49, 110. A. Cody posits that 1 Sam. 1.9 calls attention to Eli's low status and to the secondary role of the Shiloh sanctuary (*A History of Old Testament Priesthood* [AnBib, 35; Rome: Pontifical Biblical Institute, 1969], p. 69), while L.M. Eslinger proposes that the reference to Eli's sitting down highlights his passive role in contrast to Hannah's active one (*The Kingship of God in Crisis* [Sheffield: JSOT Press, 1985], p. 76).

Obviously, there are only a handful of cases where *kissē'* is something other than a royal seat, and even these are not unambiguous references to ordinary chairs. Leaving aside momentarily the verses in 1 Samuel, it is instructive to assess the other examples in column 4. In 1 Kgs 2.19 Solomon had a *kissē'* brought in when his mother visited him. He was on his (royal) *kissē'* at the time. Bathsheba sat down at her son's right hand. In this context, the *kissē'* was quite likely a chair specially designed for the Queen Mother or other high-ranking person seeking an audience with the king.[3]

A *kissē'* is among the items of furniture which the Shunammite woman placed in a room for the prophet Elisha (2 Kgs 4.10). This may be the clearest example in the Hebrew Bible for a non-technical meaning for *kissē'*. Yet even in this passage it is conceivable that a *kissē'* calls attention to the prophet's special status and office.

In Zech. 6.13 Joshua ben Jehozadak, the Branch who was to build the temple, shall sit on and rule from his *kissē'*. Depending on the antecedent of 'his', a priest will either stand beside the Branch's *kissē'* or occupy his own (*w*ᵉ*hāyâ kōhēn 'al-kis'ô*). Whether one *kissē'* or two is in view, official seats are surely indicated.[4]

In the parallel passages 2 Kgs 25.28 and Jer. 52.32, the *kissē'* that Evil-merodach king of Babylon provided for Jehoiachin was more exalted than the seats of the other restored monarchs. *kissē'* in this instance signals the profound reversal of fortune for the captured Judaean ruler. A similar usage obtains in Est. 3.1 where Ahasuerus promotes Haman. In Prov. 9.14, *kissē'* is used metaphorically of Dame Wisdom's elevated position. Finally, in Neh. 3.7 the phrase *l*ᵉ*kissē'* is used in the derived sense of 'under the jurisdiction of'.

Thus, excepting one or two examples at best, even the use of *kissē'* as reflected in column 4 shows that an unremarkable household chair is

3.   See G. Molin, 'Die Stellung der Gᵉbira im Staate Juda', *TZ* 10.3 (1954), pp. 161, 163; H. Donner, 'Art und Herkunft des Amtes der Königmutter im Alten Testament', in R. von Kienle, A. Moortgat, H. Otten, E. von Schuler and W. Zaumseil (eds.), *Festschrift Johannes Friedrich* (Heidelberg: Carl Winter Universitätsverlag, 1959), p. 110; Z. Ben-Barak, 'The Status and Right of the *Gebîrâ*', *JBL* 110.1 (1991), pp. 23-34.

4.   Zech. 6.13 is a well-known crux. See the summary of positions in B.A. Mastin, 'A Note on Zechariah VI 13', *VT* 26 (1976), pp. 113-16. C. Meyers and E. Meyers treat the first *kissē'* as a royal, messianic throne and the second one as a priestly seat. See *Haggai, Zechariah 1–8* (AB, 25B; Garden City, NY: Doubleday, 1987), p. 361.

not in view. In this light, when we read that Eli was sitting *'al hakkissē'*, we should not too hastily conclude that the notation is nothing more than a mundane fact. To indicate only that Eli was casually sitting down, *yāšab* without any mention of the object on which the priest sat would have been sufficient.[5] Even if Fabry is correct that there are few references to common furniture in the Hebrew Bible, it is not difficult to find vocabulary for either regular furniture (e.g. *môšāb*) or the simple act of sitting.[6] But in light of the general technical use of *kissē'*, being told that Eli was sitting *'al kissē'* immediately attracts attention, as though someone has said in a matter-of-fact way, 'Mr Jones came into the room and sat on the *throne*'! The nuance denotes more than the simple act of sitting. Polzin, in my view, was correct to see this.

At the same time, I believe Polzin misses the point when he casts Eli as a royal figure on the strength of these references. In fact, the narrative is rather straightforward in presenting Eli as a priest who also 'judged' Israel (1 Sam. 4.18). He and his sons are consistently called *kōhᵃnîm* (1.3, 9; 2.11, 13-15 [implied], 28 [Eli's ancestor]); they preside at an annual religious feast and at the temple where people pray (1.3, 9, 25); they engage in sacerdotal functions (2.13-17); their family had been elected to be priests (2.27-28); and their successors will be another priestly line (2.35). The evidence for a priestly role is so extensive that it would take considerably more than what Polzin has offered to interpret Eli as a royal figure and therefore a paradigm for the monarchy in Israel.

Whatever the significance of the references to Eli's having sat on the *kissē'*, it seems not to lie along these lines. In the story, Eli's priestly character and function are pervasive, whereas seeing him as a royal figure requires that one slight what the text plainly portrays. The issue turns on whether the references point to a more natural and obvious explanation than Polzin has put forward.

II

If Eli's *kissē'* is not a royal seat, but is more than an ordinary chair, as its general usage in the Hebrew Bible and its particular usage in DH suggest, then how should it be characterized? The answer lies in the fact

5. This is standard in the Hebrew Bible. See Gen. 18.1; 19.1; 21.16; 23.10; 27.19; 37.25; 38.14; 43.33. Thre are many more examples of this usage.
6. Fabry, *'kissē'*, p. 258.

that Eli in 1 Samuel is portrayed not only as a priest but as the leader of Israel (1 Sam. 4.18). From a historical perspective, Shiloh in pre-monarchic times may have been an insignificant, local sanctuary over which an undistinguished priestly family presided. But from the perspective of the present story, Eli's importance transcended any local setting. After all, Yahweh had elected Eli's family to exercise sacerdotal authority over Israel (2.27-29). Furthermore, this divinely chosen priestly house was to have ruled in perpetuity (2.30, 35).

Besides being priests, Eli and his family functioned as Israel's primary leaders during this period. For this reason, C. Meyers and E. Meyers understand the references to Eli's *kissē'* as his 'judicial and sacramental' seat.[7] Eli's leadership derived from his being simultaneously a 'judge' and a specially called priest. In some ways, Eli was actually superior to the other judges. Yahweh raised up the judges when a crisis arose, but in Eli's case his exercise of office was rooted in Yahweh's election prior to Israel's arriving in the land and having any need of deliverers. In addition, the future of Eli's house had been divinely sanctioned, whereas in the case of the judges their duties did not extend to the future.[8]

The *kissē'* on which Eli sat, therefore, should be seen as symbolic of his priestly and ruling office. These references to the *seat* are not intended to provide verisimilitude, but to call attention to the fact that in this era Israel is being presided over by a family of priests. When Eli encountered Hannah at the temple and later waited anxiously for news of the ark, he was exercising an office. Whether he was positioned inside the *hêkāl* or not makes no difference. Jehoshaphat, King of Judah, was said to be on *his* royal *kissē'* though he was not in Jerusalem at the time (1 Kgs 22.10). The *kissē'* was in effect portable. When Eli was observing Hannah at the temple and waiting for word about the ark's fate he was 'presiding'; when he fell from *hakkissē'* he was *deposed*, literally and metaphorically.

This office that Eli and his sons occupied had become thoroughly corrupted. This meant in turn that leadership in Israel had become corrupted. No longer were sacerdotal or other duties being properly executed. The Elides tragically continued the pattern of moral deterioration

7. *Haggai, Zechariah*, p. 361.
8. See A. Malamat, 'Charismatic Leadership in the Book of Judges', in F.M. Cross, W.E. Lemke and P.D. Miller, Jr (eds.), *Magnalia Dei: The Mighty Acts of God* (Festschrift G.E. Wright; Garden City, NY: Doubleday, 1976), p. 162.

that was evident in the successive deliverers whose exploits are recounted in Judges. Their having occupied *hakkissē'* in Israel had not reversed this ominous trend.

III

In my view, Eli's falling *mē'al hakkissē'* is as crucial to the story as his having sat *'al hakkissē'* in the first place. His fall signals more than a literal reaction to the stunning news of the ark's capture, Israel's resounding defeat at the hand of the Philistines, or even the death of his two sons (1 Sam. 4.17). It also signals that the priest and his house no longer preside over Israel and that a transition of leadership is both necessary and imminent. In light of the fact that the Elides were under divine condemnation (1 Sam. 2.27-36; 3.11-14), Israel's ignominious defeat, the death of Hophni and Phineas, the humiliation of the ark's having been captured, and Eli's fall *mē'al hakkissē'* all function as judgment against Israel and its priestly ruling family.

The transition of leadership from Eli and his house to Samuel (1 Sam. 3 [and Samuel's house? cf. 8.1-3]) is highlighted because the transition is not simply from one man or family to another, but from one *kind* of leadership, namely priestly, to another *kind*, namely prophetic. This is put in even bolder relief by the fact that initially Samuel was in Eli's employ and was apparently being trained as an apprentice. Samuel ministered as Eli's assistant (2.11, 18; 3.1), wore an ephod (2.18), offered sacrifices (even after being established as a prophet; cf. 7.9-10), built an altar (7.17), and later was expected to carry out routine priestly functions (16.2-5).[9]

But at the same time that Samuel was being groomed as a priestly aide, there are indications that he was destined to be primarily a prophet. His priestly duties were subordinated to his position as prophet. S.D. Walters has argued that even before Samuel's birth his mother Hannah assumed the role of a prophetess, thus adumbrating her son's future vocation.[10] Also, when Samuel was under the tutelage of Eli, his mother proleptically outfitted him in prophetic garb by bringing him a robe (*mᵉ'îl*) during her annual visits (1 Sam. 2.19). This garment was

9. See J.T. Willis, 'Cultic Elements in the Story of Samuel's Birth and Dedication', *ST* 26 (1972), p. 47 n. 50; cf. Cody, *Old Testament Priesthood*, pp. 72-80.

10. S.D. Walters, 'Hannah and Anna: The Greek and Hebrew Texts of 1 Samuel 1', *JBL* 107 (1988), pp. 385-87, 410-11.

decisive in the scene at Endor when Saul finally recognized Samuel's shade (28.14). Previously, when Saul tore Samuel's $m^{e\cdot}il$, this was a prophetic illustration that God had torn the kingdom from the hapless monarch (15.27). In Samuel's case, the prophetic robe eventually replaced the priestly ephod.[11]

Of course, nothing emphasizes more the transition from priestly to prophetic leadership in Israel than Samuel's call in 1 Samuel 3. At the end of this pericope, all Israel knew that Samuel had been established ($ne^{,e}m\bar{a}n$) as Yahweh's prophet (3.20). Ironically, the judgment pronounced against the Elides as revealed to Samuel was that the guilt incurred could not be removed by sacrifice or offering, the very means that were central to sacerdotal practice and which the priestly family had been overseeing (3.14). The prophetic word had become efficacious (3.19) while the priestly rituals—at least as carried out by the Elides— had become ineffectual. In the end, it was Samuel and not Eli who 'opened the doors of Yahweh's house' (3.15). Even while Eli was still on *hakkissē'* and before he had been *unseated* in fulfilment of Yahweh's word, the newly appointed prophet Samuel provided Israel's access to the sanctuary.[12]

IV

Israel's new prophet functioned as its new leader; as Eli the *priest* had, so Samuel the *prophet* also 'judged' Israel (1 Sam. 7.15). However, this particular religious leader occupied no *kissē'* as Eli had. Rather, Samuel's role was to insure that whoever next occupied the *kissē'* in Israel was appropriate. So Samuel's involvement was strategic when Israel demanded a king in reaction to the prophet's old age and the corruption of his sons (8.1-2). Still, the king who would occupy the *kissē'* would not be just any king. The Torah that was to guide Israel in the land (see Josh. 1.7-8) had specified that Israel's ideal king would not be

11. Depending on context, $m^{e\cdot}il$ can depict royal clothing (1 Sam. 18.4; 24.5, 12). Polzin contends, erroneously in my judgment, that Samuel's robe was a priestly garment. See *Samuel and the Deuteronomist*, p. 42.

12. J.G. Janzen connects this phrase with the motif of closing and opening wombs in 1 Sam. 1. Whether or not he has made his case, almost certainly he is correct that the reference to Samuel's opening the doors is not incidental. See ' "Samuel Opened the Doors of the House of Yahweh" (1 Samuel 3.15)', *JSOT* 26 (1983), pp. 89-96.

known for multiplying horses, wives or money, but rather for heeding Torah while sitting *'al kissē' mamlaktô* (Deut. 17.14-20). The term 'seat of his kingdom' is used only in one other place in DH, 2 Sam. 7.13, which specifies the Davidic dynasty as the legitimate holder of Israel's royal seat.

In this light, it is intriguing that Saul, Israel's first king, is never once said to have sat on the *kissē'*. Eli's occupation of the *kissē'* was ephemeral and in the final analysis illegitimate. The inadequacy of Saul as holder of the 'seat of the kingdom' is underscored by his never having sat on the *kissē'* in the first place. Saul was, as it were, a king without a throne.[13] Though anointed by God, Saul was in the end unsuitable as king. To be sure, there were non-Davidic kings who would occupy the royal *kissē'* in Israel, not to mention unworthy Davidic dynasts. Indeed, the contrast between the ideal Torah-king who would sit on the *kissē'* and the king who would multiply horses, wives and wealth, an allusion almost certainly to Solomon, is already present in the 'law of the king' (Deut. 17.14-20). Nevertheless, it was the Davidic dynasty in its ideal rather than its 'historical' form that was the model for Israelite kingship. This ideal king is represented in 2 Samuel 21–24.[14] In DH no Israelite king ever occupies the *kissē'* until *after* the Davidic dynasty has been established.

Likewise, no other 'ruling family' could sit on the *kissē'* either. Saul could not and had not. And even the great Samuel could not and had not. Eli's sitting on the *kissē'* was thus doomed from the outset. He and his family could function as priests and leaders, but they could not sit on Israel's *kissē'*. It is no accident that every single occasion where Eli is described occupying the *kissē'* is cast in a negative light. When Eli is first depicted sitting on the *kissē'*, he is so inept and devoid of insight that he cannot distinguish between a drunken woman and a praying one

---

13. 1 Sam. 28.23 is interesting in the light of Saul's kingship. The LXX translates *kissē'* with *diphros* several times (Deut. 17.18; 1 Sam. 1.9; 4.13, 18; 2 Kgs 4.10; Prov. 9.14). Curiously, it uses the same term to translate *miṭṭâ*, 'bed' in 1 Sam. 28.23—the only time *miṭṭâ* is so translated. Aquila renders *miṭṭâ* with *klinē*, as one would expect. Does this suggest that there was a Hebrew *Vorlage* that had *kissē'* where MT has the curious *miṭṭâ*? If so, it emphasizes that the MT carefully avoids ever having Saul on a *kissē'* even when there was another Hebrew tradition where he did indeed sit on it.

14. See B.S. Childs, *Introduction to the Old Testament as Scripture* (Philadelphia: Fortress Press, 1979), pp. 272-72, 278.

(1 Sam. 1.12-15). He is next pictured sitting on the *kissē'* helplessly and pathetically *watching* for the ark even though he is blind at the time (3.2; 4.15). Finally, he falls from the *kissē'* in a tragic motion that symbolizes his senility and immobility, his distance from the center of Israelite activity[15] and, most poignantly, his removal from the *kissē'* (4.18), which not only signals that priestly leadership is giving way to prophetic leadership in Israel but also that he has been occupying the *seat* that has been reserved for someone else. The prophet will have a role in the establishment and maintenance of Israel's king that no priest could have. Perhaps only in the eschatological future could a priestly and messianic figure both occupy the *kissē'* (Zech. 6.13) and exercise legitimate, co-operative and complementary authority. But for DH that day has not yet come. Eli's empty *kissē'* testifies to that.

15. This is suggested by the fact that Eli is last to get the news about the capture of the ark. Further, the narrative puts distance between Eli and the action by using the verb *bā'* five times in a brief space to slow the process by which he hears the news. The messenger first enters (*wayyābō'*) Shiloh in 4.12. He enters Eli's 'space' in 4.13, where the text notes where Eli is sitting and the state of his anxiety. But the messenger seems to run right past the priest, for he has entered (*bā'*) to inform the city. After the city's loud reaction, which Eli hears, the messenger hurries to come to tell Eli (4.14; *wᵉhā'îš mihar wayyābō' wayyaggēd lᵉ'ēlî*). The text retards the action even more by inserting at this point the note about Eli's age and the condition of his eyes. At last, when the messenger is finally face to face with Eli, with maddening deliberation he tells the priest first that 'I am the one who comes (*habbā'*) from the battle line... and I fled from the battle line today' (4.16). It is as though there were no urgency to informing Israel's head about what had transpired. I am indebted to Stanley Walters of Toronto in a private communication for his observation on this feature of the text.

JSOT 26 (1983), pp. 61-76

VIEWPOINTS AND POINT OF VIEW IN 1 SAMUEL 8–12

Lyle Eslinger

For over 200 years now the five chapters in 1 Samuel 8–12 have been displayed in introductions and textbooks as a showcase example of the value of historical-critical literary analysis for the improvement of our understanding of biblical literature. Pointing to conflicting opinions and supposed redundancies within these chapters, historical critics have suggested that the way to understand such ill-framed writing is to determine how it got into such a confused state. Encouraged by the established results of pentateuchal source analysis, scholars such as Otto Thenius (1842) and Karl Budde (1902) approached the literary complexities of 1 Samuel 8–12 with a predisposition to understand these literary phenomena as the traces of a long and varied process of composition. Artur Weiser's remarks are characteristic: 'In view of the diversity of motives and points of view in the passages under discussion we must on the contrary take into account a many-stranded process of utilizing and shaping the traditions which developed over a long period and set at different points and different times' (1961: 161).

The opening sentence of Bruce Birch's re-evaluation of 1 Samuel 7–15 exhibits the continuing predominance of the genetic approach to biblical literature, which Birch presents as a matter of fact: 'Any careful examination of the doublets, tensions and varying points of view in 1 Samuel will lead to the conclusion that it is not a literary unity' (1976: 1).[1]

---

1. More detailed presentation of the argument was subsequently published in L.M. Eslinger, *Kingship of God in Crisis: A Close Reading of 1 Samuel 1–12* (Sheffield: Almond Press, 1985); *idem, Into the Hands of the Living God* (JSOTSup, 84; Sheffield: JSOT Press, 1989). The latter is a study of the 'key speeches' in the Deuteronomistic narrative and presents a revised version of the 1985 analysis of Samuel's 'key speech' in 1 Sam. 12.

There are primarily two features of 1 Samuel 8–12 that have stimulated genetic explanation: 1. Two apparently opposing views of the monarchy are expressed at various places in the narrative. A classical example of a division of these chapters according to their pro- or anti-monarchic stance is that of Julius Wellhausen (9.1–10.16; 11.1-11, 15 being pro-monarchic, and chs. 7–8; 10.17-27; 12, anti-monarchic [1973: 249-56]). 2. The action of elevating Saul to the position of king is presented in three seemingly redundant rehearsals (in 9.1–10.16; 10.17-27; and ch. 11). The first problematic feature is a problem of point of view, or focus; the second is a comparatively simple matter of perceived redundancy and contradiction.

As the problem of 1 Samuel 8–12 is twofold, so the historical-critical mode of reading had two explanatory poles that bracket the various explanations of how the narrative got into such a confused state.

At the one end of the spectrum Wellhausen subordinates the problem of the three redundant accounts about Saul's inauguration to the criterion of whether a given scene is pro- or anti-monarchic. Wellhausen supports this arrangement with the observation that two accounts of Saul's investiture, 9.1–10.16 and ch. 11, are pro-monarchic, integral scenes in one presentation; what seemed to be two accounts of the investiture is, in fact, one. In 9.1–10.16, Saul is only king *de jure*; he becomes king *de facto* when he proves himself in ch. 11 (1973: 250). What remains of chs. 8–12 is the anti-monarchic account in 10.17-27, which is linked with the other anti-monarchic material in chs 7–8 and 12.

Weiser, at the opposite end of the spectrum, subordinates the issues of pro- or anti-monarchic points of view to the question of the relationship among the three separate accounts of Saul's investiture. He points out that neither of Wellhausen's literary strands exhibits a consistent point of view, whether pro- or anti-monarchic. Taking the so-called anti-monarchic strand as an example, Weiser finds that ch. 7 exhibits no anti-monarchic point of view (1962: 27); ch. 8 is critical only of the non-Israelite model of kingship proposed by the people, and not of kingship *per se* (1962: 27); 10.17-27a presents the election of Saul as God's will, and differs from ch. 8 in the representation of the setting and reason for the request (1962: 62); and ch. 12 differs from both ch. 8 and 10.17-27a in its description of the setting and reason for the request (1962: 80).

In Weiser's view, these disagreements outweigh any similarity of viewpoint that the separate traditions are said to share. The complex diversity of perspectives in this narrative leads him to regard it as a conglomeration of literary compilations, incorporating traditions from diverse times and places (1961: 159-61). Each contrasting point of view reflects a unique socio-historical compositional setting. The contrary points of view expressed in 1 Samuel 8–12 are to be viewed as the result of a process of literary compilation in which traditions 'are not so much intermingled with each other as strung after each other, partly on a very loose thread' (1961: 162).

Subsequent study has produced a variety of syntheses based on the approaches advocated by Wellhausen and Weiser.[2] Though theoretical presuppositions about the compositional history of the narrative have become more sophisticated—viewpoints and redundancies are now understood in terms of traditions, redactors, and successive redactional layers—it is still axiomatic that such literary features should be regarded as products of the narrative's literary history.

Underlying this historical presupposition are two literary pre-suppositions:

1. Behind each identifiable viewpoint expressed in a narrative stands an individual author, redactor, compiler, or tradent (e.g. Veijola 1977: 115-22);
2. Any given event that is reported two or more times in a narrative complex is evidence of two or more composers who have reworked tradition in different ways (e.g. Halpern 1981: 64).

When these common assumptions of historical-critical literary analysis are viewed in the wider methodological context of comparative literary theory, especially narrative theory, however, it soon becomes apparent that they need revision. In a handbook (*Theory of Literature*) published forty years ago, Rene Wellek and Austin Warren state, 'The central problem of narrative method concerns the relation of the author to his work'.[3] The work on this problem in the fields of literary theory and

---

2. Proliferation of reviews of this scholarship is undesirable in view of the many existing reviews: B. Birch (1976: 1-10); H.J. Boecker (1969: 1-10); B.S. Childs (1979: 263-77); V. Fritz (1976: 346-49); T. Ishida (1977: 26-29); E. Jenni (1961: 136-41); J. Kegler (1977: 56-70); F. Langlamet (1970: 161-200; 1978: 277-300); A.D.H. Mayes (1977: 322-31; 1978: 1-10); P.K. McCarter, Jr (1980: 12-14); A.N. Radjawane (1973–74: 190-200); A.D. Ritterspach (1967: 16-53); L. Schmidt (1970: 58-63); H.J. Stoebe (1973: 32-52); J.R. Vannoy (1978: 197-225); T. Veijola (1977: 5-14); H. Wildberger (1957: 442-46).

3. 1975: 222; cf. P. Lubbock (1921: 251), 'The whole intricate question of method, in the craft of fiction, I take to be governed by the question of the point of

comparative literature has not yet been applied with any consistency to the study of 1 Samuel 8–12, or, for that matter, to many other biblical narratives.[4]

One recent analysis of the problem of point of view, perhaps better described as the generic problem of 'mediacy of presentation' or 'focalization', concludes that there are no less than seven narrative elements that determine the total narrative perspective presented to a reader.[5] Of the seven, three are especially important:

Person: identity or non-identity of the worlds of the fictional characters and of the narrator. These terms correspond to the traditional but ambiguous differentiation between first- and third-person narration.

Perspective: internal or external. A differentiation that largely coincides with the conventional distinction between omniscience and limited point of view.

Mode: transmission by teller-character or by reflector-character. This distinction *partly* covers the general differentiation between 'showing' and 'telling', between scenic presentation and descriptive summary.[6] In view of the relative complexity of such an analytical framework in comparison with the simplicity of historical-critical analysis of point of view it seems advisable to re-examine the division of 1 Samuel 8–12 into pro- and anti-monarchic components using more sensitive analytical concepts.

The second historical-critical criterion for the differentiation of strata in 1 Samuel 8–12, it will be recalled, is the presence of multiple accounts

---

view—the question of the relation in which the narrator stands to the story'.

   4.   Applications are beginning to appear, however, e.g., M. Perry and M. Sternberg (1968–69: 263-92; Eng. summary pp. 452-99); S. Bar-Efrat (1978: 19-31; 1980: 154-73); R. Polzin (1980; 1981); R. Alter (1981); and studies cited by Bar-Efrat (1980: 154 n. 1).

   5.   The term 'mediacy of presentation' is favoured by F.K. Stanzel (1978: 247-64). 'Focalization', on the other hand, is one of G. Genette's improved descriptions for the phenomenon called point of view (1972: 203-11; 1980: 185-94).

   6.   Stanzel (1978: 249); cf. B. Uspensky (1973: 6): 'we may consider point of view as an ideological and evaluative position; we may consider it as a spatial and temporal position of the one who produces the description of the events (that is, the narrator, whose position is fixed along spatial and temporal coordinates); we may study it with respect to perceptual characteristics; or we may study it in a purely linguistic sense (as, for example, it relates to such phenomena as quasidirect discourse); and so forth'.

   Stanzel's analytical categorization of mediacy of presentation is also closely paralleled by Genette's categories. See D. Cohn (1981: 157-82).

about Saul's investiture as king in the narrative. Setting aside, momentarily, the question of whether the three scenes in question (9.1–10.16; 10.17-27; 11) are, in fact, parallel descriptions of the same event, it should first be recalled that repetition of words, phrases, motifs, scenes, and symbols is a common and valued technique in literature. Commenting on his use of repetition, Emile Zola says,

> In my view it [repetition] gives more body to a work and strengthens its unity. The device is somewhat akin to the motifs in Wagner, and if you will ask some musical friend of yours to explain his use of these, you will understand pretty well my use of the device in literature.[7]

Alter's discussion of the uses of repetition and scenic parallelism reveal the pervasiveness of these techniques in biblical narrative and suggests that the biblical writers placed a premium value on this technique as a means of providing unobtrusive exposition (1981: 6, 10, 21, 47-62, 88-113, 166-69, 179-83).[8]

Without the support of the perceived differences in viewpoint that are suggested for each scene, the division according to supposedly redundant parallel scenes is weak. Wellhausen's argument for the linkage of ch. 11 with 9.1–10.16 is neither stronger nor weaker than Halpern's

7. Quotation from E.K. Brown (1950: 28). Discussion of the uses and effects of repetition in literature may be found in Brown; S. Chatman (1978: 78-79); E.M. Forster (1976: 146-50); G. Genette (1972: 145-82, esp. 147-48; 1980: 113-60, esp. 115-16); K.H. Hartmann (1979: 4-30). For considerations from the perspective of the phenomenology of the reading process, see G.N. Leech and M.H. Short (1981: 257-59).

8. It is, incidentally, entirely open to question whether the three scenes in 1 Sam. 9–11 are parallel descriptions of the same event. There are important differences: 9.1–10.16 portrays the private designation and prophetic confirmation of Saul as 'designate' (*nāgîd*); 10.17-27 presents Saul's public installation, which arouses some dissension; and ch. 11 describes the events leading up to the unanimous, joyful acceptance of Saul as king.

It would involve, however, too large a digression from the focus of this article to rehearse the arguments of a study now being revised for publication in favour of a sequential reading of not only chs. 9–11, but even 1 Sam. 1–12. Though I disagree with many of his views on 1 Sam. 8–12 and with all of his excisions from the text, M. Buber has also presented a case for a sequential reading (1956: 113-73); cf. his essays in his *Werke* (1964: 727-845). The attempts to divide the narrative into pro- and anti-monarchic sources in which ch. 11 is linked either to 9.1–10.16 (e.g. Wellhausen [1973: 251]) or to 10.17-27 (e.g. Halpern [1981: 64-67]) are proof enough that even readers on the lookout for disjunction have seen aspects of the sequentiality that exists in the narrative.

opposing alignment when judged by the sole criterion of logical or causal concatenation of events. The reason for this stalemate is that the existing narrative presents the reader with numerous linguistic, literary, logical, and causal links between ch. 11 and both 9.1–10.16 and 10.17-27.[9] Wellhausen's argument seems to gain the upper hand, however, when the criterion of viewpoint is considered, which explains why the majority of historical-critical readers have seen a connection between 9.1–10.16 and ch. 11, both supposedly pro-monarchic.

Unfortunately, the presence of pro- and anti-monarchic opinions in 1 Samuel 8–12 is incapable of supporting the analytical weight that Wellhausen and others have placed on it (cf. Halpern 1981: 70). A quick review of the division into pro- and anti-monarchic segments with an eye on the simple question of who says what to whom reveals some interesting correlations between evaluation stances and characters:

Scene 1[10] (ch. 8, so-called anti-monarchic).

1. Omniscient narrator: supplies a critical description of Samuel's sons' behaviour in office (vv. 1-4), which verifies and hence supports the elders' justification of their request for a king. Otherwise, he is neutral.

2. Characters (in order of appearance): a. Samuel: is displeased by the request (v. 6) and critical of the institution of monarchy (vv. 11-18). b. Israel: is critical of Samuel's sons' behaviour and favours a king 'like the nations' (vv. 6, 19-20). c. Yahweh: is critical of the request (vv. 7-8) but willing to install a designated monarch (vv. 9, 22).

Scene 2 (9.1–10.16, so-called pro-monarchic).

1. Omniscient narrator: provides neutral description of first Yahweh's (9.1-17; 10.9), then Samuel's (9.17–10.8), and finally Saul's actions, all of which result in Saul's secret elevation to the status of 'designate' (*nāgîd*).

---

9.   Scattered references to these interconnections are made throughout the secondary literature on 1 Sam. 8–12. For specific discussion of ch. 11 in this regard see J.M. Miller (1974: 157-74) and Vannoy (1978: 114-30).

10.   Birch (1976: 132) has observed, correctly in my opinion, that the customary historical-critical divisions of chs. 8–12 have been made on the basis of subject matter, not critical analysis. In fact, the customary divisions are largely in accord with the chapter divisions which, in turn, seem to be based on the narrator's division of story into scenes.

2. Characters:[11] a. Yahweh: favours the elevation of Saul to the position of anointed designate as a response to his people's cry (vv. 15-17). b. Samuel: agrees with Yahweh's move and anoints Saul as Yahweh's designate (9.19–10.8).

Scene 3 (10.17-27, so-called anti-monarchic).

1. Omniscient narrator: provides neutral description of the assembly and lottery (vv. 17-27). He uses a negatively toned, technical term (*b⁽e⁾nê b⁽e⁾lîyā'al*) for transgressors of covenantal or legal stipulations to describe those Israelites who refuse to accept the kind of monarchy that Yahweh has arranged and to which they have, knowingly or not, given their assent (v. 27).[12] (This usage makes him, if anything, 'anti-renegade'.)

2. Characters: a. Samuel: is critical of the request for a king 'like the nations' but presents himself as willing to accede to it (v. 19). Instead, he gives them Saul, Yahweh's designate, and extols the latter's virtues (v. 24).[13] b. Israel: unanimously in favour of Saul when they have been led to believe he is what they asked for (v. 24); there are, however, mixed reactions to Samuel's proclamation of the new monarchic constitution in v. 25 (vv. 26-27).

Scene 4 (ch. 11, so called pro-monarchic).

1. Omniscient narrator: supplies neutral descriptive summaries and linkages of individual events.

2. Characters: a. Israel: Israel's initial despair upon facing an outside threat reveals a lack of trust in and recognition of their new king (vv. 1-5). When Saul proves his utility and the viability of the theocratically subordinated monarchy, however, the people give him their complete support (v. 15). b. Samuel: supports the people's expressions of allegiance to Saul, Yahweh's king (v. 14).

Scene 5 (ch. 12, so-called anti-monarchic).

1. Omniscient narrator: supplies neutral description of Samuel's speech.

---

11. Only those characters that express an opinion, whether in thought, word, or deed, on the issue of monarchy are included in this summary.

12. On this reading of *b⁽e⁾nê b⁽e⁾lîyā'al* see W. Caspari (1926: 118); Stoebe (1973: 214); B. Otzen '*b⁽e⁾liyya'al*', *ThWAT*, I, cols. 656-57 (ET, *TDOT*, II, 134).

13. Buber (1956: 127-28; 1964: 737-38; 1960: 60-70) discusses the importance of the difference between what was requested—a king like all the nations—and what was given—Yahweh's anointed designate.

2. Characters: a. Samuel: criticizes the request for a king as totally unwarranted, as a rejection of God (vv. 1-3, 5-12). He expresses some hope for Israel and its new king if they are obedient and loyal to Yahweh. b. People: cowed by the thunderstorm and in fear for their lives, they recant.

Even this superficial review of the narrative reveals serious deficiencies in the segmentation of the text according to pro- and anti-monarchic viewpoints. Only one character, Samuel, voices absolute opposition to the idea of a human king over Israel, and that is only an initial reaction (8.6, 11-18, 22). Once Yahweh explains the concept of a designate to Samuel (9.15-16), Samuel is all for Saul and continues to be critical only of the request for a king 'like all the nations' on account of the motivation for such a request. Yahweh is willing to appoint a royal designate from the beginning, and is critical only of the request that would replace him with a king 'like all the nations' (8.9, 22; 9.15-17; 12.17). What the reader hears even in the voices of these *characters* cannot be described as anti-monarchism. Rather, what Yahweh and Samuel are critical of is the anti-covenantal sentiment they hear in Israel's request.

Turning to the voices favourable towards monarchy one must first make a distinction between two different pro-monarchic positions. On the one hand, the reader hears the voice of Israelites who prefer a king 'like the nations' to the fading leadership of Samuel and the corruption of his sons. In opposition to the pro-monarchic sentiment of this request, on the other hand, is the voice of Yahweh who favours instituting a monarchy that will remain subordinate to the theocracy (8.9, 22; 9.15-16) in response to Israel's request. Yahweh is later joined in his particular brand of pro-monarchism by Samuel (9.15; 12), and eventually even by Israel (11.15). One must distinguish, therefore, between two different pro-monarchic voices in 1 Samuel 8–12. Israel is eventually won over to Yahweh's version of pro-monarchic sentiment by a combination of Samuel's subtle rhetorical manipulations (10.17-27), demonstrations of worthiness by the spirit-empowered Saul (ch. 11), and Yahweh's heavy-handed demonstration of power (12.16-19).

When we pay attention to the question of who says what, we can easily see the insensitivity of the division of the narrative into pro- monarchic and anti-monarchic scenes. In every scene both pro- and anti-monarchic attitudes are expressed or displayed by a variety of characters. Shifts in attitude occur, with Samuel moving from adamant anti-monarchism to one brand of pro-monarchism. Israel undergoes a transition from the pro-monarchism of the request, to a mixed reaction to the designate, Saul, to a final position in favour of the designated monarchy allowed by Yahweh. The historical-critical net was woven to catch big fish, the pro- and anti-monarchic authors (or sources, traditions, tradents and redactors). It allows the smaller fry, the characters and their separate voices to slip through, untouched. What, at first glance, looked like a few big fish, however, turned out to be schools of individual, smaller fish.

It is fairly easy to predict the historical-critical response to this metaphoric situation. If what we have here are smaller fish then all we need is a net with a finer mesh; granting that these observations about the complexity of the voices in 1 Samuel 8–12 hold, we need only refine our literary dissection to obtain a truer picture of the text's compositional history. Extrapolating from the existing trend in historical-critical analysis of 1 Samuel 8–12, there may come a time when the narrative is regarded as the conglomerate product of three or even five individual composers, one for each character voice heard in the narrative.[14]

By far the most neglected dimension in the interpretation of the voice structure of 1 Samuel 8–12 is the voice of the omniscient narrator.[15] Ironically, it is the historical-critical quest for the historical authors of the narrative that has led to the total disregard of the nearest thing, generically speaking, to an explicit authorial voice in the narrative, the voice of the omniscient narrator. It is the narrator's voice, heard both in the explicit narratorial diegesis—the summaries, explanations, comments, and identification tags attached to direct quotations of characters—and in the patterned order, commonly called the 'plot',[16] in which the story is related, that provides the overarching framework to which all elements of the story are subordinated. The narrator's voice creates this framework and is conditioned by it; the character's voices speak from within the framework and are relative to their occurrence within the context. Since the reader stands with the narrator outside the narrated

14. The trend is already visible in the analysis of the deuteronomistic history, of which 1 Sam. 8–12 is part. M. Noth (1967) suggested that the history resulted from one redaction; Veijola (1977) suggests that only two redactions can explain the pro- and anti-monarchic views; and R. Smend (1978: 123) now finds three redaction layers in the history. Will anyone say four?

15. For discussion of voices and voice structure in narrative see J.C. LaDrière (1953: 441-44); K. Morrison (1961–62: 245-55).

16. See, however, M. Sternberg's (1978: 8-14) cautious discussion about the use of the term 'plot' to describe the order of presentation in narrative.

events, looking back on them through preterite verbs and structured plots, the reader also comprehends those events *with* the narrator so long as the latter does not betray the reader's confidence in his reliability (cf. Stanzel 1971: 6, 47). For the majority of biblical narratives, with their undisputed omniscient narrators, and certainly for 1 Samuel 8–12, narrator reliability is unquestionable.[17]

The narrator of 1 Samuel 8–12 appears to maintain a steadfast neutrality towards the subject of monarchy. Only the characters are given to extreme expressions of favour towards the idea or rejection of it. The narrator's apparent neutrality is consistent with his position outside the narrated events. He looks back on these events with a balanced view— pro- and anti-monarchic sentiments are seen in perspective as oppositions that result in a new synthesis—provided, it seems, by the intervention of an indeterminate number of years between the narrated events and the time of the narrator.[18]

There are only two instances in 1 Samuel 8–12 where the narrator supplies his readers with editorial evaluations (8.2-3; 10.27). In both cases, the narrator breaks the evaluative silence of descriptive narration to direct his reader's attention to renegade transgressions of law and

17. According to W. Booth, who is largely responsible for the discussion about narrator reliability, a narrator is reliable 'when he speaks for or acts in accordance with the norms of the work (which is to say the implied author's norms), unreliable when he does not' (1961: 158-59). When a narrative makes no direct reference to its implied author, the question of the narrator's reliability does not arise because there is no comparative scale by which the narrator's utterances may be measured. In this narrative situation, which, to my knowledge, pertains throughout biblical narrative, there can be no distinction between implied author and the undramatized narrator (Booth [1961: 151-52]; cf. T. Yacobi [1981: 113-26]).

18. The impression of distance between the narrator and the events he describes is created primarily through a consistent use of the preterite, which temporally separates the narrated events from the event of narration. A second means for the creation of this impression is exemplified by the antiquarian note in 9.9, in which the narrator purposefully displays the fact that he stands outside of the story he tells (cf. Bar-Efrat [1978: 21]). Of the effect of the narrator's temporal distance from the story, Stanzel says it calls 'attention to the presence of the narrator, his now-and-here [*sic*] in the act of narration. The reader takes this now-and-here of the narrator for the basis of his or her spatio-temporal orientation in the fictional world. The point which is spatially and temporally fixed in this way in the reader's imagination will be called the reader's center of orientation. In the case of the authorial narrative situation the center of orientation is always identical with the now-and-here of the author in the act of narration' (1971: 27).

covenant. Samuel's sons, though judges (*šoph^eṭîm*, 8.2), are perverting justice (*mišpāṭ*); the *b^enê b^elîyā'al*, though they have acclaimed Saul and are legally bound to his kingship (10.24-25), spurn Saul.

These exceptions to the narrator's customary evaluative silence are important clues which, in combination with a careful examination of the order and inter-relation given to the narrated events, cue the reader to the narrator's stance. They reveal the narrator's point of view, and it is only the narrator's point of view that is addressed to the reader.

> In the analysis of a speech or literary composition, nothing is more important than to determine precisely the voice or voices *presented* as speaking and the precise nature of the address (i.e., specific direction to a hearer, an addressee); for in every speech reference to a voice or voices and implication of address (i.e., reference to a process of speech, actual or imagined) is a part of the meaning and a frame for the rest of the meaning, for the interpretation of which it supplies an indispensible control (LaDrière 1953: 441-42, my emphasis).

As readers we are privileged to overhear the characters voicing their views, but those views are addressed to other characters in the narrative; they have a narrative context. We stand outside the narrative and are addressed by the narrator, who is also exterior to the narrated events; we listen to his voice which supplies the controlling frame for the comprehension of events and voices in the story. When we dispense with the controlling frame of the narrator's voice in our pursuit of the meaning of a narrative, we dispense also with the existing narrative. The results are at hand in the creation of new narratives and new narrators such as Otto Eissfeldt's 'L' and 'J' (1931; 1965: 274-75) or the multiple deuteronomists of Veijola.

The omniscient narrator does exist in 1 Samuel 8–12 and he must be reckoned with. Standing silently behind every *way^ehî* and *wayyō'mer*, the narrator's mediation of all descriptions and quotation in the narrative is a constant reminder of his intermediary position between the story and the reader. The guide is always there to lead the reader through the intricate maze of detail and opinions expressed by characters in his story.

It should come as no surprise that those adventurous readers who attempt to get through without the narrator's guidance are quickly bewildered. Lost in diverse details and opinions, such readers find themselves on the same plane as the characters in the narrative. Instead of standing outside the narrated events with the narrator, they jump inside with the characters. On that level of the narrative various opinions, multiple perspectives, and missing logical connections are natural and characteristic of human existence. When readers choose to view with the characters, they cannot expect anything else. If, on the other hand, they seek meaning and order, readers must submit to the creator of such things, the omniscient narrator.

E.M. Forster's advice to readers of modern English literature is equally valuable to readers of biblical narrative:

> So next time you read a novel do look out for the 'point of view'—that is to say, the relation of the narrator to the story. Is he telling the story and describing the characters from the outside, or does he identify himself with one of the characters? Does he pretend that he knows and forsees everything? Or does he go in for being surprised? Does he shift his point of view—like Dickens in the first three chapters of *Bleak House*? And, if he does, do you mind? I don't (1976: 187).

BIBLIOGRAPHY

Alter, R.
1981   *The Art of Biblical Narrative* (New York: Basic Books).
Bar-Efrat, S.
1978   'Literary Modes and Methods in the Biblical Narrative in View of 2 Samuel 10–20 and 1 Kings 1–2', *Immanuel* 8: 19-31.
1980   'Some Observations on the Analysis of Structure in Biblical Narrative', *VT* 30: 154-73.
Birch, B.
1976   *The Rise of the Israelite Monarchy: The Growth and Development of 1 Samuel 7–15* (SBLDS, 27; Missoula, MT: Scholars Press).
Boecker, H.J.
1969   *Die Beurteilung der Anfange des Königtums in der deuteronomistichen Abschnitten des I. Samuelbuches* (WMANT, 31; Neukirchen–Vluyn: Neukirchener Verlag).
Booth, W.
1961   *The Rhetoric of Fiction* (Chicago: Chicago University Press).
Brown, E.K.
1950   *Rhythm in the Novel* (Toronto: University of Toronto Press, 1950).
Buber, M.
1956   'Die Erzählung von Sauls Königswahl', *VT* 6: 113-73.
1960   *The Prophetic Faith* (New York: Harper & Row).
1964   'Der Gesalbte', *Werke*, II (Munich: Kosel; Heidelberg: Lambert): 727-845.
Budde, K.
1902   *Die Bücher Samuel* (KHC, 8; Tübingen: Mohr).
Caspari, W.
1926   *Die Samuelbücher* (KAT, 8; Leipzig: A. Deichert).

Chatman, S.
1978   *Story and Discourse: Narrative Structure in Fiction and Film* (Ithaca, NY: Cornell University Press).

Childs, B.S.
1979   *Introduction to the Old Testament as Scripture* (Philadelphia: Fortress Press).

Cohn, D.
1981   'The Encirclement of Narrative: On Franz Stanzel's *Theorie des Erzählens*', *PT* 2.2: 157-82.

Eissfeldt, O.
1931   *Die Komposition der Samuelbücher* (Leipzig: J.C. Hinrichs).
1965   *The Old Testament: An Introduction* (trans. P.R. Ackroyd; New York: Harper & Row).

Forster, E.M.
1976   *Aspects of the Novel* (Markham: Penguin Books).

Fritz, V.
1976   'Die Deutung des Königtums Sauls in der Überlieferungen von seiner Entstehung I. Sam 9–11', *ZAW* 88: 346-62.

Genette, G.
1972   *Figures III* (Paris: Seuil).
1980   *Narrative Discourse: An Essay in Method* (trans. J.E. Lewin; Ithaca, NY: Cornell University Press).

Halpern, B.
1981   'The Uneasy Compromise: Israel between League and Monarchy', in B. Halpern and J.D. Levenson (eds.), *Traditions in Transformation: Turning Points in Biblical Faith* (Winona Lake, IN: Eisenbrauns): 59-96.

Hartmann, K.H.
1979   *Wiederholungen in Erzählen* (Stuttgart: J.B. Metzler).

Ishida, T.
1977   *The Royal Dynasties in Ancient Israel: A Study on the Formation and Development of Royal-Dynastic Ideology* (BZAW, 142; Berlin: de Gruyter).

Jenni, E.
1961   'Zwei Jahrzehnte Forschung an den Büchern Josua bis Könige', *TRu* 27: 1-32, 98-146.

Kegler, J.
1977   *Politisches Geschehen und theologisches Verstehen* (Stuttgart: Calwer).

LaDrière, J.C.
1953   'Voice and Address', in J.T. Shipley (ed.), *Dictionary of World Literature* (New York: Philosophical Library, rev. edn).

Langlamet, F.
1970   'Les récits de l'institution de la royauté (1 Sam 7–12); de Wellhausen aux travaux récents', *RB* 77: 161-200.
1978   Review of R. Smend, 'Das Gesetz und die Völker', T. Veijola, *Das Königtum in der Beurteilung der deuteronomistichen Historiographie*, and B. Birch, *The Rise of the Israelite Monarchy*, *RB* 85: 277-300.

Leech, G.N., and M.H. Short
1981   *Style in Fiction. A Linguistic Introduction to English Fictional Prose* (London and New York: Longman).
Lubbock, P.
1921   *The Craft of Fiction* (New York).
Mayes, A.D.H.
1977   'The Period of the Judges and the Rise of the Monarchy', in J.H. Hayes and J.M. Miller (eds.), *Israelite and Judaean History* (Philadelphia: Fortress Press): 285-331.
1978   'The Rise of the Israelite Monarchy', *ZAW* 90: 1-19.
McCarter, P.K.
1980   *1 Samuel* (AB, 8; Garden City, NY: Doubleday).
Miller, J.M.
1974   'Saul's Rise to Power: Some Observations Concerning 1 Sam 9.1–10.16; 10.26–11.15 and 13.2–14.46', *CBQ* 36: 157-74.
Morrison, K.
1961–62   'James' and Lubbock's Differing Points of View', *Nineteenth Century Fiction* 16: 245-55.
Noth, M.
1967   *Überlieferungsgeschichtliche Studien* (Tübingen: Max Niemeyer, 3rd edn).
Perry, M., and M. Sternberg
1968–69   'The King through Ironic Eyes: The Narrator's Devices in the Biblical Story of David and Batsheba and Two Excursuses on the Theory of the Narrative Text', *Ha-Sifrut* 1: 263-92 (English summary, 452-99).
Polzin, R.
1980   *Moses and the Deuteronomist: A Literary Study of the Deuteronomic History* (New York: Seabury).
1981   'Reporting Speech in the Book of Deuteronomy: Toward a Compositional Analysis of the Deuteronomic History', in B. Halpern and J.D. Levenson (eds.), *Traditions in Transformation: Turning Points in Biblical Faith* (Winona Lake, IN: Eisenbrauns): 193-211.
Radjawane, A.N.
1973–74   'Das deuteronomistische Geschichtswerk', *TR* 38: 177-216.
Ritterspach, A.D.
1967   'The Samuel Traditions: An Analysis of the Anti-Monarchical Source in 1 Samuel 1–15' (PhD thesis; Graduate Theological Union and the San Francisco Theological Seminary).
Schmidt, L.
1970   *Menschlicher Erfolg und Jahwes Initiative* (WMANT, 38; Neukirchen–Vluyn: Neukirchener Verlag).
Smend, R.
1978   *Die Entstehung des Alten Testaments* (TWI; Stuttgart: Kohlhammer).
Stanzel, F.
1971   *Narrative Situations in the Novel: Tom Jones, Moby-Dick, The Ambassadors, Ulysses* (trans. J.P. Pusack; Bloomington: Indiana University Press).

1978   'Second Thoughts on Narrative Situations in the Novel: Towards a "Grammar of Fiction"', *Novel* 11: 247-64.

Sternberg, M.
1978   *Expositional Modes and Temporal Ordering in Fiction* (Baltimore: Johns Hopkins University Press).

Stoebe, H.J.
1973   *Das erste Buch Samuelis* (KAT, 8; Gütersloh: Gerd Mohn).

Thenius, O.
1842   *Die Bücher Samuels* (KeH, 4; Leipzig: S. Hirzel).

Uspensky, B.
1973   *A Poetics of Composition* (trans. V. Zavarin and S. Wittig; Berkeley: University of California Press).

Vannoy, J.R.
1978   *Covenant Renewal at Gilgal: A Study of 1 Samuel 11:14–12:25* (Cherry Hill, NJ: Mack).

Veijola, T.
1977   *Das Königtum in der Beurteilung der deuteronomistischen Historiographie: Eine redaktionsgeschichtliche Untersuchung* (Annales academiae scientiarum Fennicae. Series B, 198; Helsinki: Suomalainen Tiedeakatemia).

Weiser, A.
1961   *The Old Testament: Its Formation and Development* (trans. D.M. Barton, New York: Association Press).
1962   *Samuel: Seine geschichtliche Aufgabe und religiöse Bedeutung. Traditiongeschichtliche Untersuchungen zu I. Samuel 7–12* (FRLANT, 81; Göttingen: Vandenhoeck & Ruprecht).

Wellek, R., and A. Warren
1975   *Theory of Literature* (New York: Harcourt, Brace, Jovanovich, 3rd edn [1942]).

Wellhausen, J.
1973   *Prolegomena to the History of Ancient Israel* (repr.; Gloucester: Peter Smith [1957]).

Wildberger, H.
1957   'Samuel und die Entstehung des israelitischen Königtums', *TZ* 13: 442-69.

Yacobi, T.
1981   'Fictional Reliability as a Communicative Problem', *PT* 2.2: 113-26.

JSOT 24 (1982), pp. 27-46

THE HEROISM OF SAUL: PATTERNS OF MEANING
IN THE NARRATIVE OF THE EARLY KINGSHIP

Thomas R. Preston

Biblical scholars tend to divide into discrete narrative units the vast
amount of material in the two books of Samuel and the first two chapters of the first book of Kings: the Samuel story, the ark narrative, the
rise of David story or, as P. Kyle McCarter recently has called it, the
apology of David, and the court or succession narrative. These blocks of
material may represent originally independent narratives, each unified by
the points of view of editors or individual authors.[1] From a literary perspective, however, originally discrete narrative units make little difference, for in its final form the whole comprises one continuous narrative
detailing the end of the judgeship era and the rise of the Israelite monarchy through the death of King David. At the surface level, the narrative
tells the story of political transition in ancient Israel: it relates the rise of
the early kingship. But the narrator, in traditional literary terms, the final
persona or voice that tells the tale,[2] is more interested in the persons

---

1. For excellent summaries of the various scholarly arguments, see P.K.
McCarter, Jr, 'The Apology of David', *JBL* 99 (1980), pp. 489-93; R.P. Gordon,
'David's Rise and Saul's Demise: Narrative Analogy in 1 Samuel 24–26', *TynBul*
31 (1980), pp. 37-39; H.W. Hertzberg, *I and II Samuel: A Commentary*
(Philadelphia: Westminster Press, 1976), pp. 17ff. All biblical quotations in this
essay are from the Revised Standard Version.
2. Whether the narrator used early and late sources for various episodes (see
Hertzberg, *I and II Samuel, passim*) is also finally unimportant when trying to
understand the literary meaning of the finished work. For recent discussion of one
final author of Joshua–Kings, see the excellent essay by F.M. Cross, 'The Themes
of the Book of Kings and the Structure of the Deuteronomistic History', in
Canaanite Myth and Hebrew Epic (Cambridge, MA: Harvard University Press,
1973), pp. 274-89. Helpful discussions of the narrator and the narrative as finished

causing the political transition than in the transition itself. At a deeper level, then, the narrator tells the story of Samuel, Saul, and David. He places their lives in the foreground, making the political transition a background, important and interrelated, but nevertheless a background for their tragedies and triumphs.

Scholarly interest in the Davidic materials leaves the impression that David is the main protagonist of 1 Samuel–1 Kings 1–2. Studies like those of Norman Whybray and David Gunn make clear, however, that while David dominates the narrative, if only because his exploits are recounted at greater length than those of Samuel or Saul, he does not emerge as the hero evoking the reader's admiration.[3] To use Whybray's terms, in the final chapters 'the figure of David looms like an evil genius' over the other characters.[4] The conclusion would seem to be that 1 Samuel–1 Kings 1–2, like Thackeray's *Vanity Fair* or many modern novels, forms a novel without a hero. Yet I do not think such is really the case. When the various literary units are read as interdependent parts of an artistic whole, as one narrative of the early kingship, we can discern that the narrator has established a unified structure in which the lives of Samuel, Saul, and David are all intertwined in such a way that they follow the same basic pattern, foreshadowing and reflecting each other as the narrative progresses. And in this mirroring of lives, Saul emerges as the hero of the story.

The pattern established by the narrator emerges clearly in Hannah's song, opening ch. 2 of 1 Samuel:

> The bows of the mighty are broken,
>   but the feeble gird on strength.
>
> The Lord makes poor and makes rich;
>   he brings low, he also exalts.

work appear in Gordon, 'David's Rise and Saul's Demise', p. 42, and D.M. Gunn, *The Fate of King Saul* (JSOTSup, 14; Sheffield: JSOT Press, 1980), pp. 13-19. See also his discussion of genre in *The Story of King David* (Sheffield: JSOT Press, 1978), *passim*, and the various discussions of fictionalized history and historicized fiction in R. Alter, *The Art of Biblical Narrative* (New York: Basic Books, 1981), pp. 23-46 especially.

3.   R.N. Whybray, *The Succession Narrative* (Naperville, IL: A.R. Allenson, 1968), pp. 48-49 especially; Gunn, *King David*, pp. 85-111 especially.

4.   Whybray, *The Succession Narrative*, p. 27.

He raises up the poor from the dust;
  he lifts the needy from the ash heap,
to make them sit with princes
  and inherit a seat of honor (1 Sam. 2.4, 7-8).

This pattern can be called the 'rise of the lowly, fall of the mighty' (or in New Testament terms, the 'first shall be last, the last first'). It is a familiar pattern in the Old Testament, and with its explicit enunciation early in the story, the narrator evokes its past history: lowly Abraham called to be the father of a great nation; the Israelite rabble called to be the people of God; Jacob, the younger born, blessed over Esau, the first-born; Joseph, for all practical purposes the youngest, called to rule over his older brothers; Ephraim, the younger, blessed by Jacob over Joseph's elder son, Manasseh; Moses, a fugitive from Egyptian justice, called to lead Israel. The incidence of the pattern seems almost endless, and the mere recollection of its deep embodiment in Israelite history assures the reader that the story to be unfolded reaches back to the most ancient traditions; indeed that it will echo them, reaffirm them, and renew them in this later time. Perhaps the narrator's most significant contribution to this ancient pattern is his logical extension of it to mean that the lowly individual who rises to become mighty may also be the very mighty individual who falls; that the lowly having been exalted may again be brought low; that one who has been lifted from the ash heap to sit with princes may find the seat of honor to be lost to the ash heap again. In any event, the narrator selects this variation as his pattern for Samuel, Saul, and David, using his treatment of their three falls from power to illumine the heroism of Saul.

The 'rise of the lowly, fall of the mighty' pattern is, of course, implicit in Hannah's barrenness, recalling as it does the barrenness of Sarah and Rebekah, who later gave birth respectively to Isaac and Jacob, the inheritors of Yahweh's promise to Abraham. To establish his pattern, however, the narrator also uses the old priest, Eli. As Samuel rises from the position of lowly servant in the shrine at Shiloh to become priest, prophet, and judge, he is also displacing Eli and ensuring that Eli's worthless sons do not succeed him, thereby preventing them from forming a dynastic priesthood. Samuel's progress to greatness, then, involves the fall of Eli and his sons. This part of the pattern is repeated later in Samuel's own life, when he is displaced by Saul, and Samuel's own worthless children are also prevented from succeeding him and founding a dynastic priesthood or judgeship. With Samuel's displacement or fall the narrator initiates his variation on the pattern, while the sub-pattern of rejected sons foreshadows the rejection of Saul's sons and the founding of a dynasty as well as the rejection of David's sons, Absalom, Amnon, and Adonijah. David, of course, does found a dynasty, but the succession of Solomon over his older brothers, an act that ironically mimics the 'rise of the lowly' pattern, occurs with such violence and intrigue that it does not bode well for the ultimate success of the dynasty.

Just as Samuel's rise to power meant the displacement of Eli, so Saul's rise to power means the displacement of Samuel. The narrator's strategy is superb. He relates the rise of Samuel and fall of Eli, concluding this opening section (1 Sam. 1–4) with Samuel clearly in control of the situation: 'And Samuel grew, and the Lord was with him and let none of his words fall to the ground. And all Israel from Dan to Beersheba knew that Samuel was established as a prophet of the Lord' (1 Sam. 3.19-20). But instead of continuing with Samuel's story and his rise to further greatness as judge, the narrator interposes at 1 Samuel 4 the story of several Israelite battles with the Philistines and the capture of the ark. This narrative continues through 1 Samuel 7, during which the ark is restored, Samuel offers sacrifice at Mizpah, and cities captured by the Philistines are restored to Israel. 1 Samuel 7 ends with the depiction of Samuel's power as judge that the reader would at first expect to have come earlier: 'Samuel judged Israel all the days of his life. And he went on a circuit year by year to Bethel, Gilgal, and Mizpah; and he judged Israel in all these places' (1 Sam. 7.15-16).

The interposition of the battle–ark story between Samuel's establishment as prophet-priest and his establishment as judge over all Israel creates two powerful and dramatic effects. First, it introduces the clear and present danger of the Philistines, emphasizing that even though Israel regains some lost cities, it needs a leader who can rid Israel of the Philistines once and for all. In effect, the interposed story prepares for the monarchy by initiating the theme of Israel's movement from a direct dependence on Yahweh to dependence on an institution of temporal leadership. Second, by separating Samuel's role as prophet–priest, a spokesman for Yahweh, from his role as judge, the interposed story implies that to Samuel the judgeship itself has come to mean just such an institution of temporal leadership, one that Samuel exercises by the continuous interpretation of Israel's laws and the administration of justice. Clearly absent from the narrative is the older idea of the judge as a charismatic personality only temporarily raised up by Yahweh to

conquer Israel's enemies. The irony, however, is that Samuel's institutionalized judgeship cannot provide the military leadership, however
temporary, of the charismatic judgeship. It becomes inevitable, then, that
the judgeship be displaced as the institution of temporal leadership and
that Samuel be displaced as temporal leader.

By placing Samuel's success as a judge in a brief paragraph after the
interposed narrative, the narrator underscores the irony of Samuel's
displacement, for the narrator immediately moves from Samuel's judgeship to Israel's request that Samuel step down and that a king be created: 'When Samuel became old, he made his sons judges over Israel...
Yet his sons did not walk in his ways, but turned aside after gain; they
took bribes and perverted justice' (1 Sam. 8.1, 3). The echoes of Eli's
situation reverberate, and the elders of Israel at first use Samuel's
worthless sons as the reason for requesting a king. But their real reason
emerges after Samuel recites for them the political oppression that will
follow upon a kingship: 'But the people refused to listen to the voice of
Samuel; and they said, "No! but we will have a king over us, that we
also may be like all the nations, and that our king may govern us and go
out before us and fight our battles"' (1 Sam. 8.19-20).

With their desire to be like other nations, especially in relying on a
temporal leader, the elders of Israel come perilously close to rejecting
Israel's call to holiness, which Leviticus repeatedly asserts will derive, in
part, from Israel's refusal to be like other nations.[5] At the same time,
Israel is clearly requesting neither an oriental kingship like that described
by Samuel nor the destruction of the covenanted tribal league; rather it
wants a king who will continue its traditions but who will be a military
commander able to defeat its enemies.[6] Saul thus enters at this time of
political-military crisis. To emphasize, however, that his story will follow
the same pattern as Samuel's the narrator opens the next section
(1 Sam. 9) with the lines: 'There was a man of Benjamin whose name
was Kish, the son of Abiel, son of Zeror, son of Becorath, son of
Aphiah, a Benjamite...' (1 Sam. 9.1). These lines echo the very opening
lines of 1 Samuel: 'There was a certain man of Ramathaim-zophim of
the hill country of Ephraim, whose name was Elkanah the son of

5.   See, for example, Lev. 18.1-5. But also see Gunn's argument that being like
other nations became necessary: *King Saul*, p. 145 n. 1.
6.   For a most helpful analysis and treatment of the military kingship idea, see
Cross, 'The Ideologies of Kingship in the Era of the Empire: Conditional Covenant
and Eternal Decree', in *Canaanite Myth and Hebrew Epic*, pp. 219-73.

Jeroham, son of Elihu, son of Tohu, son of Suph, an Ephraimite' (1 Sam. 1.1).

Saul's rise to power follows the pattern established by Samuel, but in the details of his rise and fall the narrator creates the story of a tragic hero who towers above the man who will displace him, David.[7] The seed of Saul's ultimate fall lies in the basis of his rise—his lowliness. When he is introduced into the narrative, Saul's physical attributes receive primary attention: Saul is a 'handsome young man. There was not a man among the people of Israel more handsome than he; from his shoulders upward he was taller than any of the people' (1 Sam. 9.2). This emphasis on Saul's physique, which will be echoed later in the rise of David, focuses the reader's attention on the main reason Israel demanded a king: to lead it in battles. Almost immediately thereafter, however, the narrator focuses on Saul's lowliness. When told by Samuel that he is to be king, Saul instinctively replies: 'Am I not a Benjamite, from the least of the tribes of Israel? And is not my family the humblest of all the families of the tribe of Benjamin? Why then have you spoken to me in this way?' (1 Sam. 9.21). Saul's sense of his own lowliness, his own unworthiness, becomes a mental block that prevents him from psychologically ever becoming a king. The narrator observes that 'God gave him another heart' (1 Sam. 10.9), hence the potential to become a real king, but Saul remains basically a farm boy who accepts the kingship only very reluctantly.

The narrator insists on this 'farm boy–reluctant king' aspect of Saul. When Saul finally asks Samuel how to find his father's asses, it is significant that Saul has no money on him and has to borrow from his servant to pay Samuel (1 Sam. 9.7-10). At the time Saul is formally elected king, he cannot be found, and only an oracle from Yahweh tells Israel, 'Behold, he has hidden himself among the baggage' (1 Sam. 10.22). The narrator reminds us right after Saul's formal election that

7. Various aspects of Saul's tragic stature are treated from a psychoanalytic point of view by D.F. Zeligs, 'Saul, The Tragic King', in *Psychoanalysis and the Bible: A Study in Depth of Seven Leaders* (New York: Bloch, 1974), pp. 121-59. See also E.M. Good, 'Saul: The Tragedy of Greatness', in *Irony in the Old Testament* (Philadelphia: Westminster Press, 1965), pp. 56-80; J.D. Levenson, '1 Samuel 25 as Literature and as History', *CBQ* 40 (1978), pp. 11-28; W.L. Humphreys, 'The Tragedy of King Saul: A Study of the Structure of 1 Samuel 9–31', *JSOT* 6 (1978), pp. 18-27. Gunn's study of Saul as a 'tragedy of fate' remains the most impressive interpretation of the tragic nature of the Saul story. See *King Saul*, pp. 28-30, 115-116, 129-31 especially.

some in Israel doubted Saul's ability, saying, '"How can this man save us?" And they despised him, and brought him no present' (1 Sam. 10.27). After the election, Saul returns home to farm; he is discovered 'coming from the field behind the oxen' (1 Sam. 11.5) when the news of the Ammonite threat to Jabesh-gilead arrives. It is this very back-wardness (or modesty?) that causes Saul to issue injudicious military orders like those forbidding the army to eat, orders that could sentence Jonathan to death (1 Sam. 14); it is his sense of unworthiness that prevents him from carrying out Samuel's commands to 'utterly destroy' the Amalekites. He admits finally to Samuel that he failed in this last duty because he 'feared the people and obeyed their voice' (1 Sam. 15.24).[8] Samuel's words to Saul on his failure to utterly destroy the Amalekites sum up the problem: 'Though you are little in your own eyes, are you not the head of the tribes of Israel?' (1 Sam. 15.17).

By building up this 'farm boy–reluctant king' side of the early Saul, the narrator establishes him as a very sympathetic character in the reader's eyes. Further, the narrator makes clear that even if Saul is backward and even if he is a reluctant king, he will at least try to act as king and primarily as the military king Israel demanded. The narrator dramatizes Saul's desire to act as military king in his account of the inspired way Saul puts down the Ammonite threat (1 Sam 11.5-15). This victory concludes with Israel's desire to kill those who earlier had 'despised' Saul and with Saul's gracious declaration, 'Not a man shall be put to death this day, for today the Lord has wrought deliverance in Israel' (1 Sam. 11.13). Saul's lines here will reappear ironically later in the mouth of David, but the significant point is that Saul tries to be a military leader. After Jonathan leads the defeat of the Philistines at Michmash, the narrator reaffirms Saul's stature as a military king:

> When Saul had taken the kingship over Israel, he fought against all his enemies on every side, against Moab, against the Ammonites, against Edom, against the kings of Zobah, and against the Philistines; wherever he turned he put them to the worse. And he did valiantly, and smote the Amalekites, and delivered Israel out of the hands of those who plundered them (1 Sam. 14.47-48).

8.   As Gunn points out (*King Saul*, pp. 52-55, 69), 'fear' should be translated 'honor' or 'respect', thus underscoring Saul's attitude that he is a king only in the sense of the military leader of the covenanted tribal league. The people are the true rulers.

The early Saul, then, emerges as a reluctant king who tries to fulfill his military leadership role and who is, in large part, successful.

The narrator clearly lets the reader know that for his failures, especially for his failure to obey Samuel and Yahweh in dealing with the Amalekites, Saul must fall from the kingship. The breath-taking scene occurs, of course, when Saul tears Samuel's robe and Samuel retorts: 'The Lord has torn the kingdom of Israel from you this day, and has given it to a neighbor of yours, who is better than you' (1 Sam. 15.28). Yahweh 'would have established... [Saul's] kingdom over Israel for ever' (1 Sam. 13.13), but it will not be established, as Samuel's prophetship was 'established' (1 Sam. 3.20), although not forever, and as David's 'throne shall be established for ever' (2 Sam. 7.16). But these careful and open admissions of Saul's guilt do not detract from the sympathetic figure the narrator had created. In fact, they only strengthen the heroic aspect of Saul's character that finally emerges in the course of Saul's fall from power.

The seeds of Saul's downfall, as suggested earlier, lie in his 'farm boy–reluctant king' approach to his leadership. In no small measure, however, this approach is desired by Israel and is tragically reinforced by Samuel. Samuel seemingly loves Saul: he remains to pray with Saul after the Amalekite fiasco, so that Saul will not be dishonored before the elders of Israel (1 Sam. 15.30); and he grieves over Saul after pronouncing Yahweh's sentence of doom (1 Sam. 15.35; 16.1).[9] Despite this apparent love for Saul, however, Samuel's own fall has undercut Saul's rise from the very beginning. If Saul is a reluctant king, Samuel is a reluctant king-maker. Not only does he paint a lurid picture of kingly oppression to the elders of Israel; at the time of Saul's enthronement ('renewal of the kingship') at Gilgal, Samuel delivers a self-justifying speech that completely undermines any chance Saul might have had to become a truly effective king. Samuel's speech forces Israel to admit that he had been a good judge. But its insidious nature lies in its juxtaposing good judges to this untried and rebellious kingship:

> And the Lord sent Jerubbaal and Barak, and Jephthah, and Samuel, and delivered you out of the hand of your enemies on every side; and you dwelt in safety. And when you saw that Nahash the King of the Ammonites came against you, you said to me, 'No, but a king shall reign over us', when the Lord your God was your king. And now behold the

---

9. Samuel's grieving may, however, be interpreted as other than sympathetic to Saul. See Gunn, *King Saul*, pp. 146-47 n. 8.

king whom you have chosen, for whom you have asked; behold, the Lord
has set a king over you (1 Sam. 12.11-13).

Samuel then performs the miracle of sending the rain, showing he still
has Yahweh's favor and forcing Israel to admit openly, 'we have added
to all our sins this evil, to ask for ourselves a king' (1 Sam. 12.19).

A defense of his administration as judge is certainly in order, but
Samuel turns it into a self-serving speech that puts the kingship and the
new king into an impossible situation.[10] Samuel's continued presence on
the scene further serves to remind Saul and the reader that the kingship
is to be a conditional office, depending on continued faithfulness to the
covenant and to the covenanted tribal league. And it is such a king that
Saul clearly wants to be. But Samuel's continued presence also serves to
keep Saul off balance and insecure; it keeps Saul a reluctant king politically as well as psychologically. Samuel's deliberate undercutting of Saul
stands out most poignantly in the scene where Saul awaits Samuel's
arrival at Gilgal. Samuel does not arrive at the time he had appointed,
and, with his army deserting, Saul offers sacrifice himself. At that very
moment Samuel appears on the scene: 'As soon as he had finished
offering the burnt offering, behold, Samuel came...'(1 Sam. 13.10). The
structure of the sentence indicates that the narrator wants the reader to
infer that Samuel was in fact close by, waiting to catch Saul and then to
reprove him, as Samuel immediately does.[11]

Saul's downfall proper begins in the middle of 1 Samuel 16. The narrator prepares for it very carefully. The chapter opens with Yahweh's
command to Samuel to anoint one of Jesse's sons king. Samuel is well
aware that such an act would be high treason: 'How can I go? If Saul
hears it, he will kill me' (1 Sam. 16.2). But he does go to Bethlehem,
and in the moment of anointing David (vv. 13-14) the narrator details
the beginning of the end: 'and the Spirit of the Lord came mightily
upon David from that day forward... Now the Spirit of the Lord
departed from Saul, and an evil spirit from the Lord tormented him'
(1 Sam. 16.13-14). The chapter ends with David's arrival at Saul's tent
to soothe Saul's 'evil spirit' by playing on the lyre. The irony of this
chapter is incalculable: treason leads to Yahweh's Spirit descending on
David; Yahweh's Spirit leaves Saul and is replaced by an evil spirit;
David, who is to displace Saul, who has treasonably been anointed king,
becomes the means of relieving Saul's tormented mind.

10. For a related interpretation, see Gunn, *King Saul*, pp. 65-66.
11. See also Gunn, *King Saul*, pp. 34-52.

Saul's downfall is finally caused by an 'evil spirit from the Lord', what we would today call melancholia or more accurately very agitated depression. It makes little difference what terms are used, for the important point is that the narrator uses Saul's illness to heighten the pathos of his fall and to absolve him from the crimes he commits under the influence of the depression or evil spirit. In his depression—madness—Saul becomes jealous of David's military successes and his favor in the eyes of Israel, asking, with only a touch of paranoia, 'what more can... [David] have but the kingdom?' (1 Sam. 18.8). Saul's depression leads him to make several attempts on David's life, to murder the priests and people of Nob, to drive David into becoming a fugitive and a guerrilla leader—actions that culminate in this mad pursuit of David and his troops instead of focusing his attention on the Philistine threat all around him. Yet in the midst of this madness the narrator continually projects a sympathetic, even loving, portrait of Saul, preparing us for the final heroism at Gilboa.

The two scenes where Saul on his mad pursuit meets David are perhaps the most effective. In the first scene, after David has cut off the skirt of Saul's robe and from a distance made his speech to Saul (1 Sam. 24.1-15), the narrator allows Saul a moment of sanity, portraying him as a loving father, and a father who knows his 'adopted' son David will have the throne:

> When David had finished speaking these words to Saul, Saul said, 'Is this your voice, my son David?' And Saul lifted up his voice and wept. He said to David, 'You are more righteous than I; for you have repaid me good, whereas I have repaid you evil... So may the Lord reward you with good for what you have done to me this day. And now, behold, I know that you shall surely be king, and that the kingdom of Israel shall be established in your hand' (1 Sam. 24.16-20).

This speech, so full of pathos, is yet replete with ironies. Saul's weeping and his address to David as 'my son' will be echoed in the later scene when David weeps over the death of his real son, Absalom, who has attempted to seize the throne from David, as Saul perceives David trying to do from him.[12] Moreover, Saul's sincere tribute to David's 'goodness' and his self-accusation contrast with what can only be called David's suspect sincerity. It is one thing for David to refuse the opportunity of killing the 'Lord's anointed'. That would indeed be noble. But

---

12. For discussion of the repeated use of 'my son', see Gunn, *King Saul*, pp. 104-105, and Gordon, 'David's Rise and Saul's Demise', p. 48.

as soon as David makes his 'goodness' public, in front of his own and Saul's men, David is immediately open to charges of self-serving, at least of 'blowing his trumpet before him'. The second scene, probably a doublet,[13] in essence recapitulates the first scene, and again David's suspect sincerity, in making his ability to kill the king public to his own and Saul's troops, is contrasted with the genuine sincerity of Saul's confession: 'I have done wrong; return, my son David, for I will no more do you harm, because my life was precious in your eyes this day; behold, I have played the fool, and erred exceedingly' (1 Sam. 26.21).[14]

These moments of sanity in madness effectively foreshadow Saul's final breakdown and then heroic stance at Gilboa. 'When Saul saw the army of the Philistines, he was afraid, and his heart trembled greatly' (1 Sam. 27.5), so that Saul resorted to dreams, the priests, and prophets to discover his chances in the upcoming battle. The failure of Yahweh to speak drives Saul to the witch of Endor. Here we have one of the most poignant scenes of Saul's mental deterioration. The witch conjures up the spirit of Samuel, who coldly and remorselessly foretells Saul's defeat at the hands of the Philistines, making him fall on the ground in fear: 'the Lord has torn the kingdom out of your hand, and given it to your neighbor, David...tomorrow you and your sons shall be with me; the Lord will give the army of Israel also into the hands of the Philistines' (1 Sam. 28.17-19). The coldness of Samuel, however, is contrasted by the warmth and tenderness of the witch:

> 'I have taken my life in my hand, and have hearkened to what you have said to me. Now therefore, you also hearken to your handmaid; let me set a morsel of bread before you; and eat, that you may have strength when you go on your way.' He refused, and said, 'I will not eat.' But his servants, together with the woman, urged him; and he hearkened to their words. So he arose from the earth, and sat upon the bed...and she put... [a meal] before Saul and his servants; and they ate (1 Sam. 28.22-25).

Saul's hunger and need of nourishment for the upcoming battle ironically recall the much earlier scene in which he forbade his army to eat.

---

13. But see Gordon, 'David's Rise and Saul's Demise', pp. 53-61, who argues for theme and character development from one scene to the other and explains the probable meaning of David's cutting the hem of Saul's robe.

14. Saul's use of the word *fool* probably associates him with Nabal. See Gordon, 'David's Rise and Saul's Demise', pp. 50-51 and *passim*, for a discussion of the word and of the Nabal–Saul relationship.

But the structure of the scene itself is most revealing: Saul has, in effect, arrived at his final collapse, an almost complete breakdown, in which he has become a child again, with the witch serving as mother figure, advising, comforting and nursing him.[15]

From this depth of breakdown, this symbolic return to childhood, Saul gains the strength to rise to his heroic end. The suspense is brilliantly maintained by the interposition of the story of the Philistines sending David home and David's revenge on the sackers of his city, Ziklag. This interposed story creates the suspense needed to give Saul his finest hour; at the same time it reminds the reader that David is repairing his personal fortunes as Saul goes to his death. When Saul commits suicide, he makes clear that his reason is to prevent the 'uncircumcised', unbelievers, from mocking the Lord's anointed while he is still alive, though wounded. Saul thus kills himself for a noble reason, the same reason in essence that David had given earlier for refusing to kill Saul:

> The battle pressed hard upon Saul, and the archers found him, and he was badly wounded by the archers. Then Saul said to his armorbearer, 'Draw your sword, and thrust me through with it, lest these uncircumcised come and thrust me through, and make sport of me'. But his armorbearer would not; for he feared greatly. Therefore Saul took his own sword, and fell on it (1 Sam. 31.3-4).

Saul dies on the battlefield, doing the job he had been anointed and elected to do—leading the army of Israel against its enemies. Through all the reluctance, failure, and madness, he kept his bargain to the end, dying as the military king. Emphasizing this point, the narrator concludes the death scene and 1 Samuel by having the people of Jabesh-gilead retrieve Saul's body from the Philistines and give it proper burial. We recall that Saul's first act as military king was the rescue of Jabesh-gilead from the Ammonites.[16] Saul's death scene looms large in the narrative and grimly points forward to the very different death scene of David.

The narrator inserts between the death of Saul and David's establishment as king of Judah and finally as king of all Israel David's touching elegy for Saul and Jonathan. The refrain of this elegy pointedly reminds the reader of the 'rise of the lowly, fall of the mighty' pattern: 'How are

---

15. For a related interpretation of the witch, see Gunn, *King Saul*, p. 109.

16. Gunn, *King Saul*, pp. 90, 122, reminds us that the people generally remain loyal to Saul and never ask for his removal.

the mighty fallen!' (2 Sam. 1.19). One time the refrain ends 'in the midst
of battle' (2 Sam. 1.25), and another time 'and the weapons of war perished' (2 Sam. 1.27). These conclusions to the refrain, alluding to war,
point forward to David's own fall, his displacement, reaffirming the
same pattern for David's life but suggesting, since he does not die in
battle, the very unheroic nature of his death.

As Saul's rise to power meant the fall of Samuel, so David's rise to
power means the fall of Saul. And as Saul's rise was accompanied by
Samuel's long-term presence, so David's rise is accompanied by Saul's
long-term presence. Like Samuel and Saul, David enters the narrative in
a lowly position: 'And Samuel said to Jesse, "Are all your sons here?"
And he said, "There remains yet the youngest, but behold, he is keeping
the sheep"' (1 Sam. 16.11). Yahweh specifically tells Samuel not to look
for great appearance or height in the one to be anointed in place of Saul,
'for the Lord sees not as man sees; man looks on the outward appearance, but the Lord looks on the heart' (1 Sam. 16.7). Yet when David
finally appears before Samuel, he is 'ruddy', has 'beautiful eyes', and is
'handsome' (1 Sam. 16.12), this last adjective being the exact term used
to describe Saul in 1 Sam. 9.2. Despite what the Lord says, David is
physically attractive, and by using the same adjective 'handsome' to
describe both Saul and David, the narrator carefully associates David
with Saul and suggests that the 'rise–fall' pattern will be repeated in
David.

The key to David's fall appears in his dialogue with Abigail, who is
trying to restrain him from avenging himself on her husband, Nabal.
Abigail courteously but carefully rebukes David:

> Pray forgive the trespass of your handmaid; for the Lord will certainly
> make my lord a sure house, because my lord is fighting the battles of the
> Lord; and evil should not be found in you so long as you live... And
> when the Lord has done to my lord according to all the good that he has
> spoken concerning you, and appointed you prince over Israel, my lord
> shall have no cause of grief, or pangs of conscience, for having shed
> blood without cause or for my lord taking vengeance himself (1 Sam.
> 25.28-31).

Abigail has put her finger on David's main weakness: David fights the
Lord's battles, but he is really more interested in being king in the style
of Samuel's warning against kings, and he does want to take vengeance
on those who thwart this ambition.[17] The narrator has carefully noted

17. Levenson, '1 Samuel 25', p. 23, sees this scene with Abigail as the 'first

that Samuel's prophetship and judgeship were established by Yahweh; he has carefully noted that Saul's throne was not established by Yahweh. In the famous ch. 7 of 2 Samuel he will carefully note that Yahweh has established David's throne forever. But this establishment of David's throne is viewed as a rather ambiguous matter, and David himself is projected as a failure both as king and father.[18]

David's view of the kingship is carefully rendered by the narrator. David's rise in public favor and his ultimate success in achieving the throne are firmly based on his early military victories. The David and Goliath story is, of course, celebrated. But we also remember the refrain that haunts 1 Samuel and helps drive Saul madder: 'And the women sang to one another as they made merry, "Saul has slain his thousands, and David his ten thousands." And Saul was very angry, and this saying displeased him...' (1 Sam. 18.7-8). When Abner begins to negotiate for a union of the northern tribes under David, it is clear that he and Israel are thinking of David as a military king in the style of Saul, not in the style of Samuel's warning:

> And Abner conferred with the elders of Israel, saying, 'For some time past you have been seeking David as king over you. Now then bring it about; for the Lord has promised David, saying, "By the hand of my servant David I will save my people Israel from the hand of the Philistines, and from the hand of all their enemies"' (2 Sam. 3.17-18).

Moreover, when the northern tribes do come over to David, they plainly accept him publicly as military king, even making a covenant with him, suggesting that his kingship is, as Saul's was, to be one that carries on the covenant and the traditions of the covenanted tribal league: 'In times past, when Saul was king over us, it was you that led out and brought in Israel... So all the elders of Israel came to the king at Hebron; and King David made a covenant with them at Hebron before the Lord, and they anointed David king over Israel' (2 Sam. 5.2-3). But what does David think a king should be? Certainly David is a great military leader, and he seems to enjoy battle, as his capture of the two hundred Philistine foreskins suggests. Nor does he have any intention of seizing the crown after Saul's death. As Gunn has noted, David wants the crown offered to

revelation of evil in David's character', but Gordon, 'David's Rise and Saul's Demise', pp. 53-57, disagrees.

18. For an excellent study of the conflict in David between his public life as king and his private life, see K.R.R. Gros Louis, 'The Difficulty of Ruling Well: King David of Israel', *Semeia* 8 (1977), pp. 15-33.

him.[19] What, in fact, the narrator suggests is that David holds conflicting views of the kingship: one view is that of military leader, the other that of oriental despot. What the narrator reveals is David's gradual acceptance of the oriental despot view.

The narrator constructs a literary strategy that reflects the kingship conflict in David's mind. Immediately after Saul's death, the narrative develops a sense of ominousness about David's future reign; the man who brings news to David of Saul's death is put to death; Abner kills Asahel; civil war ensues; Joab kills Abner; Ishbosheth is murdered; the two brothers who kill Ishbosheth are put to death by David. This bloodshed does not bode well for David's reign, but all is quickly resolved as the northern tribes unite under David. Even David's public renunciation of any part in Abner's murder is accepted, although the narrator leaves David's part in it ambiguous: 'And all the people took notice of [David's fast for Abner's death], and it pleased them; as everything that the king did pleased all the people' (2 Sam. 3.36).[20] After the union of the crowns of Judah and the North, David's reign begins to glow, recalling the beginning of Saul's reign. David captures Jerusalem; wages successful battle against the Philistines; removes the ark to Jerusalem; achieves further military victories; receives Jonathan's son into his household (a not altogether altruistic act, since he now has the lone claimant to Saul's throne under virtual house arrest); and achieves further military victories (2 Sam. 4–10). In the midst of these successes, in which David appears to be accepting the military leadership view of kingship, two important scenes occur. The first is brief and ominous: David builds himself a great palace with the help of Hiram king of Tyre and he takes more concubines and wives from Jerusalem (2 Sam. 5.11-16), innocent enough actions on the surface, but suggestive of oriental kingship. The second scene occurs in 2 Samuel 7, the famous prophecy that David's 'throne shall be established for ever' (2 Sam. 7.16). This is by far the longer and more elaborate scene and presumably confirms Yahweh's favor to David. Yet there is ambiguity, for the nature of

19. See his fine analysis of the 'gift–seizure' motif in the David story, 'David and the Gift of the Kingdom', *Semeia* 3 (1975), pp. 14-45.

20. On David's probable guilt and his probable activities as an enemy of Saul, even setting himself up as a rival monarch in Hebron, see J.C. VanderKam, 'Davidic Complicity in the Deaths of Abner and Eshbaal: A Historical and Redactional Study', *JBL* 99 (1980), pp. 521-39.

David's throne is questioned by the juxtaposition of the scene suggesting oriental despotism.

The crisis and the beginning of David's fall occur with the opening lines of ch. 11, the chapter in which David seduces Bathsheba: 'In the spring of the year, the time when kings go forth to battle, David sent Joab, and his servants with him, and all Israel; and they ravaged the Ammonites, and besieged Rabbah. But David remained at Jerusalem' (2 Sam. 11.1). These haunting sentences indicate that David's crime with Bathsheba, revolting though it is, is not his major crime. It is rather that he has capitulated to the oriental despot view of kingship. Kings go forth, but David remains in Jerusalem and sends his henchmen instead. David has in essence abandoned the concept of king as military leader, upholder of the covenant, and sustainer of the covenanted tribal league. His seduction and seizure of Bathsheba violates several laws of the covenant; but it is primarily the act of an oriental despot, the kind of king Samuel railed against earlier in the narrative.

David's next treacherous act, sending Uriah, Bathsheba's husband, into the forefront of battle with the intention of having him killed, sends tremors through the narrative. It recalls Saul's act of sending David for one hundred Philistine foreskins because he 'thought to make David fall by the hand of the Philistines' (1 Sam. 18.25). David recapitulates Saul's action, but what Saul did in madness, David does coldly and calculatedly. Nathan's response to David's treachery renders even more ambiguous Yahweh's earlier prophecy that David's 'house and...kingdom shall be made sure for ever before me... [his] throne shall be established for ever'. Nathan now threatens David and his 'house' with perpetual disarray: 'You have smitten Uriah the Hittite with the sword... Now therefore the sword shall never depart from your house, because you have despised me...' (2 Sam. 12.9-10). After Nathan finishes his denunciation of David, he affirms that Yahweh forgives David. But the curse still stands, and the ambiguity increases. The earlier promise made by Nathan for Yahweh was that David's house (meaning his dynasty) would be made sure forever. Does the curse mean that the sword will never depart from David's dynasty or merely that it will not depart from his current family? The history narrated in the books of Kings, and indeed the subsequent history of Israel, suggests that 'house' in the curse means David's dynasty. In any event, the curse takes effect immediately in David's family.

David's fall is rapid and dramatic, ironically reversing in outline the fall of Saul. A mere recitation of the events makes the horror of the fall clear. In effect, the narrator returns the reader to the bloodshed and treachery that opened David's reign, thus confirming the ominous forebodings of those scenes. First comes Amnon's rape of Tamar (2 Sam. 13), an action that recapitulates David's own 'rape' of Bathsheba and that ironically reverses the action whereby Saul gives his daughter Michal to his 'adopted' son, David. Two years later the rape is avenged by Absalom, who kills his half-brother Amnon to avenge his sister Tamar (2 Sam. 13). After finally being forgiven by David, Absalom carries out another part of Nathan's curse: 'Thus says the Lord, "Behold, I will raise up evil against you out of your own house; and I will take your wives before your eyes, and give them to your neighbor, and he shall lie with your wives in the sight of the sun"' (2 Sam. 12.11). David's 'neighbor' is, of course, his son Absalom, but the term chillingly recalls Samuel's assertion to Saul that the kingdom would be given to Saul's 'neighbor' (1 Sam. 15.28), who was David.

Absalom fulfills the curse when he revolts against his father, seizing Jerusalem and sleeping on the roof of the palace with David's concubines, while David flees (2 Sam. 16.20-23). As suggested earlier, David's lament for Absalom recalls Saul's weeping for David. But the death of Absalom is, in fact, a more striking and ironic reversal of Saul's situation with Jonathan. While Jonathan allied himself with David, he had never defected from his father. He dies heroically on the battlefield with Saul while David is busy avenging himself on the sackers of Ziklag. In contrast, Absalom has rebelled against his father, and, while hanging ignominiously in a tree, is butchered by Joab and other soldiers. The juxtaposition of the two scenes is almost shocking.

The narrator allows David some pity and even dignity during his flight from Jerusalem.[21] But even this sympathy is shattered by Shimei, a contemptible man whose railing at David, however vulgar, is still punctuated by truth: 'See, your ruin is on you; for you are a man of blood' (2 Sam. 16.8). David never really recovers from Absalom's revolt, as indicated by the fact that Joab has to recall him to his kingly duties: 'Now therefore arise, go out and speak kindly to your servants; for I swear by the Lord, if you do not go, not a man will stay with you this night; and this will be worse for you than all the evil that has come upon

21. On the piteous David in flight, see Hertzberg, *I and II Samuel*, pp. 341-46, and Gunn, 'David and the Gift', pp. 26-28.

you from your youth until now' (2 Sam. 19.7). As commentators have suggested, David's sorrow over Absalom is sympathetically presented.[22] It is even in one sense admirable. But it is also a private sorrow, and as such the narrator opposes it to David's public duty as king, a duty he not only accepted, but elaborated as far as he could into oriental despotism. The moral collapse of David is further detailed in David's return to Jerusalem, a return that ironically echoes Saul's victory over the Ammonites at Jabesh-gilead. David refuses to kill Shimei, saying, 'Shall any one be put to death in Israel this day?' (2 Sam. 19.22). But there is a grim difference between Saul's and David's magnanimity: Saul meant it, whereas David, on his death-bed, effectively orders Shimei's murder. The events of David's early reign, finally, are recalled at the very end of 2 Samuel, where Joab, recapitulating his murder of Abner, kills Amasa, his latest rival as commander of David's armies (2 Sam. 20.9-10).

David's death scene, narrated in 1 Kings 1–2, completes his 'rise of the lowly, fall of the mighty' pattern.[23] It is a sad scene and a vulgar scene, standing in unheroic contrast to Saul's death scene. Old and dying, David lies in bed, suffering from constant chills. His servants bring him Abishag, a young girl, to keep him warm in bed: 'The maiden was very beautiful; and she became the king's nurse and ministered to him; but the king knew her not' (1 Kgs 1.4). The ironies of this scene are abundant. First, unlike Saul, who dies heroically on the battlefield, David, the celebrated soldier, lies unheroically dying in a bed, old and infirm, but in oriental despot fashion, comforted by a girl from the harem. But the irony increases, for he is not comforted in a sexual way, for David 'knew her not'. He is instead nursed by a beautiful girl whom he is not physically able 'to know'. The final irony, however, is that the punishment fits the crime. The 'hot' David who seduces Bathsheba, and thereby sets in motion his downfall, suffers from cold chills, not able to repeat his sexual prowess any more effectively than his former military prowess.

As David lies dying we also remember that one of his daughters, raped by his son, remains a desolate woman in her brother's house; one

---

22. See, especially, Hertzberg, *I and II Samuel*, p. 361, and Gros Louis, 'The Difficulty of Ruling Well', p. 31.

23. The concluding chapters (21–24) of 2 Samuel are clearly an appendix, not part of the main narrative. See Hertzberg, *I and II Samuel*, pp. 380ff. Lines in this appendix seek to absolve David's failure to continue as military leader by explaining that the army feared he might be killed in battle. See 2 Sam. 21.15-17.

son has been murdered by another son; the next son in line for the throne has rebelled against his father, and has been killed by Joab. David goes to his death a broken and totally unheroic figure. But the unheroic, indeed degraded, circumstances of his death are not the complete story. Court intrigue makes him the victim of Nathan and Bathsheba, who convince David that he has promised the throne to Solomon instead of Adonijah, who is the next in line for the throne and who assumes he will be king.[24] David's death speech completes his physical, psychological and moral deterioration. In the midst of pious exhortations for Solomon to walk in Yahweh's statutes, David intrudes the vengeful heart that Abigail had warned him against early in his career: Solomon is to kill Joab for his early crime of killing Abner and his late crime of killing Amasa, crimes that David conveniently overlooked when they supported his throne; Solomon is to kill Shimei for his attacks on David during the flight from Jerusalem, even though David had promised his safety (1 Kgs 1.2).

The degradation of David's death stands in revelatory contrast to the heroic death of Saul. The narrator is aware that Samuel, Saul, and David have now completed the same pattern, although in greatly differing ways. He is also aware that the pattern is to begin anew, but now with even more grimness. Solomon, for all the wisdom that is later ascribed to him, is not truly in line for the throne. He is again the lowly rising to the seat of the mighty. His early reign will recapitulate the bloodshed of David's early reign: the deaths of Joab, Shimei, and his brother Adonijah; the exile of the priest Abiathar. But unlike David, there will be no conflict about views of kingship: his will be unreservedly that of an oriental despot. And for all the praise of Solomon's reign, it is ultimately undercut by the revolt of the northern tribes against his successor, Rehoboam. Solomon is repudiated by the assembly of Israel, who say to Rehoboam, 'Your father made our yoke heavy. Now therefore lighten the hard service of your father and his heavy yoke upon us, and we will serve you' (1 Kgs 12.4). The narrator in this section clearly rejects the oriental despot view for Israel's kings. David's house, thus, may be established forever—but under the curse of the sword. A reluctant king, rejected by Yahweh, and yet faithful to the ideal of a military king supporting the covenant and the covenanted tribal league, Saul emerges as

---

24. Solomon, in effect, seizes the crown, which David thinks he is giving to Solomon. See Gunn, 'David and the Gift', pp. 30-31.

the narrator's hero—a hero who was also a failure, but a failure who in completing the 'rise of the lowly, fall of the mighty' pattern also died on the battlefield in defense of Israel, not in his bed with the moral fabric of Israel crumbling around him.

JSOT 20 (1981), pp. 47-73

CHIEFS IN ISRAEL*

James W. Flanagan

I

In 1962 Elman Service delineated four stages through which societies evolve as their socio-political organization develops from simpler toward more complex forms. Although drawing comparisons among societies which are spatially and temporarily separated as Service has done does not enable complete and flawless reconstruction of a single society's history, his conclusions have proved useful for analyzing a variety of primitive and archaic civilizations. Ancient Egypt and Mesopotamia have been tested, but neither he nor others have used the cultural evolutionary hypothesis for studying a secondary society such as Israel. The fact that Israel developed under the influence of foreign polities, however, need not prevent comparing its evolution to that of other groups. To exclude Israel would isolate the nation from cross-cultural comparisons, a practice which has proven to be counterproductive in the past.

In this essay, I propose to make the comparisons previously avoided. Israel's evolution from tribal organization toward full kingship will be reviewed in the light of cultural evolutionary theory, such as that of

* I first presented evidence regarding chiefs in Israel in a paper delivered before the Pacific Northwest Region of the Society of Biblical Literature in April 1979. A second draft was delivered in the Israelite History Section of the SBL meeting in November of the same year. I am grateful to colleagues who offered encouragement and suggestions at those sessions. (Author's note: between the time this article first appeared [1981] and this reprinting [1997], Service's stages have been challenged for their seeming rigidity. Because the stages provided only a framework for my reading of the biblical genealogies, the challenges do not directly affect the argument or conclusions presented here. For further references see pp. 49-50 [and bibliography] in my 'Finding the Arrows of Time', *Currents in Research: Biblical Studies* 3 [1995]: 37-80.)

Service, and in comparison with the processes of succession to high office outlined and described by social anthropologists (Goody 1966). The comparisons will aid not only in outlining the stages of evolution, but also in identifying the principal prime movers that affected the nation's changing social organization (see Vogt 1968: 555) and in explaining the origins of hereditary inequality that eventually led to monarchy (see Flannery 1972). The patterns in Israel, however, cannot be constructed solely on the basis of comparisons supported by isolated bits of information. Such a mosaic would be little more than conjectural history. Rather, the pattern of evolution must truly be in Israel, and the comparisons must be used as a heuristic device which helps us understand and describe the processes that were at work in the ancient society. In sum, we must be careful to discover the evolutionary pattern rather than anxious to create it.

Service's analysis of bands, tribes, chiefdoms, and states, and his description of the factors which move a society along its evolutionary trajectory have been so compelling and the cross-cultural comparisons so strikingly consistent that scholars from many schools of thought within several disciplines have adopted his summary with little or no modification. Sahlins (1968), Sanders and Price (1968), Flannery (1972), and E.O. Wilson (1978) adopted the paradigm in their analyses of varied and scattered civilizations. Fried (1967), while agreeing with a four-part division in the evolutionary process, has differed with Service over the description of the stages and the role which stratification plays in bringing about a centralized monopoly of force (Fried 1968; Service 1978; see Redman 1978: 201-13). Like Fried, others have disagreed with portions of Service's description while accepting the general outline of his four stages (Renfrew 1974; Peebles and Kus 1977; see Cohen 1978a; 1978b; and Claessen and Skalnik 1978a).

The impact of the 1962 study has overshadowed modifications Service introduced in 1975. By distinguishing primitive societies known through ethnographic studies from ancient societies that can be retrieved only by prehistoric archaeology, he reduced the discernible phases in the latter to three by combining bands with tribes in a single stage (1975: 303-305). For ancient, prehistoric societies, Service now prefers a new classification with different nomenclature, namely, a tripartite division of segmental (i.e., egalitarian) society, chiefdom, and archaic civilization. Even in the new division, however, he has left his description of chiefdom intact and has continued to insist upon its universality in the evolutionary schema of both primitive and archaic societies (1975: 87). He now admits though that, while chiefdoms can be distinguished from segmented societies with relative ease, discriminating between them and the archaic civilizations is a more difficult task (Service 1975: 305; Sanders and Marino 1970: 9; Claessen and Skalnik 1978b: 629).

Because of the universal claims that have accompanied the discussion of chiefdoms, it is well to note several limitations which cultural evolutionists place upon their assertions. First, a predictable evolutionary schema does not guarantee that every human society has evolved to full statehood. This is an obvious but easily forgotten limitation, especially when one is attempting to discern the boundaries between chiefdoms and kingdoms. Second, not all archaic civilizations and states reflect the same patterns of social organization (i.e., not all were monarchies). And finally, evolutionary schemata do not imply that every developing society changes at the same rate or exhibits all the characteristics which another society exhibits at its parallel stage of development. Human societies are not so easily typed, and thus the factors interrelating processual phenomena militate against facile generalizing (Vogt 1968: 535; Leach 1968: 344).

Secondary societies whose development is influenced by polities outside their borders call for additional caution beyond that needed when studying primary or pristine civilizations (Price 1978). In them, the developments already achieved in the alien influential group affect the formation of the subordinate or neighboring society, especially if the secondary group is caught in the throes of tumultuous and unstable conditions.

Caveats such as these explain why few scholars have considered the possibility of chiefs in ancient Israel. Anthropologists have chosen to ignore the Syro-Palestine region even when considering Egypt and Mesopotamia because they prefer to draw evidence from primary societies where the 'natural' processes of development can be tested without concern for acculturation from the outside.[1] Biblical scholars, on the other hand, have accepted the dominant view of the biblical tradition, namely, that Israel moved immediately from tribal confederation to monarchy. Only recently have they begun to analyze the socio-political forces that accompanied the change.[2]

---

1.   Professor R.A. Rappaport, Chairman of the Department of Anthropology at the University of Michigan, first suggested this reason to me.
2.   Norman Gottwald made occasional references to Israel's tendency toward

II

Our investigation of Israel's steps toward monarchy may begin with the statement of Service's thesis on the origins of states:

> [The thesis] locates the origins of government in the institutionalization of centralized leadership. That leadership, in developing its administrative functions for the maintenance of the society, grew into a hereditary aristocracy. The nascent bureaucracy's economic and religious functions developed as the extent of its services, its autonomy, and its size increased, Thus the earliest government worked to protect, not another class or stratum of society, but itself. It legitimized itself in its role of maintaining the whole society (1975: 8).

Here Service argued that the prominence and success of a leader contributes directly to his authority so that, in effect, the community creates its own leadership by becoming dependent upon an individual's charismatic talents. A reciprocal and spiraling relationship is established in which a leader's traits inspire the group's dependence. The dependency in turn enhances the role of the leader so that his success guarantees even greater dependence, and so on, until the role becomes institutionalized in an office.

The gradually ascending authority invested in leadership makes it difficult to draw definite boundary lines between the organizational stages. 'Big man' leadership characteristic of segmental society embodies traits of an embryonic chieftaincy (Service 1975: 75), and a chief is himself an initiatory 'king' whose office may develop into the centralized monopoly of force typically found in the subsequent stage of early state and archaic civilization (Service 1975: 86). So, while a chiefdom stands between segmental society and coercive state, it exemplifies traits of both.

Describing chiefdoms in this fashion introduces a problem which Service sought to avoid. Inherent in discussions of evolutionary processes is the implication that intermediate stages do not have a status of their own, that is, that they are only intermediate and cannot be examined in their own right. But to assume this about chiefdoms would be a fallacy and would jeopardize understanding the nature and role of chiefs in society (Renfrew 1974: 71; Earle 1978: 1).

chiefdom in his study of Yahwistic tribes even though the subject fell outside the scope of his work (1979: 297-98, 322-23). Frank Frick (1979) has drawn attention to evidence, literary and archaeological, supporting a chiefdom hypothesis.

Still, descriptions of chiefdoms in anthropological literature tend to be lists of similarities and differences comparing and contrasting them with preceding and succeeding phases. Unlike tribes, chiefdoms exhibit sumptuary rules and taboos surrounding the chief (Service 1962: 145). They have ranking systems which add a new structural principle to kinship ties whereby those nearest the chief assume the status of nobility (Service 1962: 141). An emphasis is placed upon the leader as redistributor or, in Harris's terminology, as warrior-intensifier-redistributor (1979: 94). Theocratic claims which are lacking in tribal societies are made on behalf of the chief, and a dichotomy between the chief's center and the dependent settlements develops (Sahlins 1968: 7).

In contrast with states, chiefdoms lack social stratification into classes based upon occupational specialization. They also lack the ability to impose coercive physical sanctions and have to rely upon non-legal enforcement (Flannery 1972: 403). The government of a state is more highly centralized, with a professional ruling class including priests and bureaucrats who function as substitutes for the king in his many expanded roles (Sahlins 1968: 9). In chiefdoms, such tasks are shared by the chief personally.

The character of chiefdoms has been conveniently summarized by Renfrew (1974: 73) who listed twenty traits which distinguish chiefdoms from egalitarian societies:

1. ranked society
2. the redistribution of produce organized by the chief
3. greater population density
4. increase in the total number in the society
5. increase in the size of individual residence groups
6. greater productivity
7. more clearly defined territorial boundaries or borders
8. a more integrated society with a greater number of socio-centric statuses
9. centers which coordinate social and religious as well as economic activity
10. frequent ceremonies and rituals serving wide social purposes
11. rise of priesthood
12. relation to a total environment (and hence redistribution)—i.e., to some ecological diversity
13. specialization, not only regional or ecological, but also through the pooling of individual skills in large cooperative endeavors
14. organization and deployment of public labor, sometimes for agricultural work (e.g., irrigation) and/or for building temples, temple mounds, or pyramids

15. improvement of craft specialization

16. potential for territorial expansion—associated with the 'rise' and 'fall' of chiefdoms

17. reduction of internal strife

18. pervasive inequality of persons or groups in the society associated with permanent leadership, effective in fields other than the economic

19. distinctive dress or ornament for those of high status

20. no true government to back up decisions by legalized force

Chiefly authority, therefore, is rooted in skills of warfare, dancing, solidifying allegiances, and redistributing goods. These exhibit the chief's charisma and inspire confidence and a sense of solidarity in his followers (Service 1975: 74). Eventually, the people begin to expect and hope that the chief's exceptional qualities will be passed on to his sons so that, over time, a system of succession gradually develops with devolution of office to the chief's offspring, usually to the eldest male. Successful and successive handing on of leadership within the chief's family (dynasty) eventually leads to primogeniture as a binding custom (Service 1962: 293).

Studies on succession have demonstrated that in spite of the stability which presumption of primogeniture brings to the transmission of office, no system of succession is completely automatic even where next-of-kin procedures are thought to be in force (Goody 1966: 13). Succession to chieftaincy is often a highly competitive process with contenders vying for the paramount role both during and after the incumbent's reign (Robertson 1976). Struggles for power often leave a string of assassinations, frustrated pretenders, and exiled losers in their wake so that turbulence rather than tranquility governs the transferral of office in these cultures (Barth 1961: 84).

The competition and tension surrounding high office affects the relationship not only of incumbent to potential successors, but also of competing rivals to each other. The encroachment and usurpation that competing chiefs and successors perpetrate upon one another is so extreme at times that in monadic societies groups often migrate in order to find a strong chief who can bring a modicum of peace to their lives (Barth 1961: 85).

Goody (1966: 5-37) has identified four principal variables affecting the tranquility of successions: uniqueness of the office, time of succession, means of selecting a successor, and relationship between successive office holders. He has found that it is typical for societies to manipulate these in order to cope with disruptions that accompany the transferral of office.

The combined options available to a society are many. When a unique office is open to a number of potential successors, the tension among the eligibles can be reduced by restricting the pool of eligibles or by dividing the office or territory. Tension both between incumbent and successors and among successors can be regulated by adjusting the time of succession making it either pre-mortem or post-mortem in order to bring a strong leader to power at a convenient time. Interregnums, stand-ins, stake-holders, and co-regencies are typical forms of partial transfer of office which are employed in order to stabilize government and to insure continuity of mature leadership.

Even when the pre-mortem traumas of dethronement, abdication, and usurpation are not factors, the means of selecting successors is often not left to chance. Procedures vary according to the needs of the office. Where special qualities are required, the selection is apt to be highly regulated so that even where primogeniture plays a major role, divination, appointment, and force—always the final arbiter (Goody 1966: 18)—are also used. The time of selection (not to be confused with the time of accession) can also be adjusted as a ploy for decreasing indeterminancy and diminishing competition among rival successors.

The relationship between successive office holders impinges upon other aspects of indeterminate succession. For example, the larger the pool of eligible successors, the greater the distance between the incumbent and his successor and, therefore, the less the tension within the organization itself (Goody 1966: 23). On the other hand, the greater the indeterminacy of succession, the greater the tension among eligibles and the more frequent the struggles for power.

Seen in the light of such variables, the customs and practices which societies including Israel have adopted assume new meaning. For instance, dynastic shedding can be recognized as a common practice whereby a dynasty or group of eligibles is reduced. This can be accomplished in several ways. In some systems females are automatically excluded from office while distant males are not, or in others sons of a ruler's siblings are excluded so that the system limits succession to the lineal (vertical) line by transferring rights from father to son to grandson, and so on. In lateral systems, however, office is passed along within a single generation before being transferred to the next generation, making it highly unlikely that all males in each generation will survive long enough to assume office. In either system, rather than determining the priority of the sons themselves, elimination among a sibling group may be accomplished by designating a favored mother whose son will succeed. This practice, reminiscent of Bathsheba's choosing Solomon, arises where polygamous marriages make seniority by birth hard to determine or where office is restricted to sons born after the father assumed office (Goody 1966: 33; 1976: 86-98; Cuisenier 1980: 13-14).

A general movement in history from hereditary toward appointive office has accompanied the growing complexity of society and the consequent need for technical competence (Goody 1966: 44). But because appointment is seldom the sole means of selection for high office, in systems where hereditary practices are deeply rooted, appointive (or elective) procedures usually modify rather than replace them. In most cases, however, a candidate's economic and military resources affect his chances more than his access to royal ancestors (Goody 1970: 637).

Although the conditions described here apply to other high offices as well as to chiefdoms, they illustrate forces by which limited access to office can transform the kinship structures of a society in ways that affect succession (Service 1962: 155). Two principal effects which are important for understanding the affairs of Saul and David can be noted: the formation of conical clans and the emergence of ramage descent groups (Service 1975: 79). The former are unilineal kin groups in which, because of primogeniture, certain members are considered closer to the central line and have greater status and access to common property than do others (Alland and McCay 1973: 165). Since unequal access to property and office is a characteristic of ranked society, conical clans signal a move away from segmental social organization.

A ramage descent group is one type of kinship structure caused by limited access. Where first-born sons are expected to succeed their fathers, other sons splinter off to begin their own lineages with themselves as heads of the ramages or 'branches' (Service 1962: 158). Although they retain rights in the central line, the sons' inheritance and office are passed on to their own sons rather than reverting to the father's line. However, if the first-born's line is truncated by the death of all heirs, a childless marriage, or other causes, the right of succession moves laterally to the second son's lineage, or as necessary, to the third and so on. An individual's relative position in this structure is ranked and regulated by genealogy (Earle 1978: 168). Shifts in genealogies therefore reflect shifts in the relative position of eligibles. Fluctuations in the priority list can be frequent and complex because of polygamous marriages and power struggles which can change the eligibility of individuals rapidly.

Optative affiliation can also affect kinship patterns by placing an exogamous male in line for succession, even in an unilineal descent group (Service 1962: 162; Earle 1978: 175). This is a strategy societies employ in order to insure heirs and successors where male descendants are lacking (Goody 1976: 93-96). The phenomenon, first identified by Firth, combines traits of the epiclerate (substitution of a daughter for a son) and adoption. It allows newly married couples to choose which parental group they will affiliate with, and usually includes a choice of residence as well (Service 1962: 153). The couple generally elects the family that will bestow the higher status upon them. If it is the wife's family, her husband may be taken into her kin group and eventually inherit the title and name of her father. Through this form of adoption, the children of the couple fall in line of succession with the maternal grandfather's line, so descent technically remains patrilineal. The practice will be recalled below when discussing David's marriage to Michal and the latter's barrenness.

III

This brief summary of the circumstances accompanying the development of chiefdoms and the transferral of high office in chiefly societies provides the background for examining pre-monarchic Israel. To compare the development of chiefdoms in other societies with the evolution of Israelite leadership, we need not delay to defend the existence of an egalitarian, segmental phase among the Yahwists. This stage has been amply documented by the biblical writers and has been extensively analyzed in studies by Noth (1966) and Gottwald (1979). The end of the Israelite tribal period coincided with a series of events that brought the Yahwists under Philistine domination and initiated the rise of a centralized leadership. For our purposes we may assume that the end of the segmental stage is symbolized in the Bible by the loss of the ark reported in 1 Samuel 4.

The literary record portrays the period following the loss of the ark in terms that can only be read as tumultuous and chaotic, an atmosphere which seems to have persisted until the completion of Solomon's succession and the slayings of Adonijah, Shimei, and Joab in 1 Kings 1–2. Beginning with Samuel's vacillation between legitimating the growing pressures toward centralized rule and refusing to sanction them, deeply felt tensions divided the communities of his, Saul's, and David's days (1 Sam. 5–8).

Saul's election and rule did little to stabilize the situation or to reassure the people. Even when we allow for intentional discrediting by later anti-Saul biblical writers, we are left with a picture of a tragic individual (Gunn 1980: 23-31). A tall, handsome agriculturalist who emerged as a leader because of his military prowess, Saul enjoyed some ability to evoke support of a militia (1 Sam. 9.2; 11), but he eventually failed and stood defenseless before his enemies and slayers, the Philistines (1 Sam. 31). He was a warrior and an intensifier who apparently performed rituals, a duty he shared with the priests (1 Sam. 13.8-15), and who took part in ecstatic religious movements (1 Sam. 10.9-14), although he eventually was chastized for cultic violations (1 Sam. 14.31-35).

In retrospect his leadership can be recognized as having been handicapped from the start. Unlike the Philistines, Saul seems to have lacked the Iron Age technology needed to exploit the potential of the cattle and plough agriculture of his day or to wage effective war (1 Sam. 13.19-22). He also suffered from periods of depression and jealousy so severe that a musician's service was required to calm him (1 Sam. 15.23). Although history eventually confirmed that Saul's fear of those around him was justified, it prevented him from gaining a useful perspective upon his situation and crippled him when he was forced to compete. His personal weakness contributed directly to David's success, a situation which is typical of chiefs competing for the paramount power.

By comparison, David was a much stronger person and an obvious potential successor. He was handsome, prudent, well-spoken, and one who made a good first impression (1 Sam. 16.12-19). He was a musician and poet (1 Sam. 16.16; 2 Sam. 1.22). He was a successful warrior as well as a popular leader of armies and of the oppressed (1 Sam. 22.1-2; 27; 30). He created solidarity by his personal traits and by redistribution, and he enhanced his popularity on many occasions by sharing his booty with friends, allies, neighbors, and suzerains (1 Sam. 21; 25; 27.9; 30).

David's life was closely identified with Saul's house even though his personal relationship with Saul eventually deteriorated to the point of open hostility. He married Saul's daughter Michal after having been refused the hand of Merab and after paying the agreed bride price (1 Sam. 18); he struck a covenant with Jonathan, Saul's eldest son (1 Sam. 18). On separate occasions, both Michal and Jonathan helped David escape from their father's wrath (1 Sam. 19; 20). Later, although David retained affection for Jonathan and his son (2 Sam. 9), he appears to have reduced Michal to a pawn who could be used in whatever manner he found advantageous (2 Sam. 3.12-16; 6.20-23).

As would be expected of competing chiefs, the animosity between Saul and David spilled over into their houses and their entourages. After Saul died at the hands of an enemy David served, a long war was waged between their two houses (2 Sam. 3.1). The conflict led to the treasonous negotiations between David and Abner, who bargained away the crown of Ishbosheth, Saul's son and successor (2 Sam. 3).

The rift between the factions deepened when David permitted the wholesale slaughter of Saul's family in a blood feud with the Gibeonites. The massacre cost the lives of all surviving male heirs in Saul's house except for Jonathan's son, the crippled Mephibosheth, and his son Micah (2 Sam. 21; 9). The consequences were widespread. Shimei, a supporter of Saul's house, cursed David for his complicity in the deaths, and the long-standing feud fed the imaginations of Absalom and Sheba who organized rebellions to topple David (2 Sam. 15; 16.5-8; 20).

Although the attempted pre-mortem succession by rebellion failed for Absalom and Sheba, Adonijah, presumably the eldest survivor among David's sons, tried again when his father became incapacitated by old age (1 Kgs 1). His efforts were quashed, however, by the appointment of Solomon, the son of the favored wife Bathsheba. With Nathan, she arranged for her son to be named successor-designate.

This survey illustrates the competitiveness which characterized the emergence of centralized leadership in Israel and demonstrates how eligibles were pitted against incumbents and against each other: Saul feared David and warned Jonathan that his rights of inheritance were in danger; Ishbosheth's succession was challenged by the betrayal of his strong man and cousin, Abner; David's accession in Hebron after Ziklag was during a time of instability in the North and must have had the tacit approval of the Philistines. Absalom's revolt, Sheba's rebellion, and Adonijah's accession, linked with the murder of all the principal actors in the drama of succession except David, fit with other events to form a long chain of intrigues which reached from the early years of Saul down to the appointment of Solomon. When the murders of Joab (son of David's sister), Shimei, and Adonijah had been accomplished, a monopoly of force finally replaced chiefly rule in ancient Israel.

IV

This summary derived from the narrative portions of the books of Samuel can be tested against information retained in the genealogical sections of Ruth, Samuel, and Chronicles. There the counters in the chiefly games can be seen: kinship, politics, economics, and religion, the four rubrics anthropologists use to organize their discussions of primitive and archaic societies. Since narratives and genealogies are not subjected to the same reinterpretations at the hand of traditional scribes, parallels and agreements between the two types of literature make a particularly compelling case for the stages of development in an ancient society.

I am examining several of the genealogies elsewhere (Flanagan 1983) and have found that their function in Israel parallels genealogies in other cultures. A. Malamat (1973) and R. Wilson (1977) have demonstrated similar parallels for other sections of the Yahwistic tradition. Here, I rely heavily upon these earlier studies, and my own, for what I have to say about genealogical evidence.

It is important to understand the function of genealogies in early pre-literate and literate societies and to be familiar with several of their most common traits. Genealogies typically exhibit a characteristic called 'fluidity', that is, a moving of names within, onto, or off genealogical lists when the relationship of the named individuals or groups changes. Since genealogies record and regulate relationships in the domestic, politico-jural, and religious spheres of life, fluidity is demanded in order for a genealogy to remain functional. If genealogies were not adjusted as relationships changed, they would lose their meaning and would soon be lost (Wilson 1977: 27-54). As groups migrate, individuals die, or persons' statuses change, the effects of each are reflected in the genea-logical record.

A comparison of 1 Sam. 14.49-51, 1 Sam. 31.2 (= 1 Chron. 10.2), 2 Sam. 21.7-8, 1 Chron. 8.33-40, and 1 Chron. 9.39-43 illustrates how Israel's records were adjusted in order to keep them abreast of the rapidly changing alliances outlined above. Consequently, the genealogies serve as guides for reconstructing the history of the period and for trac-ing the fate of Saul's house. In diagram form, the genealogies appear in Table 1.

Table 1

GENEALOGIES OF SAUL'S HOUSE

1 Samuel 14.49-51

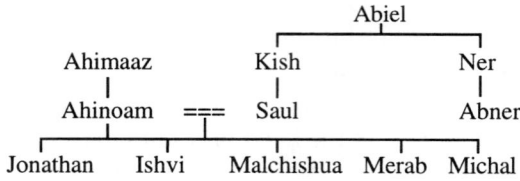

```
                              Abiel
                    ┌───────────┴───────────┐
   Ahimaaz         Kish                     Ner
      │             │                        │
   Ahinoam  ===    Saul                     Abner
 ┌────┴────┬────────────┬──────────┬────────┐
Jonathan  Ishvi     Malchishua   Merab   Michal
```

1 Samuel 31.2 (= 1 Chronicles 10.2)

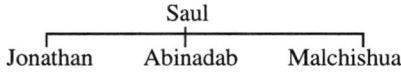

```
                  Saul
         ┌─────────┼──────────┐
      Jonathan  Abinadab   Malchishua
```

2 Samuel 21.7-8

```
(A)                    (B)                    (C)
Saul                                          Aiah
  │                                             │
Jonathan          Merab = Adriel            Rizpah   ( = Saul)
  │              ┌──┬──┬──┐              ┌──────┴──────┐
Mephibosheth       (five sons)         Armoni   Mephibosheth
```

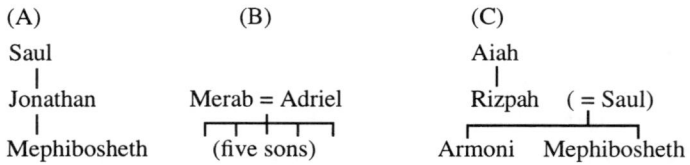

1 Chronicles 8.33-40 and 9.39-43

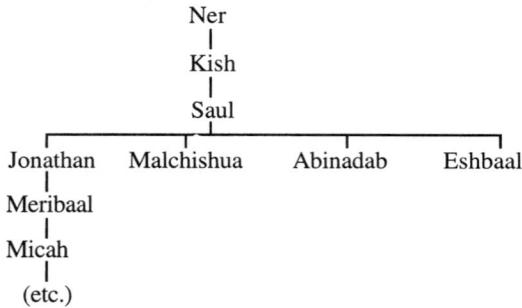

```
                        Ner
                         │
                        Kish
                         │
                        Saul
       ┌─────────┬────────┴────────┬─────────┐
    Jonathan  Malchishua       Abinadab    Eshbaal
       │
    Meribaal
       │
     Micah
       │
     (etc.)
```

In the diagrams, we see that when Abner lost his life, and consequently neither he nor his lineage continued to figure prominently in the affairs of Israel, his name was dropped from the genealogy (compare 1 Sam. 14 with 1 Chron. 8 and 9). Ner, on the other hand, was elevated to the vertical line above Kish and Saul, probably because his importance had already been deeply implanted in the consciousness of the community. Even though the reasons for his prominence are no longer evident to us, we might conjecture that as head of a ramage, Ner had been 'ranked' because he stood high among the pool of eligibles if all male successors to Saul in the vertical line should have been eliminated. Unlikely as this may have seemed in the early days of Saul's reign, the eventual violent deaths of Saul's sons and grandsons made the possibility of lateral succession much less remote. Indeed, it appears as if Abner might have succeeded Ishbosheth if he (Abner) had been successful in the intrigues he initiated.

The order in the birth sequence of Saul's sons changed over time as their rank fluctuated (cf. 1 Sam. 14, 31; 1 Chron. 8, 9). The elusive Ishvi/Eshbaal (elsewhere Ishbosheth/Ishbaal) moved between fourth- and second-born position, and Abinadab and Malchishua traded positions several times. It is important to observe, however, that Jonathan was consistently ranked as first-born, even after his death and the succession of Ishbosheth. His unwavering prominence demonstrates that the genealogists remembered that Jonathan's line had continued through Meribaal/Mephibosheth, Micah, etc. (cf. 1 Chron. 8 and 9). Because of his physical handicap, Mephibosheth did not succeed Saul, and as a result his name was not firmly set nor his generation clearly remembered (compare 2 Sam. 21 with 1 Chron. 8 and 9). Nevertheless, after the Gibeonite massacre of Saul's house, his name was retained as an important link between Saul and later eligibles in Saul's lineage. The retention of the records of Jonathan's descendants explains why Mephibosheth expected the house of Israel to give him back the kingdom of his father when David was forced into exile by Absalom's coup (2 Sam. 16.3). He assumed that David had been a stand-in who led in place of his wife Michal perhaps for one generation or until Micah achieved majority. Michal's barrenness was connected to Mephibosheth's fortunes because it contributed to the uncertainty of whether the office would pass on in her father's line or in David's through a son born of another wife. If Michal had had a son, the competitors might have chosen different sides.

David's marriage to Michal and his insistence that she be returned before negotiations with Abner could begin must be viewed in the light of the intrigue and indeterminacy that was caused by the deaths and disabilities in Saul's house. The daughter's importance for David's rise within the North can hardly be overestimated. In ways similar to the case of Zelophehad's daughters in Numbers 27 and 36, the issue was inheritance and succession rights of brotherless daughters (cf. Jobling 1980: 203-204). In David's case, he cleverly employed optative affiliation as one ground upon which he could appeal to northern support.

Political factors also figured prominently in David's competition for the paramount chief's role. For instance, when Saul forced him to withdraw to a remote outlying area, he used the distance to build a personal power-base and to begin his own lineage while waiting for another chance at the chieftaincy. The circumstances were typical of a losing contender. David's rise in Ziklag was as vassal to the Philistines, the arch enemy of Israel, and his accession in Hebron must have been with Philistine support or acquiescence. Because the biblical writers spent no time trying to connect these successes with David's affinity to the house of Saul, we must conclude that his rise in the South was predicated on different grounds than his succession in the North where optative affiliation played a part that it did not in the affairs of Judah. This may explain why there is no genealogy in the Samuel material connecting the house of Jesse to the house of Saul even though there is narrative evidence of Jesse's sons serving Saul (1 Sam. 17–18). As a losing contender, David had begun his own ramage with its own rights. When the North was finally forced to turn to him for leadership, he accepted their charge from a position of strength and made no effort to subvert Judah to the primacy of Israel. Instead he maintained two bases of power (centered in a 'neutral' Jerusalem) which he could juggle to his own advantage. In effect, he laid the foundation for the tortuous days that were to follow in the history of Israel and Judah.

The economic as well as the political manoeuvres which took place in David's house are evident in the genealogical records of his family. These are found in lists preserved in Ruth 4.18-23, 1 Chron. 2.9-17, 2 Sam. 17.24, 2 Sam. 3.2-5, 2 Sam. 5.13-16, 1 Chron. 3.1-9, 1 Chron. 14.3-7, and 2 Samuel 11 (see Table 2).

Table 2

GENEALOGIES OF DAVID'S HOUSE

Ruth 4.18-23

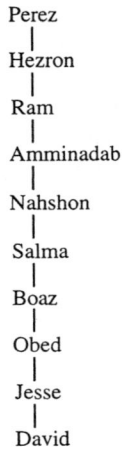

Perez
|
Hezron
|
Ram
|
Amminadab
|
Nahshon
|
Salma
|
Boaz
|
Obed
|
Jesse
|
David

2 Samuel 17.24

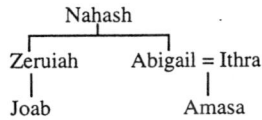

Nahash
|
Zeruiah   Abigail = Ithra
|
Joab   Amasa

1 Chronicles 2.9-17

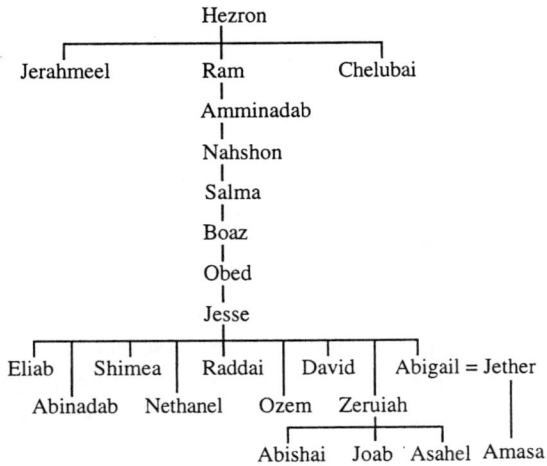

Hezron

Jerahmeel   Ram   Chelubai
|
Amminadab
|
Nahshon
|
Salma
|
Boaz
|
Obed
|
Jesse

Eliab   Shimea   Raddai   David   Abigail = Jether
Abinadab   Nethanel   Ozem   Zeruiah
Abishai   Joab   Asahel   Amasa

2 Samuel 11

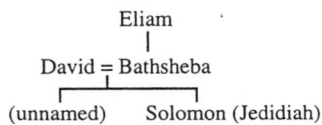

Eliam
|
David = Bathsheba
(unnamed)   Solomon (Jedidiah)

Table 2 (continued)

2 Samuel 3.2-5 (Hebron)		1 Chronicles 3.1-9 (Hebron-Jerusalem)	
son	mother	son	mother
Amnon	Ahinoam	Amnon	Ahinoam
Chileab	Abigail	Daniel	Abigail
Absalom	Maacah	Absalom	Maacah
Adonijah	Haggith	Adonijah	Haggith
Shephatiah	Abital	Shephatiah	Abital
Ithream	Eglah	Ithream	Eglah

2 Samuel 5.13-16 (Jerusalem)		1 Chron. 14.3-7 (Jerusalem)
Shammua	Shimea	Shammua
Shobab	Shobab	Shobab
Nathan	Nathan	Nathan
Solomon	Solomon (4 by Bathshua)	Solomon
Ibhar	Ibhar	Ibhar
Elishua	Elishama	Elishua
	Eliphelet	Elpelet
	Nogah	Nogah
Nepheg	Nepheg	Nepheg
Japhia	Japhia	Japhia
Elishama	Elishama	Elishama
Eliada	Eliada	Beelida
Eliphelet	Eliphelet	Eliphelet

Here again, we must point out several characteristics of genealogies, even though we must limit our remarks to those traits which show the chiefly nature of the early Davidic reign. Foremost is the difference between linear and segmental genealogies. Linear genealogies such as found in Ruth 4 serve to legitimate the last name by connecting it with the names of individuals, groups, or places (sometimes mixed together in the same list) which stand above it. Unlike segmental genealogies, the linear do not rank in priority a pool of eligibles who might all be competing for office simultaneously.

This difference has several causes, but here we may concentrate upon the different socio-political situation reflected in the two types. Segmented genealogies belong to segmented societies where kinship ties are stressed, while linear genealogies belong to societies where inheritance and succession are not determined completely by familistic concerns.

Since chiefdoms hang in the betwixt and the between, we must avoid making universal claims about this difference, but we can expect to find linear genealogies in ranked societies and segmental ones in egalitarian communities. A shift from one dominant form to the other, therefore, suggests a change in the socio-political organization of the time.

In David's case, we find both segmental and linear genealogies. For instance, in 1 Chron. 2.9-17, which is similar to the linear genealogy in Ruth 4, segmented and linear genealogies are combined to trace David's lineage from Hezron (from Perez in Ruth) and to record his position as youngest male among seven sons and two daughters of Jesse. In 2 Samuel 17, however, a segmented genealogy has been used to list his sister Zeruiah as mother of Joab, and Abigail as wife of Jether/Ithra, father of Amasa.

In other lists (2 Sam. 3 and 5; 1 Chron. 3 and 14) the names of David's children have been recorded, but not without some discrepancies. The variations, however, are strikingly consistent. The sons born at Hebron were listed with their mothers' names, whereas those born in Jerusalem are listed without mothers. The dropping of mothers' names indicates that David was a chief at Hebron where the order within his ramage, ranked according to mothers because of polygamous marriages, had to be maintained for determining statuses and succession rights; but once the bureaucracy of a monarchy in Jerusalem made primogeniture less relevant for succession, the mothers' names were no longer remembered. Here Israel's genealogies functioned in the same manner as those in other societies. The only mother from Jerusalem who was named was Bathshua/Bathsheba, identified as mother of four sons, one of whom was Solomon (2 Sam. 11 and 1 Chron. 3). In the Court History, even Solomon's name was confused with a variant, Jedidiah.

Dropping the mothers' names when the capital moved from Hebron to Jerusalem is typical of transitions from chiefdoms to archaic states. But the continuing competition for David's office after the relocation indicates that full statehood was not achieved at once. During the transitional period, succession remained indeterminate even though the growing complexity of the leader's tasks required candidates who were capable of administering the expanding bureaucracy of an empire. By the time Solomon had succeeded David, pre-mortem, appointive measures complemented heredity as a means of stabilizing the situation. Solomon was chosen from among Bathsheba's sons, and almost as an echo from the past, her name was recorded because of his prominence.

V

Service and others stressed the role which redistributing, organizing, and military leadership play in a chief's rise. Although we have no record of Saul's generosity, the narratives suggest that he was a solidifier who finally failed to knit firm alliances between the village populations and his central administration (Mendenhall 1975: 162). This factor contributed to the decline in his popularity and to the growth of David's public favor. As a result, Saul was unable to establish a state of dependency through redistribution, which otherwise might have stabilized his leadership. The fact that Ishbosheth was forced to lead from afar, probably with only a fraction of Saul's following, also indicates the extent of Saul's failure. He was too weak to rout the Philistines, and they rather than he controlled many of the economic resources.

In contrast, David's rise was closely identified with his role as warrior-intensifier-redistributor. He distributed booty from his raids to his own followers, to the oppressed, to Achish of Gath, and to the elders of Judah—in effect, to those whom he depended upon for his rise. Yet in spite of this record, the difference between such earlier acts of generosity and the later parasitical dependency of his Jerusalem administration upon the resources of the people is striking. The lists of his Jerusalem court officers included commanders of armies and of the forced labor (2 Sam. 20.23-26), and the census he ordered must have been intended as a basis for the taxation and conscription needed to staff and support these forces. The list and the census both reflect a dramatic shift in the values and organization of the Yahwistic community. David the chief had begun to act like a king.

As we would expect in chiefdoms, the religious functions mentioned in the biblical narratives also indicate that Saul's and David's reigns were theocracies. Both individuals were anointed by Samuel; both performed cultic rites; both used priests and prophets. In short, religion was used by both to legitimate their authority and to help maintain social control.

This is especially obvious in David's case where the role of religion was displayed at every major step in his rise. He consulted Yahweh when considering the move to Hebron; he transferred the ark to Jerusalem; he took part in a ritual dance in order to legitimate his new center; and he relied upon a dynastic oracle to assure the continuation of his line. But do these religious functions suggest a chiefdom or a monarchy? Two episodes demonstrate that the people's religious feelings restrained a rapid, total transition to kingship during David's Jerusalem years. The first of these was the prohibition against building a temple (2 Sam. 7). The second was the punishment meted out to David for his taking the census (2 Sam. 24). Each episode was a limitation upon David's power, the likes of which were not evident later when Solomon completed the evolution to full monopoly of force. They suggest that David stood on the boundary line between chiefdom and kingdom.

VI

A review of the royal terminology associated with Saul's and David's reigns reveals a pattern of usage that parallels the stages of cultural evolution outlined here. Although the term is still under study and open to debate, we may suggest that *nāgîd* stands for the chiefly role of Saul and David.

A great deal of ambiguity has accompanied recent studies of the term. Since Albrecht Alt's classic study of the formation of the Israelite state, most scholars have followed him in assuming that *nāgîd* described the religious calling to leadership while *melek* designated the office conferred by the peoples' acclaim (Alt 1968: 274-80). The distinction according to Alt was between religious and political functions which were present simultaneously in a leader's reign.

Studies made since Alt have helped to clarify the meaning of the term, but they have not completely resolved the confusion between *nāgîd* and *melek*. Evidence from the Sefire treaties (Fitzmyer 1958: 459; 1967: 112-13) and the Nora stele (Peckham 1972: 457-68) have influenced Cross's translation of *nāgîd* as 'commander' (Cross 1973: 220-21). For Cross, the term emphasized both the continuity with leadership in the time of the judges and the covenantal character of appointment to leadership roles. He distinguished its use from that of the later term, *melek*, which he believed was used to describe the 'routinized' or dynastic kingship of David and Solomon.

Richter (1965) distinguished three phases in the development of the term. *Nāgîd* in the pre-Davidic period meant a type of military leader specially chosen and installed. During the Davidic monarchy, the title was applied to the king and was equated with *melek*. In the post-Davidic age, it became a title for religious functionaries and administrative officials.

A more recent examination of the term in 1 Samuel by McCarter takes up Mettinger's suggestion that a reigning king could designate a crown-prince, a *nāgîd*, to be his successor (Mettinger 1976: 151-84). McCarter's preference is for 'king-designate' because 'In every case the *nāgîd* is an individual singled out from among others as leader' and because the term is usually applied to a king before he begins to reign (McCarter 1980: 178-79).

As a group these studies have shown that *nāgîd* underwent its own evolution corresponding to stages in the overall development of Israel's socio-political organization. They have agreed upon the need for a distinction between *nāgîd* and *melek*, but they have also claimed that the terms cannot be completely separated. For these scholars, the words apply either to different aspects of a leader's authority or to different times in the office holder's reign. This confusion can be explained by the gradual evolution in the role of the *nāgîd* as chiefdom gave way to monarchy.

The case for chiefs in Israel does not stand or fall with the meaning of *nāgîd*, but its use in the books of Samuel fits the developmental scheme I have outlined for chiefdom in the North. One of the earliest narrative traditions in the Samuel material is that of Samuel the seer in 1 Sam. 9.1–10.16 which systematically avoided the use of *melek* in favor of *nāgîd* whenever referring to Saul. McKenzie (1962) suggested that the usage reflected the pro-Davidic prejudice of the biblical scribes who reserved *melek* for David who was for them the first true king. The explanation ignores Saul's historical role as chief and overlooks the fact that the term was used when Yahweh rejected Saul (1 Sam. 13.14) and when the tribes of Israel selected David to be their *nāgîd* (2 Sam. 5.2) as Abigail, wife of Nabal, had predicted (1 Sam. 25.30). Each is an early use describing the historical role of Saul and David as chiefs.

David's role as *nāgîd* was also recalled when he chastized Michal (2 Sam. 6.21) and in the Davidic oracle (2 Sam. 7.8). Both references were made in connection with David's relationship to the house of Saul or with his humble pastoral origins. The passages recall David's early role before going on to celebrate and to symbolize his movement toward kingship. The ritualistic quality of these passages makes them especially important for analyzing the social structure of the period, but it also makes them exceptionally complex. Although they require more investigation than can be given here, we may emphasize that at the point of transition between Hebron and Jerusalem, between chief and king, between house of Saul and house of David, the ritualistic transfer of the ark and the utterance of the dynastic oracle were recalled. As in other societies, ritual was used to mediate the transitions and developments which were played out on the stage of history.

VII

To summarize and conclude: the literary record of the reigns of Saul and David reports a period of trauma and uncertainty when individuals competed forcefully for the paramount role. Murders, broken and restored alliances, marriages and separations, sharing of booty, unifying and leading militia, kinship ties, redistribution, and appeals to religious legitimacy all figured as strands in the warp and woof of the social, political, economic, and religious fabric of the day. Studies of the cultural evolutionary and succession patterns of other societies have described similar transitional circumstances and have concluded that such times were periods when the society was led by chiefs. The descriptions drawn from those non-Yahwistic and primary societies fit the evidence found in the literature of Yahwistic, secondary Israel. In fact, most of the elements on Renfrew's list of twenty characteristics of chiefdoms cited above can be documented in Israel. These indicate both the presence of chiefs and the absence of a strong centralized monopoly of force equipped with laws during the time of Saul and the early years of David. Since the parallels between Renfrew's list and the biblical evidence are not random, and because the evolutionary process outlined by Service is clearly evident in Israel, the cross-cultural comparisons are valid and productive. They have helped us understand the processes at work in ancient Israel and have aided in dismissing conjectures about the immediate transition from tribal league to full-blown monarchy.

In retrospect, we can see that Michal's childlessness left the future of Saul's house unclear, and it raised a question which optative affiliation usually did not raise: Should David's successor be from his house or Michal's? As would be expected, two views prevailed, one perhaps northern and pro-Saulide, the other southern and pro-Davidic. The appointment of Solomon temporarily resolved the question in favor of David by shifting the line of succession away from its northern Yahwistic roots. The outcome has left us to wonder what difference a male child born to David and Michal would have made for the history of Israel. But perhaps we do not have to conjecture. Solomon solidified kingship and a schism was avoided, but only for a generation.

BIBLIOGRAPHY

Alland, A., and B. McCay
    1973   'The Concept of Adaption in Biological and Cultural Evolution', in
                Handbook of Social and Cultural Anthropology (ed. J.J. Honigmann;
                Chicago: Rand McNally): 143-78.
Alt, A.
    1968 [1930] 'The Formation of the Israelite State in Palestine', in *Essays on Old
                Testament Religion* (trans. R.A. Wilson; Garden City, NY: Doubleday):
                223-310.
Barth, F.
    1961   *Nomads of Southern Persia* (Boston: Little, Brown).
Claessen, H.J.M., and P. Skalnik
    1978a   'The Early State: Theories and Hypotheses', in *The Early State* (ed.
                H.J.M. Claessen and P. Skalnik; The Hague: Mouton): 3-29.
    1978b   'Limits: Beginning and End of the Early State', in *The Early State*
                (ed. H.J.M. Claessen and P. Skalnik; The Hague: Mouton): 619-35.
Cohen, R.
    1978a   'Introduction', in *Origins of the State* (ed. R. Cohen and E.R. Service;
                Philadelphia: Institute for the Study of Human Issues): 1-20.
    1978b   'State Origins: A Reappraisal', in *The Early State* (ed. H.J.M. Claessen
                and P. Skalnik; The Hague: Mouton): 31-75.
Cross, F.M.
    1973   *Canaanite Myth and Hebrew Epic* (Cambridge, MA: Harvard
                University Press).
Cuisenier, J.
    1980   'Structural Anthropology and Historical Anthropology', mimeo-
                graphed.
Earle, T.
    1978   *Economic and Social Organization of a Complex Chiefdom* (Ann
                Arbor: Museum of Anthropology, University of Michigan).
Fitzmyer, J.
    1958   'The Aramaic Suzerainty Treaty from Sefire in the Museum of
                Beirut', *CBQ* 20: 444-76.
    1967   *The Aramaic Inscription of Sefire* (Rome: Pontifical Biblical Institute).
Flanagan, J.W.
    1983   'Succession and Genealogy in the Davidic Dynasty', in *The Quest for
                the Kingdom of God* (ed. Herbert B. Huffmon *et al.*; Winona Lake, IN:
                Eisenbrauns): 35-55.
Flannery, K.V.
    1972   'The Cultural Evolution of Civilizations', *Annual Review of Ecology
                and Systematics* 3: 399-426.
Frick, F.S.
    1979   'Religion and Sociopolitical Structure in Early Israel: An Ethno-
                Archaeological Approach', in *Society of Biblical Literature 1979
                Seminar Papers* (ed. P.J. Achtemeier; Missoula, MT: Scholars Press):
                233-53.

Fried, M.H.
1967   *The Evolution of Political Society* (New York: Random House).
1968   'The State, the Chicken, and the Egg; or What Came First?', in *Origins of the State* (ed. R. Cohen and E.R. Service; Philadelphia: Institute for the Study of Human Issues): 35-47.
Goody, J.R.
1970   'Sideways or Downwards?', *Man* 5: 627-38.
1976   *Production and Reproduction* (Cambridge: Cambridge University Press).
Goody, J.R. (ed.)
1966   *Succession to High Office* (Cambridge: Cambridge University Press).
Gottwald, N.K.
1979   *The Tribes of Yahweh* (Maryknoll, NY: Orbis).
Gunn, D.M.
1980   *The Fate of King Saul: An Interpretation of a Biblical Story* (JSOTSup, 14; Sheffield: JSOT Press).
Harris, M.
1979   *Cultural Materialism* (New York: Random House).
Jobling, D.
1980   'The Jordan A Boundary', in *Society of Biblical Literature 1980 Seminar Papers* (ed. P.J.Achtemeier; Chico, CA: Scholars Press): 183-207.
Leach, E.
1968   'VI. The Comparative Method in Anthropology', in *International Encyclopedia of the Social Sciences*, 1: 339-45.
McCarter, P.K., Jr
1980   *1 Samuel* (AB, 8; Garden City, NY: Doubleday).
McKenzie, J.L.
1962   'The Four Samuels', *BR* 7: 3-18.
Malamat, A.
1973   'Tribal Societies: Biblical Genealogies and African Lineage Systems', *Archives européenes de sociologie* 14: 126-36.
Mendenhall, G.E.
1975   'The Monarchy', *Int* 29: 155-70.
1978   'Between Theology and Archaeology', *JSOT* 7: 28-34.
Mettinger, T.N.D.
1976   *King and Messiah: The Civil and Sacral Legitimation of the Israelite Kings* (Lund: Gleerup).
Noth, M.
1966 [1930] *Das System der zwölf Stamme Israels* (Darmstadt: Wissenschaftliche Buchgesellschaft).
Peckham, B.
1972   'The Nora Inscription', *Orientalia* 41: 457-68.
Peebles, C., and S. Kus
1977   'Some Archaeological Correlates of Ranked Societies', *American Antiquity* 42: 421-48.

Price, B.J.
1978   'Secondary State Formation: An Explanatory Model', in *Origins of the State* (ed. R. Cohen and E.R. Service; Philadelphia: Institute for the Study of Human Issues): 161-86.
Redman, C.L.
1978   *The Rise of Civilization* (San Francisco: W.H. Freeman).
Renfrew, C.
1974   'Beyond a Subsistence Economy: The Evolution of Social Organization in Prehistoric Europe', in *Reconstructing Complex Societies* (ed. C.B. Moore; Cambridge, MA: American Schools of Oriental Research): 69-88.
Richter, W.
1965   'Die *nāgîd*-Formel', *BZ* 9: 71-84.
Robertson A.F.
1976   'Ousting the Chief: Deposition Charges in Ashanti', *Man* 11: 410-27.
Sahlins, M.D.
1968   *Tribesmen* (Englewood Cliffs, NJ: Prentice-Hall).
Sanders, W.T., and J. Marino
1970   *New World Prehistory* (Englewood Cliffs, NJ: Prentice-Hall).
Sanders, W.T., and B.J. Price
1968   *Mesoamerica* (Englewood Cliffs, NJ: Prentice-Hall).
Service, E.R.
1962   *Primitive Social Organization* (New York: Random House, 2nd edn).
1975   *Origins of the State and Civilization* (New York: Norton).
1978   'Classical and Modern Theories of the Origins of Government', in *Origins of the State* (ed. R. Cohen and E.R. Service; Philadelphia: Institute for the Study of Human Issues): 21-34.
Vogt, E.Z.
1968   'Cultural Change', *International Encyclopedia of the Social Sciences* 3: 555-58.
Wilson, E.O.
1978   *On Human Nature* (Cambridge, MA: Harvard University Press).
Wilson, R.R.
1977   *Genealogy and History in the Biblical World* (New Haven: Yale University Press).

JSOT 30 (1984), pp. 67-84

'IS THERE ANYONE LEFT OF THE HOUSE OF SAUL...?'
AMBIGUITY AND THE CHARACTERIZATION OF DAVID
IN THE SUCCESSION NARRATIVE*

Leo G. Perdue

I. *Introduction*

Recent assessments of the David character in the Succession Narrative
have led to significantly different portrayals. Walter Brueggemann's
David is 'a fully responsible, fully free man' due to the mutual trust that
shapes his relationship with God.[1] In describing the characterization of
David, Brueggemann focuses on the contrasting views of human nature
held by David, Shimei, and Abishai. According to Brueggemann, Shimei
affirms an irrevocable causal nexus between sin and divine retribution as
well as an immutable fate that incapacitates human freedom, while
Abishai rejects the possibility of divine intervention which orders human
existence, believing instead that 'history is a totally human enterprise'.[2]
Strikingly different is Brueggemann's David who breaks with the
convention of fate while still affirming God's participation in the shaping
of human affairs. The pivotal point in David's existence, thinks

---

* An earlier draft of this paper was presented to the Biblical Literature section
of the American Academy of Religion during its annual meeting in 1980. I wish to
thank David Gunn for his careful reading of this paper and for making a number of
insightful suggestions which have improved this essay in several key areas.

1. 'The Trusted Creature', *CBQ* 31 (1969), p. 487. Cf. his 'David and His
Theologian', *CBQ* 30 (1968), pp. 156-81; 'Kingship and Chaos', *CBQ* 33 (1971),
pp. 317-32; 'Life and Death in Tenth Century Israel', *JAAR* 40 (1972), pp. 96-109;
'On Trust and Freedom', *Int* 26 (1972), pp. 3-19; 'On Coping with Curse: A Study
of 2 Sam. 16.5-14', *CBQ* 36 (1974), pp. 175-92; and *In Man We Trust* (Atlanta:
John Knox Press, 1972), pp. 29-77.
2. 'On Coping with Curse', p. 187.

Brueggemann, is the combination of human freedom and responsibility with trust in God's providence and grace.

A totally different portrait of David is drawn by Jared Jackson, who centers on the king's interaction with Joab as the key to characterization.[3] According to this interpretation, Joab is the hardened military warrior who carries out his lord's commands decisively and discreetly, all the while despising the king's languor and enervation. David, by contrast, is the weak, snivelling, and vacillating ruler who is prone to anger, but unable to act decisively. The narrative, in Jackson's opinion, reaches its climax in the confrontation between David and his general in 2 Samuel 18–19 when Joab flagrantly disobeys the royal instructions by murdering Absalom and later humiliating the distraught father. According to Jackson, 'David has been reduced by the weakness and vacillation of his own character and the resultant disasters which have befallen him, to a shell of a man, covering his face and mourning for the dead son, and this at the moment of external triumph...'[4]

Fokkelman's reading of this narrative concentrates on David's sin and its consequences as the dominant center of the story. While Fokkelman avoids a systematic treatment of the David character, the character who may be extracted from his reading is a complex king of multiple dualities (strong–weak, king–father, and so forth) who perhaps may not have been 'equal to his onerous function, the kingship'. Fokkelman also points to character contrast as a major technique of characterization, especially operative in the scenes he names the 'David-Ziba-Mephibosheth triangle'. In this series of scenes, Fokkelman sees Mephibosheth as the one whose 'detached and principled' behavior follows the highest ideals of *ḥesed*, for he is the one who is unconditionally loyal to David and expects no material benefit in return. By contrast David is the compromising ruler, the psychologically disabled, often 'hindered by frustrations and fears'.[5] For instance, David knows that Jonathan's son is not truly involved in the Absalom revolt, and yet he still fears that this physically disabled man, who has a son, may indeed be a threat to his throne. On the other hand, David is aware that Ziba is a calculating liar who nevertheless gave him material aid during his

---

3.   'David's Throne: Patterns in the Succession Story', *CJT* 11 (1965), pp. 183-95.

4.   'David's Throne', p. 194.

5.   J.P. Fokkelman, *Narrative Art and Poetry in the Books of Samuel*. I. *King David* (Studia Semitica Neerlandica, 20; Assen: Van Gorcum, 1981), pp. 39-40.

flight. David, unable to match the idealistic, unconditional loyalty of Mephibosheth, makes the morally reprehensible decision to divide Saul's estate between the two. Crucial for Fokkelman's portrayal is David's sin of adultery and murder. For it is this sin which transforms the king, the initiator of action, into the passive ruler who is ultimately overcome by a series of devastating disasters.

A more convincing delineation of the David character has been made in separate studies by Kenneth Gros Louis and David Gunn. Gros Louis, who takes into consideration the entire David story, begins with the double introduction of the young David in 1 Samuel 16 and 17 and proceeds to argue that the entire narrative is patterned on the tensions between the private and public David.[6] David excels when public or private duties are clearly defined, but when personal desires and public responsibilities conflict, as in the Bathsheba affair, or when they have equal validity, as in David's relationships with Saul and Absalom, he errs. The David narrative, then, is a reflection on the complexity of kingly rule which involves the struggle between personal desire and the public good. Unlike Prince Hal in Shakespeare's *Henry V*, David's failures result from his inability to suppress his personal desires for the good of the nation. The narrative ends with 'members of his court struggling to achieve their personal desires, even at the expense of the state'.[7]

David Gunn also emphasizes the tension between the private and political spheres of the king, though he limits his discussion to the Succession Narrative.[8] Central are the effects, often adverse ones, that David's private life has on the political: the adultery with Bathsheba, the murder of Uriah, the failure to punish Amnon for his rape of Tamar, and so on. On the political level the story of David has two major themes: David's acquisition and tenure of power and his founding of a dynasty, while the private level has two parallel themes: sexual intrigue involving taking, and paternity. Thus, David's acquisition of power on a public level is paralleled by his sexual possession of Bathsheba, while David as the founder of a dynasty corresponds privately to David as father. According to Gunn, the primary mode of these themes is giving and

6. 'The Difficulty of Ruling Well: King David of Israel', *Semeia* 8 (1977), pp. 15-33.

7. 'The Difficulty of Ruling Well', p. 32.

8. 'David and the Gift of the Kingdom (2 Sam. 2–4, 9–20, 1 Kgs 1–2)', *Semeia* 3 (1975), pp. 14-45; this analysis is developed in *The Story of King David* (JSOTSup, 6; Sheffield: JSOT Press, 1978).

grasping. When David gives he is most successful, but when he grasps the results are disastrous. The point is that power must be given; it cannot be taken. Gunn's David is the most complex of those briefly described. This David is neither an 'ideal' character nor a 'villain', but rather one who acts out of mixed motives about which we are often unclear. For example, Gunn notes in David's dealings with Mephibosheth in ch. 9 that there is 'a delicate irony in the possibility that in 16.1-4 Ziba's gesture of generosity to the dispossessed David may be no less devious than David's to the dispossessed Mephibosheth'.[9] It is this ambiguity of David as a technique of characterization that, in my estimation, deserves further amplification.

II. *Point of View, Ambiguity, and Narrative Fiction*[10]

One of the major difficulties in assessing the David character results from the type of narrator in the Succession Narrative. In literary criticism, point of view has to do with the involvement of the narrator in the story, coupled with his or her knowledge of events and characters. Any writer of fiction may have his or her narrator assume any one of several

---

9.   *King David*, p. 97.

10.   Since the seminal study by R.N. Whybray (*The Succession Narrative* [SBT, 2.9; Naperville, IL: Alec R. Allenson, 1968]), the early consensus that this document is historical narrative has given way to two approaches which deny that the document is historiography. See especially L. Rost, *Die Überlieferung von der Thronnachfolge Davids* (BWANT, 3.6; Stuttgart: Kohlhammer, 1926); ET, *The Succession to the Throne of David* (Introd. by E. Ball; Historic Texts and Interpreters, 1; Sheffield: Almond Press, 1982); and G. von Rad, 'The Beginnings of Historical Writing in Ancient Israel', in *The Problem of the Hexateuch and Other Essays* (London: Oliver & Boyd, 1966), pp. 166-204. The 'redactional approach', taken by E. Würthwein (*Die Erzählung von der Thronfolge Davids—theologische oder politische Geschichtsschreibung?* [Theologische Studien, 115; Zürich: Theologischer Verlag, 1974]), T. Veijola (*Die Ewige Dynastie* [Helsinki: Suomalaisen Kirjallisuuden Kirjapaino, 1975], p. 130), and F. Langlamet ('Pour ou contre Salomon? La rédaction prosalomonienne de I Rois I–II', *RB* 83 [1976], pp. 321-79, 481-528), considers the text to be originally anti-Solomonic (or Davidic) propaganda which was then subjected to one or more pro-Solomonic (or Davidic) redactions. The 'literary approach', exemplified in the previously cited works of Gros Louis and Gunn, along with the analyses by C. Conroy (*Absalom Absalom!* [AnBib, 81; Rome: Biblical Institute Press, 1978]) and H. Hagan ('Deception as Motif and Theme in 2 Sam. 9–20; 1 Kgs 1–2', *Bib* 60 [1979], 301-26), regards the Succession Narrative as more akin to literary fiction than to history-writing or propaganda.

very different postures.[11] However, regardless of the posture of the narrator, he or she may be as fictional as any character portrayed in the narrative, even when he or she is not dramatized. Even so, the narrator becomes the medium through whom the events and characters are processed and by whom the reader's reactions to the story are strongly influenced, if not determined. Of course the narrator's influence is largely based on whether he or she appears to be truthful, unbiased, and knowledgeable. However, the fact that a narrator may be portrayed as omniscient should not be taken as evidence that he or she is biased, since this would incriminate the great majority of narrators in ancient and modern fiction.

The type of narrator chosen by the author figures prominently in the writer's efforts to impose his or her fictional world upon the reader and to control the latter's response, though 'in some narratives the author tries to control the reader's response more fully than in others'.[12] In line with this observation, writers of fiction tend to adopt one of two rather broad approaches: 'telling' or 'showing'.[13] In 'telling', the author constructs a first- or third-person narrator who authoritatively describes and evaluates characters by means of commentary and descriptions and who passes judgment on the significance of events. In this case the reader tends to be passive, accepting the statements of the narrator as true, unless there emerges some legitimate suspicion that the narrator is biased or in error.[14]

11. See especially N. Friedman, 'Point of View in Fiction: The Development of a Critical Concept', *PMLA* 70 (1955), pp. 1160-84; W. Booth, *The Rhetoric of Fiction* (Chicago: University of Chicago Press, 1961); and R. Alter, *The Art of Biblical Narrative* (New York: Basis Books, 1981), pp. 63-87.

12. R. Scholes and R. Kellogg, *The Nature of Narrative* (New York: Oxford University Press, 1966), pp. 82-159.

13. Booth, *The Rhetoric of Fiction*, pp. 3-20.

14. Whybray bases part of his argument that the document is pro-Solomonic propaganda on the conclusion that the narrator is biased (*The Succession Narrative*, pp. 50-55). The same holds true, though in the reverse, for the conclusion by Würthwein, Veijola, and Langlamet that the narrative is anti-Solomonic (or Davidic) and later redacted by royalists (cf. note 8). However, it certainly is not clear in whose favor the document as it now stands is written. Further, the 'redactional approach' that attributes 'pro- or anti-monarchical' remarks to different writers is not only simplistic, but also succeeds in turning a stimulating narrative into an insipid, anti-royal, political pamphlet which for whatever reason was appropriated by royalists who then inserted their own sympathies into the text. But why would propagandists of a royal inclination choose only to add pro-royal sentiments and not also suppress

By contrast, 'showing' involves the withholding of overt evaluations and commentary by the narrator. Thus the reader is forced to scrutinize very carefully the actions and statements of characters, always searching for clues about motive and intentionality, virtue and vice. Of course narrators often move between these two approaches in relating the story.

When one examines the narrator's stance in the Succession Narrative, it is obvious that he does more 'showing' than 'telling'. True, the point of view is on occasion neutral omniscience, that is, the narrator is a privileged bystander who speaks in the third person, selectively tells us about private conversations (e.g. 2 Sam. 13), and even seems to know the mind of God (2 Sam. 11.27–12.1; 12.24; and 17.4). In several instances he chooses to describe the mental states and internal feelings of his human characters, for example, Amnon's love-hate desire for Tamar (2 Sam. 13.2, 15). However, he is reluctant to engage in explicit evaluations of his characters.[15] Two exceptions are his remark about Adonijah's political hubris (1 Kgs 1.5) and Sheba's description as a 'base fellow' (2 Sam. 20.1). What is more, he usually declines to provide the motives behind the characters' actions,[16] a key to characterization often present in other Hebrew narratives, especially in the form of internal monologue.[17] While this narrator will set the scene, narrate actions and dialogue, and summarize events, he is reticent to pass judgment or provide motives. This forces the reader to attempt to discover the characters' intentions and then to draw his or her own conclusions.[18]

---

incriminating accusations? Obviously the Chronicler had no reservation in removing the entire Succession Narrative from his pro-monarchical 'history'. Again, the fact that a narrator is omniscient is not in itself evidence that he or she is biased.

15. By contrast note the narrator's evaluations in Job 1.22; 2.10.

16. See, for example, the exception in 2 Sam. 15.11.

17. Interior monologue is often signaled by the expression, 'said in his heart' (e.g. 1 Sam. 27.1 and Qoheleth).

18. 'For the most part, the narrator is content to show the characters as they talk and act; this dramatic presentation leaves it up to the reader to infer the motivations of the characters and to form a judgement on their actions' (Conroy, *Absalom Absalom!*, p. 105). Nevertheless, Conroy goes on to argue in his delineation of the character of David in 2 Sam. 13–20 that 'the narrator's presentation of David...is sympathetic but not uncritical'. This complexity of the narrator's treatment of David, argues Conroy, should make the interpreter less inclined to see the narrator as suffering from a pro- or anti-Davidic bias (*Absalom Absalom!*, p. 112). Gunn underscores the difficulty the interpreter has in judging characters: 'Characteristically...the narrator refuses to allow us the luxury of making simple judgements. We are left with a perception of the ambivalence of events' (*King David*, p. 97; cf. p. 138 n. 7).

A final point should be made at this juncture. The narrator frequently uses speeches and dialogue as the major catalyst for the sequences and movement of the plot.[19] However, the absence of commentary by the narrator forces the reader to decide about motives and the degree of veracity present, all the while keeping in mind the remark by Mark Harris: 'I shall allow you to eavesdrop on my people, and sometimes they will tell the truth and sometimes they will lie, and you must determine for yourself when they are doing which'.[20]

With these points in mind, I propose that the narrator's characterization of David is intentionally ambiguous so that two very different interpretations of David may emerge, depending on the reader's own assessment of the motives resting behind the king's actions and speeches.[21] I am not suggesting that the author is indifferent to the two different ways his character may be read. Rather, the storyteller's design is to demonstrate the complexity of David.

III. *David as Dynamic Character*

In interpreting the David character, one approach, following Auerbach,[22] is to search for a dynamic character who changes within the unfolding of the tragic plot that entwines private and public catastrophes. With this approach one assumes that David's speeches are truthful and that the motives at least for his public actions are usually altruistic. In this case, the narrator presents in David two contrasting views on how to rule a nation: with brute force and ruthlessness or with compassion and forgiveness. The technique used by the narrator to exploit this tension is the series of encounters between David and the sons of Zeruiah, Joab and Abishai.[23] These two warriors believe that proper rule expresses itself in

19. See H.-J. Hermisson, 'Weisheit und Geschichte', in H.W. Wolff (ed.), *Probleme biblischer Theologie* (Munich: Chr. Kaiser Verlag, 1971), pp. 136-48.

20. 'Easy Does It Not', in G. Hicks (ed.), *The Living Novel* (New York: Macmillan, 1957), p. 117.

21. A detailed analysis of ambiguity is made by W. Empson, *Seven Types of Ambiguity* (New York: Meridian Books, 1955). For an assessment of the proclivity of Henry James towards ambiguity in characterization, see E. Wilson, 'The Ambiguity of Henry James', *Hound and Horn* 7 (1934), pp. 385-406.

22. E. Auerbach, *Mimesis* (Garden City, NY: Doubleday, 1957), pp. 1-43. For a recent discussion of biblical characterization, see Alter, *The Art of Biblical Narrative*, pp. 114-30.

23. See Gunn's treatment of this conflict (*King David*, pp. 39-40).

the unreserved, even callous use of power when it is expedient, while compassion and forgiveness are viewed as potentially disastrous for the nation. By contrast, David avows, at least through most of the story, that proper rule should combine compassion with forgiveness in order to keep together a strife-ridden, divided nation. While on occasion David's private desires tend to obstruct his public altruism, on the whole he rejects brute force as the appropriate means for ruling wisely and well.

The opening scene (2 Sam. 9), which typically is the most important in revealing notable dimensions of characterization, focuses on David's public speeches.[24] The scene begins with David asking if Saul has any surviving descendants to whom he may 'show חסד [kindness, mercy, loyalty] for Jonathan's sake'. Twice more David publicly reasserts his intention to show חסד to surviving Saulides, first to Ziba, Saul's former servant, and then to Mephibosheth, Jonathan's lame son. And David seemingly makes good on his pledge by returning to Jonathan's son his grandfather's estate, appointing Ziba and his house as personal servants, and providing a royal pension in Jerusalem. This threefold repetition of חסד appears to be the narrator's method of underlining David's public affirmation of his principle of rule.[25] While the king's self-avowed motives are not confirmed by the narrator, the reader may choose to believe that his statements are truthful and his actions gracious.

The second scene (2 Sam. 10) opens in a similar fashion, but ends with different results. David once more publicly vows to show חסד, this

24. Alter makes the important observation: 'In any given narrative event, and especially at the beginning of any new story, the point at which dialogue first emerges will be worthy of special attention, and in most instances, the initial words spoken by a personage will be revelatory, perhaps more in manner than in matter, constituting an important moment in the exposition of character' (*The Art of Biblical Narrative*, p. 74).

25. חסד occurs eight times in this narrative, and occupies a strategic position in key texts (2 Sam. 9.1, 3, 7; 10.2 [twice]; 15.20; 16.17; and 1 Kgs 2.7). Even when the actual word does not occur, its connotations of 'kindness', 'mercy', and 'loyalty' are often at issue. חסד, therefore, serves as the major *Leitwort* which thematically weaves together the entire narrative. For the nature and function of *Leitwörter* in Hebrew narrative, see M. Buber, 'Über die Wortwahl in einer Verdeutschung der Schrift', in *Werke*. II. *Schriften zur Bibel* (Munich: Kösel, 1964), pp. 1111-74; and J. Licht, *Storytelling in the Bible* (Jerusalem: Magnes, 1978), pp. 51-95. For detailed analyses of the meanings of חסד see N. Glueck, *Das Wort Ḥesed* (BZAW, 47; Giessen: Töpelmann, 1927); and K. Sakenfeld, *The Meaning of Ḥesed in the Hebrew Bible: A New Inquiry* (HSM, 17; Missoula, MT: Scholars Press, 1978).

time to Hanun, the new Ammonite ruler, who has recently replaced his deceased father on the throne. The basis for David's intended gracious- ness is his former relationship, presumably formalized in a treaty, which he had with the dead king. However, the Ammonite counsellors, suspi- cious of David's intentions, convince Hanun that the Israelite emissaries sent by David are in reality spies sent to prepare the way for invasion. Thus, David's ambassadors are humiliated and returned in disgrace to Jerusalem. The Ammonites then align themselves with Syria and begin to mobilize. David, 'despising' the Ammonites for their contemptuous behavior, sends Joab and the 'mighty men' into battle. Ultimately the victory is won. Again, we may accept David's self-expressed motive and his speech as truthful and blame instead the Ammonite king and his foolish counsellors for the war.

David's private desires which lead to the betrayal of Uriah and ulti- mately his murder present a rather shocking contrast to a king's attempt to rule on the basis of kindness and mercy. But David, once discovered, does publicly repent. But has his view of rule been seriously altered by this disgraceful course of events occasioned by private lust? The answer resides in the crucial confrontation between Shimei and David in ch. 16, the next place in the story where the king comes to center stage. Shimei, a Saulide, curses David for his slaughter of Saul's sons. Abishai, one of David's loyal commanders, hears the curse and then urges the king to allow him to execute Shimei on the spot. David, however, restrains Abishai, stating that perhaps God indeed may be behind the curse. Later, following his victory over Absalom (2 Sam. 19.17-24), David is returning in triumph to Jerusalem when Shimei prostrates himself before the king and begs for forgiveness. Once again Abishai wishes to execute the Saulide for cursing the Lord's anointed, a capital offense. But David rebukes him, saying: 'What have I to do with you, you sons of Zeruiah, that you should become adversaries to me on this day? Shall anyone be executed in Israel this day? Do I not realize that I am this day king over Israel?' Consequently David publicly pardons his rival, and we may assume it is due to his insistence on compassion and forgiveness as the basis of his rule.

In the confrontation between Joab and David in 2 Samuel 18–19, once again the contrast between views of rule is revealed. David had instructed his troops, including Joab, to show mercy to Absalom, hoping perhaps even yet to effectuate a reconciliation with his rebel son. Yet, in defiance, Joab executes the hapless Absalom, even though he is reminded beforehand of David's order. Then, when David is incapacitated by his grief over his son's death, Joab berates the sorrowing king for his weakness, accusing him of loving his enemies and hating his supporters. And, to the point, Joab threatens the king that not one man, including himself, will remain loyal, unless he gives an oration to sway support to his side. Here is the classic encounter between the soldier who sees no place for compassion, forgiveness, or even grief in royal existence, since these features often hinder decisive and firm action, and a king whose compassion and desire to forgive have been thwarted by the soldier's treachery.

In the concluding episode involving David in 1 Kings 1–2, the opening description of David bears notice, for it is the first time that a physical depiction of David is provided. Here David is portrayed as old and declining rapidly in health, a description that should signal one to look for a dénouement that results from a transformation in the king's understanding of the proper way to rule. While court factions are attempting to place their successor on the throne, David proclaims Solomon as his successor. Is the king deceived by Nathan and Bathsheba's plot, or is he angry that Adonijah, like Absalom, is attempting to wrest the throne away? Again the narrator does not inform us. However, there is no doubt about David's speech in the final deathbed scene in 1 Kgs 2.1-9, when he instructs Solomon in the proper way to rule. Echoing the language of the sons of Zeruiah (2 Sam. 10.12), David instructs Solomon to use cunning and brute force in executing the dynasty's real or potential enemies. Ironically the first victim of David's changed view of rule is Joab. Then, breaking his earlier public oath and negating his pardon, David orders Solomon to use treachery in order to find a basis for executing Shimei, for the same reason twice offered by Abishai: he had cursed the king.

In this reading, the narrative's portrayal of David centers on the proper way to rule the kingdom. Against the background of the plot involving the private and public disasters of the king, David at the end of his life repudiates his earlier principles of compassion and forgiveness, חסד, and adopts the political cynicism of the sons of Zeruiah: only the use of merciless power may effectively quell internal discord and create a united kingdom.[26]

---

26. Gunn's observation is unquestionably correct: 'In reality David, Solomon, and Joab all now belong totally to the same world' (*King David*, p. 107).

IV. *David as Static Character*

It is my contention, however, that the David character is ambiguous, so that a very different picture may emerge, one that consistently binds together deceit, treachery, and ruthlessness. Accordingly, David's practice of rule is far more insidious than the one openly proclaimed by the sons of Zeruiah. The specific technique used by the narrator is the frequency of deceptive speeches by the king which involve explicitly or implicitly the motif of חסד, especially taken in the sense of 'loyalty'.[27] In matters public as well as private, one may argue that David is consistently motivated by self-interest, not altruism. This approach regards David as a static character who does not inwardly change and develop within the movement of the plot.[28]

The first scene (2 Sam. 9) opens with David's public speech: 'Is there still anyone left of the house of Saul that I may show him an act of loyalty for Jonathan's sake?'. When Ziba, Saul's former servant, is presented to the king, David repeats his question, only fashioning it in an even more persuasive manner, perhaps designed to overcome what could be the servant's justified scepticism: 'Is there not still someone of the house of Saul to whom I may show an act of divine loyalty?' The third repetition, nuanced by a slight change, occurs when Mephibosheth is ushered in before the king: 'Do not fear,' says David, 'for I will *most certainly* show an act of loyalty for the sake of your father Jonathan'. This third instance heightens (with the addition of an infinitive absolute) the king's claim to act on the basis of חסד. Thus David twice appeals to the loyalty that seals the bonds of human friendship and once to the loyalty uniting God to his chosen people in his attempts to convince his hearers of the truthfulness of his pledge and the integrity of his motive. This folkloristic threefold repetition, coupled with an increasing intensification of the claim of truthfulness, immediately attracts attention.

27. Alter's following point is most important: 'Although a character's own statements might seem a straightforward revelation of who he is and what he makes of things, in fact the biblical writers are quite as aware as any James or Proust that speech may reflect the occasion more than the speaker, may be more a drawn shutter than an open window' (*The Art of Biblical Narrative*, p. 117).

28. Hagan's study of the motif of deception is flawed by his failure to recognize David's own involvement in treachery and deceit. According to Hagan, with the exception of the Bathsheba episode, David is the victim, not the perpetrator, of deception. In his analysis, Hagan thinks that David, though weak, triumphs because of his love for and trust in the Lord ('Deception as Motif and Theme', pp. 324-25).

But it also draws one's suspicion for three reasons. First, there is an increasing emphasis placed by the king on his veracity, reflected in the slight but significant changes he makes in each repetition. Second, a rather common literary technique that exposes deception is a character's repeated affirmation of his or her integrity and goodwill.[29] And third, the isolated narrative describing David's eradication of the sons of Saul, save for Mephibosheth, by giving them into the hands of the Gibeonites (2 Sam. 21) is obviously in the background of this narrative (cf. 2 Sam. 16.8) and well explains both Mephibosheth's fear and the necessary heightening of emphasis on the king's integrity in ch. 9. Nevertheless, David does turn over to Saul's grandson the former king's lands as well as his family servant. However, the privilege to eat at the king's table was on occasion extended to political prisoners.[30] Is David not afraid that surviving Saulides might occasion a revolution, and thus is prompted to identify potential threats from the house of Saul? Is his motivation in giving Mephibosheth a royal pension not that of making Jonathan's son a political prisoner? David's suspicions are exploited by Ziba who later accuses his new master of royal ambitions (2 Sam. 16.1-5).

In ch. 10 David once again makes a public declaration in which חסד is prominently featured: 'I will deal loyally with Hanun, the son of Nahash, even as his father dealt loyally with me'. This time חסד refers to the loyalty that binds two rulers to the stipulations of a political treaty. However, the motif of deceit is provided by the Ammonite advisors who warn their new king that David's true intention is one of treachery: the emissaries are spies of a king lusting after Ammonite land. David is angered by the rebuff that is compounded by both a public affront and war preparations, but, ever the opportunist, he uses this occasion to bring the Syrians to their knees and the Ammonites within his expanding empire.

The next complex of quickly moving vignettes, centering on the Bathsheba affair and its aftermath, reinforces on a private scale this emerging picture of a deceitful king, for these scenes contrast the deception and treachery of the lustful king who sleeps with his absent soldier's wife with the total loyalty of Uriah to king, nation, and fellow warriors, a loyalty that ironically comes from a Hittite mercenary. This loyalty of a foreigner is emphasized twice more in the behavior of Ittai and Hushai. Perry and Sternberg have exposed the multiple ironic levels of this

29. T. Todorov, *The Poetics of Prose* (Ithaca, NY: Cornell University Press, 1977), pp. 59-61.
30. See 2 Kgs 25.29 (= Jer. 52.33).

narrative section in regard to the exchanges between David and Uriah.[31] However, I would add that the deceit and treachery of the king is further emphasized in the exchange of messages between David and Joab (2 Sam. 11.14-25). Joab so badly mishandles David's order to effectuate Uriah's death in battle that a number of the king's servants are killed. Fearing David's reaction, Joab carefully coaches his messenger in a bit of rhetorical psychology designed to avert the king's anticipated wrath. But, in comic fashion, the messenger, perhaps frightened, bungles his mission, awkwardly blurting out the entirety of his message. But most striking is the realization that Joab's fears of an angry response do not materialize. In spite of the messenger's poor performance, David responds with his own deceitful message to take back to Joab: 'Do not let the affair concern you, for the sword consumes now one and then another. Rather, strengthen your attack against the city and overthrow it.' The messenger's news has evoked neither anger nor remorse over the death of the king's servants. In fact David's only concern seems to be with the care he takes not to intimate to the messenger that anything devious or underhanded has transpired. And as Joab begins to follow the king's order to take the city, David proceeds to possess the wife of the ill-fated Uriah, the final treachery.

In the scene that follows, the prophet Nathan uses his own rhetorical deception in the guise of a parable that tricks the king into self-condemnation (2 Sam. 12.1-15). Caught in his own deceit, David confesses that he has sinned and even engages in the traditional mourning ritual on behalf of his stricken, innocent child (2 Sam. 12.15-23). But is this true remorse? What attracts one's suspicion about the motive of David's lamentation are his break with tradition and the lack of a father's normal emotional reaction to hearing the news of the death of his child. David, hearing the child is dead, arises, washes himself, anoints his body, changes clothes, and eats. The king's stunned servants, who had anticipated he might do himself harm upon hearing the news of the child's death, express their amazement. Then David explains: 'While the child was still alive I fasted and wept; for I said, "Who knows, perhaps the

---

31. M. Perry and M. Sternberg, 'The King through Ironic Eyes: The Narrator's Devices in the Biblical Story of David and Bathsheba and Two Excursuses on the Theory of the Narrative Text', *Hasifrut* 1 (1968), pp. 263-92 (English summary, pp. 449-52); and 'Caution, a Literary Text! Problems in the Poetics and the Interpretation of Biblical Narrative', *Hasifrut* 2 (1970), pp. 608-63 (English summary, pp. 679-82).

Lord will be gracious to me so that the child may live?" But now that he is dead, why should I fast? Can I bring him back again? I shall go to him, but he will not return to me.' Are these the words of a grief-stricken father, or of a callous ruler realizing he had failed to negate Nathan's prophecy predicting trouble from the king's own house, a prediction whose initial sign was the death of the child?

The Absalom complex (2 Sam. 13–19) is also filled with examples that exploit the tension between loyalty and treachery, devotion and deceit. But what concerns us most are the significant encounters and dialogues between David and his loyal servants that focus on the motif of loyalty. The first of these involves David's rhetoric designed to test the loyalty of the Gittite leader, Ittai, and his band of compatriots. Ittai responds by swearing loyalty even to death to David and accompanies the king in his flight from Absalom (2 Sam. 15.19-22).[32] The second case involves David's commission to Hushai. Telling his Canaanite counsellor that his presence would only impede the royal escape ('be a burden to me'), David exploits Hushai's loyalty by sending him back to Absalom as a spy and almost to certain death. In words characteristically revealing, David says to his advisor: 'If you return to the city and tell Absalom: "I shall be your servant, O king; as I had been your father's servant, so now will I be your servant", you will bring to naught for my sake the counsel of Ahithophel' (2 Sam. 15.33-34). Indeed, when Hushai returns to act as David's spy, he publicly swears his loyalty to the new king, even though Absalom had suspiciously asked: 'Is this your loyalty (חסד) to your friend?' (2 Sam. 16.17). Thus Hushai's deceitful counsel to an unsuspecting Absalom results in the saving of David's life and crown, but the text's ominous silence following Absalom's discovery of the spy suggests the price this loyal servant had to pay to be the 'king's friend' (2 Sam. 15.32–17.23).[33]

The third and most dramatic example of treachery and loyalty begins

32. Unfortunately the Hebrew reading in v. 20 is problematical, with the result that the exact meaning of David's use of חסד is obscured. The versions also differ widely, as noted by *BHS*. I suggest that the difficult expression, והשב את־אחיך עמך חסד ואמת, is best translated: 'take back with your brothers loyalty and faithfulness'. From the context it appears that David is attempting to persuade Ittai and the Gittites to return to Jerusalem and swear allegiance to Absalom.

33. Of course Hushai's title, 'the king's friend', points to his official position of royal advisor (T.N.D. Mettinger, *Solomonic State Officials* [ConBOT, 5; Lund: Gleerup, 1971], pp. 62-69). However, that his relationship to David also involves the loyalty of friendship is noted in Absalom's suspicion expressed in 2 Sam. 16.17.

to unfold just before the fateful encounter between the armies of David and Absalom. David has just received the public expression of loyalty from his troops, who vow their willingness to die for their sovereign, while refusing to allow him to risk his own life in battle. Now the king publicly instructs his troops: 'Deal gently (לאֵט), for my sake, with the young man Absalom' (2 Sam. 18.5). While David, presumably intentionally, uses the synonym for חסד, Joab, nevertheless, has heard David's speeches and messages before and has learned to recognize the king's rhetorical deception, especially when he mentions kindness and loyalty. Ironically Joab takes the speech to be a deceitful one, thinking perhaps that David knew that his loyal commander would understand the true intent of the statement. Hence, Joab murders Absalom, all the while thinking he has carried out David's true wishes.

The irony of the king who falls victim to his own deceit is revealed in David's devastated reaction to the news of the Cushite messenger. A messenger, one should note, was used quite often by the king in effectuating his treachery. However, the genuineness of David's grief is this time underscored by the narrator's remark that 'the king was deeply moved' (2 Sam. 19.1). Yet one must ask, Where is the king's remorse over the death of 20,000 warriors? That Joab is confused by David's reaction is revealed in his berating of the king's lack of loyalty to his own family and faithful servants. Joab accuses David of being willing to sacrifice them all if only he could have his beloved traitor back. Then Joab persuades the king to use his powerful gift of rhetoric to recapture the support of his followers, a skill at which the king is all too adept. Otherwise David faces abandonment and the loss of his empire.

When the king is returning victoriously to Jerusalem, he once again employs those skills in swearing by public oath to pardon Shimei for his curse. But is this not evidence once again of a deceitful speech, necessitated by the fact that this Saulide had with him a thousand men from Benjamin (2 Sam. 19.17-24)? David surely recognizes it is not an auspicious time for dispatching his rival, but he also knows that one day a better, more convenient occasion would surely arise for settling old debts. Even David's partial forgiveness of Mephibosheth, implicated in the revolt, is surely based on expediency, for the king must have known that the execution of Jonathan's son would only alienate the tribe of Saul. Nevertheless, by giving to Ziba half of his former master's land to repay his loyalty, David reminds Mephibosheth who now has the real power in Israel (2 Sam. 19.25-31).

The final scenes in 1 Kings 1–2 are replete with contrasts between loyalty, at least self-professed, and treachery, between faithfulness and deception. The plot by Nathan and Bathsheba to place Solomon, not Adonijah, on David's throne succeeds because of the prophet's strong emphasis on his and Bathsheba's loyalty, coupled with that of Benaiah and Solomon. By contrast Nathan points to the treachery of Adonijah and his party, who are plotting to take the throne. Thus David, consumed with his own passion for loyalty from his subjects, selects Solomon as his successor. Once again the king is no match for the scheming wit of this prophet of Yahweh.

But the royal deceiver engages in one final act of treachery. On his deathbed, David orders Solomon to 'use his wisdom' (i.e., engage in political deception) to find a legal means by which to execute the ever-dangerous Joab and Shimei. Joab, David's most loyal and devoted servant, the one who won his victories in the name of the king, who saves David's throne on at least two occasions, and who discreetly carries out the royal execution orders, is ironically repaid with betrayal in the form of David's execution order to Solomon. Likewise David's shameless lie in regard to his earlier oath of pardon given to Shimei is clearly evidenced in his instruction to Solomon to find a legal basis to execute his old enemy. Then the king instructs his successor to repay Barzillai for his loyalty during the Absalom rebellion by allowing his sons to eat at the king's table. With the echo of loyalty (חסד) and the reference to eating at the royal table we are at full circle. With this obvious closure the narrator ends his story of David. Indeed, Solomon carries out David's instructions to the letter, even adding to them in executing Adonijah and exiling Abiathar. However, the sons of Barzillai are not again mentioned. Do they refuse the king's offer to eat at the royal table, knowing the ambiguous nature of such a 'reward', or is it that Solomon, like Joab, has heard his father's deceitful speeches about loyalty and thus dismisses this part of the instruction?

In this second reading, David is consistently deceitful, ruthless, and treacherous, with self-interest the driving force behind his speeches and actions. His final oration to Solomon then is not surprising. This speech corresponds to David's statements and actions throughout the narrative. And now Solomon, like his father before him, initiates his reign with the same callous deceit, treachery, and brutality. Indeed, a new David sits on the throne of Israel.

V. *Conclusion*

Of the two portraits of David just drawn, which one do we choose? Do we select the David who valiantly attempts to rule his kingdom with compassion and forgiveness, changing only at the end of his life when, as an old, embittered, and dying man, he comes to recognize that ruthless force is the only way to suppress revolution? Or is the other David more convincing, the king who is consistently deceitful, treacherous, and ruthless, demanding loyalty from his subjects, but repaying it only if it promotes his own self-interest? But must we choose? Robert Alter has stated in regard to biblical characterization: 'We are compelled to get at character and motive...through a process of inference from fragmentary data, often with crucial pieces of narrative exposition strategically withheld, and this leads to multiple or sometimes even wavering perspectives on the characters. There is, in other words, an abiding mystery in character as the biblical writers conceive it, which they embody in their typical methods of presentation.'[34] I would only add here that the type of ambiguity surrounding the David figure in the Succession Narrative is the result of skilful craftsmanship.

But is the ambiguity of the David character merely a typical feature of biblical narrative, or is there some intention on the author's part in portraying David in such a manner? Since an author's intention is often well concealed, one may only speculate. But is it not possible that the double portrait of David reflects the ambiguity many Israelites held about the institution of monarchy in general, an ambiguity reflected in many biblical texts? 'Is there anyone still left of the house of Saul, that I may show him an act of kindness for Jonathan's sake?'[35]

---

34. *The Art of Biblical Narrative*, p. 126. Gunn has suggested in private correspondence that Alter may be placing too much emphasis on mystery as an intrinsic feature of human nature, when mystery may instead be more a matter of (our) perception.

35. P. Miscall's book (*The Workings of Old Testament Narrative* [SBL Semeia Series; Philadelphia: Fortress Press, 1983]) appeared after this essay was finished. It is significant, however, that he has argued for a similar reading of David in 1 Sam. 16–22 (cf. pp. 47-138). The 'undecidability' of the David character (i.e. David is at the same time 'good' and 'bad') is especially clear, argues Miscall, in the Goliath episode (ch. 17). Miscall writes: 'David is a cunning and unscrupulous schemer, and he is also an innocent "man of destiny" for whom all goes right. The text supports a spectrum of portrayals of David and thereby does not support any one definitive or probable portrayal' (p. 83).

JSOT 55 (1992), pp. 39-59

DESIRE, RIVALRY AND COLLECTIVE VIOLENCE
IN THE 'SUCCESSION NARRATIVE'

Hans J.L. Jensen

1. *René Girard: A Theory of Desire, Rivalry and Collective Violence*

The fundamental themes in Girard's anthropological theory[1] (or 'hypo-thesis'[2]) are *desire, rivalry, conflict*, and solutions of conflicts by means of *expulsion*. According to Girard, humans are basically *mimetic*; the greatly increased predisposition for mimetic behaviour distinguishes humankind from all other living beings. This predisposition to mimetic behaviour and mimetic reactions—in short, *mimesis*—is the precondition for culture, even for language. But mimesis can destroy a culture just as easily as it can build it up. Mimetic reactions—or *mimetism*—running wild will make everybody the enemy of everybody else. Imitating another person means also to imitate the other's objects and the other's

---

1.   R. Girard, *Deceit, Desire, and the Novel* (trans. Y. Freccero; Baltimore: Johns Hopkins University Press, 1965); *Violence and the Sacred* (trans. P. Gregory; Baltimore: Johns Hopkins University Press, 1977); *The Scapegoat* (trans. Y. Freccero; Baltimore: Johns Hopkins University Press, 1986); *Things Hidden Since the Foundation of the World* (trans. S. Bann and M. Metteer; London: Athlone Press, 1987); *Job, the Victim of his People* (trans. Y. Freccero; London: Athlone Press, 1987). In this paper there is no room for a methodological discussion concerning the relevance of Girard's works for Old Testament exegesis in general. But condemnations *ex cathedra* like the one in Walter Kornfeld's presidential address to the 1980 IOSOT Congress in Vienna, '*QDŠ* und Gottesrecht im Alten Testament' (in J.A. Emerton [ed.], *Congress Volume, Vienna 1980* [VTSup, 32; Leiden: Brill, 1981], pp. 1-9), which tries to preclude any discussion by referring to the categorically sacrosant status of *the sacred*, are difficult to take seriously.

2.   Strongly underscored in Girard, *Things Hidden*, pp. 437-38.

wishes; and so imitation, at least between individuals not too distant from one another, is always in danger of becoming rivalry. Therefore, culture can survive only if it possesses means to prevent 'bad mimesis', that is, conflicting desires. No culture can exist without *prohibitions* whose function is to channel desire in different directions in order to avoid rivalry and prevent violence.

Anger can be imitated as easily as can desire.[3] A group of human beings can be hit by a general crisis against which it has no rational means of defence. In that situation everybody will become everybody else's enemy and the group will be in danger of destroying itself in general violence. But there is another possibility: a situation of rivalry between two persons can be imitated by others, and by virtue of mimesis the enemy of a single person can become a public enemy. A general crisis can be solved, or at least the group can obtain a temporary decrease in tension, by the expulsion of the common enemy, the scapegoat. According to Girard, one can imagine *ritual* to have originated as an artificial crisis in which prohibitions are transgressed, but where the resulting aggression is directed towards an artificial common enemy, typically a sacrificial victim. Nobody can doubt that sacrifices 'work'; it is much more difficult to explain why they do so. Girard's answer is that their very real effect is caused by their symbolized scapegoating—and scapegoating works, at least as long as it is not recognized as such.

These themes are also—such is my thesis—the themes of the so-called 'Succession Narrative'. This Old Testament literary work is a reflection—in narrative form, of course—on basic phenomena in the human world.

2. *Observations on the 'Succession Narrative'*

The Succession Narrative is generally recognized as a coherent literary work; there are some doubts about its delimitation, but normally it is defined as covering 2 Samuel 9–20 and 1 Kings 1–2.[4] The designation

---

3.   Cf. R. Schwager, *Brauchen wir einen Sündenbock?* (Munich: Kösel, 1979), pp. 16-17.

4.   Scholars who do not want to get involved in a discussion about the redactional dimensions of the Succession Narrative normally choose this definition; so, e.g., R.N. Whybray, *The Succession Narrative: A Study of II Sam. 9–20; I Kings 1 and 2* (London: SCM Press, 1968), p. 8; H. Hagan, 'Deception as Motif and Theme

'Succession Narrative' is the traditional one that goes back to the classical study of L. Rost; it is not at all satisfying, since the main theme in the
story does not seem to be 'succession' in the strict sense; one may
prefer to regard the story as a 'court history'[5] or perhaps 'the story of
King David'.[6] But despite its disadvantages, 'Succession Narrative' has
become a generally accepted designation for this story.

As David Gunn remarked in his book, *The Story of King David*,
everybody seems to agree that the Succession Narrative is a work with
a clear-cut tendency; however, there is not quite the same consensus on
what that tendency is.[7] We do not know who the author or authors of
the work were and we do not know when it was written. It could be

in 2 Sam. 9–20; 1 Kings 1–2', *Bib* 60 (1979), pp. 301-26; D.J.A. Clines, 'Story and
Poem: The Old Testament as Literature and Scripture', *Int* 34 (1980), p. 120; F.E.
Deist, 'David: A Man after God's Heart: An Investigation into the So-Called
Succession Narrative', in W.C. van Wyk (ed.), *Studies in the Succession Narrative*,
De Ou-Testamentiese Werkgemeenskap in Suid-Afrika (*OTWSA*) 27 (1984) and 28
(1985), pp. 99-129; L.G. Perdue, '"Is There Anyone Left of the House of Saul…?"
Ambiguity and the Characterization of David in the Succession Narrative', *JSOT* 30
(1984), pp. 67-84 (pp. 167-83 in this volume); W. Brueggemann, *David's Truth in
Israel's Imagination and Memory* (Philadelphia: Fortress Press, 1985), p. 41;
J. Ackerman, 'Knowing Good and Evil: A Literary Analysis of the Court History in
2 Samuel 9–20 and 1 Kings 1–2', *JBL* 109 (1990). Others claim a new consensus
on including 2 Sam. 2.8(12)–4.12 (perhaps with vv. 5, 3a) in the Succession Narrative: so O. Kaiser, 'Some Observations on the Succession Narrative', in van Wyk
(ed.), *Studies*, p. 132, with references to H. Schulte, *Die Entstehung der Geschichtsschreibung in Israel* (BZAW, 128; Berlin: de Gruyter, 1972); D.M. Gunn, *The
Story of King David* (JSOTSup, 6; Sheffield: JSOT Press, 1978); and J. Van Seters,
In Search of History (New Haven: Yale University Press, 1983).

5.   E.g., Van Seters, *In Search of History*; J. Rosenberg, *King and Kin: Political
Allegory in the Hebrew Bible* (Bloomington: Indiana University Press, 1986),
p. 101; Ackerman, 'Knowing Good and Evil'.

6.   E.g., J.W. Flanagan ('Court History or Succession Document', *JBL* 91
[1972], pp. 172-81) assumed an earlier stratum (without 1 Kgs 1–2 and the
'Solomonic' sections of 2 Sam. 9–20—the 'succession' stratum proper), which he
regarded as a 'court history'. Modern interpreters normally avoid the designation
'Succession Narrative' (e.g., Gunn, *Story of King David*; J.P. Fokkelman, *Narrative
Art and Poetry in the Books of Samuel*. I. *King David* [Assen: Van Gorcum, 1981];
Van Seters, *In Search of History*).

7.   Gunn, *The Story of King David*, p. 23; followed by Perdue, '"Is There
Anyone Left?"', p. 82; Brueggemann, *David's Truth*, p. 121.

from the Solomonic period[8] or it could be much later;[9] it could be based upon historical facts, but it could also be regarded as an almost purely *literary* work. And this in fact is more or less the view of Gunn,[10] and on this point I shall follow him. In any case, this subject is not very controversial; probably few would deny that there might be a good deal of historical information in the Succession Narrative (the problem being only how to specify it)—and nobody will deny that the Succession Narrative is primarily a literary work.[11]

8.   According to L. Rost, *Die Überlieferung von der Thronnachfolge Davids* (Stuttgart: Kohlhammer, 1926); many follow him (e.g., G. von Rad, 'Der Anfang der Geschichtsschreibung im alten Israel' [1944], repr. in *Gesammelte Studien zum Alten Testaments* [Munich: Chr. Kaiser Verlag, 1958], pp. 148-88; Whybray, 'Succession Narrative'—the redaction critics—and everyone else who sees in the Succession Narrative a piece of political propaganda).

9.   Most radically Van Seters (*In Search of History*), who regards the Succession Narrative as a post-deuteronomic work.

10.   On the other hand, for Rost (*Die Überlieferung*), as for von Rad ('Anfang'), there was no conflict between the Succession Narrative as a historical document and as a work of literary art. Whybray (*Succession Narrative*) stressed the literary side more than the historical, but ended up with a hypothesis of the Succession Narrative as a work of political propaganda (see the criticism in Gunn, *Story of King David*, p. 21). In order to avoid a too narrow focus on the text as historical information and/or as biased, which inevitably would bar access to the text's stylistic and thematic qualities, Gunn insisted on the text as a narrative in its own right. Gunn, however, avoided the term 'literary' and preferred 'work of art' because he wanted also to emphasize the significance of the traditions—oral or otherwise—which had functioned as the material for the present literary work (Gunn, *Story of King David*; on this last specific point Gunn is—from different viewpoints—criticized by Fokkelman [*Narrative Art*, p. 11] and Van Seters [*In Search of History*, p. 287]). Nevertheless, Gunn is (correctly) counted among those who, in the footsteps of Whybray, invigorated the literary investigations of the Succession Narrative (see Hagan, 'Deception', p. 301; Clines, 'Story and Poem', p. 120). A strictly literary point of view—with the resulting overestimation of the sacrosanct 'work of art'—is taken by, e.g., Fokkelman, *Narrative Art*. Of course, redaction criticism (Flanagan, 'Court History'; E. Würthwein, *Die Erzählung von der Thronfolge Davids* [Zürich: Theologischer Verlag, 1974]; F. Langlamet, 'Pour ou contre Salomon? La rédaction prosalomonienne de I Rois, I–II', *RB* 83 [1976], pp. 321-79, 481-528; T. Veijola, *Die Ewige Dynastie: David und die Entstehung seiner Dynastie nach der deuterono-mistischen Darstellung* [Helsinki: Suomalainen Tiedeakatemia, 1975]) also insists on the text's literariness—but from a totally different perspective, namely in order to stress the text's heterogeneity, not its basic homogeneity.

11.   A somewhat modified 'literary approach' (in the sense that it takes the

In fact, the Succession Narrative has always been praised for its out-standing *literary qualities*.[12] Now, since I am going to investigate some details in the Succession Narrative from the 'Girardian' point of view that I have just presented, it is perhaps interesting to mention that, according to Girard,[13] the knowledge of the mimetic character of desire and the mimetic rivalry to which mimetic desire leads is to be found not in academic philosophy or in psychology, but first and foremost in the great European *literature*. So in advance one is tempted to ask whether the most obvious literary part of the Old Testament may not deal with the same matters—that is, with mimetic desire, mimetic rivalry and so on.

Gunn proposed two major patterns in the Succession Narrative. First, 'it is possible to describe the story as one of accession, rebellion and succession. It is a story about David as king.' Secondly, the 'pattern of intrigue, sex and violence in the Bathsheba episode is played out at length in the subsequent story within David's own family'.[14] This is quite true. But what is the role of the story of Sheba's rebellion in 2 Samuel 20? It fits only the first of Gunn's two patterns as an instance of 'rebellion', and in this respect it is very different from Absalom's rebellion as well as from Adonijah's *coup d'état*; and it does not seem to have any part in Gunn's second pattern—it does not take place within David's family, and it has nothing to do with sex.[15] I shall presently

connection between text and 'history' seriously, even if it is by stressing the text's function not as historical report, but as interpretation) is found in J. Rosenberg, *King and Kin*.

12. Strongly emphasized by Rost (*Die Überlieferung*) and (with perfect justice) repeated by everybody else.

13. See e.g. R. Girard, *'To Double Business Bound'* (Baltimore: Johns Hopkins University Press, 1978), p. 89; cf. *idem*, *A Theater of Envy: William Shakespeare* (Oxford: Oxford University Press, 1991), p. 18.

14. Gunn, *Story of King David*, p. 89.

15. 2 Sam. 20 (vv. 2b-3 are probably redactional additions) has caused problems for exegetes. It is inevitably regarded as belonging to the sub-unit, chs. 13–20 (e.g. Flanagan, 'Court History'; C. Conroy, *Absalom! Absalom! Narrative and Language in 2 Sam. 13–20* [AnBib, 81; Rome: Pontifical Biblical Institute, 1978]). S. Bar-Efrat (*Narrative Art in the Bible* [Bible and Literature Series, 17; Sheffield: Almond Press, 1989], pp. 136-37) sees a 'block of narratives' in 2 Sam. 11–20, namely a story that 'begins with David's sin of adultery with Batsheba'; but also in this *narratively* defined and delimited textual unity there is no real room for the Sheba story (except for the curious coincidence that a 'daughter of Sheba' opens the unity and a 'Sheba' closes it). But for what reason then is ch. 20 always regarded as so closely connected with the preceding chapters—if we for methodological reasons

return to the question of the actual role of sex in the overall structure of the Succession Narrative; for the moment I propose a hypothetical reformulation of Gunn's three points: the Succession Narrative is primarily about *desire* (rather than 'sex'), *rivalry* (rather than 'intrigue') and *collective violence* (rather than merely 'violence'). If this proposal is to any extent to the point, then it follows that a 'Girardian' point of view on the Succession Narrative should be of some interest. For these three themes are, of course, the three basic themes of Girard's work.[16]

2.1. *Desire and Rivalry in the Succession Narrative*
Undoubtedly, an overall concern of the Succession Narrative is the phenomenon of *desire*. As a matter of fact, in the episodes that deal with David and his family, we shall find nothing but desire. And—what is even more important—the desire is in each and every instance pictured in the shape of *triangles*.

a. In the story of David and Bathsheba (2 Sam. 11–12), the triangle consists of David (the subject of desire), Bathsheba (the object of desire) and Uriah (the 'obstacle', the rightful possessor of the desired object). Uriah is the obstacle for the desire of David and so desire leads to rivalry and violence; David gets Uriah killed in a battle during the siege of Ammonite Rabbah.

discard the hypothesis of a *historical* connection between Absalom's and Sheba's rebellions—except for the purely negative fact that this chapter too is *not* about Solomon (that is, it does not belong to the 'succession theme' *stricto sensu*)? Certainly there are strong similarities in style and worldview between this chapter and the preceding ones; on the other hand the same thing could be said about its relations to 1 Kgs 1–2 or to 2 Sam. 3–4 (or even to 1 Kgs 12). The 'Sheba theme' (vv. 1-2a, 14-22, which is easily extracted from the rest of the chapter as an independent literary unit) does not have closer connections to the Absalom story than to any other part of the Succession Narrative (cf. H.J. Stoebe's review of Fokkelman, *Narrative Art*, in *TLZ* 109 [1984], col. 108). An equally good case could probably be made for its close *thematic* connections with 2 Sam. 21 and 24.

16. It should be mentioned that many of the observations on the Succession Narrative in what follows are not at all 'original'; on the contrary, they can be found many times in the exegetical literature. The point is not just to make the observations but to insist on their thematic (not necessarily their literary) coherence. By doing so I shall take the consequences of some observations made in the process of research especially by Gunn (the above-mentioned characterization of the themes of the Succession Narrative), by B.O. Long ('A Darkness between Brothers: Solomon and Adonijah', *JSOT* 19 [1981], pp. 79-91) and by Ackerman ('Knowing God and Evil').

b. In the second sequence of the Succession Narrative, the story of Amnon and Tamar, the triangle consists of Amnon (the subject of desire), Tamar (the object) and Tamar's brother Absalom. Once again desire leads to rivalry and violence. First, Amnon has to take Tamar by force, and, secondly, after a couple of years of silent resentment Absalom takes vengeance and kills Amnon.

In these two instances desire is undoubtedly *sexual*—so perhaps desire in the Succession Narrative is basically sexual, after all? Do we in the Succession Narrative meet a preoccupation with sex fitting our Freudian twentieth century, and does the Succession Narrative in this way suggest that behind all desire and rivalry, behind all violence and murder, sexual desire is to be found? We are for a moment tempted to ask: is sexuality the hidden reality behind everything, according to the Succession Narrative?[17]

The sexual desire is in these narratives not in the least 'hidden', nor is it in any way 'suppressed'. So we are probably not in the world of Freud, at least. This impression is corroborated by the two final sequences taking place within David's family.

c. In the story of Absalom's rebellion, desire once again is triangular. Absalom is the desiring subject; kingship is the object of his desire, and the third pole of the triangle is David himself. The wish to be the king is ultimately the wish to be what David already is; so David is a perfect example of a 'model' in the 'Girardian' sense. But Absalom certainly cannot be what he desires to be without removing his own model; the model becomes the *obstacle*, the admirer becomes the *rival*. Accordingly, Absalom does everything that David did himself. Absalom establishes himself as the just judge that David is said to be in the immediately preceding chapter;[18] he goes to Hebron and becomes king there, as David did;[19] with an army he goes to Jerusalem and takes the

---

17. As a proposal for thematic unity in the Succession Narrative, J. Blenkinsopp ('Theme and Motif in the Succession History [2 Sam. xi 2ff] and the Yahwist Corpus', in J.A. Emerton *et al.* [eds.], *Congress Volume, Geneva 1965* (VTSup, 15; Leiden: Brill, 1966], pp. 47-48) suggested exactly this. As we saw, Gunn is in the same line.

18. 2 Sam. 15.2-6; cf. 14.1-22.

19. 2 Sam. 15.7-12; cf. 2.1-4; Fokkelman (*Narrative Art*, p. 171) sees the parallel.

city, as David did;[20] ultimately he enters David's harem and lies with his father's concubines. So far, Absalom is David's *double*. The conflict between Absalom and David is caused not by the differences between the two fighting parties, but by the *similarities*. They are identical because they want the same object and therefore act identically.

In Absalom's case, desire is precisely non-sexual; on the surface it is rather desire for *power*—so perhaps here the Succession Narrative has shifted from Freud to Nietzsche? The description of Absalom's desire, however, does not indicate that in Absalom there lies hidden a deep-rooted desire for *power*. What Absalom actually does is to imitate his father. The text does not tell us Absalom's motives for his rebellion. We could of course look for a historical explanation: Absalom as leader of a certain political faction or the like. But on the literary level of the narrative we are left to ponder. Freudians would of course make an easy case with Absalom's rebellion against his own father.[21] Nietzschians would have no difficulty in ascribing a fundamental desire for power to the all-too-human subject of Absalom.[22] However, the rationale of both these explanations is based on modern theories, even if they have become vulgarized to the extent that their status has shifted from theory to—more or less—unconscious ideology. Certainly, Girard's model is no less a modern theory than Freudianism and Nietzscheanism; moreover, it presents itself as a direct challenge exactly to Freudianism and Nietzscheanism. And it is no doubt true that the text does not say that Absalom's desire is 'mimetic' in the Girardian sense.

Yet the Girardian explanation has one big advantage. Even if the text

20. 2 Sam. 16.15; cf. 5.6-9. These verses do not belong to the Succession Narrative as a literary unity; but certainly David's capture of Jerusalem is presupposed by the Succession Narrative; see, e.g., Gunn, *Story of King David*, pp. 69-70; Van Seters, *In Search of History*, p. 285.

21. And in a way, Absalom is actually a better case than Oedipus as an antique emblem for the 'Oedipus complex'; for what Oedipus does due only to a misunderstanding, Absalom does openly.

22. To Fokkelman (*Narrative Art*) also there is no doubt about Absalom's motives; true to his individualistic-moralizing approach, Fokkelman has no problems in talking about Absalom's 'pride, his ambitions and his rebelliousness—in short, his ego... His bid for power' (p. 242); similarly, Amnon's desire is caused by his bad character: 'Amnon's act of violence reveals him as someone incapable of contact and as an uncouth egoist' (p. 108). It is the strong individualistic bias in Fokkelman's interpretation that makes it natural for him to consider the chains of events as originating in the characters' 'karma'.

or its author does not have any conscious idea of 'mimetism' as such, the text shows mimetism at work. And this is decisive. We do not need a pre-established idea of any ultimate reason for desire, such as infantile sexuality or a desire for power. The mere fact of Absalom's imitation is enough to explain his desire and thereby the rivalry in which he becomes involved. Therefore the Girardian model is more appropriate than any other in Absalom's case.

Since Absalom's model is a king, that is, a person invested with power, Absalom desires power. We see this fact clearly in the role that sexuality plays in the story. Sexuality is not absent from the story of Absalom's rebellion; Absalom indeed enters his father's harem. But certainly it was not sexual desire that made Absalom begin his rebellion in the first place. Absalom does not imitate his father because he wants to lie with his father's wives; he lies with his father's wives because he imitates his father. Moreover, Absalom does not enter the harem on his own initiative, but only after the advice of Ahithophel. The story of Absalom's rebellion is not 'about' sex, as the formulation of Gunn seemed to indicate, because sex is simply not important in it. The story is about mimetic desire, at least in the sense that it demonstrates the effects of mimetism. Eventually, what Absalom wants is to *be* David;[23] if the desire to imitate the mediator grows strong enough—if the mediator is within the reach of the subject—and if the mediator accepts the challenge from the imitator, conflict will inevitably be the result.

d. In the last of the four episodes of the Succession Narrative that take place within David's family, the struggle between Adonijah and Solomon for the succession to the throne of David once again is mimetic. First, Adonijah is presented as Absalom's double.[24] Adonijah is good looking—so was Absalom; Adonijah gathers a party around him— so did Absalom; Adonijah is illegally proclaimed king—as Absalom was. Solomon, for his part, is no less a *double*, namely of Adonijah; Solomon too gathers a party around him, Solomon too goes to a spring outside Jerusalem, Solomon too is proclaimed king.

Rivalry issues in violence. With his father's support, Solomon is the stronger party, and Adonijah gives up. Later, Adonijah asks Solomon for permission to marry Abishag the Shunammite. Solomon understands

---

23. This is what Girard (*Deceit, Desire*, p. 55) calls 'metaphysical desire'.

24. The parallels between Absalom and Adonijah are stressed, e.g., by Long, 'Darkness between Brothers', and Bar-Efrat, *Narrative Art*, pp. 87-88, 176.

this wish as a hidden threat against himself—as a part of a plan of Adonijah to build himself up once again with royal prerogatives; and Solomon reacts by ordering the death of Adonijah. Once again, Adonijah and Solomon are becoming too alike; coinciding desires produce personal similarities, which rouse rivalry; only a violent solution can re-establish the hierarchy and the differences which peace presupposes.

Also in this instance, sexuality is involved. But just as in the case of Absalom, here too sexuality is not the primary factor. Solomon interprets the desire of Adonijah not as sexual, but as mimetic; Adonijah wants to resemble David as much as possible—that is, to resemble the king as much as possible, and that means also to resemble Solomon, the actual king. Adonijah wants to go on with the play of the doubles, and the result is the violent termination of mimetic rivalry.

In the first two episodes, sexual desire was the starting point. At least on the surface of it, neither David's desire for Bathsheba nor Amnon's desire for Tamar was either mimetic or explained in any other way. David simply sees a very beautiful woman bathing and he desires her. This is not mimetic desire, but desire of the more basic sort, 'objective desire' (or 'physical desire', as Girard puts it), desire caused by the intuitively recognized 'value' of the object. The woman 'is' very beautiful, and so David desires her, and that's that. 'David's son Absalom had a beautiful sister named Tamar, and David's son Amnon fell in love with her'—so, what's the problem?[25] Nevertheless, there is a detail in the story of Amnon that suggests a more complicated reality. After the rape, Amnon does not want Tamar any more. He 'was filled with intense revulsion; his revulsion for her was stronger than the love he had felt; he said to her, "Get up and go"'. If it had been the girl's beauty that roused the desire of Amnon, then why does he not want her any more? Has her beauty disappeared? Of course not. So perhaps it was not her beauty after all that made Tamar so interesting for Amnon.[26] Here we

25. In his commentary on the Song of Songs (*Ruth: Das Hohelied* [BKAT, 13; Neukirchen–Vluyn: Neukirchener Verlag, 1981 (1965)], pp. 73-74), G. Gerlemann compares Amnon's love for Tamar with the love scenes in the Song of Songs; cf. Blenkinsopp, 'Theme and Motif', p. 54; P.K. McCarter, Jr, *2 Samuel* (AB, 9; Garden City, NY: Doubleday, 1984), pp. 320-22; and Ackerman, 'Knowing Good and Evil', p. 45.

26. Amnon's sudden shift from desire to repulsion has of course puzzled the interpreters. 'There is excess of love in the beginning, excess of hate at the end', says Gunn (*Story of King David*, p. 100); according to McCarter (*2 Samuel*, p. 324),

seem to be in the field of what D. de Rougemont described as the love for the *obstacle* of love.[27] And we are in the presence of what Girard has called the 'romantic lie'—the lie, namely, that desire is caused by the natural value of the object.[28] Only Girard asks more precisely about the obstacle of love. He is not satisfied with the mere concept of the obstacle as such, but proceeds with a very concrete question: not *what* is the obstacle, but *who* is the obstacle (that is: who is the mediator, who is the one to become a rival). And it should not be too difficult to find a

'A number of poets and psychologists could be cited on the readiness with which love—especially of the acute, grasping variety—turns to hatred and the intensity of the hatred thus produced. Accordingly, most commentators have thought it adequate to explain Amnon's sudden change of heart by reference to general truths of human behavior.' But the simple observation *that* great desire turns to deep repulsion is still no explanation of *why* it does so. To Fokkelman (*Narrative Art*), the text's rhetoric in itself serves as an explanation (p. 107); in accordance with his whole moralizing approach, to Fokkelman there is nothing so different as hate and love: 'Just as the hatred excludes the love...' (p. 113).

Girard has the one great advantage of actually offering a theoretically acceptable explanation. If desire is really mimetic (that is, 'metaphysical' in the sense that the true reason for desire is the desire to be what the model is), then the object in itself is only a pretext:

> Even in the most favorable cases, the physical qualities of the object play only a subordinate role. They can neither rouse metaphysical desire nor prolong it; moreover, the absence of physical enjoyment does not cause the disappointment in Stendhal's and Proust's hero when he finally possesses the object of his desire. The disappointment is entirely metaphysical. The subject discovers that possession of the object has not changed his being—the expected metamorphosis has not taken place. The greater the apparent 'virtue' of the object, the more terrible is the disappointment... (Girard, *Deceit, Desire*, p. 88).

Amnon's desire is not mimetic, at least not on the surface of it; yet, the paradox is that without a mimetic foundation for his desire his hatred against Tamar seems impossible to explain. I do not say that Girard's theory *therefore* is 'true'; what I imply is that *without* this explanation we are left with no explanation at all; and more or less well-turned circumlocutions like Gunn's, Fokkelman's and McCarter's can not serve as explanations. The paradox then is that even if Amnon's desire is not presented as mimetical in the text, all the surrounding texts point in no other direction; everything that belongs to the theoretical 'scenario' of Girard is present here: triangles, brothers in conflict, actions that are repetitions of each other, and—as we shall see—even the all-against-one scene (that is, ultimately the scapegoating scene).

27. D. de Rougemont, *Love in the Western World* (trans. M. Belgion; New York: Schocken Books, 1983), p. 37.

28. Girard, *Deceit, Desire*, pp. 2, 16, *et passim*.

candidate for an obstacle, a mediator, a rival, in Amnon's own brother. Mimetic rivals or not, Amnon and Absalom are certainly an example of the *'frères ennemis'*, the 'enemy brothers', no less than Adonijah and Solomon[29] (or Cain and Abel, Esau and Jacob, Joseph and his brothers[30]). But perhaps there may be more than one obstacle in this narrative? And one can equally well make a good case for mimetic desire also in the case of David's desire for Bathsheba. At least this possibility is hinted at by Joel Rosenberg in his *King and Kin*.[31]

However this may be, so far we can with some certainty conclude that the Succession Narrative is a *sort of investigation* into the phenomenon of desire, and that in all instances it shows how *desire leads to rivalry and to violence*. But do we find the second cornerstone in Girard's theory—that is, collective violence—in the Succession Narrative as well?

29. The significance of the 'mythical', 'archetypical' 'enemy brothers' motif for the Succession Narrative is stressed by Long ('A Darkness between Brothers'; cf. already Blenkinsopp, 'Theme and Motif', p. 51); Long notices that the series of violent acts 'after all, gives birth to an era of public stability (1 Kings 3–10)' (p. 89), a structure which he considers as a representation of 'a mythic pattern in the idiom of a historical narrative', the 'mythic pattern' being 'cosmos—chaos—cosmos' (p. 90), and its roots presumably going 'deeply into the ancient Near Eastern culture' (p. 91). A mythic pattern it certainly is, but it has absolutely nothing to do especially with 'ancient Near Eastern culture'; on the other hand, it has—of course—everything to do with religion (myth, ritual) as such; or, in other words, its level of abstraction belongs not to a historical, but to an anthropological discourse. So I agree deeply with Long in seeing more than mere fortuitous events in the Succession Narrative; I even agree on seeing a mythical pattern in them; but I differ from Long when it comes to the evaluation of this pattern. In itself the pattern is no explanation at all, but itself remains in need of an explanation. This explanation is—partly—given by the Succession Narrative itself, namely, in its demythologizing analysis of how conflicts come into being and how they can be solved.

30. The similarities between the Succession Narrative and the Yahwistic patriarchal narratives have been observed more than once; see, e.g., Blenkinsopp, 'Theme and Motif'; P. Gibert, *Bible, mythes et récits de commencements* (Paris: Seuil, 1986), pp. 118-23.

31. 'Uriah's position as one of David's *gibborim*...should cause us to modify somewhat our conventional picture of Uriah as a humble foot soldier... One whose dwelling is located so near "the king's house" is very likely an honored member of royal-military circles, one well enough known to the king's courtiers, if not to the king himself, that his naked wife seen from an adjacent rooftop would trigger astonishment of a rather precise nature' (Rosenberg, *King and Kin*, p. 129). I propose to qualify the nature of this 'astonishment' as mimetic desire.

2.2. *Collective Violence in the Succession Narrative*

a. The rivalry between Absalom and David (in fact, David does not want
any rivalry, but he is forced into it) has ended up with two armies facing
each other. In the battle Absalom is isolated from his supporters, and as
he rides his mule, his head is caught in the boughs of a large oak where
he is left hanging between heaven and earth. Joab, David's general, drives
three javelins into Absalom's chest, after which ten young men surround
(סבב) Absalom and kill him. Absalom's body is flung into a large pit, and
a great cairn of stones is raised over the grave.

This scenario—the image of a king, or rather a false king—hanging
between heaven and earth and killed by a circle of warriors—has too
many resemblances to the image of King Pentheus in Euripides' *The
Bacchae*, and too many similarities with African sacred kings in (for
example) Frazer's *The Golden Bough*,[32] to escape the suspicion that it is
more than just another factual account of 'what really happened'.[33]

The closest parallel to Absalom's death in the Old Testament is probably the report of the death of Achan in Joshua 7. Here too we find the
great cairn of stones over the body of a victim of collective killing. And,
as in the case of Achan, where 'the Lord's anger was abated', the death
of Absalom really leads to a solution of the conflict. The reason for the
conflict is gone and the two armies can return, reconciled and in peace.
Absalom's death is a paradigmatic example of the blessings of collective
violence, in which general violence is done away with by its transformation into an 'all versus one' scene, that is, by the elimination of one
single victim.

The death of Absalom is not the only instance in the Succession
Narrative where this mechanism is shown at work. Just as in the case of
desire, where we found no less than four instances that showed how
important this theme was for the text, so we have more examples of the
same mechanism of collective violence. Repetition (or redundancy) is
emphasis, as we all know.

---

32. Cf. the Old Norse myth of King Vikar's death (*Gautreks Saga* 7); cf. Saxo
Grammaticus, *Gesta danorum*, VI.

33. The sacrificial connotations in the scene are also strongly underscored by
Ackerman ('Knowing Good and Evil', p. 50), who compares Absalom's death with
the sacrificial scene in Gen. 22; but the biblical and theological parallel obviously
hinders Ackerman from seeing that in the Absalom scene the 'sacrifice' is *also*
demythologized—as an 'all versus one' scene.

b. In 2 Samuel 20—the story of Sheba's rebellion—the conflict is solved in exactly the same way. Joab and his troop of soldiers, loyal to David, have pursued Sheba and his followers up to the town of Abel in the northernmost part of Israel. Joab besieges the town where Sheba has taken refuge. But then a woman among the people in the town of Abel intervenes; and she is especially qualified as a *wise* woman, an אשה חכמה. She proposes to hand over Sheba in order to save the rest of the town, a proposal that is immediately accepted both by the population of the town and by Joab outside. So Sheba is beheaded, his head is thrown over the wall to Joab, the enemy army disperses and the town is saved.[34]

c. A third example of the same mechanism is to be found in the advice that Ahithophel gives Absalom after David's flight from Jerusalem:

> Ahithophel said to Absalom, 'Let me pick twelve thousand men to go in pursuit of David tonight. If I overtake him when he is tired and dispirited I shall cut him off from his people and they will all scatter; I shall kill no one but the king. I shall bring all the people over to you as a bride is brought to her husband. It is only one man's life that you are seeking; the rest of the people will be unharmed.'

And Ahithophel is qualified, if not as a 'wise' man (with the root חכם), as the *counsellor* (יועץ), whose counsel (עצה) was considered almost divine in those days. It is an interesting detail that Ahithophel (2 Sam. 15.12) is described as a sacrificial priest; one may then conclude that he knows what he is talking about. This is a rather important point, in a way. For according to the Gospel of John, exactly this way of thinking was the reason for the death of Jesus:

> Caiaphas, who was the high priest that year, said, 'You have no grasp of the situation at all; you do not realize that it is more to your interest that

---

34. McCarter (*2 Samuel*, p. 431) clearly sees the connection between Absalom's fate and Sheba's death: 'the masquerading wise woman of chap. 14, who has been told by Joab what to do (14.33), persuades David to set aside the interests of the society as a whole in favor of the interest of one man, and the result is a rebellion. In the present chapter the wise woman of Abel, who tells Joab what to do, counsels the sacrifice of one man in the interests of the society as a whole, and the result is the prevention of a rebellion.' But by this (correct) argument, McCarter supports *nolens volens* the analysis here presented of these chapters: no doubt the word *sacrifice* about Sheba's death was no more than a slip of the pen, but... Obviously, of course, McCarter belongs to the great majority of exegetes who always find it appropriate to reprimand David severely for his momentary lack of interest in 'the society as a whole'.

one man should die for the people, than that the whole nation should be destroyed'.

However, if there were any reminiscences of sacred violence and human sacrifice in the killing of Absalom, these connotations have completely disappeared in the killing of Sheba and in Ahithophel's wise advice. In a way, what we have here is a good example of a cultural transformation from a sacred to a non-sacred or a profane understanding of what a sacrifice is. Leave out the sacred interpretation and you have an act of 'statesmanship' left, which catches up with Machiavellianism, when it is at its best—and which, by the way, is celebrated with astonishing frequency by Old Testament scholars. Very seldom, or never, have they anything critical to say about the death of Absalom or the death of Sheba; on the other hand, almost all scholars are extremely critical of the non-violent, non-combative David whom we see in these chapters.[35] We have certainly learned to master the hermeneutic of suspicion; today, it is child's play to suspect dark motives behind a seemingly pious person, and there is rarely a more comforting position than to be able to demonstrate one's lack of naive credulity towards the biblical text...by repeating what everybody else says.

d. Two more examples with traces of an 'all versus one' scene should be noticed. *The death of Uriah* (2 Sam. 11) is staged as an incident so that neither David nor any Israelite can be considered guilty. Yet they all are, of course. Placing the victim between the army and the enemies and then leaving him alone by moving back looks very much like an

---

35. The height of this practically unanimous tendency among exegetes is probably reached by Fokkelman (*Narrative Art*), who never gets tired of telling his reader what David should have done and what he ought not to have done; he even finds it appropriate to consider David a *masochist*, and he sees a sado-masochistic relationship between David and Joab (e.g. pp. 263, 278). On its own premises the legitimacy of this point of view can not be denied; it is pure Nietzscheanism and as such adequate for our time. An attitude according to which one lost sheep is more important than the ninety-nine others seems to be absolutely incomprehensible to modern exegesis. David's love for Amnon and for Absalom can be decoded as weakness, as masochism...everything seems acceptable except one thing—love. There certainly is an 'evangelic' thematic in these chapters, and even Fokkelman cannot help making associations with the Passion Narrative: 'If Joab is unsuccessful in getting another person to do his dirty work for ten pieces of silver...' (p. 245). Metaphors like this one are not only 'rhetorical'—they are indications of the common problematic in the Succession Narrative and the Passion Narrative.

inversion of more palpable forms of collective killing, such as stoning, pushing the victim from a cliff and the like.[36] In all cases the result is the same: the victim is killed and no single member of the persecuting group has caused the victim's death.[37] Similarly, *the death of Amnon* (2 Sam. 13) is arranged in such a way that Absalom himself is not personally guilty. He orders his servants to kill Amnon in the middle of a feast. The result is that Absalom is less guilty than if he himself had slain his brother, and the servants are less guilty than they would have been had they performed the misdeed totally on their own initiative (cf. the Nuremberg process!). Even the scenario of the murder of Amnon has some resemblances with a scapegoating scene: everyone is assembled, the drinking is heavy, the eldest brother—and probably the crown prince—is killed. We should not identify the scene with an archaic scapegoating process (as, for example, in the story of Achan's death); what we see here is a 'de-sacralized' version of the sacrificial death. It belongs to the same thematic group as the other instances of collective killings in the Succession Narrative with the same tendencies to a 'secularization' of the killing of a single victim; but the circumstances of that killing have not totally departed from their more sacral origins.

But do we have the other extreme on the axis of collective violence in the Succession Narrative as well?—that is, an instance of collective killing or victimization, which not only looks like a ritual killing of a sacred king, as in the instance of the death of Absalom, but which actually is an example of the killing of a sacred king? We do not have it in the Succession Narrative proper, according to the definition that scholars normally assign to this narrative. On the other hand, we may find it in the closest possible proximity to the Succession Narrative, namely in the two narratives about David which close 2 Samuel. At this point, we shall see a 'Greek connection' appear on the horizon.

3. *Plague, Hunger—and a Greek Connection*

a. In the story about David and the plague, 2 Samuel 24, we have a story that in many respects strangely resembles a very well known

36. Equivalent forms; cf. R. Hirzel, *Die Strafe der Steinigung* (Abhandlungen der Philologisch-Historischen Gesellschaft der Wissenschaften, 27; 1909 [repr. Darmstadt: Wissenschaftliche Buchgesellschaft, 1967]), pp. 223-66, especially pp. 227-28.

37. Fokkelman (*Narrative Art*) notices the parallel between Uriah's and Absalom's death—but not that they both are 'all-against-one' scenes.

episode from a very well known Greek myth: the central episode of the myth of Oedipus, the plague over Thebes.[38] In both narratives a king (David, Oedipus) commits a sin (by establishing a census, by unknowingly killing his father and marrying his mother); a public catastrophe breaks out (in both cases a plague); in both cases the king 'is guilty', and in both cases a prophet tells the king about the reason for the plague and the king willingly admits his guilt; in the Greek myth Oedipus is expelled from Thebes, whereas in the David story the death of David is avoided by establishing a sacrificial cult on the threshing-floor of Araunah; in both cases the plague disappears.

So, if we reduce the specific details of ch. 24, we have a very traditional scheme of *the sacred king*; probably the king's responsibility for public disasters is a little more than a mere consequence of the concept of a sacred king. Most scholars would like to have it that way—if they mention this 'dimension' at all—but in reality it could very well be the hidden truth of sacred kingship as such.[39]

In connection with the death of Absalom, we observed certain parallels to the death of Achan in Joshua 7; here, in the story of David and the plague, we are once again brought back to Achan. (1) Just as Achan willingly admits his guilt, David readily accepts that he is the guilty one; (2) just as Achan was not killed alone, but with his whole family, so David here proposes not only himself as a victim, but his whole family as well:

> When David saw the angel who was striking down the people, he said to the Lord, 'It is I who have sinned, I who committed the wrong; but these poor sheep, what have they done? Let your hand fall on me and on my family.'

b. This 'Oedipus pattern' probably belongs to a very widespread ideological scheme in the East-Mediterranean world—including Greece—as W. Burkert has demonstrated.[40] But perhaps this 'Greek connection' could be more intimate than that.[41] In the cycle of legends about Thebes

---

38. Girard, *Deceit, Desire*; see esp. pp. 29-30.

39. Girard, *Violence*, pp. 103-18 *et passim*; *Job, the Victim*, pp. 86-90.

40. W. Burkert, 'Transformations of the Scapegoat', in *Structure and History in Greek Mythology and Ritual* (Berkeley: University of California Press, 1979), pp. 59-77.

41. Another 'Greek connection'—from a purely literary point of view—is proposed by J. Van Seters, 'Love and Death in the Court History of David', in J.H. Marks and R.M. Good (eds.), *Love and Death in the Ancient Near East:*

to which the Oedipus myth belongs, the story of Oedipus was followed by two other stories. The one was about the 'enemy brothers', Eteocles and Polyneices, who fought for the throne of Thebes—a theme abundantly present in the Succession Narrative, especially in the concluding section about Adonijah and Solomon. But the other story was the story about Antigone. Although we do not have an 'Antigone story' in the Succession Narrative nor in its neighbourhood, we do have the very same motif of a woman guarding the body of her dead but unburied relative against the wild animals:

> But Polyneices, a dishonoured corse,
> (So by report the royal edict runs)
> No man may bury him or make lament—
> Must leave him tombless and unwept, a feast
> For kites to scent afar and swoop upon (*Antigone* 26-30).[42]

Compare 2 Samuel 21:

> Rizpah, daughter of Aiah took sackcloth and spread it out as a bed for herself on the rock, from the beginning of harvest until the rains came and fell from the heavens on the bodies. She kept the birds away from them by day and the wild beasts by night (v. 10).[43]

Certainly 2 Sam. 21.1-14 should be read 'in the context of religious primitivism'; Kapelrud was undoubtedly right in understanding the events narrated in this story in the light of a very ancient and very 'primitive' conception of sacral kingship.[44]

Essays in Honor of Marvin H. Pope (Guildford, CT: Four Quarters Publishing, 1987), pp. 121-24.

42. *Sophocles, with an English Translation by F. Storr*, I (LCL; London: Heinemann, 1981 [1912]).

43. The connection between Rizpah and Antigone has already been seen by others, e.g., by R. Kittel in his *Geschichte des Volkes Israels*, II (Stuttgart: Kohlhammer, 1925), p. 131.

44. A.S. Kapelrud, 'King and Fertility: A Discussion of 2 Sam. 21.1-14', in *God and His Friends in the Old Testament* (Oslo: Universitetsforlaget, 1979), pp. 41-50. In the whole complex of 2 Sam. 21–24, W. Brueggemann ('2 Samuel 21–24: An Appendix of Deconstruction?', *CBQ* 50 [1988], pp. 383-97) prefers to see a *criticism* of the sacral pretensions of the Davidic dynasty. This, however, he can only achieve by neglecting the inherent rationality of 2 Sam. 21 and 24; he recognizes this by admitting that his reading is 'not necessary exegetical' (p. 386). But it is not possible to do away with the most natural reading of a text by qualifying it as reading 'innocently' and 'in the context of religious primitivism'. Moreover, in this article

The relationship between the stories about the Saulides in 2 Samuel
21 and about David and the plague in 2 Samuel 24 and the Succession
Narrative proper is assured by the choice that David has to make in
ch. 24. As R.A. Carlson already saw in his *David, the Chosen King*, the
choice between three years of famine, three months of flight from the
enemy and three days of pestilence is a choice between the three
proverbial plagues of the prophets: sword, hunger and pestilence; and, as
Carlson rightly pointed out, the 'sword' referred back to the Succession
Narrative, the famine to ch. 21, and the pestilence to ch. 24 itself.[45] But
this series of plagues is interesting also for another reason. For these
three crises—war, famine and pestilence—are paradigmatic instances of
a situation where a society will turn to sacrifice in order to re-establish
the normal order—and that means: these three crises are typical for situations in which a society will turn to scapegoating. Here the sacred
king—so dear to the Scandinavian school—gains a new meaning. The
sacred king became very important in such crises; and these texts in
2 Samuel confirm this impression. For the pestilence is done away with
by King David's victimization of himself;[46] the famine is done away with

Brueggemann's conception of the role of kingship is much too narrow. There is, for
example, no reason to discard A.R. Johnson's understanding of the נר־ישראל in
21.17 (*Sacral Kingship in Ancient Israel* [Cardiff: University of Wales Press, 2nd
edn, 1967], pp. 1-2) by seeing it instead as an indication of the superfluity of the
king—as if the role of the king in Israel consisted solely in making war. It is difficult
to avoid the impression that behind Brueggemann's (and others') aversion to reading
a text like 2 Sam. 21.1-14 as 'primitive', as it in fact *is*, lies an apologetic and ideological interest which certainly would prefer that 'les israélites ne sont pas comme les
autres'.

45. R.A. Carlson, *David, the Chosen King* (Stockholm: Almqvist & Wiksell,
1964), pp. 197, 212.

46. In David's speeches in 2 Sam. 24.10, 17, Brueggemann ('2 Samuel 21–24',
p. 393) sees 'a staggering theological confession' and a 'dramatic move' which 'is
stunningly beyond our expectations...David here has forsaken that mode of royal
pretension and now speaks as a child of the covenant'. Brueggemann's view seems
to presuppose that the disasters in the Succession Narrative and in 2 Sam. 21 and 24
were due to David's overestimation of sacral kingship. This is not the fact; the
Bathsheba incident and Amnon's death had nothing to do with sacral kingship. More
important, however, is that David's confession is *not against the ideology of sacral
kingship, but totally in conformity with it*. What David is doing here is exactly what
he, as a sacral king, was supposed to do—namely, to take the responsibility for a
public disaster against which no rational means existed. This point is proved by the
basic structural identity with the Oedipus myth. Here, Brueggemann's (and many

by killing seven of Saul's sons and grandsons; and the war between Absalom and David is ended by the death of Absalom, the king's son, the false king—a death worthy of an African sacral king, and a death like the death of the sons and grandsons of a former king, and a false king: Saul.

4. *Conclusion*

Regardless of the opinion one may have on the literary unity of the Succession Narrative, it is a *thematic* unity—not in the sense of being totally without internal inconsistencies and so forth, but in the more significant sense of dealing with the same subject or the same circle of subjects, which are: desire (objective and mimetic), rivalry, collective violence and scapegoating. Redundance is insistence: the narrative repeats itself with variations; over and over again desire leads to rivalry and rivalry leads to violence—collective violence against a single person. Accordingly, the theme of the narrative is not only these sub-themes but rather their connection. In this way, the Succession Narrative is an anticipation of the Girardian anthropology, or, if you prefer, a contribution to the investigation of the relationship between mimetism, desire, rivalry and violence. And as such, besides being a work of art, the Succession Narrative performs a kind of 'phenomenological' investigation in the realm of human behaviour and reactions. The indisputable 'literary' or 'artistic' qualities of a text should not exclude the possibility that it could possess also real insights into human phenomena—not in spite of, but because of these same qualities.

Is it then by mere coincidence that what is probably the most outstanding example in the Old Testament of a text which deals with the thematic complex of desire, mimetism, rivalry and collective killing—so impressively investigated by Girard, the teacher of literature—also happens to be what is, according to a widespread scholarly consensus, the most 'literary' text in the whole Old Testament?

others') fundamental error is not to allow for the negative (one may say 'dark other') side of sacral kingship. Surely 2 Sam. 24 is not an instance of 'primitivism' pure and simple—this is assured by the fact that the events are seen through the eyes of David, the king; but the basic logic of the events, be they in accordance with the 'covenant', as Brueggemann puts it, or not, has not changed.

JSOT 59 (1993), pp. 25-36

JUDGING THE WISDOM OF SOLOMON:
THE TWO-WAY EFFECT OF INTERTEXTUALITY

Hugh S. Pyper

In his recent article in *JSOT* on 2 Kgs 6.24-33 (Lasine 1991), Stuart
Lasine raises the issue of the relationship between that story and the
Judgment of Solomon in 1 Kings 3 and how our reading of 2 Kings 6 is
illuminated by our knowledge of 1 Kings 3. This response to that article
is a tribute to the stimulation Lasine's work has been to me in trying to
understand the interaction of such stories and the effect of this on the
reader. In this case, however, I want to draw attention to an aspect of
the matter that I believe Lasine has not examined: the influence of
2 Kings 6 on our reading of 1 Kings 3.

Lasine's article follows a series in which he has explored the social
function of judgment stories such as 1 Kings 3 (Lasine 1987; 1989a;
1989b: 63-65), seeking to understand what the ancient reader might
have made of them. Essentially, he represents 1 Kings 3 as a comforting
story that reassures the ancient audience by illustrating 'how a human
being with "god-like" wisdom might be able to overcome human cognitive limitations' (1989a: 61). It serves a social function in allaying the
anxieties of ordinary people over their inability to tell who is or is not
deceiving them, an anxiety linked with the epistemological gap between
the divine and human, which Lasine sees as a fundamental postulate of
the Old Testament (1987: 252; 1989a: 73-74). Its readers are set in a
world where they are not only open to deceit and betrayal by their
inscrutable neighbours, but they are confronted by a God who has an
insuperable advantage over them in an infallible knowledge of human
nature. As Lasine reads it, what gives reassurance to the audience of the
story of Solomon's judgment is its demonstration of an inherent stability
of human nature. Solomon's ruse can only work if he can depend on

the compassionate self-sacrifice of a genuine mother's response as an unquestionable assumption in this otherwise baffling situation. Confronted by two women disputing the possession of a child, he threatens to kill the child, relying on the deep natural impulses of maternal feeling to impel the natural mother to renounce her claim if this will save the child's life. By telling such a story, the existence of these stable categories of relationship can be affirmed in times of social strain or transition.

If 1 Kings 3 is given this weight of epistemological and social significance, it is not surprising that 2 Kings 6 should have to be dealt with. Lasine quotes R.D. Nelson's view of it as a 'grim analogical contrast'[1] to 1 Kings 3 as he details the similarities between the two stories (1991: 41). In both, two mothers have each given birth. One of the children has died and the mothers are arguing over their claims to the living child.

In 1 Kings 3, however, the argument is between two women who both want possession of a living child. In 2 Kings 6, the argument is over the gruesome use of the child as an item of food. At first sight, this story appears to gainsay the comforting assumptions of 1 Kings 3. It turns upon the willingness of mothers to make a deal in which their children become mere meat. Not much compassion is shown here, and no compunction at all about the death of a child. Where is the natural response of the mothers now? The irony is compounded because this is not a situation where the social fabric has completely disintegrated. The woman still acknowledges the king as a figure to whom she can make an appeal to redress an injustice. She still has a sense of justice and of social cohesion; mothers may kill their children, but they should keep their promises, and the king, who can do nothing else, is still the figure to whom she can appeal to ensure that the words of her treacherous companion should be transformed into deeds.

Obviously, this presents problems for Lasine's reading of 1 Kings 3. As he himself puts it, 'even Solomon's god-like insight into human nature would be useless in the topsy-turvy world of this narrative' (1991: 29). The woman's behaviour 'turns upside down all expectations concerning maternal nature' (1991: 42). Does this not then undermine the assurance that Solomon's judgment was supposed to give? How

---

1. Nelson 1987: 189. In the previous sentence, Nelson describes the case as 'a *horrible parody* [my emphasis] of the sort of dispute between neighbours that kings often heard'.

much reliance can we place on a natural compassion that can be so
completely overturned?

Lasine does not address this question directly. Instead, he sees the
radical undermining of human nature as part of the *topos* of the 'world
turned upside down' as God wreaks retribution on the people for their
desertion of covenant promises. Deuteronomy 28 explicitly sees the
resort to infant cannibalization as a consequence of such disobedience,
especially in vv. 56-57. Lasine asks, however, whether the readers of
2 Kings 6 are being led to condemn the king and accept the justice of
God's punishment or whether they are being induced to question the
fairness of the divine response. Is there an implicit criticism of God's
lack of maternal compassion towards his children whom he has abandoned to this perverse parody of an ordered world? As Lasine points
out, such a reading seems to fly in the face of the generally accepted
characterization of the Deuteronomistic History as interpreting the history of the Northern Kingdom as a tale of just retribution for acts of
idolatry and betrayal. In turn, this may lead the reader to wonder just
what ideological stance is being propounded by this material (Lasine
1991: 47-49).

It is in acknowledging Lasine's sensitivity to these issues that I want to
draw attention to the aspect of the juxtaposition of these two judgment
stories that Lasine does not treat. This story in 2 Kings 6 seems to me to
entice the reader to go back and reappraise the story of Solomon's
judgment, and in particular the figure of Solomon. Lasine sees that
'readers are indeed invited to compare the two monarchs' (1991: 41),
but neither he nor the others who have looked at this story seem to
have seen this as an invitation to do anything more than measure the
king in 2 Kings 6 by the unimpeachable standards of Solomon, the all-
wise judge of 1 Kings 3.[2]

As I have recently argued in the case of two other biblical stories that
seem to stand in a similar sort of parodic relationship to one another
(Pyper 1993),[3] the existence of the parody inevitably throws doubt over

---

2.   See here for example La Barbera 1984, where the case is specifically argued
that the king in 2 Kings 6 is being held up to ridicule in comparison to Solomon:
'Whereas Solomon in his wisdom brings justice and restores a child to its mother,
the king of Israel here can do nothing but tear his garments, revealing underneath the
sack-cloth of distress or repentance, conditions traceable to unwise behavior' (1984:
646). As we shall see, the question is: whose unwise behaviour?

3.   In this paper I sought to demonstrate the way in which the story of David's

the 'original' story. As John Miles (1990) puts it, parody shows up the conventions that underlie a text and, in the case of a satirical or ironic parody, the target is not so much the original text itself as the audience that takes its conventions at face value.

Lasine himself is well aware of the illumination that can come from the juxtaposition of analogous stories. In his own investigation of Judges 19 (Lasine 1984a), he argues that for the present reader of the text an awareness of the analogous aspects of Genesis 19 and Judges 19 is very important in bringing the reader to recognize that the kingless world of Judges is itself 'inverted'. The callous actions of the old man in Judges 19 who thrusts out the Levite's concubine to be raped and murdered are, so to speak, a parody of the actions of Lot in Genesis 19 in response to the threats made against his guests by the men of Sodom. Where I would part company with him is in his view that this is an instance of what he calls 'one-sided literary dependence'. He explains this concept as follows:

> By literary dependence I mean that Judges 19 presupposes the reader's awareness of Genesis 19 in its present form, and depends on that aware-ness to be properly understood. The dependence is one-sided because a reader can fully understand the story of Lot's hospitality in Sodom with-out knowing the story of the Levite's concubine, whereas the events described in Judges 19 must be viewed together with Genesis 19 for the intended contrast between the two situations to make the reader aware of the topsy-turvy nature of the 'hospitality' in Gibeah (Lasine 1984a: 38-39).

The question this prompts me to ask is how Lasine here can be so confident that the reader 'fully understands' the Genesis passage with-out reference to Judges. His whole case in his reading of Judges 19 rests on the contrast he makes between Lot's 'hospitality' in Genesis 19 in offering his virgin daughters to save his guests' honour, and the inhospi-tality of the old man of Judges 19 who includes the Levite's own

encounter with the woman of Teqoa in 2 Sam. 14 is a parodic counterpart to his encounter with Nathan in 2 Sam. 12, which throws doubt on the sincerity of David's repentance and on the status of the prophet himself. In addition, between the two stories, a hermeneutical model is at the same time proposed and undermined, leading to a questioning of the reader's own competence and status. I acknowledge in this the insightfulness of Lasine's paper on Nathan's parable (Lasine 1984b), but here again, the destabilization of a text by its parodic counterpart is an aspect that he does not comment upon. These issues are further explored in my recent book, *David as Reader* (Pyper 1996).

concubine in the deal. Is there no sense in which this story in Judges serves to reinforce what one would hope was a fairly obvious message in the Genesis material itself: that there is something dishonourable—to say the least—in men sheltering behind women in this way, Lot included?[4]

It is obvious that Lasine's claim that the dependence between the two stories is unidirectional is not based on the chronological order of the stories, or even the order of sequential reading. 1 Samuel 11 stands in a very different relation to Judges in this regard, and he argues that Judg. 19.29 'presupposes the reader's awareness of the incident recorded in the given text of Samuel, and requires that awareness in order to be fully appreciated' (1984a: 41). So a story that would be read later can have a retroactive effect.[5] Though this time Lasine is not explicit in describing the dependence as one-sided, he again refers only to one direction of influence. Is there not a case here, too, for arguing that the increase in understanding operates in both directions? Surely the savagery of the dismemberment of the concubine throws a shadow over Saul's analogous action in summoning the people with the fragments of his oxen, especially in view of his association with Gibeah and Benjamin, the scene of the outrages of the last chapters of Judges.

The crucial issue seems to be how we are to make judgments as to what constitutes 'full appreciation' of a text. Part of the excitement of reading these texts, and the reason why three millennia after their composition they are still provoking the arguments of commentators, is that

---

4.   Lasine's disregard of the treatment of the women in this story is notable, though he is rightly concerned to understand it within what can be gleaned of the social mores of the times. That the biblical narrator is not quite so unconcerned may be seen in the subsequent behaviour of these daughters towards the father who offered them to the mob. Is Lot really any more a paragon of hospitality in these texts than of any other virtue?

5.   It is, I hope, clear that by phrasing the matter in this way I am placing no weight on any putative order of composition of the texts. I write as a present-day reader of a canonized text in book form. Lasine also in the article in question is concerned with the 'reader of the Old Testament in its present form' (1984a: 37). This contrasts with his discussion of the judgment stories where he is concerned with the ancient reader. While I do not doubt the interest or the plausibility of his results, I find it challenge enough to read the texts from my own standpoint. The point is that if Lasine's ascription of dependence here is valid in his own terms, there is no *a priori* reason to exclude the possibility of such a retroactive dependence of 1 Kgs 3 on 2 Kgs 6 in the same terms.

we can never be assured of having fully appreciated them. Indeed it is an illusion to suppose that any text can be fully appreciated, let alone one possessing the allusive complexity common among texts of the Old Testament. Any text that one could fully appreciate would be unlikely to be worth the effort. On that basis alone one would be justified in looking at 1 Kings 3 in the light of the analogue in 2 Kings 6. When in addition the suspicion of a parodic intent behind a text arises, we may feel that this is as clear an invitation as the text can give us to reappraise the text or genre that is being highlighted.

In the remainder of this paper I propose to read 1 Kings 3 in the light of 2 Kings 6 and at least make a case that the illumination is not all one way. My basic contention will be that in doing so, we are led to see that there is more consistency to the ideology of the final form of the books of Kings than Lasine seems to allow. I will argue that along with its depiction of the glory of the Solomonic empire, the text is always aware of the way in which that empire contains the seeds of its own destruction. Ultimately, the disasters that lead to the destruction of the monarchy are the product of its own internal dynamics as much as they are the result of God's vengeance or the activities of Israel's political enemies. The social and political disaster of 2 Kings 6 has its roots in the inevitable negative aspects of monarchic rule. The very assumptions underlying Solomon's judgment lead to the situation that reduces a king of Israel to tearing his garments in despair when confronted with the perversion of social values.

The Judgment of Solomon is presented to us by the narrator in 1 Kgs 3.28 as the proof, in the eyes of Israel at any rate, of his wisdom and his fitness to judge. It follows on from the representation of God's gift of wisdom to him and the highest expressions of God's favour. In this context, it may seem perverse to argue that there is a negative side to this portrayal.[6] It may, however, be significant that this high praise of Solomon is represented as a dream. Whatever the historical facts, the text presents this information in such a way that its only possible source is Solomon himself. We should at least bear in mind the strictures against taking a person's own testimony as the final word. All the reader

---

6. For a persuasive advocate of such an evalutation, see Eslinger (1989: especially pp. 129-49). The overall thrust of his argument supports my thesis of the ambivalent attitude to wisdom and to the monarchy in these texts. His reading of 1 Kings 3 has many points in common with my analysis, although the wider resonances with 2 Kings 6 are not part of his discussion.

actually knows is that Solomon has reported that the LORD has granted
him wisdom and high favour. We might observe also that the LORD
appears to him at Gibeon, just after he has sacrificed a thousand burnt
offerings at the chief high place in Israel (1 Kgs 3.4-5). Is it not odd that
the previous verse has explicitly stated that it was his propensity for
sacrificing at high places that led to Solomon falling short of David's
statutes? Just what is the status of this dream? In any case, there is a
disquieting echo of the promise the serpent made to Eve in Gen. 3.5.
That story certainly puts a question mark over the appropriateness of
desiring wisdom, the very desire that led Eve to eat the fruit.[7]

Of course, the word 'wise' has been applied to Solomon before this.
His father refers to his wisdom twice in the charges he gives him as he
prepares to 'rest with his fathers' (1 Kgs 2.6, 9). This is the kind of
wisdom that will let him know what to do to Joab and to Shimei. In this
scene, of course, David is getting as near to contradicting his own previous oath to Shimei and to signing his right hand man's death warrant as
he can without explicitly stating it. Solomon's wisdom is the kind of
statecraft that allows a king to renege on promises without actually
exposing himself to the charge of breaking his word; a useful gift, perhaps, but dangerous and not particularly admirable.[8]

Having raised some of these general questions, let us turn to the
specific case of the two prostitutes. The first question might be: what are
two prostitutes doing in the court of Israel's wisest king? Quite apart
from the social stigma of prostitution, which is difficult to gauge in the
biblical text, there is a standard connection between prostitution and the
kind of dubiously orthodox setting in which the king has just been
having his dream. There has been some disagreement among commentators about the significance of the status of these women. It can be seen
as affirmation of the impartiality of Solomonic justice that was available
to the lowest of the low (De Vries 1985: 61). It could also be seen as a
narratological necessity (Deurloo 1989: 20). In what other setting than a

---

7.   I am aware that many modern commentators seek to show that this Genesis
story is in itself not painting as negative a picture of Eve's actions as some traditional
readings would have it. Be that as it may, the consequences of her actions are rather
drastic, leading to the expulsion from Eden. We might then speculate on the relationship between Solomon's model of kingship and the eventual expulsion of the people
from the land.

8.   See here Rosenberg's description of this wisdom as the 'bad faith that sus-
tains all statecraft of a "cumbersome people"' (1986: 186).

brothel could such an unfortunate incident happen without witnesses? Where else would two mothers be sleeping together without a man around? Though both of these arguments have some force, the fact remains that the one act of justice recorded of the king involves these prostitutes. At the presumed peak of Israel's fortunes under the monarchy, such women are accorded some degree of royal indulgence. When we go on to consider the strictures found elsewhere in the text against Solomon's own interest in women, and foreign women at that,[9] a class that much biblical material seems to regard as practically synonymous with idolatry, the reader may begin to suspect that it is not purely accidental, nor entirely in Solomon's favour, that he is given such a setting in which to exercise his god-given wisdom.

If the picture of Solomon's god-given wisdom is not quite so straightforward, neither is the contrast between the women in 1 Kings 3 and the women of 2 Kings 6. Both stories contain a woman who shows compassionate instincts and a woman who seems shamelessly devoid of them. The woman who opts for the child to be divided in1 Kings 3 may thereby show herself not to be its mother, but the case relies on her response as much as it does on the natural mother's. Why did both women not protest to the king about the killing of an innocent child by renouncing their claims? Of course, this would have scuppered Solomon's ploy. Solomon seemingly can depend just as reliably on the fact that a woman will be quite prepared to see someone else's child killed as he can on the fact that a mother will sacrifice her own desires to ensure her child's survival. What does this say about human nature and social values in Solomon's kingdom?

In 1 Kings 3, the polarization of attitudes is clear enough as we hear the two contradictory voices. The voice of maternal compassion is not heard explicitly in 2 Kings 6, but the problem at issue between the two cannibal mothers has arisen because one of them has refused to give up her son. The woman who complains to the king has not shown any compunction, but the second woman, though capable both of suggesting the deed to the other and of joining her in the meal, has, when it has come to the point, hidden her own son. Strictly speaking, of course, we are not told whether she has hidden the living boy to protect him, or

---

9. Is it a coincidence that 1 Kgs 3 begins with the information that Solomon has concluded a political marriage with the daughter of Pharaoh, especially in view of the mileage made of that fact in 1 Kgs 11? She is named first among the horde of foreign women who lead him astray into building new high places.

whether she has hidden the corpse so that she can have it all to herself. One possible clue may be the reciprocal use of the formula 'give up your son' by the two women, which would perhaps indicate that the children were either both alive or both dead when they were to be handed over. The former seems more likely—given the choice, a freshly killed child must have advantages over eating a child that has died of who knows what disease, in a land without refrigeration.

If this is so, maternal instincts are not completely abolished in 2 Kings 6 and there is little doubt that human nature has a pretty dark and uncaring aspect in 1 Kings 3. Perhaps there has not been such a revolutionary change as all that. Rather, circumstances have conspired to bring out the different aspects of a common but complex human nature.

The difference in the responses of the two kings when they are confronted with the respective complainants may also bear scrutiny. Solomon's willingness to arbitrate between the two prostitutes entails acceptance of the callousness of the woman who is not the mother as a natural fact on which he can depend. In this regard, the king of Israel in 2 Kings 6 may actually come out better than Solomon. He acknowledges his own impotence, and faced with the inhumanity of the woman who pleads with him he tears his garments, revealing the fact that he is wearing the clothing of a penitent. Though this may have a comic aspect, it is also something that it is hard to imagine Solomon ever doing, whatever the circumstances. It can scarcely be claimed that Solomon had nothing to repent over.

In addition, amid all the cares and worries of his situation, he stops to listen to the pleas of an importunate woman, and seems prepared to take his time in reaching what conclusion he can until he hears the abhorrent tale she has to tell. In contrast to this, Solomon's encounter with the prostitutes looks like a rather stage-managed virtuoso exercise, in which the feelings of the mother and the life of the child become legitimate material for the king to use in the demonstration of his superiority. He is capable of using a ruse to differentiate between the women, but the cleverness of this, rather than the establishment of justice, is the focus of the story. We look in vain for the ruling on what the due punishment of the callousness of the false claimant should be. It is at least arguable that the criticism is not all one-sided as we look at these two stories.[10]

10. Another line of argument, for which there is not enough space to pursue here fully, is also opened up by Lasine himself when he looks at the story of David's three contradictory judgments between Mephibosheth and Ziba (Lasine 1989b).

Rather than seeing the contrast between the situations of these two kings as the picture of a world turned upside down, I see it more in line with the kind of picture that García-Treto paints in his recent article (1990) on 2 Kings 9 and 10, which he treats in terms of Bakhtin's concept of carnivalization. He prefaces this paper with this epigraph:

> 'I saw a topsy-turvy world', he replied, 'the upper [*class*] underneath and the lower on top'.
> 'My son', he observed, 'you saw a clear world' [*Pes.* 50a] (1990: 47).

García-Treto writes of the fall of the house of Ahab as a critique, not just of Israel and the Samaritan establishment, but of all religious and political institutions. Out of the chaos of their collapse, however, there are seeds of new hope and revived fortunes.

In the same way, the world of 2 Kings 6 may actually be Solomon's world with the skin off, so to speak, a world where the assumptions and pretensions of kings are shown up for what they are—a world where Solomon's unbending harshness, epitomized in his willingness to divide the child, has led to the division of his kingdom under his son Rehoboam, whose weak attempts at bullying tactics are a parody in themselves of his father's strength. It is a world, moreover, where the dalliance with foreign women and with alien gods, which Solomon also initiated, has led both to the political weakness and the religious crisis that issue in the destruction of the kingdom. Far from being a crazy reversal of the normality of Solomon's world, it is the 'clear world', the one where the real impulses of human conduct are revealed. In that revelation, it indicts the world of Solomon—that depends on 'wisdom' for its continuance—as unreal and inadequate.

Yet it is also a world where some order, some decency survive, though hopelessly beleaguered. It is a world where a mother *in extremis* may still hide her son rather than eat him, and where a king *in extremis* can be horrified and wear garments of repentance, while railing against

---

David's ultimate solution of dividing the property is often compared to Solomon's, especially since Mephibosheth then renounces his claim to a share in a way not totally dissimilar to the response of the genuine mother. Lasine makes the point that this so-called 'Solomonic' judgment of David is in the end a demonstration of his inability to judge fairly or consistently on this matter, which Lasine contrasts with the brilliance of Solomon's verdict (1989b: 63). Once again, however, the comparison is one-sided. When we see Solomon adopt the same strategy in 1 Kgs 3, might this not give us pause and lead us to wonder whether he may not be following his father's example all too closely?

the agent of a God who has allowed such chaos to come about.

On faithfulness in such decency will depend in the end the survival of those in exile. Just as the mother who is prepared to give up her son in the end has him restored to her, so God is prepared to give up his people and let them be taken into exile, rather than subject them to the destruction they have brought on themselves. The people must indeed also be willing to give up their land and their temple, together with their political and religious institutions, and observe instead the remnants of human decency that lead to compassion for all God's children, not just one's own family, and this will preserve them as a community in exile, with the hope of a return to a renewed kingdom.

By allowing 2 Kings 6 to inform our reading of 1 Kings 3, then, we may be able to understand more fully the subtlety of the portrayal of the monarchy in these texts, not as something either bad or good, but as something that failed as all human enterprise must fail. In that failure, the writers of Kings see revealed both the glory and the shame of human nature, and they seek to indicate the way in which God may use such failure to deepen Israel's understanding of the conditions for its continued existence as a community.

BIBLIOGRAPHY

Deurloo, K.A.
    1989   'The King's Wisdom in Judgment: Narration as Example (1 Kings 3)', *OTS* 25: 11-21.
De Vries, S.J.
    1985   *1 Kings* (WBC; Waco, TX: Word Books).
Eslinger, L.
    1989   *Into the Hands of the Living God* (JSOTSup, 84; Bible and Literature Series, 24; Sheffield: Almond Press).
García-Treto, F.O.
    1990   'The Fall of the House: A Carnivalesque Reading of 2 Kings 9 and 10', *JSOT* 46: 47-65.
La Barbera, R.
    1984   'The Man of War and the Man of God: Social Satire in 2 Kings 6.8–7.20', *CBQ* 46: 637-51.
Lasine, S.
    1984a   'Guest and Host in Judges 19: Lot's Hospitality in an Inverted World', *JSOT* 29: 37-59.
    1984b   'Melodrama as Parable: The Story of the Poor Man's Ewe-Lamb and the Unmasking of David's Topsy-Turvy Emotions', *HAR* 8: 101-24.

1987   'Solomon, Daniel and the Detective Story: The Social Functions of a
Literary Genre', *HAR* 11: 247-67.

1989a   'The Riddle of Solomon's Judgment and the Riddle of Human Nature
in the Hebrew Bible', *JSOT* 45: 61-86.

1989b   'Judicial Narratives and the Ethics of Reading: The Reader as Judge of
the Dispute between Mephibosheth and Ziba', *Hebrew Studies* 30: 49-
69.

1991   'Jehoram and the Cannibal Mothers (2 Kings 6.24-33): Solomon's
Judgment in an Inverted World', *JSOT* 50: 27-53.

Miles, J.R.

1990   'Laughing at the Bible: Jonah as Parody', in Y.T. Radday and
A. Brenner, *On Humour and the Comic in the Hebrew Bible*
(JSOTSup, 92: Sheffield: JSOT Press): 204-15.

Nelson, R.D.

1987   *First and Second Kings* (Interpretation; Atlanta: John Knox).

Pyper, H.S.

1993   'The Enticement to Re-read: Repetition as Parody in 2 Samuel',
Biblical Interpretation 1: 153-66.

1996   *David as Reader: 2 Samuel 12:1-15 and the Poetics of Fatherhood*
(Leiden: Brill).

Rosenberg, J.

1986   *King and Kin: Political Allegory in the Hebrew Bible* (Bloomington:
Indiana University Press).

JSOT 59 (1993), pp. 37-53

THE UPS AND DOWNS OF MONARCHICAL JUSTICE:
SOLOMON AND JEHORAM IN AN INTERTEXTUAL WORLD

Stuart Lasine

In 'Judging the Wisdom of Solomon: The Two-Way Effect of Intertextuality', Hugh Pyper argues that the story of the king and the cannibal mothers in 2 Kgs 6.24-33 is a carnivalesque parody of 1 Kgs 3.16-28 which 'entices the reader to go back and reappraise' Solomon. The reader will then recognize that 2 Kings 6 'indicts the world of Solomon that depends on "wisdom" for its continuance as unreal and inadequate'. Pyper prefaces his discussion of these texts with briefer remarks on other 'similar' narratives. In each case, the idea of the 'two-way effect of intertextuality' seems to offer interpreters the prospect of solving the thorny problems associated with narrative analogy and inner-biblical exegesis in a swift and sweeping fashion. Unfortunately, the concepts of 'intertextuality', 'ideology' and 'the world upside-down *topos*' (as well as the other related concepts I employ in the articles from which Pyper produces his *antitheton*) are quite a bit more complex and elusive than he implies. The same can be said for 1 Kgs 3.16-28 and 2 Kgs 6.24-33 and their many contexts. My response will focus on the most important interpretative issues raised by Pyper's essay. I will discuss in detail the various ways in which the concepts of 'intertextuality', 'narrative analogy' and 'inverted world' are understood and used by biblicists, literary critics and social scientists. This will allow me to clarify what one is actually doing when one reads 1 Kings 3 and 2 Kings 6 'backwards' in Pyper's sense. In the process I will draw some broader conclusions about the significance of intertextuality for both synchronic and diachronic interpretations of narrative analogies in the Hebrew Bible.

1. *Intertextuality*

'But my thesis isn't about that', said Persse.
'It's about the influence of T.S. Eliot on Shakespeare.'

The first thing to note is that the kind of narrative analogies discussed by Pyper are not examples of intertextuality in its widest sense. In this sense, intertextuality is 'everything, be it explicit or latent, that links one text to others' (Worton and Still 1990: 22), if not all the ways in which a text participates 'in the discursive space of a culture' (Culler 1981: 103). Here intertextuality involves not only 'the dominant relations of production and the socio-political context' which influence the writer (who is first a reader of texts), but reading that text through a process of 'cross-fertilization' which 'involves all the texts which the reader brings to it' (Worton and Still 1990: 1-2). While my own discussions of Solomon's judgment (Lasine 1987; 1989a) do not attempt to be intertextual to *this* degree, they do acknowledge a number of factors that play no role in Pyper's understanding of intertextuality: that the story can be viewed as a *Gerichtsrätsel* comparable to other law-court riddles and thematically similar folktales, as a way of coping with 'cognitive anxiety' (the same anxiety expressed by a variety of other biblical texts [including laws, psalms and proverbs] and modern formulaic fiction), as an example of interest and strain ideology, and so on. Similarly, I viewed the story of Jehoram and the cannibal mothers as part of an intertextual network that includes Assyrian and Aramaic treaty curses, reports of—and myths about—cannibalism in ancient Greek and modern traditional societies, other examples of the world upside-down *topos* in biblical and extra-biblical texts, and so on (Lasine 1991). All these approaches—the attempts to view the stories in terms of their possible social functions for various audiences in ancient Israel (before and after their inclusion in the Deuteronomistic History as we now have it) *and* the synchronic analyses of the rhetorical functions served by the stories for ancient readers of the DH (and for later readers of the 'Hebrew Bible')—qualify as 'intertextual analysis'. In *this* sense, the 'effect' of intertextuality is not 'two-way', but 'all-ways' and always.

As Daniel Boyarin points out, virtually all discussions of intertextuality assume that it is 'part of the structure of the literary text as such', not a 'characteristic of some texts as opposed to others'. He notes further that because 'every text is constrained by the literary system of which it is a part...every text is ultimately dialogical in that it cannot but record the

traces of its contentions and doubling of other discourses' (1990a: 14).
Boyarin believes that the Bible is 'a preeminent example' of a text that
contests its own assertions in this way (1990a: 12). This intertextual
'contestation' can itself be viewed in a number of different ways,
depending in part on whether the interpreter's interests are primarily
diachronic or synchronic. If, like Pyper, one views a pericope like 2 Kgs
6.24-33 as 'contesting' the ideology projected by a naive reading of
1 Kgs 3.16-28, one can view the contest in a quite literal sense. 2 Kings
6 'contests' the notion of the monarchy dormant in 1 Kings 3 and is
designed to debunk it by inviting readers to re-view it from the supposedly critical view of kingship inspired by a reading of 2 Kings 6. In
Pyper's reading 1 Kings 3 is compositionally prior to 2 Kings 6 but
must surrender the sceptre of interpretative priority to 2 Kings 6
for readers who have reached that point as they proceed through
1–2 Kings, revising their interpretations of monarchy as they go along.
One can take Pyper's approach even further and speculate that the final
editors of 1–2 Kings placed the stories in their present positions in order
to tempt readers of 1 Kings 3 to share the same uncritical enthusiasm
for the apparently wise king as is displayed by the Israelites in 1 Kgs
3.28, only to disabuse the reader of this glittery propagandistic notion of
monarchy through the deflating influence of 2 Kings 6. Here the intertextual artistry would be provided by an editor rather than the composer
of 2 Kings 6.

   The fact that the Hebrew Bible is such a heavily redacted collection of
writings is one reason it is indeed a 'preeminent example' of a textual
arena filled with contesting voices. Pointing to the 'intratextual' interpretative strategies that 'the' Bible 'itself' manifests, Boyarin remarks
that 'the very fractured and unsystematic surface of the biblical text is
an encoding of its own intertextuality' (1990a: 15). For Michael Fox the
fact that 'redaction is the epitome of intertextuality' means that 'critical
readers' of composite texts like the books of Esther should not only
engage in a synchronic 'literary reading' of one of the 'final forms' of
the text, but 'read redaction' using the conceptual 'key' of intertextuality (1991: 150-52). In other words, intertextuality not only involves the
discursive space of the culture of any particular writer, or of any particular reader of any of the individual forms of a text, but the process
through which specific biblical authors and redactors simultaneously
affirmed and negated already existing intertexts. Appealing to Bloom's
notion of intertextuality as the anxiety of influence, Fox stresses the

paradoxical nature of intertextual redaction, in which a later text both incorporates its precursor and lives upon it symbiotically in a process of 'antithetical completion' (1991: 152).

Fox's approach highlights the fact that 'intertextuality' is just as crucial for diachronic studies of biblical texts as it is for 'literary' synchronic ones. In some of the articles cited by Pyper I have attempted to demonstrate that it is crucial to investigate the discursive space of ancient Israelite culture (including prevailing literary conventions, ideological codes, social strains, etc.) even when the primary object of study is the narrative rhetoric of a given textual block in any given 'final form' or the entire biblical corpus viewed as 'scripture' (when 'scripture' is understood to be an overarching genre designation). While Pyper seems to assume that all of my cited articles presuppose the same monolithic notion of one-way intertextuality, only a few focus on the narrow concept of 'one-sided literary dependence', a term I coined when arguing against the way 'literary dependence' has been understood and employed in diachronic studies of narrative analogues like Genesis 19 // Judges 19,[1] Exodus 32 // 1 Kings 12 // Deuteronomy 9, and Numbers 11, 14, 20–21 // Deuteronomy 1–3.[2] In such studies specific features of the two narratives are often conscripted by historians to serve as evidence for priority of composition (i.e. proving which *author* was in a position of 'literary dependence') without first considering whether the author/redactor might have had rhetorical reasons for designing one of the texts to be read by an audience that was already familiar with the other (so that the author is 'depending' upon the *audience* knowing one

---

1.   Pyper's remarks on my treatment of literary dependence in Judg. 19–Gen. 19 fail to take this into account. (For an example of the effective use of my concept of 'one-sided literary dependence' in a synchronic and diachronic analysis of Judg. 19, see Brettler 1989: 411-12.) In addition, Pyper seems to think that I regard Lot as something of a 'paragon of hospitality' about whom there is nothing 'dishonourable', in spite of the fact that I discuss at some length the ludicrous and comical aspects of Lot's character and behavior (1984: 40) and his lack of trust in God (1984: 53-54). Perhaps Pyper does not share my opinion that one of the functions served by the humor in both stories is to prompt the audience to acknowledge and to condemn 'dishonorable' and immoral behavior on the part of the male protagonists.

2.   On Exod. 32 and 1 Kgs 12, see Lasine 1992. My study of Num. 11–21 and Deut. 1–3 and 9–10, entitled 'The Leader Explains His Followers: Responsibility and "Original Sins" in Deuteronomy 1–3, 9–10', was presented at the annual meeting of the CBA, Los Angeles, August 1991.

text when encountering the other).[3] Whenever the specific features of the dependent text have been crafted to serve this rhetorical function, those features cannot be used to determine historical priority without taking their 'literary' functions into account. Failure to investigate whether this is the case—using both literary and historical tools—has led not only to unfounded conclusions about compositional priority, but to unwarranted assumptions about the level of literary and moral 'refinement' and 'sophistication' of the hypothetical audiences for whom the redactors (if not the 'original' authors) rhetorically designed these intertexts (see, e.g., Lasine 1984; 1992).

Interpreters of narrative analogues often become tentative or uncertain when it comes to labeling specific elements as evidence of compositional priority or artistic 'echoing'. For example, Berlin chides 'literary' readers like Alter and literary-diachronic readers like Damrosch for failing to distinguish between narrative analogues that actually 'exist' (1991: 127) and perceived similarities that are actually nothing more than products of their own imaginative eisegesis. She believes that they are mistaking a midrashic hermeneutical procedure for a compositional poetics, confusing 'something in the mind of the reader' for something in the mind of the writer (1991: 124; cf. 120).[4] Historians have also expressed suspicion concerning the many alleged echoes heard by these literary readers. In reviewing Damrosch's *The Narrative Covenant*

3.   The statement by David Lodge's character Persse which serves as my epigraph ('my thesis...[is] about the influence of T.S. Eliot on Shakespeare' [Lodge 1984: 51]) only sounds 'backwards' because he too is referring to 'influence' on the audience rather than influence on the author. When his rival Dempsey had heard that Persse did his 'research on Shakespeare and T.S. Eliot', he had declared that with the help of a computer 'you could precisely quantify the influence of Shakespeare on T.S. Eliot'. Persse then makes the statement quoted above, adding 'what I try to show...is that we can't avoid reading Shakespeare through the lens of T.S. Eliot's poetry' (1984: 52).

4.   It should be noted that Berlin's distinction between 'the strategies that *the Bible uses* in composing *its* narratives and the strategies that the reader uses to interpret them' (1991: 120; italics mine) is not unproblematic. One cannot draw a firm line between the human composers' strategies and their readers' interpretative strategies. Authors weave into their texts cues to direct their target audiences to employ specific interpretative strategies, strategies with which they expect those audiences to be familiar. While Berlin does attack cases of narrative analogy that fail to yield a large exegetical gain as a hermeneutical strategy (1991: 124), most of her criticisms are directed to cases in which biblical scholars draw conclusions about compositional priority solely on the basis of narrative analogies generated by their own hermeneutic.

(1987), Van Seters notes that 'while Damrosch seems to believe that the ancient authors actually intended the audience or readers to be fully aware of these "echoes", they can only be discovered by a "close reading" and were scarcely noticed by several generations of biblical scholars and commentators' (1990: 342; cf. Lasine 1989b: 62-63).[5]

For example, if 2 Kings 6 has the backlash 'effect' on the meaning of 1 Kings 3 described by Pyper, why has it been so ineffectual in leading ancient and modern 'close readers' to re-hear 1 Kings 3 in that way?

Indeed, how *is* one to distinguish between 'echoes' that are little more than symptoms of synchronic tinnitus and those that should be viewed as rhetorical devices designed by an author or redactor to be heard by a reader in order to make a point—whether the point is to drown out the text heard first, harmonize with it, or use the dissonance to convey a message to which both contribute but which could be made by neither alone? Take, for example, Pyper's assertion that 1 Kgs 3.5-15 includes 'a disquieting echo of the promise the serpent made to Eve in Genesis 3.5' in 1 Kgs 3.5-15, where Solomon receives 'high praise' from God for having desired judicial wisdom. Now, one can hear this 'echo' only if one goes along with Pyper's assumption that 'the text' presents the 'information [in 1 Kgs 3.5-15] in such a way that its only possible source is Solomon himself', because the praise he receives 'is represented as a dream'. In other words, one can hear the echo only if one interprets the passage as a modern narcissist's report of a wish-fulfilment fantasy. Yet the ancient authorial audience was far more likely to interpret 1 Kgs 3.5-15 in terms of the conventions shared by the intertexts with which that audience was familiar, namely, the revelatory dream reports found elsewhere in the Bible and other ancient Near Eastern texts (see Gnuse 1984: 81-84 and *passim*). Moreover, to say that the contents of Solomon's dream could only have been reported by the dreamer is to ignore the many instances in which biblical narrators report privileged divine communications with humans, be they awake, asleep or incubating.

Admittedly, Eslinger (1989: 135) has shown that it is not necessary to

---

5. Addressing the possibility that ancient audiences could 'read redaction' in the manner described by Damrosch, Greenstein notes that 'the method of interpretation that follows from source analysis that Damrosch claims is critical for understanding biblical narrative is something that has only begun to be applied in recent centuries. What did an ancient audience do? There is no evidence that ancient readers analyzed; there is evidence, in fact, from Chronicles and elsewhere that they harmonized' (1988: 352-53).

doubt the narrator's testimony that Yahweh spoke to Solomon in 1 Kgs 3.5-15 if one wants to conclude that 1 Kings 3 alludes to Genesis 3 and that the allusion serves to debunk Solomon's godlike wisdom.[6] In spite of their difference concerning the dream report, Eslinger's basic conclusions anticipate those of Pyper because they both begin with a number of interpretative assumptions that make it possible to hear 'subversive' echoes of Genesis 3 in 1 Kings 3. First, both assume that the negative overtones of Solomon's lethal 'wisdom' in 1 Kgs 2.6, 9 will necessarily carry over to every other mention of the king's wisdom later in the narrative. Second, both assume that readers will have made a negative judgment concerning the woman's desire for wisdom in Gen. 3.6 and that this will lead them to view Solomon as displaying 'an Eve-like will to power' (Eslinger 1989: 135). Third, both assume that readers will evaluate Solomon's desire for judicial wisdom in terms of the distant echo from Genesis 3 and not in terms of the narrator's repeated references to Solomon's desires later in the Solomon narrative itself—references that would direct their attention to a very different group of intertexts.[7] Finally, both put a cap on the king's potential for wisdom by

6.   Far from doubting that Yahweh said the words attributed to him in 1 Kgs 3.5-15, Eslinger focuses on those words. One of his main interpretative goals is to expose the nefarious role played by the character Yahweh. According to Eslinger, Yahweh says these tempting words to Solomon as part of an elaborate trap he has set in order to snare the king and thereby provide a way for him to get 'out of his obligation to David' (1989: 135-37). While I have increasingly found reason to believe that sections of the DH do make it possible for readers to challenge the fairness or logic of Yahweh's actions (e.g. in his relations with Jehoram [Lasine 1991: 44-49], Saul, Jeroboam *and* Solomon [Lasine, 1992; 1993]), I find insufficient grounds for making subversive irony the key to understanding Dtr's evaluations or the ways in which Dtr presents the character Yahweh.

7.   While many ancient Near Eastern royal inscriptions and royal narratives describe the ways in which gods and humans give kings what they desire—including vast amounts of gifts and tribute—1 Kgs 5–10 develops this theme in a distinctive way. In 1 Kgs 5, 9–10 the narrator uses the terms *ḥpṣ* and *ḥšq* to refer to the way Solomon and other monarchs fulfil one another's desires/pleasures. Hiram king of Tyre fulfils all Solomon's desires (5.22, 24; 9.11). The Queen of Sheba says to Solomon, 'Blessed be Yahweh your God who has taken pleasure in you' (10.9) and then gives him an enormous quantity of desirable gifts (10.10). For his part, Solomon (5.23, 25) fulfils the desires of Hiram (at least initially; cf. 9.12-13), and gives the Queen of Sheba all her desire, whatever she asks (10.13; cf. 3.5, 13). In addition, Solomon fulfils all his own desires for his own pleasure (9.1, 19). The narrator not only stresses the fact that Solomon's wealth—and wisdom—exceed that

assuming that he would have gone ahead and chopped the baby in two if the true mother had not called out (Eslinger 1989: 138). Every one of these assumptions is open to question.[8] Until additional support is provided for these assumptions, one cannot even *begin* to analyze the rhetorical function of the alleged analogy.

Of course interpreters who are accused of hearing phantom intertextual echoes can always respond by saying that they are reading according to the interpretative rules of midrashic intertextuality described by scholars like Bruns and Boyarin. According to these rules the Bible is a 'self-glossing book', with 'later texts...throwing light on the earlier, even as they themselves always stand in light of what precedes and follows them' (Bruns 1987: 626-27). Here interpretation is 'the laying bare of an intertextual connection between two signifiers which

possessed by anyone else (5.10-11; 10.7, 12, 23-25) but the fact that the very people who are most impressed by his unequaled wealth and wisdom give him even more. By the end of ch. 10 Solomon's inflated 'wisdom' is no longer judicial, proverbial or economic. It is simply the indeterminate element of Solomon's 'character' that makes him desirable, attracting gift-bearing admirers like a magnet.

The way in which the narrator of 1 Kgs 5, 9–10 develops the themes of Solomon's desires and wisdom clearly has little to do with the woman in Eden. It has much more to do with the early warning signs of monarchical *hubris* described by many Greek writers. These symptoms are *koros* (satiety) and *pleonexia* (the desire for more, when 'more' is what belongs to someone else). As Solon puts it, 'satiety breeds arrogance when much prosperity follows humans whose mind is not right side up' (5.9; text in Edmonds [ed.] 1961: 116). The author of Deuteronomy shows just as much awareness of the dangers of satiety as does Solon—including the danger of satiety leading the king into *hubris* and idolatry (Deut. 6.11-12; 8.7-14, 17-18; 11.15-16; 31.20; 32.15; cf. especially 8.13-14 with 17.17, 20). In this context, the writer/redactor of 1 Kgs 3–11 appears to be describing a Solomon who is force-fed the ingredients of *hubris* as though he were a royal veal calf. From this perspective it is remarkable that Solomon never engages in the kind of violence against others that is the hallmark of a true tyrant. Nor does he suffer the alternative fate typical of the tyrant, that is, he never becomes the scapegoat of those who fatten him up (namely, everyone else in the story, from the *corvée* workers to rival monarchs to Yahweh) like the leader in Aristophanes' *Knights*. That political idol is fed and maintained by the people ('Demos') only to be sacrificed and eaten at a cannibal feast when he is 'full' (1111–150). For a detailed discussion of Solomon's desires and wealth in the biblical and ancient Near Eastern contexts, see Lasine 1993.

8.   On the possibility that Solomon's wisdom has different connotations in 1 Kgs 2 and 1 Kgs 3, see below. On the references to Solomon's desires within 1 Kgs 3–11, see the preceding note. On the question whether Solomon would have cut the baby in two if the true mother had not cried out, see Lasine 1989a: 65-66.

mutually read each other' (Boyarin 1990b: 223). Or they can respond by acknowledging that their reading is a 'misprision', but only in the Bloomian sense of a 'strong' misreading. However, to adopt this ratio-nale one must still grapple with all the issues connected with intertextual-ity in its widest sense. As Culler puts it,

> Bloom and others have shown us that one can often produce heat and light by rubbing two texts together... [E]ven when the proponents of interpretation call their activity 'misreading' and announce that 'strength' is the criterion of success, a question arises about the source of strength. And to answer that question one must engage with all the pragmatic presuppositions, the conventions of discourse, and the sedimentation of prior texts designated by 'intertextuality'. Strength comes from a strategic positioning in the discourses of a culture, and to produce a strong dis-course one must be an acute analyst of intertextuality (1981: 118).

In other words, when one cuts out and rubs together two 'similar' biblical pericopes in the peace and quiet of pure synchronic space the acuity of one's hearing and the strength of the sound (if not the 'heat and light') produced in this fashion will be limited because one has not come to terms with their larger reverberating intertextual matrix. That is, one has not come to terms with the vexing variables that strongly affect a culture's discursive space—variables like social strain, warring ideologies (including antithetical *types* of ideology), economic exigencies and the varying degrees of literary competence possessed by the hypo-thetical audiences for whom the authors and redactors want to design their texts (if not the audiences that actually heard and continue to hear those compositions).

Are the similarities between 1 Kings 3 and 2 Kings 6 noted by myself and Pyper strong enough for 2 Kings 6 to effect a transformation of a reader's earlier evaluation of Solomon based on 1 Kgs 3.16-28? I think it is safe to say that if 2 Kgs 6.24-33 were the only element prompting readers to become suspicious of the way Solomon's wisdom is portrayed in 1 Kgs 3.16-28, the king's image as ideal judge would remain untar-nished—and the story would continue to be viewed as similar to the many texts describing a king's judicial wisdom produced by Israel's monarchical neighbors. Would the idea that 2 Kings 6 subverts the interest ideology projected by the judgment story even *occur* to anyone if there were not much stronger reasons for readers to doubt Solomon—reasons located much closer to home, that is, within 1 Kings 3–11 itself (as has been recognized by scholars with vastly different interpretative methods like Miller and Hayes [1986: 189] and Eslinger [1989: 123-81])? Whatever else one might say about Eslinger's view that Dtr uses devastating (and of course undisconfirmable) irony to deflate and to destroy the image of Solomon's divine wisdom in 1 Kgs 3.16-28 (1989: 138-40), it does not appeal to (or need) 2 Kings 6 to do so.

Moreover, the questions raised about Solomon's desires and his wisdom in 1 Kings 3–11 do not necessarily undermine the depiction of judicial wisdom in 3.16-28 itself. If the judgment story conveyed a comforting message about the stability of monarchical justice before it was inserted into 1 Kings 3–11 (either in an earlier written version or in any of the forms in which it may have circulated orally), the ways in which it has been interpreted since its inclusion in the DH indicate that for some audiences it has retained its integrity and vitality as a folktale 'sound bite'. Many readers are aware that the story stands out from its present context for a number of reasons (e.g. a difference in tone, the abrupt switch from a king's audience with God to a prostitutes' audience with the king). These readers recognize that the final editors have allowed the seams of the text to show. They are then in a position to 'read redaction' in Fox's sense. This may entail interpreting the story in terms of the larger intertextual contexts I outlined earlier, or it may lead one to conclude that this example of Solomon's god-like wisdom was placed in its present location in order to provide a stark contrast to the bloody human 'wisdom' described in 1 Kgs 2.6, 9.

Clearly, the importance of narrative analogues must be determined on a case by case basis, whether one is primarily interested in how the ancient authors and redactors prepared their work for their target audiences or how modern readers of the canonical collections approach the 'same' stories. I consider the complex relationships between Exodus 32 and 1 Kings 12 and between Genesis 19 and Judges 19 to be quite significant. The similarities between 1 Kings 3 and 2 Kings 6, on the other hand, are of much less significance for both diachronic and synchronic interpretations. As correctly noted by Pyper, 2 Kings 6 plays little role in my analyses of 1 Kings 3. Similarly, only a minor portion of my article on 2 Kings 6 is devoted to the relationship between this narrative and the judgment story. All these papers are much more concerned with the larger intertextual issues just discussed.

2. *Inversion*

Does this mean that I was engaging in false advertising when I chose for the subtitle to my article on Jehoram and the cannibal mothers 'Solomon's Judgment in an Inverted World'? Not really. The 'inverted world' depicted in 2 Kgs 6.24-33 is not limited to—or even based on—its relationship to 1 Kings 3 in isolation. In fact, much of the paper traces the symbolic value of parental cannibalism and the 'world upside-down *topos*' in terms of a much broader intertextual network which includes 1 Kings 3—along with many other biblical passages, narrative and non-narrative, other ancient Near Eastern texts, and so on.

In order to discuss the range of possible functions served by the world upside-down *topos* in cases of narrative analogy I must first correct Pyper's apparent assumption that the 'carnivalesque' and the world upside-down *topos* serve different functions. Pyper describes the carnivalesque as using parody to take the 'skin off' the normal world to expose its perversity, while the world upside-down *topos* merely offers a 'crazy reversal' of normality which fails to indict the *status quo*. A brief review of the evidence will show that this is a false distinction. It will also show that inversion does not always entail subversion in *either* the inverted world topic *or* the carnivalesque. Thus, one cannot assume that turning upside down or parodying an upright authority figure in a society will necessarily undermine the foundations of the social order which lend that figure his or her right(eous)ness.

Many of the symbolic inversions expressed through the inverted world topic (examples of which can be found in my papers on Judg. 19, 1 Kgs 3, 2 Kgs 6 and Job) also play key roles in carnival and the genres of carnivalesque and grotesque literature. However, the terms 'world upside-down *topos*' and carnivalesque are not interchangeable. Nor can one category be subsumed under the other. While analysts of carnival like Allon White at times imply that the 'world upside-down' and 'reversible world' are simply 'phrases used to denote the way in which carnival inverts' community rules and customs (White 1989: 164), on other occasions he and his colleague Peter Stallybrass refer to the world upside-down *topos* as the 'broader' and 'more general' concept (Stallybrass and White 1986: 18, 20). However, the anthropologists and literary critics who study the cultural and literary expressions of the upside-down world topic and the carnivalesque do agree that *neither* the inversions characteristic of the former *nor* those found in carnival consistently have a subversive effect. In discussing 1 Kings 3, 2 Kings 6 and other texts I have already had occasion to point out that world upside-down motifs (as well as folk riddles, liminal rituals and cultural expressions of the disorder or 'messiness' underlying cultural categories) are capable not only of subverting social hierarchies and cultural reality-concepts but equally of supporting those categories by ventilating the pressures they generate or rendering them more flexible in times of social strain (Lasine 1986: 62-68; 1989a: 62-63, 74-75, 77-78; 1991: 36-37). The same is the case for carnival. Responding to Bakhtin's enthusiastic affirmation of carnival, Terry Eagleton notes that 'carnival, after all, is a *licensed affair*...a contained popular blow-off' (1981: 148). Roger Sales also uses the metaphor of controlled pressure-relief when pointing out that 'the fizzy, dizzy carnival spirit did not necessarily undermine authority. The authorities themselves...removed the stopper to stop the bottle being smashed altogether' (1983: 169; cf. Stallybrass and White 1986: 13).

On the other hand, the carnivalesque, like the 'world upside-down *topos*', does not always *remain* a 'licensed affair'. For example, Lucia Folena has charted the ways in which the language of inversion, which had served to neutralize and authorize 'spaces of disorder within the order of the culture' in medieval and Renaissance England, *became* subversive in Jacobean culture. Inversion 'gradually [became] synonymous with subversion', and the language of carnival was soon to be 'appropriated by the radical discourse of the Puritan revolution' (1989: 226). At times it is the authorities' fear of disorder and inversion that leads them to treat carnival and other forms of inversion as subversive, thereby making them subversive. For example, White (1989: 161) notes that one reason for the marginalization of carnival was the '"disowning" of carnival' by the middle class; that 'act of disavowal on the part of an emergent bourgeoisie...*made* carnival into the festival of the Other'. Again, a carnivalesque embodiment of misrule like Robin Hood can be simultaneously licensed *and* excluded during the same period by different power-hierarchies like the state and the church (Stallybrass 1989: 62-73).

When one is considering the possible effects of carnival and the 'world upside-down *topos*' one should not limit one's choices to licensed misrule or subversion of the 'licensing power'. Both carnival and other forms of societal inversion (e.g. the rituals cited by Victor Turner as examples of liminality and communitas [see Lasine 1986: 59-62, 67-68; 1988: 45-47]) can express the elimination or suspension of such opposing poles, including high–low, good–evil, and powerful–powerless. One must distinguish between situations in which the opposite of hierarchical order is its inverse—equally 'orderly' but upside down (e.g. the world of the cannibal complainant in 2 Kgs 6; see Lasine 1991: 48-49)—and situations in which order is opposed to disorder, chaos or 'mess' (see Lasine 1986: 56-58). Here the boundaries separating cultural categories are rendered 'permeable' rather than being allowed to be 'transgressed' in order for the underclass temporarily to 'blow off steam'. In theory at least, the cultural orders are themselves 'oxygenated' through the stripping, leveling and playful inversion of hierarchical identities and social structures that characterize carnival and communitas. As a folk riddle, the story of Solomon's judgment explores and maintains the boundary separating divine omniscience and human cognitive limitations in precisely this way.

Bakhtin's 'utopian and lyrical' descriptions of carnival (Stallybrass and White 1986: 9) are in total accord with Turner's accounts of liminality:

> All *distance* between people is suspended...carnival is the place for working out...a *new mode of interrelationship between individuals*, counterposed to...the all-powerful socio-hierarchical relationships of non-carnival life... Because carnivalistic life is life drawn out of its *usual* rut, it is to some extent 'life turned inside out', 'the reverse side of the world' (*monde à l'envers*) (1984: 123, 122).

Here what is 'counterposed' to the ruling order is not a revolutionary reversal of roles where the newly elevated rulers create themselves in the image of their former oppressors, but a temporary suspension of the master–slave relation itself. Inversions are done in the spirit of play, making fun of a world run by polar oppositions which make inversion possible and profitable for those 'on top'. Here the inverted world is not the same fractured world turned upside-down but a world that has no 'up–down' pole to invert.[9]

---

9.   In my dissertation, 'Sight, Body, and Motion in Plato and Kafka: A Study of Projective and Topological Experience' (Lasine 1977), I argue that there are two fundamental epistemological models for all human experience, one based on the model of the body as a 'kinesthetic amoeba' immersed in a fluid world in topological space, and the other based on the model of the world as before and present to a disembodied ocular knower in projective space. Projective experience, which defends against (and denies the fact of) bodily immersion in the fluid world, generates bipolar inversions, *Verkehrtheit*, and *die verkehrte Welt*. Topological experience is based on 'the primordial myth of the inside and outside'. Here the boundaries that describe such poles are osmotic and *Verkehr* across boundaries is neither inversion nor subversion.

Is there any situation in which inversion necessarily entails subversion? According to Pyper, parody is such a situation. He argues that 2 Kings 6 is a 'parody' of 1 Kings 3 that undermines the ideology (or, as I would say, ideologies) projected by the judgment story. He believes that 'the existence of the parody inevitably throws doubt over the "original" story'. Like the 'world upside-down *topos*' and carnivalistic inversion, however, parody does *not* always subvert its model. As Rose puts it, 'both by definition and structurally, parody is ambivalently critical and sympathetic towards its target' (1979: 34; cf. 28). Parody within carnival displays the same ambivalence: 'as a metaphor for Revolution, the parodistic games of the carnival represent both the satiric inversion of the world and the masking of its revolutionary purpose'. In fact, it has been used 'in the cause of counter-revolutionary movements to mock subversion' (Rose 1979: 167-69). Thus, while Jonah parodies elements of the Moses story, it does not subvert the model of prophetic intervention presented in passages such as Exod. 34.6-9; if anything, the author is attacking 'prophets' and others whose notions of prophetic intercession are viewed by the author as a travesty of the ideal represented by Moses.

Clearly, if the 'world upside-down *topos*', carnival and parody can support and suspend social orders as well as subvert them, one cannot assume that a story about a king who attempts to maintain justice in a topsy-turvy world will necessarily overturn the ideology upon which the idea of the 'just king' is based, namely, the idea that the throne 'rests firmly on', and is 'upheld by' righteousness and justice, and that through justice the king gives his country 'stability' (Prov. 16.12; 20.28; 29.4). However, re-viewing 1 Kgs 3.16-28 and 2 Kgs 6.24-33 in the light of 'intertextuality' in its widest sense has also revealed that the support–subvert dichtomy is itself reductive and inadequate to the task of charting the many possible 'effects' of these two judicial narratives.

BIBLIOGRAPHY

Armstrong, N., and L. Tennenhouse (eds.)
    1989   *The Violence of Representation: Literature and the History of Violence*
             (London: Routledge).
Bakhtin, M.
    1984   *Problems of Dostoyevsky's Poetics* (ed. and trans. C. Emerson;
             Minneapolis: University of Minnesota Press).

Berlin, A.
  1991   'Literary Exegesis of Biblical Narrative: Between Poetics and
                Hermeneutics', in J.P. Rosenblatt and J.C. Sitterson, Jr (eds.), *'Not in
                Heaven': Coherence and Complexity in Biblical Narrative*
                (Bloomington: Indiana University Press): 120-28.
Boyarin, D.
  1990a   *Intertextuality and the Reading of Midrash* (Bloomington: Indiana
                University Press).
  1990b   'The Song of Songs: Lock or Key? Intertextuality, Allegory and
                Midrash', in R.M. Schwartz (ed.), *The Book and the Text: The Bible
                and Literary Theory* (Oxford: Blackwell): 214-30.
Brettler, M.
  1989   'The Book of Judges: Literature as Politics', *JBL* 108: 395-418.
Bruns, G.L.
  1987   'Midrash and Allegory: The Beginnings of Scriptural Interpretation',
                in R. Alter and F. Kermode (eds.), *The Literary Guide to the Bible*
                (Cambridge, MA: Harvard University Press): 625-46.
Culler, J.
  1981   *The Pursuit of Signs: Semiotics, Literature, Deconstruction* (Ithaca,
                NY: Cornell University Press).
Damrosch, D.
  1987   *The Narrative Covenant: Transformations of Genre in the Growth of
                Biblical Literature* (San Francisco: Harper & Row).
Eagleton, T.
  1981   *Walter Benjamin: Towards a Revolutionary Criticism* (London:
                Verso).
Edmonds, J.M. (ed. and trans.)
  1961   *Elegy and Iambus*, I (LCL; Cambridge, MA: Harvard University
                Press).
Eslinger, L.
  1989   *Into the Hands of the Living God* (JSOTSup, 84; Bible and Literature
                Series, 24; Sheffield: Almond Press).
Folena, L.
  1989   'Figures of Violence: Philologists, Witches, and Stalinistas', in
                Armstrong and Tennenhouse 1989: 219-38.
Fox, M.V.
  1991   *The Redaction of the Books of Esther: On Reading Composite Texts*
                (Atlanta: Scholars Press).
Gnuse, R.K.
  1984   *The Dream Theophany of Samuel: Its Structure in Relation to Ancient
                Near Eastern Dreams and its Theological Significance* (Lanham, MD:
                University Press of America).
Greenstein, E.L.
  1988   'On the Genesis of Biblical Prose Narrative', *Prooftexts* 8: 347-54.
Lasine, S.
  1977   'Sight, Body, and Motion in Plato and Kafka: A Study of Projective
                and Topological Experience' (PhD dissertation, University of

Wisconsin-Madison; available from University Microfilms International, Ann Arbor, MI).

1984   'Guest and Host in Judges 19: Lot's Hospitality in an Inverted World', *JSOT* 29: 37-59.

1986   'Indeterminacy and the Bible: A Review of Literary and Anthropological Theories and their Application to Biblical Texts', *Hebrew Studies* 27: 48-80.

1987   'Solomon, Daniel and the Detective Story: The Social Functions of a Literary Genre', *HAR* 11: 247-66.

1988   'Bird's-Eye and Worm's-Eye Views of Justice in the Book of Job', *JSOT* 42: 29-53.

1989a   'The Riddle of Solomon's Judgment and the Riddle of Human Nature in the Hebrew Bible', *JSOT* 45: 61-86.

1989b   'Judicial Narratives and the Ethics of Reading: The Reader as Judge of the Dispute between Mephibosheth and Ziba', *Hebrew Studies* 30: 49-69.

1991   'Jehoram and the Cannibal Mothers (2 Kings 6.24-33): Solomon's Judgment in an Inverted World', *JSOT* 50: 27-53.

1992   'Reading Jeroboam's Intentions: Intertextuality, Rhetoric and History in 1 Kings 12', in D. Fewell (ed.), *Reading between Texts: Intertextuality and the Hebrew Bible* (Louisville, KY: Westminster/John Knox Press): 133-52.

1996   'The King of Desire: Indeterminacy, Audience, and the Solomon Narrative', *Semeia* 71: 83-116.

1997   'Solomon and the Wizard of Oz: Power and Invisibility in a Verbal Palace', in Lowell K. Handy (ed.), *The Age of Solomon: Scholarship at the Turn of the Millennium* (Leiden: Brill).

Lodge, D.
1984   *Small World: An Academic Romance* (New York: Macmillan).

Miller, J.M., and J.H. Hayes
1986   *A History of Ancient Israel and Judah* (Philadelphia: Westminster Press).

Rose, M.A.
1979   *Parody//Metafiction: An Analysis of Parody as a Critical Mirror to the Writing and Reception of Fiction* (London: Croom Helm).

Sales, R.
1983   *English Literature in History 1780–1830: Pastoral and Politics* (London: Hutchinson).

Stallybrass, P.
1989   ' "Drunk with the Cup of Liberty": Robin Hood, the Carnivalesque, and the Rhetoric of Violence in Early Modern England', in Armstrong and Tennenhouse (eds.) 1989: 45-76.

Stallybrass, P., and A. White
1986   *The Politics and Poetics of Transgression* (Ithaca, NY: Cornell University Press).

Van Seters, J.
1990   Review of *The Narrative Covenant: Transformations of Genre in the Growth of Biblical Literature*, by D. Damrosch, *JAOS* 110.2: 340-43.

White, A.
    1989   'Hysteria and the End of Carnival: Festivity and Bourgeois Neurosis',
             in Armstrong and Tennenhouse (eds.) 1989: 157-70.
Worton, M., and J. Still
    1990   *Intertextuality: Theories and Practices* (Manchester: Manchester
             University Press).

JSOT 53 (1992), pp. 75-91

SOLOMON AS PHILOSOPHER KING?
THE NEXUS OF LAW AND WISDOM IN 1 KINGS 1–11

K.I. Parker

The problem of human ordering, or how justice can be secured in the midst of scant resources and uncertain conditions, is the political problem *par excellence*. In classical political philosophy, a solution is provided by Plato in Book 5 of his *Republic*: justice is secured only when members of the state do what they are best suited for; those who are best suited to rule are the philosophers, since they alone have the capacity to know things that are important for political order. According to Plato, if the state on earth is a copy of its heavenly ideal, and if only philosophers have the time and training to contemplate this ideal, then only philosophers can rule. As Socrates tells Glaucon, 'Unless either philosophers become kings in our states or those whom we now call our kings and rulers take to the pursuit of philosophy seriously and adequately, and there is a conjunction of these two things, political power and philosophical intelligence...there can be no cessation of troubles'.[1] Therefore no law should limit the philosophers' power to mould human beings and the state in the image of the ideal.[2]

---

1.   Plato, *Republic* 473D, in *The Collected Dialogues of Plato* (ed. E. Hamilton and H. Cairns; trans. Paul Shorey; Princeton, NJ: Princeton University Press, 1969).
2.   Plato's ideal of the rule of the philosopher king has had a curious history in the West. Some, like the natural law theorists in the eighteenth century, agreed with Plato and held that society was an organic unity known to human reason but obscured by prejudice, custom and ignorance. A sovereign was needed, therefore, to translate the 'laws of nature' into political practice, and thereby eliminate prejudices such as religion, custom and tradition. Others, however, have been against Plato's proposal. Some, like Spinoza, have argued that philosophizing would be dangerous to the ruled (i.e. philosophers are not interested in the concerns of the people they

This Greek ideal is in direct contrast with the biblical ideal, according to which law is integral to the rule of the philosopher king. If law is neglected or spurned, justice is in jeopardy. In this paper I will argue that the rule of the 'philosopher king' Solomon, as presented in the Deuteronomistic History (1 Kgs 1–11), is destined to end in failure precisely because he fails to abide by the law. In so doing, I hope to demonstrate the difference between Athens and Jerusalem with respect to their political ideologies.

While it is true that the Deuteronomist's portrayal of Solomon's rule ends in disaster—the kingdom is divided and syncretism is firmly established—Solomon is initially presented as conforming to the Israelite conception of the *ideal* king. At the risk of oversimplifying a very complex problem, three salient features of the ideal king can be isolated. The ideal king is one who (a) renders justice throughout the realm (see 1 Sam. 12.3-4; 2 Sam. 8.15; 23.3-4; Ps. 72.1-4; Isa. 16.5; Jer. 21.5; 22.3-4, 15-17),[3] (b) lives according to the law of Yahweh (see Deut. 17.14-20; Pss. 18.21; 132.12),[4] and (c) is wise, that is, one who 'fears Yahweh' (see Prov. 1.7; 8.14-16; 9.10; Ps. 11.10; Job 28.28; Isa. 11.2-3a; 9.6).[5]

govern), whereas others, like Kant, have argued that ruling is dangerous to philosophizers (i.e. the possession of power corrupts the faculty of reasoning).

3.   According to Mowinckel (1954: 55) and Whitelam (1979: 33), the idea that the king is to render justice is also embedded in the pre-monarchic institution of the judges. The rise of kingship is directly attributable to the inability of anyone to render justice; it was a time when 'every man did what was right in his own eyes' (Judg. 17.6; 21.25; cf. 18.1; 19.1). Although justice is ultimately a principle that resides with Yahweh, the king must maintain and administer it if his rule is to be effective (see Johnson 1967: 4-13). By administering justice (i.e. caring for the underprivileged—the widows, orphans and poor), the king will be able to maintain the stability and the prosperity of the nation (see Eaton 1976: 141; Whitelam 1979: 29).

4.   To ensure the welfare of his people, the king must live under the laws of Yahweh, and maintain the covenantal relationship between Yahweh and Israel (Widengren 1957: 16-17). If the king breaks the law, the consequences are disastrous for the people (Mowinckel 1954: 95; Eaton 1976: 141-42). As Kenik suggests in her study *Design for Kingship*, the ideal king is one who lives according to the Torah by maintaining its statutes, ordinances and laws (1983: 84-88, 133-40, 162-69, 206-207).

5.   Wisdom is crucial to the concept of the ideal king. As one scholar claims, 'she is the power behind the throne' (McKane 1970: 348), and another remarks, 'wisdom to maintain social order and to administer justice was the essential endowment of the king, whether as the incarnate deity in Egypt, or as viceregent of God in Mesopotamia and Israel' (Scott 1971: 72). By 'fearing Yahweh', the wise king is

Naturally there is a certain amount of overlapping between the three concepts of justice, law and wisdom. Wisdom or fear of Yahweh implies obedience to the law, and by the king's obedience to the law justice is rendered to the people. For the most part, however, these concepts function as separate aspects of the ideal king. The prophets, too, anticipate the coming of an ideal eschatological king in terms of these three attributes (see especially the 'messianic' prophecies of Isa. 9.6; 11.1-5; and Jer. 21.5; 33.15). The future ideal (eschatological) king is to be noted for his ability to usher in the new age of justice, to adhere to divine law, and to possess wisdom. In his capacity as judge, the ideal king cares for the underprivileged to ensure justice is meted out (Whitelam 1979: 34-35). In his capacity as one under divine law, the king is to observe its statutes and ordinances (Noth 1966: 245). Implied in these two aspects of kingship is the notion that a divine wisdom or knowledge enables the king to execute justice and law in a manner consistent with his office (Porteous 1955: 254; Ringgren 1966: 231). Thus the ideal king is the bearer of divine law, the judge who renders justice throughout the nation, and the one who uses his wisdom to execute both justice and law. In the Deuteronomistic presentation of Solomon, the same three features of justice, obedience to the law and wisdom emerge. Solomon is able to render justice by using his wisdom to comply with the law.

Solomon as the Ideal King[6]

Unquestionably, God's revelation to Solomon in his first dream theophany embodies the ideal of kingship. The three aspects of justice, law, and wisdom are forged into an alliance, setting the stage for what follows. In 1 Kings 3 Solomon asks God for 'an understanding mind to govern' the people, and the ability 'to discern between good and evil'[7] in order

---

totally dependent upon and obedient to Yahweh (Kalugila 1980: 103).

6.   The Deuteronomistic narrative concerning Solomon in 1 Kgs 1–11 divides neatly into two parts: chs. 1–8 show Solomon as the ideal king, and chs. 9–11 show him as the apostate king. For the structural and chiastic arrangement of the sequence of events, cf. Parker 1988. For recent alternative structural arrangements, see Brettler 1991: 87-97 and especially Frisch 1991. Cf. also my reply to Frisch's article (Parker 1991).

7.   For an elaboration of the judicial background to the phrase 'good and evil', see Clark 1969: 268, Weinfeld 1972: 247 and Mettinger 1976: 240-41. Kenik also argues that the phrase has a legal background, especially when applied to Solomon (1983: 137).

to rule more effectively (3.9). Solomon, it would appear, asks for a type of knowledge that would make justice possible. God responds not by giving Solomon 'an understanding mind' (*lēb šōmēa'*), but 'a wise and discerning mind' (*lēb ḥākām wᵉnābôn*). Although Solomon's request implies an ability to listen (literally his request was for a 'hearing heart'), God grants Solomon wisdom directly. God's gift of a 'wise and discerning' mind implies knowledge appropriate to a king, both in the sense of obedience to the divine word and an ability to render justice (see Porteous 1955: 249; Scott 1955: 270; Gray 1970: 126; and Kenik 1983: 141-43). God, however, adds the important proviso that Solomon must continue to 'walk in my ways, keeping my statutes and commandments' (3.14). Solomon's ability to govern is conditional on his ability to comply with the law, and thus his wisdom and judicial perspicacity are also contingent upon his obedience to the Torah (see Weinfeld 1972: 256).

In the narrative subsequent to the dream, there is ample evidence of Solomon's wisdom and justice. In the famous story of the two harlots, Solomon is shown as the judge *par excellence*. In a passage that combines both Solomon's justice and wisdom, the Israelites perceive that 'the wisdom (*ḥokmâ*) of God was in him to render justice (*mišpāṭ*)' (1 Kgs 3.28). Solomon's judicial capacity is further emphasized by his defense of the weaker members of society—even the lowest of citizens can approach the king to ask for justice (see Kalugila 1980: 116). The story of the two harlots would thus attest both to Solomon's judicial power and to his wisdom. Justice and wisdom, however, are only effective if they are subsumed under Torah, or if they comply with Torah. When Solomon's wisdom is no longer under Torah (as in chs. 9–11), it will lose its effectiveness, even though he still may be considered wise in some sense (cf. 10.7, 23).

Under the kingship of Solomon, Israel reaches its economic and territorial pre-eminence. The text relates that the territory over which Solomon ruled extended 'from the Euphrates to the land of the Philistines, and to the border of Egypt' (1 Kgs 5.1 [RSV 4.21]). This description matches the ideal of Israel's dominion as given to Abraham (Gen. 15.18) and reiterated by Moses (Deut. 1.7) and Joshua (Josh. 1.4).[8]

---

8.   See especially the summary in Jones (1984: 146). There are some syntactical difficulties with the Hebrew, inasmuch as the phrase 'to the land of the Philistines' is believed to be a gloss in order to explain where the border of Egypt was (Montgomery 1950: 127; Gray 1970: 141 n. b). Whichever reading is preferred, the extent of Solomon's territory is unmistakable.

The boundaries of the kingdom are repeated again in 1 Kgs 5.4 (RSV 4.24), as if to emphasize that the promise to Abraham has been fulfilled during the reign of Solomon. The limits of the kingdom, coupled with the fact that 'there was peace on all sides round about [Solomon]', provide additional evidence of Solomon's portrayal as the ideal king.

Parallels between the promise to Abraham and the kingship of Solomon are also found in the portrait of the people living in the kingdom. In 1 Kgs 4.20, the Deuteronomist writes, 'the people of Judah and Israel were as many as the sand by the sea; they ate and drank and were happy'. In a similar passage in Genesis, there is a description of God telling Abraham that a sign of the blessing will be when his descendants are as numerous as 'the sand which is on the seashore' (22.17). While the metaphor of 'sand' to indicate large numbers of people is used on other occasions as well,[9] the thrust of the metaphor is that a great multitude is the sign of the covenant blessing. That the narrative consistently emphasizes great numbers of people (*'am rāb*) indicates that Solomon's kingdom represents a fulfilment of the promise to Abraham (see especially Kenik 1983: 92-96). Thus, in the matter of domestic affairs—that is, in the extent of Solomon's territory, in the quality of life of the people, and in the great numbers of people—Solomon is the ideal king, one who is the embodiment of wisdom, law and justice.

Further examples of Solomon's wisdom and justice are found in his contract with Hiram (1 Kgs 5.15-26 [RSV 5.1-12]). By virtue of the peace that surrounds him, Solomon is able to build the Temple 'for the name of the LORD my God' (5.19 [RSV 5.5]), thus fulfilling Nathan's prophecy to David (2 Sam. 7.12-13). The justice of the contract with Hiram may be inferred by the peace that ensues (1 Kgs 5.26 [RSV 5.12]; see also Mettinger 1976: 227, and Kalugila 1980: 120). Solomon's role as a wise king is confirmed by Hiram's assessment of him: 'Blessed be the LORD this day, who has given to David a wise (*ḥākām*) son to be over this great people' (5.21 [RSV 5.7]). In this speech, Solomon's position as the ideal king is made explicit: he is the leader of a 'great people' (*'am rāb*, fulfilling the promise to the patriarchs), and he is 'wise' (*ḥākām*, fulfilling God's promise of 3.12). Hiram thus reaffirms that Solomon is a great king with respect to his wisdom.[10] Solomon's

9. Josh. 7.12; 11.4; 1 Sam. 13.12; 2 Sam. 17.11; Isa. 10.22; 48.19; Jer. 33.22; Hos. 2.1 (RSV 1.10).

10. There is additional confirmation of Solomon's wisdom in 1 Kgs 5.26 [RSV 5.12]), explicitly linked to his treaty of peace with Hiram. As Montgomery writes, 'it

divinely bestowed wisdom, at this stage, is shown in an entirely positive light. This will be in sharp contrast to the description of the purposes for which his wisdom is employed in the second part of the narrative.

A second instance of Solomon's justice concerns the *corvée*, which provides the labour for the construction of the Temple (1 Kgs 5.27-32 [RSV 5.13-18]). There are a number of textual problems associated with this passage (see Montgomery 1950: 137-38), not the least of which is its lack of agreement with 9.20-22.[11] Regardless of the numbers and the nationality of the people involved in the *corvée*, a period of rest is taken into consideration in the assignment of the work. In fact, the labourers rest more than they work, since they are 'a month in Lebanon [doing the work] and two months at home' (5.28 [RSV 5.14]). Solomon's ability to initiate building projects without resorting to slave labour will stand in contrast to the slave labour required for the building projects described in 9.20-22. The institution of slavery recalls the life of the Israelites in Egypt, a situation to which the Deuteronomist is decidedly hostile (Deut. 5.15; 15.15; 16.12; 24.18, 22). The justice of Solomon's rule in 5.15-32 is therefore evident by virtue of the fact that he does not use an Egyptian model as the basis for his *corvée*.

The great achievement of Solomon was the construction of the Temple (1 Kgs 8.1-11). It is the fulfilment of the scheme laid out in Deut. 12.2-7, according to which the high places would be eliminated, and sacrifices and offerings would take place at one central location. The building of the Temple without metal tools (1 Kgs 6.7) reflects the Torah's prohibition against the use of an iron tool in constructing an altar (Exod. 20.28; Deut. 27.5). Ostensibly, the Temple is built to house the ark, which is explicitly said to contain the Law of Moses (1 Kgs 8.9). The fact that the ark is installed in the innermost sanctuary of the

is wisdom of a political character…the wisdom with which Solomon was endowed "to judge this thy great people" included diplomacy and the erection of splendid buildings' (1950: 134; see also Kalugila 1980: 119).

11. The text at 1 Kgs 5.27 (RSV 5.13) says that the *corvée* was 'throughout all Israel', yet, in 9.20-22, only non-Israelites are said to be conscripted. These discrepancies can be resolved if it is understood that two different types of forced labour are being referred to. The *corvée* (Heb. *mas*) of 5.27 (RSV 5.13) is a temporary conscription that does not involve slavery (Gray 1970: 155); the *corvée* (*mas 'ōbēd*) of 9.21, however, does involve slavery of some kind that was applied to the non-Israelites (Gray 1970: 155; Jones 1984: 158). There is also a problem in regard to the disproportionately large numbers of conscripts as given in ch. 5 and the more 'realistic' account as given in ch. 9 (Montgomery 1950: 137).

Temple implies that the ark and the law become the heart of Solomon's kingship. Thus, Torah is manifested in Solomon's kingdom both by Solomon's piety and by the physical presence of the tablets of Moses in the Temple. In his great prayer, Solomon explicitly states that he has followed God's instructions in building the Temple (8.20-21). Although the connection with his father David is obvious here (i.e. Solomon has complied with the divine plan to build the Temple and has 'walked before' Yahweh like his father [8.23; cf. 3.6 and Kenik 1983: 76-82]), there is also a connection to Moses. Solomon is the 'new Moses', or at least the one through whom the prophecies of Moses will be fulfilled (see the promise of 'rest' to the people in 8.56 and Deut. 12.9-10; and the promise of obedience to the Torah in 8.57-61 and Deut. 10.13; 11.22-23).[12]

Furthermore, the sacrifice that Solomon holds on the occasion of the dedication of the Temple recalls Deut. 12.7, 12, 18. The dedication of the house is also in line with Torah (cf. Deut. 20.5), as is the feast itself (cf. Deut. 16.13-15). The statement that 'all Israel' (1 Kgs 8.65) joins Solomon in his feast indicates that, for at least one brief moment in Israel's history, the entire nation is united under its ideal king. And by acting in accord with the Torah, the nation reaps rewards; the Deuteronomist reports that all Israel 'went to their homes joyful and glad of heart for all the goodness that the LORD had shown to David his servant and to Israel his people' (8.66). This communal participation in the joys of the sacrifice is not unlike the utopian vision of the Jubilee Year (see Lev. 25).

The narrative of 1 Kings 3–8 thus clearly presents Solomon as Israel's

---

12. The conflation of Mosaic and Davidic traditions in the person of Solomon has been suggested by Kenik (1983: 88, 169), and (in a private communication) by A.M. Cooper. As David's successor, Solomon is heir to the promise of an 'everlasting dynasty', and to the teachings, instructions and wisdom that marked David as a successful ruler. As Moses' successor, Solomon re-enacts key events in Moses' life. He judges Israel (cf. Exod. 18 and 1 Kgs 3), establishes a bureaucracy (cf. Num. 2–4 and 1 Kgs 4), disseminates the law (cf. Exod. 19–24 and 1 Kgs 8), builds Yahweh a throne (Exod. 25–31 and 1 Kgs 6), and promises reward for obedience to the law and punishment for disobedience (Deut. 12–26 and 1 Kgs 8). But, whereas Moses leads the people out of Egypt, Solomon adopts Egyptian customs and practices, thereby taking Israel symbolically back to Egypt (1 Kgs 9–11). The Deuteronomic presentation of Solomon in 1 Kgs 1–8 is one, therefore, that combines two very important traditions in Israelite history: he is the ruler *par excellence* in the line of David, and the law-giver *par excellence* in the line of Moses.

ideal king. The ideal king is illustrative of the favourable combination of wisdom and Torah that results in justice. This political ideology lies at the heart of the Deuteronomist's presentation of Solomon as the ideal king, whatever the historical reality may have been. The writer consistently emphasizes Solomon's adherence to the principles of justice, wisdom and law, in order to show that for Solomon's justice and wisdom to be efficacious, they must be subservient to Torah. In fact, Solomon's justice and wisdom are gifts from God that are contingent upon his obedience to Torah. The ideals of wisdom and law, essential for the just governing of the people, thus converge in the person of Solomon. They converge, on the one hand, because 'wisdom to govern' is given by God, and, on the other hand, because Solomon is obedient to the Torah.[13] The blend of law and wisdom, however, will soon prove to be too volatile to be contained in one man: in chs. 9–11 Solomon's wisdom will no longer be yoked to Torah, and disaster will follow.

Solomon as the Apostate King

Solomon's second dream theophany introduces the second, or anti-Solomonic, section of the narrative. The text itself explicitly recalls the first dream ('the LORD appeared to Solomon a second time, as he had appeared to him at Gibeon', 1 Kgs 9.2), and anticipates themes of the second section. Having established in the first dream that Solomon's justice and wisdom are conditional upon his obedience to Torah, the Deuteronomist focuses upon the consequences of not abiding by the condition in the second dream: if Solomon does not act in accord with Torah, his judicial wisdom is in jeopardy (9.6-9). By focusing on the condition, the writer prepares the reader for Solomon's apostasy and his characterization as the antithesis of the ideal king.[14]

13. According to a penetrating analysis of 1 Kgs 3.4-15 by Kenik (1983), the description of Solomon's obedience to the Torah serves the purpose of establishing the Deuteronomist's ideology of kingship. Kenik argues that the Deuteronomist's vision of an ideal king is contained in Solomon's first dream. Although she at times over-argues her case, Kenik demonstrates the concern with Torah in the Deuteronomist's political perspective.

14. A number of commentators have also seen a relationship between the two dreams (Montgomery 1950: 203-204; Gray 1970: 235; Jones 1984: 209; Long 1984: 108), but only Noth has discerned that the bipartite structure to the narrative is dependent upon the two dream theophanies (1981: 60; 1968: 209). Nevertheless, Noth does not work through the implications of his insight, and he even attributes the

The second dream is an intimation of disaster. The general crime of not following God's commandments and statutes is specified by the Deuteronomist in the second dream as the act of going to 'serve other gods and worship them' (1 Kgs 9.6; cf. Deut. 11.16; 17.3). For the Deuteronomist, no act could be more egregious. Solomon's subsequent worship of foreign gods (1 Kgs 11.5-8) instigates the rupture of Israel's covenant with God. And although at this stage the Deuteronomist presents Solomon's apostasy as only a possibility, not a reality, it is a possibility that is consistent with the promises and threats in Deut. 28.36-37 and 29.24-28, and with the ultimate fate of Israel as described in 2 Kings 25. The dream theophany is thus pivotal not only for the Solomonic material but for the entire Deuteronomistic History as well. It both recalls the Torah's precepts (Deut. 28–29) and points ahead to the disastrous consequences of their violation (2 Kgs 25).

Having established that the contravention of Torah will have dire consequences, the Deuteronomist now deals with the specific instances of Solomon's violations. In so doing, the author recalls two earlier episodes: the agreement with Hiram and the *corvée*. While the first contract with Hiram had been characterized by wisdom, justice and peace, the second contract is characterized by unwise dealings and injustice. Hiram is angry over the cities that Solomon has sold him, and the contract seems to be an example of bad faith on the part of Solomon. Equally, by selling cities in the land of Galilee to Hiram, Solomon relinquishes the 'ideal' territory over which he should have dominion. Any sale of land, no matter how remunerative, affects the land's integrity and undermines the promise of the Torah.[15]

The episode of the second *corvée* (1 Kgs 9.15-28) offers further evidence for the change in Solomon's character. Solomon's violations of Torah are much more explicit here, and his regime exhibits tendencies that are characteristic of a tyrannical dictatorship. Solomon institutes slavery in the form of the *mas 'ōbēd* (9.21). This is Solomon's first subtle look in the direction of Egypt. The Israelites are once again enslaved as they had been in Egypt, a situation from which Yahweh had taken great pains to rescue them. Samuel's anxieties about the cost of kingship are now realized (see 1 Sam. 8.17). Moreover, in the second *corvée*, the

composition of the two dreams to two different redactors (1968: 195).

15. See Jones, who remarks: 'the loss of territory was a heavy blow for Israel, and this account contributes indirectly to the negative assessment of King Solomon' (1984: 213).

labour is directed not to the building of the Temple, but to the building of store-cities to house Solomon's chariots and horsemen, a special house for Pharaoh's daughter, and a fleet of ships. The building of the store-cities seems to be motivated by military purposes (see Gray 1970: 243-49), the house for Pharaoh's daughter by the desire for prestige (Montgomery 1950: 210), and the fleet of ships by the desire for wealth (1 Kgs 9.28). These three concepts of 'power, prestige and money' typify the new regime, and are indicative of the extent to which Solomon has departed from Torah.

Solomon's foreign policy stands in marked contrast to his domestic policy. If his domestic policy was characterized by a concern for justice (1 Kgs 3.16-28), effective administration (4.1–5.8 [RSV 4.1-28]) and wisdom (5.9-14 [RSV 4.29-34]), the qualities of justice and good government are now conspicuously absent in the description of his foreign policy. Nevertheless, Solomon's wisdom is still operative to a certain extent (10.1-10 and 10.23-25), as can be seen in his encounter with the Queen of Sheba. While it is true that the Queen of Sheba is impressed by Solomon's wisdom, she is equally, if not more, impressed by the ostentatious display of wealth in Solomon's court. The queen's testimony confirms that God's gifts of wisdom and fame to Solomon are still in effect, but the focus of Solomon's wisdom has shifted from the rendering of justice (3.28) to entertainment and the accumulation of wealth (10.1-10). The harnessing of wisdom to Torah, which had led to the characterization of Solomon as the ideal king in chs. 3–8, is no longer evident. Solomon's wisdom is now in the service of his own self-aggrandizement. Although the wealth pouring into the king's coffers is enormous, the Deuteronomist is careful not to specify that it is used to benefit the people in any way. The writer subtly undermines Solomon's status as the ideal king by raising doubts about the use of his wisdom.

One final point that contributes to the negative portrayal of Solomon in this section concerns his explicit violations of the laws dealing with kingship found in Deut. 17.16-17. Solomon transgresses all four laws: (1) he conducts horse trading with Egypt (cf. 1 Kgs 10.28); (2) he has numerous foreign wives (cf. 1 Kgs 11.3); (3) he multiplies gold (cf. 1 Kgs 10.14); and (4) he makes 'silver as common in Jerusalem as stone' (1 Kgs 10.27). Solomon's concern with wealth, his misuse of wisdom, his failure to act in accord with the Torah, and his violation of its statutes profoundly contribute to the portrayal of him as the apostate king. In a more direct sense, Solomon's apostasy is shown by his violations of

Torah in ch. 11. Solomon's enormous harem of seven hundred wives and three hundred concubines (11.3) is an explicit violation of Deuteronomic law (Deut. 7.1-4). The fact that these wives are expressly said to be 'foreigners' (1 Kgs 11.1-2) incriminates Solomon all the more.

A curt summary of the activities of Solomon is found in 1 Kgs 11.6, where the text reads, 'so Solomon did what was evil in the sight of the LORD, and did not wholly follow the LORD, as David his father had done'. The Deuteronomic phrase, 'did what was evil in the sight of the LORD', which is first used with reference to Solomon, is also used on other occasions to indicate apostasy (see 1 Kgs 14.22; 15.26, 34; 16.19, 25, 30; 22.52; 2 Kgs 3.2; 8.27; etc.). Solomon is thus portrayed as a kind of paradigm of the infidelities to which future kings will often fall prey.

The failure to live in accordance with Torah is predicted in the second dream theophany (1 Kgs 9.1-10), and the implications of this failure to abide by Torah are demonstrated in the subsequent episodes. Through his disregard of Torah, Solomon's capacity to be Israel's ideal king is nullified. Instead, Solomon becomes, in certain ways, the prototype of an evil king. His wisdom, if not always degenerating into folly as in 11.1-6, nevertheless is not used for the benefit of the people. His justice turns to tyranny, and the kingdom is forever divided after his death. The ideal has thus become its antithesis through Solomon's failure to comply with Torah.

Conclusion

In 1 Kings 3–8 Solomon is portrayed as the ideal king. As Solomon continues to act in accord with Torah, he manifests justice and uses his wisdom for the benefit of the people. In 9.1–11.13, however, when Solomon does not comply with Torah, he becomes the ideal's antithesis. His regime is noted for its egregious tyranny, and his wisdom is directed towards his own self-aggrandizement. Such wisdom is akin to folly. With the contrast between these two portraits of Solomon, that of the ideal king and the apostate king respectively, the Deuteronomist makes a larger point about wisdom and Torah. By depicting Solomon's wisdom in the second section as being concerned with wealth, prestige or glory, and not with justice and administration, as in the first section, the Deuteronomist emphasizes that wisdom not harnessed to Torah is not beneficial or efficacious. Thus, there is an implicit criticism of wisdom, that is, of wisdom that is not concerned with Torah. This deleterious use of wisdom may account for its negative depiction in the Deuteronomistic History.

The negative assessment of wisdom in the Deuteronomistic History has been demonstrated by R.N. Whybray in two monographs, *The Succession Narrative* (1968) and *The Intellectual Tradition in the Old Testament* (1974). In his study of the Succession Narrative (1 Sam. 9–20; 1 Kgs 1–2), Whybray argues that such foolish acts as David's indiscretion with Bathsheba, Amnon's rape of Tamar, Absalom's rebellion, and Solomon's 'ruthless' accession to the throne are all associated with 'wisdom' (*hokmâ*). Thus, David tries to extricate himself from his predicament with acts of 'wisdom' (2 Sam. 11.14-25); Amnon receives counsel from Jonadab, who is 'very wise' (*hākām me'ōd*, 2 Sam. 13.3), which leads him to rape his half-sister. The wise woman of Tekoa is only superficially wise, and David easily perceives the hand of Joab behind her speech (2 Sam. 14.20). And David, by recalling Absalom and then not reconciling himself to his son, sets events in motion that have disastrous consequences. Finally, David's demand that Solomon eliminate his opponents is also considered to be 'wise'. Thus, according to Whybray, there is something of a negative assessment of wisdom in the narratives of the Deuteronomistic History. As he writes,

> the author was well aware, as were the authors of Proverbs, that not everything which passes for wisdom should be accepted at its face value, and also that wickedness can assume the character of wisdom for its own purposes (Whybray 1974: 90).

G.E. Mendenhall also argues that 'wisdom' has a pejorative meaning, especially as it is understood in the Succession Narrative and the Solomonic material (1974: 323-25). Mendenhall argues that Solomon's wisdom is incontestable, a situation that eventually leads to his establishment of a military dictatorship and to the eventual disintegration of his kingdom. He remarks that

> the arrogant stupidity of power reinforced by access to, and control of, a wide range of technical wisdom had its logical culmination in the policies of Rehoboam, which resulted not only in the complete disintegration of the empire but also in schism of the homeland itself (1974: 325).

Mendenhall further argues that the problem with wisdom is that there exists no 'control other than the limitation of technology and power', because 'wisdom as a means of achieving goals has rarely been able to evaluate itself' (1974: 331). While it may be true that an uncontrolled wisdom is a dangerous thing, the Solomonic narrative points out that the necessary control exists in the form of Torah.

The Deuteronomist thus offers a criticism of wisdom, that is, of wisdom that is not in accord with Torah. It is significant that wisdom is never again to be associated with an Israelite king, nor is it, for that matter, ever mentioned again in the Deuteronomistic History. According to the Deuteronomist, wisdom by itself is sufficient neither to effect good government, nor to allow justice to prevail. Wisdom is, however, an ideal in eschatological writings. Isaiah predicts the coming of a messiah who is to be endowed with wisdom and an ability to rule in accordance with Torah (9.6; 11.1-5), and who will usher in the new age. The association of wisdom with Torah, although never occurring again in the person of a reigning monarch, lives on as an ideal to be realized in the person of the messiah.

The development of the connection between wisdom and Torah can be seen in the writings of the Second Temple period, especially in the books of Sirach and Baruch. In Sirach, a pre-existent, immortal wisdom is hypostatized and identified with Torah (ch. 24). In the book of Baruch, the identification of Torah with wisdom is more explicit. Wisdom, who was with God from the beginning, comes down to earth where she *is* the eternal, life-giving Torah (4.1). For the authors of Sirach and Baruch, then, Wisdom becomes integrated with Torah in a creative synthesis. Wisdom traditions became strongly associated with and grounded upon Torah. Thus, just as Torah reveals wisdom (cf. Deut. 4.6), so wisdom helps to legitimate the authority of Torah in a kind of symbiosis.[16]

The pattern of the identification of Torah and wisdom was also to influence rabbinic Judaism and the New Testament writers. W.D. Davies argues that by identifying Jesus with the New Torah, Paul could also attribute ideas such as eternality and creativity, which were by then associated with wisdom, to Jesus (1948: 149-51). Furthermore, the association of Jesus with the messiah, a messiah who embodied wisdom and followed the will of God, shows that the New Testament writers were concerned to associate wisdom and Torah with an eschatological figure. In this way, the severing of wisdom from Torah, which led to the

---

16. Relevant here is Sheppard's argument, according to which wisdom for the writers of Sirach and Baruch becomes a theological category and a hermeneutical construct to interpret Torah (1980: *passim*, but esp. pp. 113-18).

ultimate failure of Solomon, is reversed as wisdom and Torah are reinte-
grated, both eschatologically and ontologically, in the person of Jesus.[17]
Thus, although the Deuteronomist regards the nexus of Torah and
wisdom as too volatile to sustain in an earthly king, the association does
persist throughout biblical literature, both in wisdom's hypostasis and
identification with Torah and as an ideal to be realized in a messianic
king.

In conclusion, when Solomon acts in accordance with Torah (as in
chs. 3–8), he is the ideal king; that is, he renders justice and uses his
wisdom for the benefit of the people. When Solomon violates the Torah
(as in chs. 9–11), he is the ideal's antithesis: he fails to render justice, and
he uses his wisdom for his own self-aggrandizement. Solomon's reign is
a watershed in the Deuteronomistic History: his political achievements
are unmatched by other kings, but his actions lay the foundations for the
division and destruction of the kingdom. These actions also have broad
theological implications in Solomon's rise and fall, and they will affect
future developments. The ideals of wisdom and Torah, which are combined both constructively and destructively in Solomon, persist throughout biblical literature, to be realized either in an eschatological figure, or
by wisdom's hypostasis and identification with Torah. Wisdom that is
not bound to Torah, as the story of Solomon shows, is almost the same
as folly.

We are now in a position to see how the biblical portrait of the
philosopher king differs from its Platonic counterpart. On the surface,
there is a remarkable similarity between the two. In Plato, the preservation of the ideal state is dependent upon philosophers becoming kings.
Similarly, in the Bible, the philosopher king Solomon establishes a short-
lived ideal state and initiates a sacrifice and a communal meal that bear a
striking resemblance to the utopian vision expressed in the Jubilee Year.
Yet, in marked contrast to its Greek counterpart, the rule of the biblical
philosopher king is doomed to failure if he does not abide by law.
Whereas the Greek philosopher king must transcend laws or customs to
get a better view of the whole, the Bible maintains the necessity of
abiding by law or custom if the rule is to be efficacious. In its own way,
the Bible maintains the validity of its customs and laws without denying
the legitimacy of the rule of the philosopher king. The fact that this rule

17. See also Brown's argument that Jesus was the mediator of the New Torah
(1979: lxxii), and his remarks concerning the personification of wisdom in the
Gospel of John (1979: cxxii-cxxvi).

is not possible from a human point of view does not alter the ideal, or the validity of an eschatological figure bound by law who would rule in the manner of the philosopher king. If Athens, then, argues that wisdom must transcend particular laws for true justice to be established, Jerusalem argues that without law there can be no true wisdom.

BIBLIOGRAPHY

Brettler, M.
　　1991　　'The Structure of 1 Kings 1–11', *JSOT* 49: 87-97.
Brown, R.E.
　　1979　　*The Gospel according to John, I–XII* (AB, 29; Garden City, NY: Doubleday).
Clark, W.M.
　　1969　　'A Legal Background to the Yahwist's Use of "Good and Evil" in Genesis 2–3', *JBL* 88: 266-78.
Davies, W.D.
　　1948　　*Paul and Rabbinic Judaism* (London: SPCK).
Eaton, J.H.
　　1976　　*Kingship and the Psalms* (London: SCM Press).
Frisch, A.
　　1991　　'Structure and its Significance: The Narrative of Solomon's Reign (1 Kgs 1–12.24)', *JSOT* 52: 3-14.
Gray, J.
　　1970　　*I and II Kings* (OTL; Philadelphia: Westminster Press, 2nd edn).
Johnson, A.
　　1967　　*Sacral Kingship in Ancient Israel* (Cardiff: University of Wales Press).
Jones, G.H.
　　1984　　*1 & 2 Kings* (NCB; Grand Rapids: Eerdmans).
Kalugila, L.
　　1980　　*The Wise King* (ConBOT, 15; Stockholm: Liber Tryck).
Kenik, H.A.
　　1983　　*Design for Kingship* (SBLDS, 69; Missoula, MT: Scholars Press).
Long, B.O.
　　1984　　*I Kings with an Introduction to Historical Literature* (FOTL, 9; Grand Rapids: Eerdmans).
McKane, W.
　　1970　　*Proverbs* (OTL; Philadelphia: Westminster Press).
Mendenhall, G.E.
　　1974　　'The Shady Side of Wisdom: The Date and Purpose of Genesis 3', in H.N. Bream *et al.* (eds.), *A Light unto My Path* (Festschrift J.M. Myers; Philadelphia: Temple University Press): 319-34.
Mettinger, T.N.D.
　　1976　　*King and Messiah: The Civil and Sacral Legitimation of the Israelite Kings* (Lund: Gleerup).

Montgomery, J.A.
    1950   *The Book of Kings* (ICC; Edinburgh: T. & T. Clark).
Mowinckel, S.
    1954   *He That Cometh* (trans. G.W. Anderson; New York: Abingdon Press).
Noth, M.
    1966   'Office and Vocation in the Old Testament', in *The Laws in the Pentateuch and Other Studies* (trans. D.R. Ap-Thomas; Edinburgh: Oliver & Boyd): 229-49.
    1968   *Könige* (BKAT, 9.1; Neukirchen–Vluyn: Neukirchener Verlag).
    1981   *The Deuteronomistic History* (trans. J. Doull; JSOTSup, 15; Sheffield: JSOT Press).
Noth, M., and D. Winton Thomas (eds.)
    1955   *Wisdom in Israel and in the Ancient Near East* (Festschrift H.H. Rowley; VTSup, 3; Leiden: Brill).
Parker, K.I.
    1988   'Repetition as a Structuring Device in 1 Kings 1–11', *JSOT* 42: 19-27.
    1991   'The Limits to Solomon's Reign: A Response to Amos Frisch', *JSOT* 51: 15-21.
Porteous, N.W.
    1955   'Royal Wisdom', in Noth and Winton Thomas (eds.) 1955: 247-61.
Ringgren, H.
    1966   *Israelite Religion* (trans. D. Green; London: SPCK).
Scott, R.B.Y.
    1955   'Solomon and the Beginning of Wisdom in Israel', in Noth and Winton Thomas (eds.) 1955: 262-90.
    1971   *The Way of Wisdom* (New York: Macmillan).
Sheppard, G.T.
    1980   *Wisdom as a Hermeneutical Construct* (BZAW, 151; Berlin: de Gruyter).
Weinfeld, M.
    1972   *Deuteronomy and the Deuteronomic School* (Oxford: Clarendon Press).
Whitelam, K.W.
    1979   *The Just King* (JSOTSup, 12; Sheffield: JSOT Press).
Whybray, R.N.
    1968   *The Succession Narrative* (SBT, 9; London: SCM Press).
    1974   *The Intellectual Tradition in the Old Testament* (BZAW, 135; Berlin: de Gruyter).
Widengren, G.
    1957   'King and Covenant', *JSS* 2: 1-32.

JSOT 50 (1991), pp. 55-62

ON KINGS AND DISGUISES*

Richard Coggins

I

The intention of this paper is to look at stories in which a distinctive motif, that of disguise, either by or in the presence of a king, is found and expressed in a particular way. There is a small number of stories, quite separate and unrelated in their context, which have the theme of a confrontation between a king and someone who is presented as the one through whom, perhaps rather unexpectedly, God's will is made known. In order that this 'making known' may come about, one of the parties disguises himself (or in one case herself), but the disguise is penetrated, and God's will is conveyed in a form which is liable to be quite unacceptable to the one seeking it.

It is surely not simply a matter of coincidence that this theme is repeated three or four times within the work we sometimes call the Deuteronomistic History; rather we may suppose that a theological point is being made here. It is, however, not one that fits into our usual categories, which may make it the more worthy of our consideration, particularly as it also relates to the current interest in narrative theology.

I say 'three or four' instances of such a story because in three instances one particular verb is used, and since it is a rare word in a form probably not found elsewhere, that gives those stories a certain coherence. But there is also another story which shares the same motifs yet without the use of that particular verb, which cannot be excluded altogether from our consideration.

---

* This paper was originally given as the Henton Davies Lecture at Regents Park College, Oxford, in February 1989; and subsequently at a seminar at the University of Exeter. I am grateful for the hospitality of both institutions and for the discussion which has led to some small changes (and, I hope, improvements) in content.

The verb in question is the reflexive or *hithpael* form of *ḥāpas*. The basic meaning of this verb is 'search', but the reflexive form always has the sense of 'disguising oneself'.[1]

II

All of the stories in question occur in the narratives relating to the monarchical period, found in either Samuel–Kings or Chronicles. First is the story of the witch of Endor in 1 Samuel 28. The context there is that Saul finds himself in a desperate position because of the Philistine threat: 'When he saw the army of the Philistines, he was afraid and his heart trembled greatly'. None of the approved means of seeking divine counsel had yielded any result, and so 'he disguised himself and put on other [that is, non-royal] garments and they came to the woman by night'— the woman being the medium who was at Endor, despite the fact that Saul himself had previously had mediums and wizards put out of the land of Israel. (This statement is usually taken as historical reportage, but the reference to Saul's putting these practitioners out of the land may be no more than a prolepsis for the Endor story.) The verb 'disguised himself' is the one that concerns us here: *ḥāpas* (*hithpael*).

The woman summons Samuel, whom she sees as an '*ᵉlōhîm* coming up from the earth'. Samuel is able to give Saul a message: 'The LORD has turned from you and become your enemy… The LORD will give Israel with you into the hand of the Philistines.' We meet Saul again only in the account of the battle on Mount Gilboa, where 'Saul died, and his three sons, and his armour-bearer, and all his men, on the same day together' (1 Sam. 31.6). His disguising himself had done him no good; the divine disfavour had reached its inevitable result in the death of Saul.

The second story is in 1 Kings 20, a collection of prophetic material relating to the northern kingdom with Elijah stories on either side of it, but itself with no reference to Elijah. As in 1 Samuel 28 the chief protagonists are a prophet-type figure and a king, and the same key verb, *ḥāpas*, is used; but there are important differences in the development of

---

1. There is an apparent exception in Job 30.18 where MT has this form, but translations and commentators are apparently unanimous in agreeing that it makes no sense in its context, and all the usual armoury of scholarly ingenuity is employed to achieve something which will make sense, either by emendation or by proposing hitherto unsuspected meanings for the verb.

the motif. One of the 'sons of the prophets', presumably a member of the prophetic bands, perhaps in royal service, which play a prominent part in the narratives from this period, persuades a passer-by to wound him by a blow, which he covers by 'disguising himself (*ḥāpas*) with a bandage over his eyes'. It is not clear whether that is meant to imply that he blinded himself, or whether it simply means that his forehead was swathed in bandages. Along comes the king; the prophet manufactures a story about his loss of a hostage whom he had undertaken to keep. The king thinks to condemn him out of his own mouth, but at that point the prophet strips off his disguise and stands revealed as a prophet. He has a message from God, that the king should not have let go the hostage he had been keeping—none other than Benhadad, the king of Damascus. As a result of the king's misplaced generosity his own and his people's lives will be forfeit.

After the Endor story, as we saw, a later episode describes the defeat of Israel and the death of the king; no such sequel occurs here, and it is not clear which king is referred to; nor are commentators agreed upon the literary relationships of these different stories at the end of 1 Kings. Nevertheless, the disguise story ends in each case with the same warning: defeat of the people in battle, and death of the king. But there is of course an important difference between this story and the earlier one. There the king had sought to trick God and his servant by disguising himself; here the 'servant of God' does the disguising, and not in any kind of attempt to trick God but to ensure that his message would be conveyed unmistakably to the king. To disguise oneself is thus not automatically a matter for condemnation; it may be a way of forwarding the divine initiative.

The third example of the device occurs in 1 Kings 22. The earlier part of that chapter describes the measures taken by the king of Israel and his southern partner to decide whether or not to engage in battle to capture Ramoth-Gilead, and the way in which they tried to discover the divine will. There what at first sight seemed to be a favourable prophetic response was reversed by the intervention of Micaiah son of Imlah. The two kings go to war against Ramoth-Gilead, and the king of Israel says 'I will disguise myself [*ḥāpas* (*hithpael*) once again] and go into battle, but you [the king of Judah] wear your robes'. This seems a sensible precaution when we hear in the next verse that the Aramaeans are commanded to 'Fight with neither small nor great, but only with the king of Israel'. But as we discover, it did the king of Israel[2] no good.

That the archer 'drew his bow at a venture' does not mean that the bow-shot was purely a matter of luck or chance. Here is the word of Yahweh spoken through the prophet Micaiah being brought into effect. Like the witch of Endor, the Aramaean archers are merely the instruments through which the result is achieved, but nevertheless instruments of a will that cannot be thwarted by human attempts at disguise.

We consider next the case of Josiah, depicted in 2 Kings as the very model of ideal kingship. Yet in the description of the Chronicler he fails to live up to a promising start. His death at the hands of the Egyptians at Megiddo, which seems to be an embarrassment to the editors of 2 Kings ('a somewhat embarrassed appendix...obscure as to detail' [Williamson 1982: 408]), is now in 2 Chronicles seen as the direct consequence of his falling away from God. Preparing to meet Pharaoh Neco, Josiah 'disguised himself' (*ḥāpas* [*hithpael*] again), and was killed. This incident provides an interesting link with the death of the king of Israel in our previous example; Williamson (pp. 409-11) suggests, surely rightly, that, from the disguise theme on, it is 'patterned closely' on the earlier account. There is of course no suggestion here of a 'bow at a venture', but the theme is again of the purpose of the God of Israel being worked out through the people's enemies.

Finally, in 1 Kings 14 is another well-known story which uses the same motif of disguise. Jeroboam's wife disguises herself at her husband's instigation to visit the blind prophet Ahijah of Shiloh because of the illness of their son. The verb *ḥāpas* does not occur (it is *šānâ* [*hithpael*], to change), but the particular motifs of these disguise stories are once again to the fore. Once again disguise brings disaster. As we have seen, it is not always the disguiser that is the victim; here it is the unfortunate child, and Jeroboam, who had initiated the idea, is punished by being pictured as left childless (v. 10, though we note that, according to a different tradition in v. 20, he was in fact succeeded briefly on the throne by his son Nadab). Relevant also is the unexpected way in which the disguise is shown to be ineffective. Ahijah is blind, so presumably the disguise would not in itself have made any difference; but he is given a direct word from God which tells him who his imminent visitor is, and

---

2. The text calls him simply 'the king of Israel'; though he is identified as Ahab in v. 20 this is generally taken as a secondary identification. Such identification in an originally anonymous story is not uncommon and is in this case historically unlikely.

thus both the limitations of his blindness and the trickery of the disguise are overcome.

III

We may now examine characteristic features of the theme. The four stories, excluding 1 Kings 14 for the moment, indisputably have in common the use of this particular verbal form: the *hithpael*, reflexive, form of *ḥāpas* occurs in them, and (with that one doubtful exception in Job) only here in the whole Hebrew Bible. But there also appear to be links which extend beyond what might be a mere chance of vocabulary usage, thematic points which illustrate something of the underlying ideology involved. In all the stories the victim is the king: Saul, the two anonymous kings of Israel in 1 Kings, Josiah, and, in 1 Kings 14, Jeroboam plus the child who might have been expected to succeed his father on the throne. In every case the story is told *at the expense of* the king. We need not engage in speculation about the pre-history of any of these traditions to recognize here that an important point is being made by the final editors concerning the ambiguity of royal status. Whether the king attempts to disguise himself (so Saul, the king in 1 Kgs 22, and Josiah), or whether he requires someone else to disguise herself on his behalf (Jeroboam), or whether he falls victim to a plot by a prophet in disguise, it is clear that bounds are set to the royal authority; it is God who will determine the course of events, whatever the king may think or attempt to bring about. The dubious mantic practices of the witch, or the bow at a venture, or the archers of the traditional enemy, Egypt, can all be put to this use.

The accounts in the Deuteronomistic History have in common the fact that it is an unacceptable line of kingship which is condemned in these disguise stories. In 1 Kings that is obvious enough; all three of the rulers there referred to are rulers of the northern kingdom, and that very fact is itself enough to ensure condemnation. Historically it is very doubtful whether Saul should be understood as a predecessor of the northern kings, but our concern here is not with history; it is the literary presentation that is significant, and there seems much to be said for the view that Saul's kingship is presented in terms comparable to those used of Jeroboam the son of Nebat and his successors as being automatically victims of the divine displeasure. Is the unacceptability of this royal line somehow implicated in the disguise motif?

But here Josiah's description in similar terms raises interesting questions concerning the Chronicler. In 2 Kings it is the wicked Manasseh who is compared with Ahab (2 Kgs 21.3, 13); in 2 Chronicles, by implication, it is Josiah, at least in his death, with whom the Ahab comparison is made. Josiah is pictured in 2 Kings in quasi-messianic terms; in 2 Chronicles the picture is very different, and questions must be raised against any understanding of Chronicles which sets great store upon an ideal king restoring the nation to ideal borders.

One point which is common to all the stories we have looked at is the 'superficiality' of the disguise. It is either seen through or proves ineffective because the one disguised is killed despite the disguise. In this respect, the Old Testament treatment of the theme differs markedly from that found in other literary contexts. In opera, for example, how different a matter it is, whether the device is used for comic or dramatic effects, in *Così fan tutte* or *Fidelio*. The contrast here with Old Testament usage is reminiscent of that made famous by Auerbach's *Mimesis* for narrative modes more generally; the apparent naivety and lack of sophistication of the biblical material which in fact conceals its own very distinctive literary art of 'realistic narrative'. When we turn to consider the character of that literary art, it seems that a point of fundamental theological significance is being made by the way in which this theme of disguising oneself is treated. Nothing is hidden from God's sight; he is presented as controlling the situation, often, as we have seen, in unexpected ways.[3]

IV

But by way of conclusion it may be suggested, if it is not too fanciful, that in the final form of the Deuteronomistic History the disguise theme had another important function. The overarching theme of that work

---

3. There is a disguise story in Gen. 27, where Jacob played a trick upon his blind father Isaac. The element of deliberate deception and trickery is far greater here than in any of the previously mentioned stories; even the king of Israel in 1 Kgs 22 seems to be presented as doing nothing more than taking sensible precautions. Yet Jacob tricks both his father and his brother, tells deliberate lies which involve bringing God into the story—and still gets away with it! It is a use of the theme in a way very different from that which we have been considering; disguise is here something positive, something through which God's own plans can be carried forward. But perhaps the main difference is that this story does not concern a king.

can fairly be said to be a description of the way in which God has worked his purpose out in and through his people. But some modern accounts of Deuteronomistic theology present that theme in very naive terms, as if the realities of every situation could be read off precisely as on a slide-rule. In fact, there is much in the Deuteronomistic understanding of God which should warn us against such oversimplification. What is really going on in any given set of events may in fact be disguised; there may be a deeper level of significance than that which appears on the surface; and the way in which frequent use is made of this disguise theme helps to reinforce that perception.

BIBLIOGRAPHY

Fokkelman, J.P.
    1986   *Narrative Art and Poetry in the Books of Samuel*. II. *The Crossing Fates* (Assen: Van Gorcum).
Jones, G.H.
    1984   *1 and 2 Kings* (NCB; London: Marshall, Morgan & Scott).
Whitelam, K.W.
    1979   *The Just King* (JSOTSup, 12; Sheffield, JSOT Press).
Williamson, H.G.M.
    1982   *1 and 2 Chronicles* (NCB; London: Marshall, Morgan & Scott).

CHRONICLES, EZRA, NEHEMIAH

JSOT 33 (1985), pp. 83-107

THE HISTORICAL RELIABILITY OF CHRONICLES:
THE HISTORY OF THE PROBLEM AND ITS PLACE
IN BIBLICAL RESEARCH*

Sara Japhet

Anyone interested in the history of research into Chronicles[1] will very soon discover two ways in which its study has deviated from that of other biblical books. Both divergences are interesting and surprising. One is the intense preoccupation with the book of Chronicles during certain phases of biblical research, a preoccupation which was actually in inverse proportion to the value attached to the book. The other is that the focus of interest in Chronicles, from the beginning of research into it and for a long time afterwards, centred upon questions of historical reliability and not upon matters of literary and theological concern, which were at the heart of the attention of biblical scholarship at the time. An examination of these two points—separately and jointly—will clarify the matter and reveal the peculiar position of Chronicles in the history of biblical research.

I

The book of Chronicles was appraised negatively from the very beginning of biblical criticism. Joseph Shelomo del Medigo, a Jewish scholar of the Renaissance, stated that the writer of Chronicles 'lived a long time

---

* A Hebrew version of this article has been published in the Seeligmann Festschrift: A. Rofé and Y. Zakovitch (eds.), *Isaac Leo Seeligmann Volume*, II (Jerusalem, 1983), pp. 327-46.

1. For the history of research on Chronicles cf. T. Willi, *Die Chronik als Auslegung* (FRLANT, 106; Göttingen, 1972), pp. 12-47. Willi is interested in the early stages of this research, up to Wellhausen, and deals only briefly with the developments from Wellhausen onwards.

after the first destruction...and therefore it was included among the Hagiographa...and you should know these post-destruction stories, how they vary, like most of the modern historiographies, where you will find no two in agreement on one single event'.[2]

Del Medigo's supposition was that the author of Chronicles was unreliable because so far removed in time from the events he described. His attitude probably influenced B. Spinoza, whose evasive statement about Chronicles was merely an excuse for the fact that he did not intend to deal with the book at all, and indeed totally disqualified it:

> Concerning the two books of Chronicles I have nothing particular or important to remark except that they were certainly written after the time of Ezra and possibly after the Restoration of the Temple by Judas Maccabaeus... As to their actual writer, their authority, utility and doctrine, I come to no conclusion. I have always been astonished that they have been included in the Bible by men who shut out from the canon the books of Wisdom, Tobit, and the others, styled apocryphal.[3]

At first Spinoza's extreme view did not exert much influence, doubtless because of two factors: one, that he obscured his intentions behind the above evasive comment and did not actually deal with the book, and the other, that interest in Chronicles at that time was at best marginal in any case, the work being assigned little significance. The one scholar actually influenced by Spinoza was G.L. Oeder, who took up the philosopher's second remark and tried to prove that Chronicles was not written through divine inspiration and therefore should be excluded from the biblical canon.[4]

The decisive change in Chronicles research occurred at the beginning of the nineteenth century with de Wette, who must be regarded as the founder of the modern study of the book. De Wette determined the character of this study—both for better and for worse—for over a hundred years, and his influence is still felt today. De Wette's work

---

2. Y.S. del Medigo, in S. Ashkenazi (ed.), *Matzref Lahochma* (Basel, 1629), p. 29b. On the man and his works cf. recently I. Barzilai, *Yoseph Shlomo Delmedigo (Yashar of Candia)* (SPB, 25; Leiden, 1974). On our subject, pp. 299-304.

3. B. Spinoza, *Theologico-Political Treatise* (1670), trans. R.H.M. Elwes, in *The Chief Works of Benedict de Spinoza* (New York, 1951), I, p. 146. On the possible connection between Spinoza and del Medigo, cf. Willi, *Die Chronik*, p. 29 nn. 97-98; Barzilai, *Yoseph Shlomo Delmedigo*, pp. 303-304.

4. G.L Oeder, *Freye Untersuchungen über einige Bücher des Alten Testament* (ed. G.L.H. Vogel; Halle, 1771), pp. 137-246; R. Smend, *Wilhelm Martin Leberecht de Wette* (Basel, 1958), p. 41.

should serve, therefore, as the point of departure for our study.[5]

The attention of the reader is drawn immediately to the importance of Chronicles in de Wette's work, an importance which was in sharp contrast to the work of his predecessors.[6] In 1806 de Wette published his *Beiträge zur Einleitung in das Alte Testament* which comprised two parts, one entitled 'Historical-critical Study of the Books of Chronicles', and the other 'Conclusions for the History of the Books of Moses and the Giving of the Law'.[7] The structure of de Wette's work and the relationship between the two parts are the keys to understanding his attitude towards Chronicles, in general and in particular.

The main question which engaged all biblical scholars of the time and which was the focus of protracted and lively debate was the question of authorship of the Pentateuch in its various aspects.[8] De Wette's view on the matter was that the Pentateuch was not written by Moses but much later, and he endeavoured to prove this not only by evidence from the Pentateuch but primarily by the history of Israel as described in the

5.   Willi deals in great detail with de Wette's role in the study of Chronicles. It seems, however, that he tends to judge his motives in a rather over-positive manner; cf. *Die Chronik*, esp. pp. 31-35. Smend emphasized the place of Chronicles in de Wette's scholarship (*De Wette*, pp. 40-45) and described it in the following words: 'The research on Chronicles is the brilliant piece among the early works of de Wette' (p. 45).

6.   An example of such an attitude is Eichhorn's *Einleitung*, which is generally regarded as the first modern introduction to the Bible and as laying the foundation of this specific genre; cf. O. Eissfeldt, *The Old Testament: An Introduction* (trans. P.R. Ackroyd; Oxford, 1965), p. 3: 'Eichhorn has been described as the founder of modern introduction to the Old Testament and rightly so'. Cf. also H.-J. Kraus, *Geschichte der historisch-kritischen Erforschung des Alten Testament* (Neukirchen–Vluyn, 1956), p. 120. In the first edition of the *Einleitung* there are only 26 pages dedicated to Chronicles and, as with the other historical books, there is a short paragraph on its 'Echtheit und Glaubwürdigkeit'. J.G. Eichhorn, *Einleitung ins alten Testament* (Leipzig, 1781–83), II, pp. 630-56.

7.   Originally 'Historisch-kritische Untersuchung über die Bücher der Chronik' and 'Resultate für die Geschichte der Mosaischen Bücher und Gesetzgebung'.

8.   Cf. Kraus, *Geschichte*, pp. 141ff. The problem of the Pentateuch revolved mainly around two issues: the question of 'who', which contained also that of 'when', and the question of 'how'. 'Who', namely: was it Moses who wrote the Pentateuch or a later author? 'How', mainly: was the Pentateuch as a whole the product of one creative author or were there sources which the author has used? There is a partial overlapping between the questions and the supposition of 'sources' is possible even when Moses is regarded as the author. Cf. Kraus, *Geschichte*, pp. 82ff.

Bible. He challenged the biblical and traditional view that the Law was given to Israel in the wilderness and formed Israel's constitution from the very beginning of its history, and posed this view as a question: Was the life of Israel in its land, from Joshua onwards, actually conducted according to the laws of Torah? Aware that a negative answer to this question would have supported and reinforced his different approach, he turned to examination of the life of Israel during the pre-exilic period, with this question serving as his guideline: Does the actual life of Israel, as recorded for that time, testify to the existence of the Torah?

Two sources were available to the contemporary biblical scholar in the attempt to reconstruct the period under discussion: the Former Prophets, from Joshua to Kings, in which are found only slight traces of the Pentateuch (mainly of Deuteronomy), and Chronicles, which describes the whole period, from David onwards, in close affinity with the laws of the Pentateuch. That affinity is especially evident in regard to worship, which is described in Chronicles with great similarity to the precepts of the Torah.[9] Until de Wette these two sources had been regarded as complementary, each describing the period from different points of view according to the different interests of their authors. The historian was expected to make use of the two sources while constantly harmonizing them. The consequence of this approach would be, of course, that the life of Israel was indeed determined by the laws of the Pentateuch. De Wette's goal, therefore, was to undermine the accepted view and base the history of Israel on one source alone: the Former Prophets. In order to attain this goal it was not sufficient to express a few doubts or hesitations regarding the reliability of Chronicles; rather it was necessary to reject completely any use of the book as a historical source, and to prove that it was absolutely unreliable. This was the purpose of the first part of de Wette's study. Thus, while his choice of title—'Historical-critical Study of the Books of Chronicles'—appears unassuming and neutral, the work was in fact directly aimed at disproving the reliability of Chronicles.

De Wette achieved this goal by the juxtaposition of the two sources: the Former Prophets on one hand and Chronicles on the other. He

---

9. Cf. W. Rudolph, *Chronikbücher* (Tübingen, 1955), pp. xiv-xv. The question which of the literary layers of the Pentateuch had influenced Chronicles most had drawn the attention of many scholars in the course of research; cf. below, n. 69, and S. Japhet, *The Ideology of the Book of Chronicles and its Place in Biblical Thought* (Hebrew; Jerusalem, 1977), p. 11 n. 20.

presented a contrast between what is close to the events, accurate, authentic, etc., and what is distant and detached, inaccurate, tendentious, etc. What is told in Samuel–Kings is presented as 'truth', 'history'; whatever deviates from it as 'forgery' and 'tendentious'.

The central place of Chronicles in the critical study of the Pentateuch explains at once the significance which the book acquired in de Wette's approach, the intense preoccupation with the problem of reliability, and the interrelationship between the two parts of de Wette's work. Indeed, at the beginning of the second part he says:

> Just as the whole of Jewish history, in its most interesting and important aspects, namely those of religion and worship, took on a completely different form after sweeping out[10] the description of Chronicles, which was…for such a long time an obstacle to the correct view and deceived the student of history, so at once the study of the Pentateuch received a completely different direction.[11]

Consequently, the first chapter of this part is called 'Revision of the Historical Evidence and the Traces of the Existence of the Pentateuch as a Written Whole'.[12]

There is an inseparable bond between the study of Chronicles and Pentateuch criticism, and it is this which illumines the history of Chronicles research from de Wette and for a long time afterwards. The interest of scholars in the book itself remained marginal, a trend reinforced by the constant efforts of biblical scholarship to prove the book's worthlessness. But its central role in the study of the Pentateuch resulted in a series of studies all dealing with the question of its reliability and with the sources at its disposal. In the fourth edition of his *Einleitung*, Eichhorn dedicated seven pages to a discussion of the reliability of Chronicles and tried to defend it against de Wette's view.[13] Among the books written at that time we should mention J.C. Dahler, *Of the Dispute about the Authority and Historical Fidelity of the Book of Chronicles*;[14] J.M. Hertz, *Are There Traces of the Pentateuch and the*

---

10. De Wette's language is very sharp, using words like 'Wegräumung' here and 'Verwerfung der Chronik' later (W.M.L. de Wette, *Beiträge zur Einleitung in das Alte Testament* [Halle, 1806], p. 136).

11. *Beiträge*, p. 135.

12. *Beiträge*, p. 136.

13. J.G. Eichhorn, *Einleitung in das Alte Testament* (Leipzig, 4th edn, 1823), III, pp. 495ff.

14. J.G. Dahier, *De Librorum Paralipomenon Auctoritate atque Fide Historica Disputatio* (Strassburg and Leipzig, 1819).

Law of Moses to Be Found in the Books of Kings? A Study on the Defence of Chronicles, as well as the Antiquity of the Law of Moses;[15] C.P.W. Gramberg, *The Historical Character and Credibility of Chronicles Examined Anew*,[16] which supports de Wette's views; and C.F. Keil, *Apologetical Study of the Books of Chronicles and the Integrity of the Book of Ezra*,[17] who again defends the traditional view.

As already stated, the close connection between the two fields of research persisted later on, its main landmarks being the studies of K.H. Graf, 'The Book of Chronicles as a Historical Source',[18] and of Wellhausen in his *Prolegomena*, published in 1878, with Chapter 6 dedicated to Chronicles.[19] That it was these two scholars who produced momentous research on Chronicles was again no accident. In the study of the Pentateuch in the nineteenth century the line of development continued via the detailed work of Graf to its climax in Wellhausen's work, which presented a final synthesis of all the lines of research followed to his time. Even today the 'Documentary Hypothesis' is often referred to as 'the Graf–Wellhausen hypothesis'.[20] The fact that these same scholars were the ones who developed and completed the line of study of the book of Chronicles is closely linked with their preoccupation with the Pentateuch. While Graf dedicated an elaborate study to the reliability of the various details in Chronicles, the synthesis is presented

---

15. J.M. Hertz, *Sind in den Bücher der Könige Spurn des Pentateuch und der Mosaischen Gesetze zu finden? Ein Versuch zur Vertheidigung der Bücher der Chronik wie auch des Alterthums der Mosaischen Gesetze* (1822).

16. C.P.W. Gramberg, *Die Chronik nach ihren geschichtlichen Charakter und ihrer Glaubwürdigkeit neu geprüft* (Halle, 1823)

17. C.F. Keil, *Apologetischer Versuch über die Bücher der Chronik und über die Integrität des Buches Ezra* (Berlin, 1833).

18. K.H. Graf, 'Das Buch der Chronik als Geschichtsquelle', in *Die Geschichtlichen Bücher des Alten Testament* (Leipzig, 1866), pp. 114-247. The book comprises two parts and the difference between their respective titles is telling. While the discussion of Chronicles focuses on the problem of historical reliability, that of the Pentateuch and Former Prophets is dedicated to the 'Components of the Historical Books from Genesis 1 to 2 Kings 25 (Pentateuch and Former Prophets)'.

19. J. Wellhausen, *Prolegomena to the History of Israel* (trans. S. Black and A. Menzies; Edinburgh, 1885), pp. 171-227.

20. Cf., for example, H.H. Rowley, *The Growth of the Old Testament* (London, 1950), p. 16. The justification of this title and the contribution of other scholars, mainly A. Kuenen, to the formation and establishment of this theory is not my interest here.

in Wellhausen's work, as a systematic presentation of the book's character and its value as a historical source.

Wellhausen regarded himself as a follower of de Wette and not of
Graf;[21] indeed, without overlooking his own contributions to the understanding of the literary character and theological concepts of Chronicles,[22]
its study was for Wellhausen, as much as for de Wette, only a means to
an end.[23] De Wette had denied the reliability of Chronicles on the basis
of what he regarded as two of its main features: negligent, inaccurate
work, and gross tendentiousness, expressed *inter alia* in the author's
preference for the Levites, his predisposition toward the cult and his love
of Judah and animosity for Israel.[24] Having abrogated the historicity of
the Chronicler's evidence, the way was clear for establishing a later
dating of the Pentateuch as a whole. In principle Wellhausen followed
the same path, but at his time the late date of the Pentateuch had already
become an accepted axiom and the main interest lay with the problem
of the 'documents' of which the Pentateuch was composed, their origins,
dates and delimitation. Given these developments, therefore, Wellhausen
related the tendentious testimony of Chronicles not to the lateness of the
Pentateuch as a whole, but more specifically to the dating of the Priestly
Code. His conclusion was that the historical description of Chronicles

21. Wellhausen, *Prolegomena*, p. 172. It is certainly noteworthy that he down-
plays the importance of Graf, both here and in his general introduction, pp. 3-4.

22. On the resemblance between Wellhausen and de Wette, cf. also Willi, *Die
Chronik*, pp. 44-45. According to Willi, 'The meaning of Wellhausen's chapter on
Chronicles in his "Prolegomena" lies only in giving a classical form to de Wette's
results, and enabling them to exert a general influence'. It seems, however, that
Wellhausen cannot be regarded only as providing form and distribution to de
Wette's work; he made a contribution of his own and added important points to our
understanding of the Chronicler's views.

23. It should not be surprising, therefore, that Wellhausen paid no attention at all
to Ezra–Nehemiah. Although he stated categorically that Ezra–Nehemiah is an
organic part of Chronicles, he referred to it only in one parenthetical sentence in the
introduction: 'Chronicles, which properly speaking forms but a single book along
with Ezra and Nehemiah, is...' (*Prolegomena*, p. 171), with no further elaboration.
Although he agreed with the prevalent view of his time regarding the relationship
between the two books, it was only Chronicles which was needed for the discussion
of the Pentateuch and therefore it alone was the subject of his study.

24. The third paragraph in de Wette's work on Chronicles is entitled: 'Lack of
Precision, Negligence, Compilatory Manner of the Author of Chronicles' (*Beiträge*,
pp. 62-77); the following paragraphs deal with the above-mentioned subjects and
with the Chronicler's love for miracles (pp. 78-133).

was thoroughly dyed with the colours of the Priestly Document and this was for him a proof that the Priestly Document had only recently come into being. The complete tendentiousness and unreliability of Chronicles were the indications by which the lateness of the Priestly Document was proven, and this in turn led to a complete theory of the history of the spiritual development and the religious institutions of Israel.[25]

The work of Wellhausen was apparently conclusive. His description of Chronicles was accepted almost without demur. An expression of this view, in an extreme form, was given by C.C. Torrey, who dedicated several of his studies to Chronicles and Ezra–Nehemiah. At the end of the nineteenth century he declared categorically:

> No fact of Old Testament criticism is more firmly established than this; that the Chronicler as a historian is thoroughly untrustworthy. He distorts facts deliberately and habitually; invents chapter after chapter with the greatest freedom, and what is most dangerous of all, his history is not written for its own sake, but in the interest of an extremely one-sided theory.[26]

II

Before turning to the next stage in the history of research, another aspect of the study of Chronicles should be clarified. This aspect may at first seem unrelated to our subject, but its relevance will quickly become evident. It is the question of the extent of the chronistic work, namely the relationship between Chronicles and Ezra–Nehemiah.[27]

25. Concerning the historical value of the book, he concludes as follows: 'The whole question ultimately resolves itself into that of historical credibility; and to what conclusion this leads we have already seen. The alterations and additions of Chronicles are all traceable to the same fountain-head—the Judaizing of the past' (Wellhausen, *Prolegomena*, p. 223). In the same vein he also opens his study: 'We shall now proceed to show that the mere difference of date fully accounts for the varying ways in which the two histories [Former Prophets and Chronicles] represent the same facts and events, and the difference of spirit arises from the influence of the Priestly Code which came into being in the interval' (pp. 171-72). He also attacks rather sharply all those who tried to defend the reliability of Chronicles with the argument that the Chronicler had made use of ancient authentic sources. Cf. esp. pp. 222-27 and below, n. 44.

26. C.C. Torrey, *The Composition and Historical Value of Ezra–Nehemiah* (BZAW, 2; Giessen, 1896), p. 52.

27. Cf. S. Japhet, 'The Supposed Common Authorship of Chronicles and Ezra–Nehemiah Investigated Anew', *VT* 18 (1968), pp. 330-71; H.G.M. Williamson, *Israel in the Book of Chronicles* (Cambridge, 1977), pp. 5-82.

The traditional view is expressed in the Talmudic statement found in *B. Bat.* 15a: 'Ezra wrote the book that bears his name and the genealogies of Chronicles up to his time... Who then finished it [the book of Chronicles]? Nehemiah, the son of Hachaliah.' The view that Ezra was the author of Chronicles was questioned by Spinoza, who claimed that 'they were certainly written after the time of Ezra'.[28] Spinoza based his argument on the list of the Davidides in 1 Chron. 3.17-24,[29] but it seems that the motive behind his argument was again related to the problem of the Pentateuch. Since Spinoza suggested Ezra as the most likely candidate for the authorship of the Pentateuch and the Former Prophets, which he regarded as one composition,[30] he could not then attribute to Ezra authorship of the book named after him, or of Chronicles. Both of these works Spinoza ascribed to much later writers.[31]

The question of the relationship between Chronicles and Ezra–Nehemiah took central place in a study of Chronicles by L. Zunz in 1832. His conclusions were that the two books were indeed composed by one author, but that this person could not have been Ezra the scribe but someone who surveyed the period from a distance and who therefore must have lived at a later date. Ezra, then, was not the author of Chronicles but rather the opposite: the Chronicler was the author of Ezra–Nehemiah. 'We see the book of Chronicles and the book of Ezra–Nehemiah as two interconnected parts of one and the same work. Thus in the book of Ezra we have the Chronicler before us, with his descriptions of the people's assemblies, festivals, and the reading of the Law...'[32]

28. Spinoza, *Treatise*, p. 146.

29. *Treatise*, p. 274 n. 19.

30. 'When we put together these considerations, namely, the unity of the subject of all the books, the connection between them and the fact that they are compilations made many generations after the events they relate had taken place, we come to the conclusion...that they are all the work of a single historian. Who this historian was is not easy to show; but I suspect that he was Ezra and there are several strong reasons for adopting this hypothesis' (*Treatise*, pp. 129-30).

31. Spinoza places at a very late date also the author of Ezra, but he does not identify him with the author of Chronicles. In addition to Ezra he ascribes to him the composition of Nehemiah, Daniel and Esther (*Treatise*, pp. 150-51).

32. L. Zunz, *Die Gottesdienstlichen Vorträge der Juden historisch entwickelt* (Berlin, 1832), p. 21. The same conclusion was reached independently by F.C. Movers, *Kritische Untersuchungen über die biblische Chronik* (Bonn, 1834), who attributed to the Chronicler only Ezra 1–10. Unfortunately I could not consult the book.

Zunz's approach and arguments were based on a literary-critical study of Ezra–Nehemiah, having—on the face of it—no direct bearing on the question of the book's reliability or its use as a historical source. Yet, in characterizing the Chronicler as the author of Ezra–Nehemiah a judgment was implied: 'Thus in the book of Ezra we have the Chronicler before us...with his love for genealogies, his exaggeration of numbers...his historical ignorance, etc.'[33] Still, from these literary conclusions Zunz did not draw far-reaching historical ones, since he attributed to the Chronicler only a small part of Ezra–Nehemiah and regarded most of Ezra–Nehemiah as consisting of sources adopted by the Chronicler.[34] He did not challenge the overall reliability of the book but tended to accept its evidence more or less at face value.

The theory suggested by Zunz was a significant point of departure for future generations of scholars. In following years this view gained in popularity, until it became a virtually unquestioned axiom.[35] Indeed, various literary studies of the time endeavoured to show that the Chronicler's part in Ezra–Nehemiah was much greater than Zunz had supposed, and the entire Ezra narrative was attributed to the Chronicler's authorship.[36] Toward the end of the nineteenth century there was an increasing tendency to deny completely the historical reliability of Ezra–Nehemiah and consequently the very fact of the restoration.[37] The most extreme view was again expressed by Torrey, who claimed that the author of Ezra–Nehemiah had at his disposal only two sources, both of which were more meagre than was generally thought,

33. Zunz, *Vorträge der Juden*, p. 21.

34. Zunz regarded the following sections as 'chronistic': Ezra 1; 3; 6.18–7.11; 10.1-17; Neh. 7.73b–10.29; and also some verses and sections in Neh. 11, 12, and 13 (*Vorträge der Juden*, p. 28).

35. Cf. Japhet, 'Supposed Common Authorship', pp. 330-33.

36. Torrey, *Composition*, pp. 14-29; *idem*, *Ezra Studies* (Chicago, 1910), pp. 238-48; A.S. Kapelrud, *The Question of Authorship in the Ezra Narrative* (Oslo, 1944).

37. One should mention here the work of Van Hoonacker, who raised doubts regarding the historical framework of Ezra–Nehemiah and placed Ezra after Nehemiah. Cf. A. Van Hoonacker, *Néhémie et Esdras* (Louvain, 1890); *idem*, *Zorobabel et le Second Temple* (Gand, 1892); *idem*, *Nouvelles Etudes sur la Restauration Juive* (Paris, 1896). Also to be mentioned is Kosters, who doubted the historical reliability of Ezra 1–4 and denied the historicity of the restoration. Cf. W.H. Kosters, *Die Wiederherstellung Israels in der persischen Periode* (trans. A. Basedow; Heidelberg, 1895) (the Dutch original was published in 1893).

and not free of later reworking. These two were Nehemiah's Memoirs and a late, worthless, Aramaic source; all the rest was of the Chronicler's free composition.[38] The basis of Torrey's stand on the matter was the combination of the two lines of research which had been developed previously: the identification of the author of Ezra–Nehemiah with the Chronicler, and a categorical denial of this author's reliability. Torrey's contribution lay in the broadest application of these principles and the drawing of the most extreme historical conclusions from them. Consequently, he rejected out of hand the historical picture portrayed by Ezra–Nehemiah and suggested his own: The exile was a limited phenomenon; there was no restoration at all; Ezra the Scribe is a fictitious figure; the edict of Cyrus and the letter of Artaxerxes are later forgeries; the story about the bringing of the Torah from Babylon is pure imagination; the expulsion of the foreign wives is an unfounded invention; and so on.[39] From the point of view of the historian, the consequences of the rejection of the historical reliability of Ezra–Nehemiah were more far-reaching than the denial of the same in Chronicles. After all, for the description of the monarchic period the book of Chronicles can be regarded as merely complementary; our main sources are to be found in earlier historiography, other biblical books and extra-biblical material. Not so the history of Israel in the Persian period, for which the book of Ezra–Nehemiah was and still is the main source. Only little can be learned from other biblical books (in particular Haggai and Zechariah), and extra-biblical material was and remains quite meagre. The total abandonment of Ezra–Nehemiah as a historical source left the historical study of the period to the scholar's whim. Thus the problem of these 'ad absurdum' conclusions about the unreliability of Ezra–Nehemiah can be regarded as a major cause for change of direction and a reconsideration of the historicity of the Chronicler.

III

The first impulse toward a moderation of attitudes, and a more careful examination of the use of Chronicles as a historical source, came from

38. The summary of Torrey's literary analysis is found in his *Composition*, pp. 49-50.

39. Torrey, *Composition*, pp. 51-65. He then elaborated these conclusions in his following studies (mainly in *Ezra Studies*, pp. 208ff.), after realizing that his first study did not make the impression he had wished for.

scholars whose main interest lay not in the study of the Pentateuch or the history of the religion of Israel, but in the reconstruction of ancient history. In the second half of the nineteenth century archaeological discoveries in the Near East were beginning to bear fruit. The newly discovered findings were brought to bear on the accepted view of the history of Israel—until then based on biblical sources alone. The discoveries also inspired increased interest in the history of Israel as such, and encouraged scholars to search for additional sources even within the Bible, to complete as far as possible the historical picture. The beginnings of a change in attitude regarding the reliability of Chronicles must be put within this framework.

It seems that the first scholar to articulate this change was Hugo Winckler, who dedicated a special study to 'Remarks on Chronicles as a Historical Source',[40] and dealt with the book on various other occasions.[41] Winckler's approach was cautious and rather reserved. He faithfully followed his predecessors in the study of Chronicles and accepted as a general rule the fact of the book's tendentiousness which by its very nature compromised reliability. Yet, following some isolated remarks made by Graf,[42] he began to re-examine the historical description, although in a very restrained manner. To begin with he disregarded the sections of the book which parallel Samuel–Kings, agreeing with his predecessors that the changes which this material underwent in Chronicles all resulted from the Chronicler's own motivations, and consequently were of no historical value. He therefore limited himself to a re-examination of the additional material peculiar to Chronicles. Even this, according to Winckler, had to be scrutinized for the characteristic views of the Chronicler, and only when these were absent could one reconsider—in each case on its own merits—the historical probability of the material. Winckler believed that the new information gathered from

40. H. Winckler, 'Bemerkungen zur Chronik als Geschichtsquelle', in *Alttestamentliche Untersuchungen* (Leipzig, 1892), pp. 157-67.

41. Cf. mainly his discussion of the deportation of Manasseh in 'Die Orakel über Nordarabien, Jes. 21', in *Alttestamentliche Untersuchungen*, pp. 122-23. His conclusion was that 'one has as much right to doubt Manasseh's deportation as his very existence'. Cf. also the discussion of the problem of the Arabs and Meunites in 'Musri, Meluhha, Mai'n', MVAG 3 (1898), pp. 42ff.

42. Cf. Graf, 'Das Buch der Chronik', pp. 187-88. Graf lists here verses and passages from 2 Chron. which are of an annalistic character and were probably excerpted from an ancient source. He states here too, however, that they are found in Chronicles in a reworked form and therefore should not be taken literally.

the discoveries in the ancient Near East caused an essential change in the very concept of 'historical probability', a change which must be brought to bear on the material in Chronicles as well.[43]

Winckler's cautious approach demonstrated the historian's need to complement his or her sources and to make use of all the material to which he or she might have access, but also the conviction that the uncompromising, categorical disqualification of Chronicles is itself rather arbitrary. Following Winckler, we can trace the same careful search for historical elements by other scholars as well, such as Benzinger, Kittel and Curtis.[44]

At the same time the examination of the problem of historical reliability was being introduced in another area, that is, the book of Ezra–Nehemiah. In 1896 Eduard Meyer published his study, *Die Entstehung des Judentums*, in which he discussed in great detail the Aramaic documents in the book of Ezra: their language, form and historical background. The conclusion he reached was that the Aramaic documents were an authentic, reliable source; as a result much greater historical value was ascribed to the whole of Ezra–Nehemiah.[45] The path taken by Meyer is a good example of the way in which generally accepted conventions forced the historical and literary study of Ezra–Nehemiah into certain avenues of research. According to the general view the Chronicler was the author of Ezra–Nehemiah and his reputation as a historian had reached its nadir; in fact he is described as a first-rate forger

43. Winckler, 'Bemerkungen', pp. 157-60.

44. I. Benzinger, *Die Bücher der Chronik* (KHAT; Tübingen, 1901), pp. x-xiii; R. Kittel, *Die Bücher der Chronik* (HAT; Göttingen, 1902), pp. x-xvi; E.L. Curtis and A.A. Madsen, *The Books of Chronicles* (ICC; New York, 1910), pp. 14-16. It should be said that Wellhausen too recognized the existence of several historical nuclei in the genealogy of Judah, following his dissertation on the subject (*De Gentibus et Familiis Judaeis* [Göttingen, 1870]). Cf. *Prolegomena*, pp. 216-18. However, he regarded as marginal the importance of these details, did not draw from them any inferences regarding the other parts of the book, and in his final conclusions simply ignored them. He stated explicitly that 'To speak of a tradition handed down from pre-exilic times as being found in Chronicles, either in 1 Chron. 1–9 or in 1 Chron. 10–2 Chron. 36, is thus manifestly out of the question' (*Prolegomena*, p. 222). Later on he justified his stand by saying: 'It is indeed possible that occasionally a grain of good corn may occur among the chaff, but to be conscientious one must neglect this possibility of exceptions and give due honour to the probability of the rule' (*Prolegomena*, p. 224).

45. E. Meyer, *Die Entstehung des Judentums* (Halle, 1896), pp. 8-71.

of history. The only way to 'rescue' the book of Ezra–Nehemiah and accept its historical outlines was by the assumption that at least the major part of the book derived from authentic, contemporary sources, and that the Chronicler's interference with these sources was minimal. At the same time, all historical inconsistencies could be attributed to the Chronicler, an academic escape route which afforded easy solutions and ample opportunity for various historical reconstructions.[46]

An important change in attitude can be traced in the first study of Albright dedicated to Ezra–Nehemiah. The article is entitled, 'The Date and Personality of the Chronicler', but it deals in fact with the question of authorship and reliability of Ezra–Nehemiah.[47] Albright was faced with a dilemma. On the one hand he admired the philological studies of Torrey and accepted unquestioningly his literary conclusions, that most of Ezra–Nehemiah, including the Ezra narrative, was composed by the Chronicler.[48] On the other hand, he followed Meyer in accepting the authenticity of the Aramaic documents, and rejected Torrey's historical conclusions that almost everything in Ezra–Nehemiah was spurious.[49] In order to solve this impasse Albright suggested that Torrey's literary conclusions did not force the assumption that the author of Ezra–Nehemiah was the Chronicler. In fact the opposite is more convincing: that Ezra was the author of both Ezra–Nehemiah and Chronicles.[50] By returning to the traditional view Albright achieved several ends: he upheld the literary conclusions of Torrey without denying the existence of Ezra himself; he considerably antedated the composition of Ezra–Nehemiah; and, while holding to the accepted view regarding the complete unreliability of Chronicles, he emphasized the reliability of Ezra–Nehemiah, the problematics of which had been his starting point. Thus he writes:

46. Torrey debated with Meyer in 'The Aramaic Portions of Ezra', in *Ezra Studies*, pp. 140ff. Cf. also the independent views of L.W. Batten, *The Books of Ezra and Nehemiah* (ICC; New York, 1913), pp. 14-24.

47. W.F. Albright, 'The Date and Personality of the Chronicler', *JBL* 40 (1921), pp. 104-24.

48. Cf. Albright, 'Chronicler', p. 106: 'Torrey's textual work is perhaps unsurpassed for brilliancy in the whole domain of Old Testament science'.

49. Albright, 'Chronicler', p. 107. In support of Meyer's view he adduced the witness of the Elephantine papyri which had come to light in the interval (pp. 107, 117-18).

50. 'Chronicler', p. 120.

> The question of the Chronicler's date is naturally of the greatest impor-
> tance for the post-exilic history of the Jews. Since he shows a total lack of
> historical sense in dealing with the pre-exilic age, he may be trusted with
> equal unreliability for the century after the Captivity, in case he lived in the
> third century BC, where the great majority of scholars...place him. On the
> other hand, since practically the whole of the old Jewish literature perished
> in 586, we can understand how a writer of the early fourth century might
> be worthless for pre-exilic conditions, and yet reliable for the century
> preceding his own time. The two problems of the date and veracity of
> Ezra-Nehemiah are therefore indissolubly connected...[51]

In a way, Albright is here at a crossroads: he is still bound to the
prevalent conclusions of his time, but his historical approach impels him
to look for new solutions. Albright proposed a view which entailed some
changes in the concept of historical reliability. Accordingly, he saw one
and the same author as unreliable for one historical period and fully
trustworthy for another, because the origin of his unreliability was not in
himself as an author, but in the lack of appropriate sources or in the
absence of a critical method.[52] In principle this view implied a rehabilitation of the Chronicler as a historian who, in spite of his tendentiousness,
could be regarded as a writer of history and not of *belles lettres*.
Albright addressed himself in this study only to Ezra–Nehemiah and not
to Chronicles, but in the article's first footnote he remarks:

> Up to the present no archaeological discoveries have confirmed the facts
> added by the Chronicler to his liberal excerpts from the canonical books
> of the Old Testament. Some of his statements, especially his lists of
> towns and clans, have doubtless historical value, though their exact source
> remains unknown... It is still however too early for a categorical denial
> of historical nuclei in these fantastic stories...'[53]

These words of Albright were actually an expression of a wish and hope
that the archaeological discoveries might indeed confirm these stories!
Indeed, in an article written almost thirty years later, in 1950, this new

51. 'Chronicler', pp. 105-106.
52. Albright refers to it in one sentence from the passage already quoted: 'since
practically the whole of the old Jewish literature perished in 586, we can understand
how a writer of the early fourth century might be worthless for pre-exilic conditions'—which implies that the cause of the late author's 'worthlessness' is only the
lack of sources and not his literary method or theological bias. At the same time
another possibility may be implied, namely that the late author could act more freely
because there was no appropriate literature which could serve as a means of control.
53. 'Chronicler', p. 104 n. 1.

direction was confirmed. The title of the article is 'The Judicial Reform of Jehoshaphat',[54] but only its second part dealt with that subject; the first, more comprehensive part, addressed itself to 'The Literary and Historical Character of the Chronicler's Work'.[55] Here Albright purposed to challenge outright the rejection of Chronicles as a historical source, for which 'archaeological evidence can now be marshalled in increasing abundance'.[56] Still, Albright finds it necessary, here too, to begin his argument with the post-exilic periods and the book of Ezra–Nehemiah. He then proceeds from the historicity of the restoration, the exile of Jehoiachin and the Elephantine papyri, to the book of Chronicles itself, making reference to the genealogies, the Temple singers, various facts from the history of the kingdom of Judah, and so forth. His final conclusion was that the total rejection of Chronicles is 'both subjective and uncritical'.[57]

Even Albright did not accept the evidence of Chronicles at face value but required a careful examination of the material before any historical conclusions could be drawn. However, in relation to Winckler, he took an important step forward. Winckler looked for reliable historical elements only in the additional material of Chronicles, and only when it was free of any characteristic tendencies of the author. Albright demanded that all the elements of the chronistic work be studied anew. Important data could be found, according to Albright, not only in the neutral stories, but also in the tendentious ones, and even there it was possible that the Chronicler was not inventing his stories but selecting what suited his purposes from alternative sources. According to Albright, Ezra edited his work 'with profound respect for what he found in books and traditions, but with scarcely the most elementary conception of critical method. It is therefore incumbent on the historian to accept his material with gratitude but sift it with care.'[58]

---

54. W.F. Albright, 'The Judicial Reform of Jehoshaphat', in *Alexander Marx Jubilee Volume* (New York, 1950), pp. 61-82.

55. 'Judicial Reform', pp. 61-74.

56. 'Judicial Reform', p. 62.

57. 'Judicial Reform', p. 74.

58. 'Judicial Reform', pp. 73-74. Cf. also the balanced statement of Rudolph: 'Descriptions in which no influence of the chronistic leading ideas can be recognized deserve full trust and form a welcomed complement to our knowledge; even where such influence can be traced we are not free from examining whether the Chronicler did not make authentic events carry the burden of his theological views even when these events are not known from any other place' (*Chronikbücher*, p. xvii).

IV

The change in Albright's attitude toward the historical reliability of
Chronicles was just one expression of a more general, manifold change
which has come about in the study of Chronicles in the present century.
This change was accelerated by several factors, of which the weightiest
in Albright's consideration was the progress in knowledge of the history
of Israel as a result of archaeological discoveries, both material and epi-
graphic. The influence of this factor can be discerned already in
Winckler's studies, and it gained impetus gradually with the accumulation and combination of various details, both large and small. The discovery of the Siloam inscription and tunnel, for example, confirmed the
evidence of 2 Chron. 32.30 and made almost impossible any understanding of this verse as a mere interpretation of 2 Kgs 20.20.[59] As early as
1905, Macalister connected the seals bearing the inscription למלך, which
were being discovered at several sites in Israel, with 1 Chron. 4.23 and
the genealogies of Judah.[60] The archaeological surveys in the Judaean
desert, which began in the 1950s, showed that the information about the
constructions of the kings of Judah 'in the desert' were not just an
expression of the Chronicler's own interests but also reliable historical
facts.[61] More examples could be cited.

Another result of the archaeological discoveries, especially in Israel,
was an increased understanding of historical geography, which led to a
new evaluation of the geographical data in Chronicles, and an emphasis
on their basic reliability. In this area one could mention the studies of
Klein, Bewer, Noth, Aharoni, Kallai and others.[62]

The force of archaeological discoveries as a factor in biblical research

59. The inscription was discovered by accident in 1880. Cf. J. Simons,
Jerusalem in the Old Testament (Leiden, 1952), pp. 179-87.

60. R.A.S. Macalister, 'The Craftsmen's Guild of the Tribe of Judah', *PEQ* 37
(1905), pp. 243-53, 328-42.

61. 2 Chron. 17.12; 26.12; 27.4; cf. F.M. Cross and J.T. Milik, 'Explorations in
the Judean Buqê'ah', *BASOR* 142 (1956), p. ii; M. Kochavi (ed.), *Judea, Samaria
and the Golan Archaeological Survey 1967–1968* (Hebrew; Jerusalem, 1972), pp.
93-94.

62. S. Klein, 'Studies in the Genealogical Chapters of Chronicles', in *Palästina
Studien* (Hebrew; Jerusalem, 1930); G. Beyer, 'Das Festungssystem Rehabeam',
ZDPV 54 (1931), pp. 113-34; M. Noth, 'Eine siedlungsgeographische Liste im
1 Chron. 2 und 4', *ZDPV* 55 (1932), pp. 97-124; *idem*, 'Die Ansiedling des
Stammes Juda auf den Boden Palästinas', *PJ* 30 (1934), pp. 31-47.

stems from its foundation in extra-biblical material, which affords a sense of objectivity. Its results were felt not only in the confirmation or rejection of isolated details, but in a more general change of attitude. This manifested itself in two ways: an overall increase in the credibility of Chronicles (thanks to the cumulative evidence of numerous details), and a more cautious stand regarding the limits of 'historical probability'. From these new points of departure the historian could now approach the historical data of Chronicles in a more moderate mood.[63]

The above considerations were, however, just one of the factors which brought about a change of attitude toward Chronicles. Another factor was the developing re-evaluation of the Chronicler himself and of his literary methods. The portrayal of the Chronicler as *the* forger of history, as a person endowed with a rigid dogma, rare literary talents, and an unrestrained audacity, whose writings were pure fiction, inspired by limited objectives[64]—this was a stereotype which could no longer be accepted. It seems that two elements in this picture caused a counter-reaction. One is the presupposition that the Chronicler had been writing his history with *a priori* evil intentions and vicious premeditations, forging his story in the service of ideological and political objectives, and the other the assumption of 'free invention': fictitious writing disguised in geographical lists, genealogical details and historical narratives. As we saw above, Albright claimed that the Chronicler (or Ezra) was a cautious editor, who described the history of Israel by means of collecting and reworking ancient sources which he handled with great respect. Another step was made at the same time by E. Bickerman, who claimed that characteristic features of the historiography of the time are expressed in the Chronicler's work. These would include the selection of data from available source material, guided by the principle of historical probability;

63. It should be emphasized that the definition of 'historical probability' is still fluid and inconclusive. We still find a complete acceptance, or almost so, of the witness of the Chronistic material (cf. for example, J. Bright, *History of Israel* [Philadelphia, 2nd edn, 1955], pp. 230-31, 248-49, 272, 283, 316, etc.) and side by side with this acceptance, a total, or almost total, denial. Cf. *inter alios*, M. Noth, *The History of Israel* (trans. S. Godman; Edinburgh, 1958) and below n. 74. Moreover, even when the bare event is accepted as historical, the debate regarding the details is still active. Cf. for example the manner in which two commentators react to Albright's attitude regarding the judicial reform of Jehoshaphat: Rudolph, *Chronikbücher*, pp. 256-58, and J.M. Myers, *II Chronicles* (AB, 13; Garden City, NY, 1965), pp. 108-109.

64. Torrey, *Ezra Studies*, pp. 227-51.

the choice of subjects in accordance with the changes in historical interest; and the description of history in line with its meaning to the author and to his generation.[65] Bickerman applied to the Chronicler the same criteria which would be applied to any historiography, and compared the Chronicler's methods to those of contemporary Greek historiographers. In contrast to the generally held view Bickerman claimed that the Chronicler's tendentiousness and his lack of critical method do not compromise his status as a historian.[66]

Another direction in the understanding of the literary phenomenon of Chronicles was being followed in the 1930s. By then, the study of biblical historiography was developing under the influence of factors which had come into play within biblical scholarship.

In the first half of the twentieth century new avenues were opening up in the study of biblical literature, and the question of the authorship of the Pentateuch was being freed from the rigid hold of the 'Documentary Hypothesis'. Following Gunkel, his contemporaries and successors, the 'documents' lost some of their centrality in the study of the Pentateuch, the composition of which was now conceived of as a process spanning many generations, and not as the exclusive enterprise of individual authors at specific historical moments.[67] In addition, the chronological landmarks in the composition of the Pentateuch had become firmly established, based on interior literary and historical considerations, and only to a lesser degree in the light of the evidence of

65. E. Bickerman, *From Ezra to the Last of the Maccabees* (New York, 1962), pp. 21ff., first published in L. Finkelstein, *The Jews: Their History, Culture and Religion* (New York, 1949).

66. This argument was brought up by various scholars over the years; cf. Graf, 'Das Buch der Chronik', p. 122; Wellhausen, *Prolegomena*, pp. 226-27; G. von Rad, *Das Geschichtsbild des chronistischen Werkes* (BWANT, 54; Stuttgart, 1930), pp. 121, 133; J.M. Myers, *I Chronicles* (AB, 12; Garden City, NY, 1965), p. xviii. On the recent expressions of this view, cf. below. Bickerman's stand is followed by M. Smith, *Palestinian Parties and Politics that Shaped the Old Testament* (New York, 1971), pp. 169-70. One may say that the decision on this issue rests less with the book's tendentiousness than with a basic definition of 'historian' on the one hand and an opinion about the literary nature of Chronicles on the other. Cf. M. Noth, *Überlieferungsgeschichtliche Studien* (Tübingen, 2nd edn, 1957), pp. 166, 172; Japhet, *Ideology*, pp. 426-31.

67. H. Klatt, *Hermann Gunkel* (FRLANT, 100; Göttingen, 1969), pp. 104-92; D. Knight, *Rediscovering the Traditions of Israel* (Missoula, MT, 2nd edn, 1975), pp. 71ff.

biblical historiography. The need to deal with the historical evidence of Chronicles as a proof of the lateness of the Pentateuch—as a whole or in part—was greatly diminished. Consequently, Chronicles ceased to be used as a tool in the service of Pentateuch criticism. It could now become an object of interest in its own right, to be studied in its proper context as one component of biblical historiography.

Further, biblical historiography in general ceased to be evaluated in terms of 'truth' and 'untruth'. This change should be attributed to the general disillusionment within the historical sciences, and to the realization that the describing of events 'as they really happened' was impossible—not just for the ancient historian. Historiosophy, the historian's concept of history, became a legitimate aspect of historiography, to be coped with and accepted. The fruits of this general disillusionment with 'objective history' can be found also in the study of Chronicles.

In 1930 von Rad published his book on *The Historical Picture of the Chronistic Work*,[68] a title which was already an expression of the change afoot. What von Rad regarded as significant was the 'historical picture' of the Chronicler, the way in which he understood the history he described, and not the 'historical truth'. In order to draw this picture von Rad made use of the sketches of his predecessors; however, he broadened the picture to include many aspects previously neglected (having no bearing on the problem of historical reliability), and he explained differently, as might be expected, their origins and meaning.[69] He also made a clear shift in the focus of interest: the specific chronistic views, which until then had been used only as proof of the unreliability of the historical description, now became objects of study in their own right. Consequently von Rad emphasized those parts which are peculiar to Chronicles and not the parallel sections[70] and in the additional material the central meaning of Chronicles was determined for him by the historiosophical aspects rather than by the historical.

Noth dedicated to Chronicles a substantial part of his book *Traditio-Historical Studies of the Historical Compositions of the Old Testament,*

---

68. Von Rad, *Das Geschichtsbild des chronistischen Werkes.*

69. Willi claims that von Rad's main merit is the proof that the Chronicler was influenced not only by the Priestly Code but by the Pentateuch as a whole and especially by Deuteronomy (*Die Chronik*, p. 46 and elsewhere). This is rather an underestimation of von Rad's work and even more so of its influence.

70. Von Rad, *Das Geschichtsbild*, p. 3.

which Are of a Collective and Editorial Nature.[71] He dealt with
Chronicles from a different point of view than von Rad, yet depended
basically on the same development in biblical studies. According to him
there were three 'historical compositions' in the Bible: the Pentateuch,
the Deuteronomistic work and the Chronistic work. It was to the last
two that he devoted his book, leaving the Pentateuch for special consideration elsewhere.

In Noth's study there is almost a full parallelism between the two
parts, which deal respectively with the Deuteronomistic and Chronistic
historiographies, and the discussion is conducted under the same headings for both works.[72] Noth emphasized in particular that the book of
Chronicles should be defined as 'historiography',[73] though by no means
should this definition obscure the book's tendentiousness (of which Noth
is very much aware), nor should it in itself lend the book any extra reliability.[74] His opening assumption is that the need to explain the past to
any present generation in meaningful terms is a common feature of historiography, and Chronicles with its idiosyncrasies is just one example.[75]

71. Above, n. 66.
72. The study of each of these compositions is divided basically into two sections: 'The Structure of the Work' and 'The Character of the Work'. The latter is
built along identical headings for each of the compositions, referring to: 'literary
peculiarity'; 'historical presupposition'; 'the stand towards the accepted traditions'
and 'leading theological ideas'. The first section, which deals with the structure of the
work, is built along different lines for each of the compositions, as determined by
their respective problems.
73. *Überlieferungsgeschichtliche Studien*, p. 172.
74. On the extent of the historical data in Chronicles, cf. Noth, *Überlieferungsgeschichtliche Studien*, pp. 131-43. Noth regards only very few passages in
Chronicles as historically reliable, and even these are not used in full when he draws
the picture of the history of Israel. Cf. above, n. 63.
75. A comparable attitude towards the Former Prophets and Chronicles is also
the general point of departure of B. Mazar, according to whom 'The character of the
books of Kings and Chronicles makes it necessary to distinguish between the elements which bear on the time of their compilers and editors and which are influenced by the religious and national views of the period of their composition, and on
the other hand the ancient sources, namely the authentic material which was written
at the time of the events themselves or somewhat later' (B. Mazar, 'Early Israelite
Historiography', in *The World Congress of Jewish Studies 1* [Hebrew; Jerusalem,
1952], p. 358). Regarding the details, however, Mazar ascribes to Chronicles a much
greater reliability than Noth and in his reconstruction of historical events he uses its
evidence abundantly. Cf. for example, B. Mazar, 'The Cities of the Priests and

It seems, then, that with regard to the problem of historical reliability two major trends were being established: one was the attempt to sift from the book maximum historical data through a cautious, critical method, in order to complement our knowledge of the history of the monarchic period and exploit as far as possible the material peculiar to Chronicles. The other was the treatment of the book as a specific section of biblical historiography with interest focused on questions of a literary and religious nature and with the question of historical reliability losing its centrality. The fruits of these two trends are found in a long series of studies published during recent years.[76]

V

To approach and evaluate with a proper perspective the most recent studies of the subject is a forbidding task. It is as yet impossible to say what are the general guidelines expressed in these studies. Yet even at risk of error I can hardly ignore some of the more recent endeavours, devoted specifically to the subject under consideration here.

I would like to mention first the monograph by P. Welten, entitled *History and the Description of History in the Books of Chronicles*, dealing with 2 Chronicles 10–36.[77] Welten accepts the results of several recent studies and regards Chronicles and Ezra–Nehemiah as two separate works[78]—a step of great significance in itself. Yet both in method

Levites', VTSup 7 (1960), pp. 197ff., also Richardson, p. 12.

76. It is beyond the scope of this study to mention all these contributions, but some of them should be listed. The first direction is demonstrated, for example, by J. Liver, 'History and Historiography in the Book of Chronicles', in *Festschrift A. Biram* (Hebrew; Jerusalem, 1956), pp. 152-61; S. Talmon, 'Divergences in the Calendar Reckoning in Ephraim and Judah', *VT* 8 (1958), pp. 48-74; F.L. Moriarty, 'The Chronicler's Account of Hezekiah's Reform', *CBQ* 17 (1965), pp. 399-406; E.L. Ehrlich, 'Der Aufenthalt des Königs Manasse in Babylon', *TZ* 21 (1965), pp. 281-86. To the second direction belong, for example, A.C. Welch, *The Work of the Chronicler* (London, 1939); G. Wilda, 'Das Königsbild des chronistischen Geschichtswerk' (Bonn, 1959); A.M. Brunet, 'Le Chroniste et ses sources', *RB* 60 (1953), pp. 481-508; 61(1954), pp. 349-86; J. Liver, *Chapters in the History of the Priests and the Levites* (Hebrew; Jerusalem, 1968); R. Mosis, *Untersuchungen zur Theologie des chronistischen Geschichtswerk* (Freiburg, 1973); Willi, *Die Chronik*; Williamson, *Israel*; Japhet, *Ideology*.

77. P. Welten, *Geschichte und Geschichtsdarstellung in den Chronikbüchern* (WMANT, 42; Neukirchen–Vluyn, 1973).

78. Cf. above n. 27; Willi, *Die Chronik*, pp. 179-84; Welten, *Geschichte*, pp. 3-4.

and in conclusions his book is closest to the work of Torrey. This is an interesting phenomenon, as Welten does not mention Torrey, and it is quite possible that he was not aware of his work.[79] Welten bases his study on a literary-linguistic analysis of the additional sections of 2 Chronicles 10–36; the gist of his historical conclusions is that the sure contribution of Chronicles to our knowledge of the monarchic period is minimal, and is exhausted in three short paragraphs from the times of Rehoboam, Uzziah and Hezekiah. To these one could add, hesitantly, two more pieces of information from the time of Rehoboam and Jehoram.[80] All the other additions in 2 Chronicles 10–36 are a free invention of the Chronicler, created in response to the circumstances of his time, the first half of the third century BCE.[81]

It seems that, in both method and results, Welten's study is an antithetical reaction to the two trends in the study of Chronicles that I have mentioned above. He consciously opposes any attempt to find in Chronicles a substantial contribution to the history of Israel in the monarchic period, criticizing systematically a number of studies written in this spirit.[82] At the same time he opposes Noth and his followers who regard the book of Chronicles as an organic continuation of biblical historiography, to be understood and evaluated in parallel to the Deuteronomistic historiography. According to Welten Chronicles is a new and unique phenomenon, which he describes as follows: 'With the books of Chronicles the historiography of Israel enters an entirely new stage; no more are traditions being collected and reworked; no more are earlier works being re-edited. The Chronicler writes history from beginning to

79. This may be explained by the fact that the author limited his reading to books concerning Chronicles and did not refer to those which deal with Ezra–Nehemiah. This is but one example of Welten's one-sided treatment of the subject.

80. The sections are: 2 Chron. 11.5b, 6-10a; 2 Chron. 26.6a, 10; 32.30 (Welten, *Geschichte*, pp. 195-96). Elsewhere he points to the possibility that also for 2 Chron. 11.22-23 and 21.1-4 a source from the monarchic period was utilized (p. 193).

81. On his view regarding the date of the Chronicles, cf. *Geschichte*, pp. 196-97. For a dispute with these views cf. Williamson, *Israel*, pp. 83-86.

82. Cf. the introduction, pp. 2-5, and in great detail throughout the book. Welten is right in claiming that the positive attitude towards the historical reliability of Chronicles is to be found mainly in non-German circles of biblical studies (*Geschichte*, p. 3). Among the German scholars his arguments are directed especially against Galling (p. 5). Cf. K. Galling, *Die Bücher der Chronik, Ezra, Nehemia* (ATD; Göttingen, 1954), pp. ii, 189-91.

end, anew and independently.'[83] Welten's definition of the phenomenon as a 'free, parabolic, writing of history'[84] is arrived at through a comparison with the book of Judith. In this way he excludes Chronicles from the very definition of historiography.

A second study on the subject is R. North, 'Does Archaeology Prove Chronicles' Sources?'[85] His answer to the question is categorically in the negative and his results are very similar to those of Welten. The third, and the most recent, is Ralph W. Klein, 'Abijah's Campaign against the North (1 Chron. 13)—What Were the Chronicler's Sources?'[86] Klein's conclusions are that all the Chronicler's sources were biblical, and nothing more. In a cautious but determined style he concludes:

> I do not wish to disparage in general the historical character of the Chronicler, or to deny that he had access at times to records that were the basis for much of his additional or divergent information. In the case of Abijah, however, the Chronicler's departures from Kings can all be explained as due to a divergent text of Samuel–Kings, to his theological viewpoints, and to his exegetical-midrashic use of an old Benjaminite list, to give concreteness to Abijah's northern victory.[87]

In view of all these studies one should ask whether the renewed scepticism regarding the reliability of Chronicles is more than a passing mood and represents a new line of approach to the understanding and interpretation of the book. This new development clearly shows that although the interest in Chronicles has certainly broadened and become much more varied, with the question of the historical reliability no longer occupying the centre of discussion, the feeling of many scholars that a certain consensus has been reached, albeit with slight variations, is far from justified. As yet, the question of the Chronicler's historical reliability cannot be considered a 'closed case'. We are still looking forward to a broadening of our knowledge, a deepening of our understanding, a clarification of our terms and definitions, an improvement of our evaluation, all of which may enlighten our use of the book of Chronicles as a source for the history of Israel.

83. Welten, *Geschichte*, p. 205.
84. 'Freie parabolische Geschichtsdarstellung' (*Geschichte*, p. 206). The term is borrowed from H. Junker, *TTZ* 70 (1961), pp. 182-85.
85. In *A Light unto my Path* (Festschrift J.M. Myers; Philadelphia, 1974), pp. 375-401.
86. *ZAW* 95 (1983), pp. 210-17.
87. 'Abijah's Campaign', p. 217.

JSOT 58 (1993), pp. 71-92

DYNASTY, PEOPLE, AND THE FUTURE:
THE MESSAGE OF CHRONICLES*

Donald F. Murray

1. *The Problem*

Does Chronicles inform its readers that the ancient promise to David of
an eternal dynasty achieved its purpose in Solomon's succession to
David and their founding of the Jerusalem temple and its cult? And does
it further imply that the promise continues valid into the readers' own
time in that their own temple and cult are the legitimate successors of
the Davidic–Solomonic institution?[1] Or does it rather invite them to
hope for a return to rule of the Davidic dynasty, and through this future
revalidation of God's eternal promise to David to look for the consummation of his purpose for Israel, only partially fufilled in the sixth-
century restoration?[2] These are, at their starkest, the contending views

---

* The following article is a revised full version of a paper read to the
International Meeting of the Society of Biblical Literature in Vienna, 7th August,
1990.
    1. The most influential exponent of this approach in the twentieth century has
been W. Rudolph (*Chronikbücher* [HAT, 21; Tübingen: Mohr, 1955], p. xxiii),
whose lead has been followed by O. Plöger (*Theokratie und Eschatologie*
[WMANT, 2; Neukirchen–Vluyn: Neukirchener Verlag, 3rd edn, 1968], pp. 52-55
= *Theocracy and Eschatology* [trans. S. Rudman; Oxford: Blackwell, 1968], pp. 39-
42) and P.D. Hanson (*The Dawn of Apocalyptic* [Philadelphia: Fortress Press,
1975], pp. 276-78).
    2. The currency of this type of view in the twentieth century has its origin in
Hänel's introduction to J.W. Rothstein and J. Hänel, *Das erste Buch der Chronik*
(KAT; Leipzig: J. Deichert, 1927), pp. x-xi, xliii-iv; but it owes much to its advocacy
by G. von Rad, *Das Geschichtsbild des Chronistischen Werkes* (BWANT, 3.4;
Stuttgart: Kohlhammer, 1930), pp. 123-24, 127.

variously nuanced by different scholars,[3] derived from readings of the dynastic promise texts in Chronicles.[4] I propose to tackle the question in a different way.[5]

2. *A Different Way into the Problem*

Let us instead ask ourselves what we could reasonably expect to find in Chronicles, if we assume in turn that each of the above views is correct, and then compare this with what we actually find in the text.[6] We shall probe first of all the hypothesis that the Chronicler understood the

---

3.   Among recent discussions, the latter type of view has been espoused by J.L. Myers, *1 Chronicles* (AB, 12; Garden City, NY: Doubleday, 1986), pp. lxxx-lxxxiii; J.D. Newsome, 'Toward a New Understanding of the Chronicler and his Purpose', *JBL* 94 (1975), pp. 201-17 (208-10, 213-14, 216); H.G.M. Williamson, 'Eschatology in Chronicles', *TynBul* 28 (1977), pp. 115-54 (*passim*); *idem, 1 and 2 Chronicles* (NCB; Grand Rapids: Eerdmans; London: Marshall, Morgan & Scott, 1982), pp. 133-34 *et alibi; idem*, 'The Dynastic Oracle in the Books of Chronicles', in A. Rofé and Y. Zakovitch (eds.), *Essays on the Bible and the Ancient World* (I.L. Seeligman Memorial Volume 3; Jerusalem: E. Rubinstein, 1983), pp. 305-18 (318). The opposite approach is taken by A. Caquot, 'Peut-on parler de messianisme dans l'oeuvre du chroniste?', *RTP* 99 (1966), pp. 110-20 (118-20); R.L. Braun, 'Solomonic Apologetic in Chronicles', *JBL* 92 (1973), pp. 503-16 (515); *idem, 1 Chronicles* (WBC, 14; Waco, TX: Word Books, 1986), p. xxvi-xxvii. S. Japhet (*The Ideology of the Book of Chronicles and its Place in Biblical Thought* [trans. A. Barber; Beiträge zur Erforschung des Alten Testaments und des Antiken Judentums, 9; Frankfurt am Main: Peter Lang, 1989], pp. 460-67, 493-504) is also broadly sympathetic to this view, though she does not express herself explicitly in the terms given above.

4.   For a recent discussion using this approach, see Williamson, 'Dynastic Oracle', *passim*. For a reading of the dynastic promise texts in Chronicles along the lines of this article, see my forthcoming book, *Claim for Power, Power for Claim: A Divine Promise in History and Theology*.

5.   Nor shall I align myself with, or directly argue towards, any of the broad categorizations, such as 'eschatological', 'theocratic' or 'hierocratic', to which Chronicles has been assigned in much recent discussion; on this see e.g. Williamson, 'Eschatology', pp. 117-33. My intention is to take a more text-immanent approach. But cf. n. 43 below.

6.   Naturally we are only concerned here with those implications of each view which can produce decisive evidence in favour of the one view and against the other. Nor need we exhaust the logical possibilities, if we can readily identify considerations powerful enough in themselves to call into question either or both views.

dynastic promise as a divine guarantee of the succession of Solomon to David in order to ensure for all time the establishment of the temple and its cult, beyond which the dynasty in itself was of no continuing significance. On this hypothesis the reader is entitled to expect from the considerable post-Solomonic history in Chronicles some justification of the long forbearance of God to a dynasty that ultimately inflicted such damage on temple and cult. For *ex hypothesi* the Chronicler regards these as the very matrix of Israel's relationship to God. Indeed, since in the writer's own time temple and cult seem to have fared so much better than in the First Temple period, precisely without the unreliable supervision of a Davidide, the issue is one that ought to have been the more acute to both writer and reader. Yet the only justification for the divine forbearance towards any of the Davidides ever made in Chronicles is a statement based on the *Vorlage*: 2 Chron. 21.7 // 2 Kgs 8.19, which concerns Jehoram and his cultic faithlessness. But this is double evidence against our *ex hypothesi* expectation that the divine forbearance to apostate Davidides would be a burning issue for our author. For first, the reign of Jehoram is not the only, let alone the most telling, occasion in Chronicles to express a view on the question,[7] and secondly, it is not the Chronicler's way to leave the exposition of his view on an important matter merely to a brief comment derived from the *Vorlage*.

But even more decisive against this way of understanding the dynastic oracle in Chronicles is the justification 21.7[8] actually gives for the divine forbearance to Jehoram: Yahweh's covenanted commitment to the dynasty for the sake of David.[9] For this would mean that the promise, *ex hypothesi* given in order to establish temple and cult, now justifies divine forbearance to one whose actions have undermined the promise's very *raison d'être*! The obvious conclusion, that the Chronicler must have seen in the promise to David a more enduring significance for the

---

7.   Apart from the generalized charges of 21.6 (// 2 Kgs 8.18) and 21.12-13, no detail of Joram's cultic apostasy is given, unlike 28.2-4 (expanding on 2 Kgs 16.2-4) of Ahaz, and with more detail 33.2-9 (// 2 Kgs 21.2-9) of Manasseh.

8.   Unless context indicates otherwise, all unspecified references are to 2 Chronicles.

9.   Chronicles has actually sharpened the issue by reading *byt dwyd* for Kings' *yhwdh* as the object of Yahweh's forbearance, and incorporating a specific reference to a covenant with David *lm'n hbryt 'šr krt ldwyd* in place of the less explicit *lm'n dwyd 'bdw*.

dynasty than this view allows, follows also from the fact that 2 Chron. 21.7 is not the only occasion in the post-Solomonic section of his work when the Chronicler appeals to a divine covenant with David. In 13.5, Abijah cites it to condemn the secessionist North; and in 23.3b, Jehoiada invokes it to justify his coup to restore the Davidide Joash to the Judaean throne in place of the Omride usurper, Athaliah. Moreover, since these two latter texts have no parallel in Kings, they must say something important enough to the Chronicler for him to have added them to the account. Thus these three reaffirmations of an ongoing divine covenant with the Davidides, two of which are peculiar to Chronicles, make it impossible that in Chronicles as a whole[10] the promise to David has continuing significance only in that, by ensuring the succession of Solomon to David, it also secured for all time temple and cult as the means of grace to Israel.

But does the preceding argument force us back onto the alternative 'messianic',[11] or 'royalist'[12] understanding of the role of the dynastic promise in Chronicles? In other words, must we conclude that the

10. There can be little doubt that in the Davidic–Solomonic section of his work, the Chronicler focuses all attention on the dynastic promise as a guarantee of the succession of Solomon the chosen temple-builder, as already seen by R.L. Braun, 'The Significance of 1 Chronicles 22, 28, and 29 for the Structure and Theology of the Work of the Chronicler' (ThD thesis, Concordia Seminary, St Louis, 1971), *passim*; *idem*, 'Solomon, the Chosen Temple Builder: The Significance of 1 Chronicles 22, 28, and 29 for the Theology of Chronicles', *JBL* 94 (1976), pp. 581-90; *idem*, *1 Chronicles*, pp. xxxiv-xxxv; and Williamson, 'Eschatology', pp. 136-37; *idem*, 'Dynastic Oracle', pp. 312-13. This is most compellingly shown, however, by the reprise of the dynastic promise (1 Chron. 17.10-14) put into the mouth of David in 1 Chron. 22.9-10. For here the dynastic promise has been conformed as much as possible to the genre of the birth announcement oracle, a point hitherto unremarked as such by scholars. But this change brings with it a formal limitation of the promise to Solomon, since it is of the essence of birth announcement oracles that they herald the birth and future career of one named individual; cf. Gen. 16.11-12 (Ishmael), Isa. 7.14-15 (Immanuel), Mt. 1.21 and Lk. 1.31-33 (Jesus), Lk. 1.13-17 (John the Baptist).

11. Von Rad himself, in his influential study of David and the dynastic promise in Chronicles (*Geschichtsbild*, pp. 119-32) applies the term 'messianic' to the Chronicler's conception; note especially 'so wird man hier [*sc.* in Chronicles] ohne Gefahr von einer *messianischen Vorstellung* reden dürfen' (p. 126, my emphasis).

12. Williamson prefers this term to 'messianic', as a way of avoiding some of the wider implications associated with the latter term ('Eschatology', p. 154; 'Dynastic Oracle', p. 305).

Chronicler cherished a hope for the restoration of the Davidic dynasty at a still future time? Given that his date is probably no earlier than the later Persian period,[13] there are three questions that one might reasonably expect Chronicles to answer, if the writer hoped to persuade his contemporaries to share his putative conviction about the future restoration of the dynasty. The first is to explain the long hiatus between the demise of the dynasty in the first quarter of the sixth century BCE and its anticipated restoration, still unrealized some two hundred years later. This issue would have been made the more pressing by the fact that, when Chronicles appeared, probably in the course of the fourth century, a community calling itself Israel had existed in and around Jerusalem for well over a hundred years, with a temple and cult that purported to continue that of the former Solomonic temple.

The two further questions in urgent need of answer arise out of this last observation. Since the anticipated restoration manifestly had not happened with the return, what circumstances would lead to the dynasty's restoration? And, since the restored community had existed, apparently quite happily, without a ruling Davidide for a century and more, what would the dynasty's restoration add to the community? For it could hardly be assumed by the writer as self-evident to his readers that such a community needed a Davidic dynast at its head. Nor would his readers see the dynasty's return to rule as a very belated completion of the restoration begun in the sixth century. The mere formulation of our three questions is enough to show that the view that has provoked them implies at least an inchoate eschatology in Chronicles. In other words, the Chronicler needed to say something quite concrete on all three questions if he wished to persuade many of his contemporaries to share this alleged hope for the future restoration of the Davidic dynasty.

3. *Rationale of Exile and Restoration: 2 Chronicles 36.11-21*

The one place in Chronicles more than any other where we could reasonably expect clear reference to the future restoration of the Davidic

---

13. The dating of Chronicles is a controversial and complex question upon which we cannot enter here. Suffice it to say that I find convincing the reasons adduced by Williamson (H.G.M. Williamson, *Israel in the Books of Chronicles* [Cambridge: Cambridge University Press, 1977], pp. 83-86; 'Eschatology', pp. 121-29) for a date in the fourth century before the Hellenistic era.

dynasty is in the work's conclusion,[14] 36.11-21,[15] which treats both of the dynasty's downfall and of the promise of future restoration of the people. Yet not only is there no citation of the dynastic promise in this concluding section, there is not even the most oblique of allusions to it. On the contrary, our author manifests a surprising lack of interest in the fate of the last Davidides, notably less than does the Kings *Vorlage*. Thus the personal fate of the very last of them, Zedekiah, is not mentioned at all in Chronicles, 2 Kgs 25.5-7 notwithstanding. His predecessor, Jehoiachin, is treated with hardly any more ceremony, since the latter's captivity is barely noted in passing (2 Chron. 36.10), and his subsequent release from close confinement is completely ignored by the Chronicler, in marked contrast to 2 Kgs 25.27-30.[16]

Altogether a curious indifference to the final days of power of the dynasty whose restoration our author is alleged to be commending to his readers as the crowning of all their hopes for the future. It would be just about explicable, if we could show that in so doing he was directing the reader's gaze away from the ignoble debacle of the dynasty's downfall towards its glorious restoration. But no such splendid prospect can be found in the context. On the contrary, the only future dynasty drawn to the reader's attention in the closing words of Chronicles is that of the Persians (36.20; cf. 36.22-23). Since the Achaemenid dynasty was to all appearances still solidly in power at the time of writing, such a concluding allusion to its inauguration is not the best calculated way to arouse hopes for the re-establishing of a rival monarchy.

What then of the three questions we posed above to the messianic-cum-royalist interpretation? Where more than here—where hard on the heels of narrating the end of the Davidic dominion the writer alludes to

14. Without entering into the details of the discussion here, I find the overall case argued by both Japhet (S. Japhet, 'The Supposed Common Authorship of Chronicles and Ezra–Nehemiah Investigated Anew', *VT* 18 [1968], pp. 330-71) and Williamson (*Israel*, Part One) for the separate authorship of Chronicles and Ezra–Nehemiah compelling.

15. On the view taken here, viz. that Chronicles was originally a separate work from Ezra–Nehemiah, only subsequently joined to form a continuous work, the vexed question of the original ending of Chronicles is a material point. However, since a strong case can be based on the text down to 36.21 (a case only strengthened by the inclusion of 36.22-23), I will confine myself to the shorter ending.

16. This observation suggests that we should be wary of reading too much into the genealogy of Jehoiachin recorded in 1 Chron. 3.17-24, even assuming it to be from the same hand; cf. Braun, *1 Chronicles*, pp. 54-55 *ad loc.*

future restoration of the people, 36.20-21—would such questions clamour for answer? But no answers are forthcoming. Moreover, the questions themselves do not even arise, because the argument's major premise, a future for the Davidic dynasty, conspicuously fails to be affirmed here, precisely where events most call it into question.

Let us now move on from asking what the text does not say to reflecting on what it does say. Williamson is right to observe that these final pages on the downfall of the Judaean kingdom are focused as much upon the destruction of the temple and its cult as upon any other aspect of the tragedy.[17] But is he justified in further claiming that 'the Chronicler has drawn a deliberate parallel between the fate of the temple and that of the *Davidic dynasty*'?[18] This presupposes that the downfall of the dynasty is as central a concern of the Chronicler here as the destruction of the temple and its cult. Yet Williamson himself acknowledges that the Chronicler's accounts of the last four Davidic kings are remarkably abbreviated, noting with Mosis that the Chronicler 'has carefully omitted from Kings the notice of the death of each king'.[19] Not only is this so, however, but the most extensive of the four accounts, that of Zedekiah, is actually more concerned with the conduct of the people and their spiritual leaders and their consequent fate (36.14-17) than with the king himself (36.11-13). But further, since this is also the climactic account of the four, one would have expected Williamson's parallel to be most in evidence here. Yet in this very instance the destruction of the temple and the plundering of its paraphernalia (36.18-19) are made parallel not to the fate of king Zedekiah, of which nothing is reported, but rather to the destruction and exile of the people (36.17, 20). Thus it appears that, at this climactic point in the narrative, the very downfall itself of the dynasty is not uppermost in the Chronicler's mind, let alone its supposed future restoration.

Nowhere is this more unambiguously demonstrated than in 2 Chron. 36.20-21, the Chronicler's 'clear indication of the way forward to

17. *1 and 2 Chronicles*, p. 412.

18. Williamson, *1 and 2 Chronicles*, p. 412, my emphasis. Williamson nowhere says as much, but it is more than likely that he makes this claim with an eye to its corollary—i.e. that restoration of the temple should by the same token imply restoration of the dynasty. But such a corollary would raise very starkly indeed precisely the unanswered questions for the messianic-cum-royalist interpretation that I defined above.

19. Williamson, *1 and 2 Chronicles*, p. 412, with reference to R. Mosis *et al.*

restoration', as Williamson has it.[20] But what is the restoration envisaged in 36.20? Does it involve the Davidic monarchy? To the contrary. The restoration is of the exiled people and their land, brought to pass by the advent of a quite different and opposed sovereignty, that of the Persian empire. Not the slightest hint, then, in 36.20 of restoration at any time of the fallen dynasty. Nor is any to be found in 36.21, with its combined allusion to the seventy-years-of-exile prophecy in the Jeremiah corpus (Jer. 29.10), and to the divinely enforced Sabbath rest for the land in the Holiness Code (Lev. 26.34-35). Again, to the contrary. Both allusions are to contexts exclusively concerned with exile as punishment for the misdemeanours of the people, and the hope for its restoration through their collective repentance. Now since kingship is not part of the universe of discourse in Leviticus 26—hardly surprising in view of its Mosaic setting—not much can be made of its absence in this allusion. The case is different, however, in Jeremiah 29, where explicit reference is made to the present exile of the Davidic monarch Jeconiah (= Jehoiachin, 29.2), and to the concomitant reign of Zedekiah in Judah.[21] Yet Jeremiah's letter to the exiles is addressed not to Jeconiah but to the representatives of the people in exile (29.1), and when the text comes to speak of restoration, as it does in 29.10-15, the oracle is in the plural, addressed to the exiles. Pointedly, neither Jeconiah nor any successor in the Davidic line is explicitly included in the restoration oracle. In other words, this concept of restoration accords no special place to a Davidide.[22]

It appears accordingly that this concluding double allusion of the Chronicler is to restoration promises that ignore, or in the case of Jeremiah 29 pointedly exclude, any role for the Davidic dynasty. Rather odd texts to be invoked by one who is supposedly so committed to a role in the restoration for a reinstated dynasty. Strong as its evidence is, however, it would be premature to conclude solely on the basis of 2 Chronicles 36 that the Chronicler saw no place in the restoration for a

20. *1 and 2 Chronicles*, p. 412.

21. Jer. 29.16 in the Hebrew further mentions the disaster impending over Zedekiah, here referred to generically as 'he who sits on the throne of David'. However, since 29.16-20 are absent from the LXX, I confine my remarks to the shorter text.

22. The Chronicler takes up part of this oracle in David's charge to Solomon, 1 Chron. 28.9b, where it is appropriately transferred to the singular. However, significantly, in all of its reprises in Chronicles it is in the plural, as in Jeremiah. See further n. 26 below.

future scion of the house of David. However, confirmation of this can be found in two earlier sections of Chronicles that share significant links with 36.11-21.

4. *From Exile to Restoration*

2 Chronicles 7.12-22

It has been recognized by commentators that the account of Zedekiah and the destruction of Judah in 36.11-21 makes a number of allusions to 7.14,[23] part of the divine response (7.12-22) to Solomon's prayer at the dedication of the temple (6.14-42). In citing the causes of the catastrophe, besides the statement of wrongdoing by both Zedekiah and the people,[24] the Chronicler castigates Zedekiah for failing to 'humble himself' before Jeremiah (*l' nkn' mlpny yrmyhw*), 36.12b, and for hardening his heart 'so as not to return to Yahweh' (*mšwb 'l yhwh*), 36.13b. Further, the people's behaviour in 36.14, 16 is characterized as high-handed and defiant, while 36.16b tells us that the people so utterly reject the divine warnings that there is no longer any chance of 'restoration' (*'d l'yn mrp'*). These are all references back to 7.14, where, in response to the people's self-humbling, prayer, seeking Yahweh's face, and turning from their evil ways, Yahweh will forgive their sins and restore their land.[25] In negating the conditions set out in 7.14, and denying the blessing entailed by their fulfilment, 36.12-16 indicates that Zedekiah and his people alike[26] are under a curse.

---

23. Notably Williamson, *1 and 2 Chronicles*, pp. 416-17, and R.B. Dillard, *2 Chronicles* (WBC, 15; Waco, TX: Word Books, 1987), p. 300.

24. Zedekiah 'did evil' (36.12a), 'rebelled' against Nebuchadnezzar (13a), became 'stiff-necked' and 'hardened his heart' (13b); the people followed the 'abomination of the nations' (14a), 'defiled' the temple (14b), 'mocked' the divine messengers, 'scoffed at' the prophets, and 'despised' God's word (16a).

25. Chronicles does not reiterate in 36.12-16 every item in this list. Only the first and last of the four conditions and the last of the divine responses are cited, thus forming an overall inclusive reference to the content of 7.14.

26. It is worth noting here, in view of my impending argument that 7.12-22 subsumes the fate of the dynasty within that of the people as a whole, how 36.12-16 refers to king and people indiscriminately matters predicated of the people alone in 7.14. Nor is this a solitary example of such promiscuity by the Chronicler. A very significant instance the opposite way around to the preceding arises from the charge given to Solomon by David in 1 Chron. 28.9-10, which is distinguished by its emphatic opening *w'th* from the preceding charge (28.8) to the state officials.

2 Chron. 36.11-21 shows further connections with 7.12-22 that should not be missed. First, there is a close verbal reminiscence of *w'th bḥrty whqdšty 't hbyt hzh* (7.16a, cf. 7.20a) in *'t byt yhwh 'šr hqdyš byrwšlym* (36.14b). Then further, 36.14 accuses Judah in the time of Zedekiah of the sin of apostasy for which 7.19-22 had threatened king and people[27] with exile and destruction of the temple, while 36.17-20 narrates events that graphically fulfil this threat. Thus 7.19-22 is important background to 36.11-21. But the connection of 7.12-22 with the conclusion of Chronicles is even more deep-seated than has yet appeared.

However, in order to see the full implications of this connection, we need to appreciate that in the passage 7.12-22[28] itself the writer is responding to two other texts. The first of them is evident enough: 7.12-22 gives the divine reply to Solomon's address and intercessory prayer at the dedication of the temple (6.4-11, 14-42), just as the parallel passage 1 Kgs 9.1-9 does to 1 Kgs 8.12-21, 23-61—this connection is already

Incorporated in it are the words *'m tdršnw ymṣ' lk w'm t'zbnw yznyḥk l'd* (28.9b), based on Jer. 29.13-14 (cf. Deut. 4.29), but here appropriately in the singular as against the plurals of Jeremiah and Deuteronomy (cf. n. 22 above). Yet every one of five subsequent allusions to this charge, all in the post-Solomonic section of Chronicles, is in the plural and refers either to king and people together (2 Chron. 12.5; 15.2, ?15) or the people alone (15.4, ?15; 24.20). These examples of the Chronicler's 'democratization' of the monarchy constitute powerful evidence against Williamson's claim ('Eschatology', pp. 141-42, 154; 'Dynastic Oracle', pp. 316-18) that for the Chronicler Solomon's monarchy was a probationary period which established the eternal validity of the dynastic promise. What had eternal validity in the eyes of our author was the principle enshrined in the charge to Solomon (1 Chron. 28.9b), and the practice enjoined by Yahweh on the people (2 Chron. 7.14), which principle and which practice were valid alike for king and people, both during the reign of Solomon and ever after. For another argument against this understanding of Solomon's reign in relation to the dynastic promise, cf. n. 45 below.

27. In the context these are the only possible referents for the second person plurals, since (1) the only direct addressee up to this point has been Solomon (*wy'mr lw*, 7.12b), and since nothing indicates a complete change of addressee, he must therefore be included in the plural reference (*contra* Dillard, *2 Chronicles*, p. 59 *ad loc.*); (2) the third person plural reference in 7.22 must be to the people, and the parallel of content between that verse and 7.19-20 indicates that they are included in the second person plural reference of 7.19. Williamson (*1 and 2 Chronicles*, pp. 224, 226) correctly refers 7.19-22 to both king and people; but for his misconstruction of the Kings parallel, see n. 30 below.

28. The following discussion comes to very different conclusions from that of Williamson, 'Eschatology', pp. 149-53.

made by Yahweh's opening words of acceptance (7.12b, cf. 1 Kgs 9.3a).
But in the Chronicler's version of the divine response the connection is
made the stronger by the immediately ensuing Chronicles plus (7.13-15),
with its explicit reference back in vv. 13-14 to 6.26-31, and to 6.40 in
v. 15. In making these particular additional links with Solomon's prayer,
and in inserting the material just here, the Chronicler has a different
point to make from his *Vorlage*. There Yahweh's initial brief word of
acceptance of the temple dedication (1 Kgs 9.3) quickly leads on to a
conditioned dynastic promise addressed to Solomon (9.4-5, with emphatic
anticipatory *w'th* 9.4a). The burden of Yahweh's response is Solomon's
first petition, concerning establishment of the dynasty (8.25-26). But then
follows an abrupt warning couched in unprepared-for second person
plurals (*'tm wbnykm*, 9.6a),[29] which spells out to king and people[30] the
consequences of failure to keep the conditions specified in the dynastic
promise to Solomon. Thus in the Kings version of the divine response,
the conditional dynastic promise is given great prominence, both as
being the first matter of substance enunciated by Yahweh, and as providing the basis for the more general threat of 9.6-9 (cf. *wl' tšmrw mṣwty
ḥqty*, 6a, with *ḥqy wmšpṭy tšmr*, 4b).[31]

29. It is not material here to consider whether this abrupt change of subject is
traceable to redactional activity in 1 Kgs 9, since vv. 6-9 were evidently already in the
Vorlage to Chronicles. The alternative adopted by S.L. McKenzie (*The Chronicler's
Use of the Deuteronomistic History* [HSM, 33; Atlanta: Scholars Press, 1984], pp.
205-206), which is to assume that the material is redactional in both texts, fails to
take account of the close structural and ideological connections between 2 Chron.
7.19-22 and 7.12-16 pointed out below.
30. That the text refers to the dynasty alone, as Williamson understands it (*1 and
2 Chronicles*, p. 224: 'just the king and his descendants', cf. p. 226; and
'Eschatology', p. 152), would be logically possible only if the subject were *'tm
simpliciter*, but the possibility is excluded by the additional *bnykm*, which on this
construction of the text is rendered both pointless and confusing, since (1) its referents would already be sufficiently comprehended in the *'tm*; (2) the generational
frame of reference implied in the compound subject *'tm wbnykm* requires *'tm* to refer
to the *current* generation in contrast to *bnykm*, which must refer to at least one future
generation. Just as in the parallel in 2 Chron. 7.19-22 (n. 27 above), Solomon's
being sole addressee in 9.3-6 and the implications of the third plurals in 9.9 combine
to indicate that *'tm* refers to both king and people. The additional *bnykm*, omitted in
Chronicles, relates to the Deuteronomistic concept of guilt accumulating over generations until the final catastrophe, a perspective not shared by Chronicles, which
regards each generation as a closed retributional system.
31. In the Kings narrative, the conditional promise 9.4-6 prepares the way for the

But the balance of the Chronicles version is quite different. This change results from the addition of 7.13-15, and its being enclosed within a double reference to the temple, 7.12b,16. For what is now thrown into prominence is no longer, as in Kings, Yahweh's response to the opening plea of Solomon's prayer (6.16-17 // 1 Kgs 8.25-26), namely that Yahweh would honour his commitment to the dynasty. Rather it is his response to what in fact bulks largest in Solomon's intercession in both versions of the prayer: the role of the temple as a centre for the *people's* response to God, with its potential for continuous revival of people and land. Moreover, this emphasis is reinforced by the repeated idea of perdurance associated with it by the *'d 'wlm* and *kl hymym* of v. 16 (// 1 Kgs 9.3). By contrast, the conditional dynastic promise, making a belated appearance in Chronicles (7.17-18), has no reference to perdurance, unlike the parallel 1 Kgs 9.5. Here the main concern is to set out the conditions under which people and temple will prosper (7.12-16) or come to grief (7.19-22). This new concern substitutes for the temple–dynasty–people nexus of the *Vorlage* at this point a people–temple nexus; that is, the temple once established is for the people directly, not mediated to them only via the dynasty. Indeed, so far as the future is concerned, the dynasty is largely subsumed into a common fate with the people. This follows from the linking of 7.12-16 to 7.19-22 as two complementary halves, which now enclose the brief conditional dynastic promise of 7.17-18. For this changes the balance noted above between the conditional dynastic promise (7.17b // 1 Kgs 9.4b) and the related general warning (7.19a // 1 Kgs 9.6a). In Chronicles the latter predominates over the former, so that the conditions for continuance of the dynasty are now simply made the same as for continuance of the people, rather than providing the basis for the latter, as in the Kings version. This significant restructuring of Yahweh's reply to the temple dedication prayer therefore relegates the conditional dynastic promise to being a subsidiary aspect of the more important question of the future of people and temple.[32]

---

account in 1 Kgs 11 of Solomon's apostasy and its consequences for the dynasty, another perspective not shared by Chronicles.

32. It also gives to the second person plurals of 7.19, so abrupt in the *Vorlage* 1 Kgs 9.6, a rather clearer referent, namely the people as a whole including the royal dynasty. Even so, the transition to second plurals is still rather unexpected. Williamson ('Eschatology', pp. 141 n. 81, 152; *1 and 2 Chronicles*, pp. 226-27) wrongly argues from the absence of *bnykm* in 7.19 that 7.19-22 contains no threat to

Thus in the Chronicler's version of the divine reply to Solomon's prayer of dedication the future of the people is not made to depend on the perpetuity of the dynasty. Rather the reverse. But this observation takes us back to our starting point in 36.11-21, for such subsuming of the fate of the dynasty into that of the people seems in all respects parallel to what we have seen of the Chronicler's handling of the downfall of the dynasty and the destruction of Judah in that passage, and to witness to the same indifference to any hope that the dynasty had a glorious future. Thus far our study of 7.12-22 bears out the conclusions we drew from an examination of 36.11-21.

In comparison with its Kings counterpart, then, the Chronicles version of Yahweh's response to Solomon's prayer at the dedication of the temple is highly 'democratized'. This Chronistic change of emphasis, with its highlighting of the interrelationship of people and temple even at the expense of the dynasty, is further convincingly demonstrated by the way Yahweh's reply in 7.12-22 relates to our second text, Psalm 132, from which the Chronicler has quoted in 6.41-42. Yet this claim may appear capricious to proponents of a 'messianic' or 'royalist' view of Chronicles. For it is pre-eminently 2 Chron. 6.42, with its plea for Yahweh's anointed on the basis of the promise to David culled mainly from Psalm 132, taken together with Yahweh's response to that plea in 7.17-18, which has been offered as the clearest proof for the Chronicler's messianic or royalist outlook.[33] Moreover, in Chronicles this quotation from the undeniably royalist Psalm 132 has replaced 1 Kgs 8.52-53, with its reference to the election of Israel, a more overtly 'democratic' passage. The justification for the claim, however, comes from perceiving the structural and conceptual connections between 2 Chron. 7.12-22 and the psalm quoted in 6.41-42, connections both more extensive and more crucial to the understanding of 7.12-22 than has previously been recognized.

---

the dynasty, and that accordingly the conditional element in the dynastic promise of 7.17-18 is intended to apply to Solomon alone. This is based on his misconceived construction of *'tm wbnykm* in 1 Kgs 9.6, on which see n. 30 above. In any case, since 7.19-22 is clearly a standing warning to all generations, then Solomon's descendants, no less than those of the rest of the people, come under its strictures.

33. So e.g. von Rad: 'Hier ist zu betonen, dass der Verfasser [*sc.* of Chronicles] durch die Zitierung des eschatologisch hochgespannten Ps. 132 die ganze Situation stark ins Messianische umgebogen hat' (*Geschichtsbild*, p. 127).

Psalm 132 takes the form of petition and response: vv. 1 and 8-10 in particular present the petition and vv. 11-18 the divine response. The petition centres on the standing with God of the Davidic dynast, and bases its plea on the sedulous efforts of the dynasty's founder to provide an appropriate 'resting place' for Yahweh (*mnwḥtk*, v. 8, cf. 14). There is an obvious correspondence between David's oath in this connection (vv. 2-5) and the oath, supporting a conditional promise of futurity for David's dynasty (vv. 11-12), which opens the divine response. For the psalmist practical proof of this divine commitment to the dynasty is found in Yahweh's endorsement of Zion, the shrine founded for him by David, as confirmed by his accepting the worship offered there (vv. 13-16, which respond to the petition of 8-9). The psalm concludes with God exalting the reigning scion of David's house (vv. 17-18), replying to the earlier petition for the dynast (vv. 1, 10) with a resounding declaration of high royal theology. In the view of this psalmist, then, dynasty and temple form an indissoluble dyad, in which David's support for Yahweh in searching out a shrine as his resting place is frankly traded off against Yahweh's support for David and his dynasty. Priests and people play merely the subsidiary role of chorus, giving their approbation to the transaction between god and king.

Why has Chronicles brought this piece of dynastic propaganda into the conclusion of Solomon's prayer? Does it indicate the writer's commitment to so high a view of the Davidic dynasty as to imply his cherishing of hopes for its future restoration? The answer to the latter question lies in probing the former. First, we observe that much of the subject matter is in common between the psalm and the narrative of the dedication of the temple. The primary function of the dedication prayer is to invoke Yahweh to accept as his shrine (6.20-21, 40) the Solomonic temple, which is the consummation of David's efforts to provide a 'resting place' for the ark (cf. 6.7-11). David's exertions to that end dominate Ps. 132.1-10. This section of the psalm includes petitions (vv. 8-9) for acceptance of the shrine that fit the occasion of the temple dedication. Accordingly, 6.41 appropriates them. The dedication prayer further makes Solomon's completion of that task the basis of a plea for Yahweh to continue to honour his promise to David (6.14-17). We have seen how in Psalm 132 the dynasty's sponsoring of the shrine for the ark is made the basis for petitions on behalf of the reigning dynast. Thus this element also is taken up into the peroration of Solomon's prayer by means of a petition, 6.42, which combines vv. 1 and 10 of Psalm 132.[34]

These observations take us further into our author's reasons for quoting from this psalm at this juncture in the narrative. For the petition–response structure of Psalm 132 resembles that of 2 Chronicles 6–7,[35] where 7.12-22 give the divine response to Solomon's petitions in 6.14-42, just as Ps. 132.11-18 do to the petitions in 132.1-10. But it is just this structural similarity and the common elements of subject matter between the psalm and 2 Chronicles 6–7 that are exploited by the Chronicler to manifest a considerable disparity of outlook between them. Whereas in the psalm the petition (132.8-9) and response (132.13-16) concerning David's shrine and its worship are subsidiary to the petition (132.1, 10) and response (132.11-12, 17-18) for the ruling dynast, in Chronicles the balance of the corresponding items is made quite the opposite. The divine response to Solomon's prayer in 7.12-22 does not, contrary even to what 6.4-10, 14-17 might have led one to expect, bring the temple into direct relation with the undertaking to the dynasty, let alone proffer the divine acceptance of the temple as evidence for that undertaking, as one might naturally suppose from the quotations from Psalm 132 in 6.41-42. Instead, the emphasis here falls on a role for the temple that in Psalm 132 is merely ancillary to its dynastic function, but which becomes pre-eminent in Solomon's temple dedication prayer: the temple as centre for the life and worship of the people. This quite different emphasis from Psalm 132 in Chronicles has already been signalled in the quotations from the psalm, where, reversing the order in Psalm 132, the petition concerning acceptance of the shrine (6.41) is placed before that for the king (6.42). Moreover, it is also responded to first by Yahweh (7.12b-16), a response of greater length than the response to the petition for the king (7.17-18), in terms that leave no doubt that the temple is first and foremost a temple for the people, not just the royal dynastic shrine of Psalm 132. Consequently, when Yahweh's response to the petition for the king finally comes in 7.17-18, it is striking that it is given a much lower priority in the Chronicles version than either the

34. It is much less certain whether 6.42 also makes allusion to Ps. 89.50-51, as von Rad (*Geschichtsbild*, pp. 126-27) argued, or to Isa. 55.3, as is vigorously maintained by Williamson ('Eschatology', pp. 143-46; *1 and 2 Chronicles*, pp. 220-21), but rejected by Dillard (*2 Chronicles*, pp. 51-52).

35. This structure is already there in the *Vorlage* 1 Kgs 8 and 9.1-9, but has been both more strongly articulated in Chronicles, and, as will appear from the ensuing discussion, also significantly modified.

equivalent response in the *Vorlage* (1 Kgs 9.4-5) or—here following the *Vorlage*—the corresponding petition in Solomon's prayer (6.16-17). This is a far cry from the priorities and preoccupations of Psalm 132, and at the same time it is a significant modification of the priorities of the temple dedication prayer inherited from the *Vorlage*.

Thus our investigation into the relation of 7.12-22 to 6.14-42 and to Psalm 132 has revealed both a repudiation by the Chronicler of the high royalist theology of Psalm 132 and a playing down of the royalist tone of the opening of Solomon's prayer, in favour of the more 'democratic' view of the temple and its cult evinced by the bulk of that prayer. In the light of these observations, it must surely be significant that, whereas the writer emphasizes by repetition (*'d 'wlm* and *kl hymym*, 7.16) the perdurance of the temple as locus for Yahweh's response to his people, no similar affirmation of the perpetuity of the dynasty appears in the conditional divine promise to Solomon (7.17). But *l'lm* is there in the *Vorlage* (1 Kgs 9.5a), and *'dy 'd* is in the corresponding response in Ps. 132.12b. In other words, there was more than enough prompting to the Chronicler to assert perpetuity of the dynasty, had it been important to him. Yet 7.12-22 is precisely a passage where the writer is transparently addressing a message to his contemporaries in the temple community of Jerusalem, concerning both their present and their future.[36] Clearly, then, for the Chronicler the perdurance of the temple is of greater contemporary concern to the people than the continuance of the dynasty.

From our discussion of 7.12-22 in the light of the two texts that have been formative influences on the passage, it has become clear that for the Chronicler the future of God's people in his own time was not inextricably bound up with a putative future for the Davidic dynasty. More, we have seen that our author has taken some trouble to articulate a non-royalist view of the matter, whereby on the question of ultimate fate the dynasty neither enjoys any privileges over the people nor mediates to it any special blessing or curse—it simply takes its place as part of the 'you' of the people, to whom are addressed the conditions of blessing and the warnings against apostasy. Such a reading of 7.12-22 is entirely consonant with what we saw in 36.11-21, where the fate of king and

---

36. One small indicator of this is that, of all the sets of circumstances entertained by Solomon in his prayer as provoking the people to turn to the temple, the author has singled out in 7.13 those most readily applicable, and repeatedly applicable, to the Jewish community under Persian sovereignty, and not, e.g., those which envisage war or defeat and exile.

dynasty, far from determining that of the people, was not an object of much interest to the author in comparison with that of people and temple. Furthermore, the restoration of people and temple anticipated in that text is without evident embarrassment inextricably bound up with the establishment of a new and opposed sovereignty, that of the Persians. We have, it would thus appear, complete convergence of these two lines of evidence from the text of Chronicles.

2 Chronicles 29.5-11; 30.6-12

This convergence is intensified by the last set of texts we shall consider, Hezekiah's address to the priests and Levites, 29.5-11, and his letter to the people of Israel and Judah and the response to it, 30.6-12. Numerous verbal and conceptual links with both 36.11-21 and 7.12-22[37] establish a strong thematic connection between the latter passages and the Hezekiah pericope in general. We find here the same characteristic conjunction of temporal exile and restoration with spiritual apostasy and religious revival, a revival centred on the temple and its cult. The blessings of the people under Hezekiah are presented as a foil to the disasters that overtake them under Zedekiah, and as a model fufilment of the conditions for blessing laid down in 7.14. The people under Hezekiah, with their religious leaders in the van (29.4-19), respond wholeheartedly to the summons to repentance, and accordingly reap the resultant blessing of revival and restoration. The people under Zedekiah, on the other hand, once again with their religious leaders in the van (36.14), persist in apostasy and rebellion, thus bringing down on themselves the curse of 7.19-22.

This contrast is not, however, primarily intended as a purely historical observation on the two reigns. It has long been recognized that the Chronicler's account of Hezekiah's reign owes as much to ideology as to history, reflecting more the writer's aspirations for his own day than the historical conditions of Hezekiah's time. This appraisal has focused on the account of the celebration of Hezekiah's Passover, but it applies no less to the two texts germane to our inquiry, 29.5-11 and 30.6-9. We observe that each is for the most part couched in very general terms, with almost no specific anchorage in the historical circumstances of

---

37. Cf. 29.5bβ with 36.14b; 29.6 with 36.12a, 14a; 29.6bβ with 36.13bα; 29.8a with 36.16b; 29.9a with 36.17aα; 29.9b with 36.20; 30.6bα with 7.14aβ, 36.13bβ; 30.7a with 36.14aα; 30.8a with 36.13bα; 30.8bα with 36.14b; 30.8bβ with 36.16b; 30.9-10 with 36.15-16; 30.11 with 7.14aα, 36.12b; also 30.18b-20 with 7.14 and 32.26a with 7.14aα.

Hezekiah's reign.[38] On the contrary, 29.8-9 fits better into the situation of the later Persian period than that of Judah at the end of the eighth century, just as the promise of 30.9 articulates hopes more appropriate to this later period. As with 7.12-22, then, we have to do with exhortations directed at the author's readers. Moreover, just as in 7.12-22, the burden of these exhortations concerns temple and people: how the people's welfare, past, present and future, is intimately bound up with their service of Yahweh in his chosen sanctuary.

But even more than 7.12-22, these exhortations bracket out any possible role for a Davidic monarch in this process of revival and restoration. Such a figure is not mentioned at all. Yet the responsibilities both of cultic functionaries (29.5, 11) and of the people (30.6-9) are clearly spelled out. Now admittedly, these words are put into the mouth of a scion of David, a veritable paragon among the post-Solomonic kings, presented by the Chronicler so as to recall both David and Solomon,[39] a king under whose hand revival and restoration are brought to pass. Is our author thereby tacitly demonstrating a role for the alleged future Davidide of his hopes? Even leaving aside the cumulative weight of our argument, such a reading of these texts would be more convincing if indirect implication and ironic understatement were characteristic of the Chronicler. However, like the Deuteronomists, the Chronicler prefers the direct approach, going in with all guns blazing, as it were, when he has an important message to impart.[40] In other words, it is far more likely that in these exhortations direct expression has been given to what was important to the Chronicler for the present and future welfare of the community of his own day. This must make significant the silence about the dynastic promise, not only in these two texts but in the Hezekiah pericope as a whole. For if the hope that the writer is said to be commending to his readers is for a future Davidic ruler from Hezekiah's mould, that is, one who incarnates both David and Solomon, then surely

---

38. Apart from the reference to the kings of Assyria in 30.6, only the charge that the 'fathers' closed the doors of the portico and extinguished the lamp (29.7) goes beyond a very general delineation of circumstances.

39. For a summary of recent discussion on this, see M.A. Thronveit, *When Kings Speak: Royal Speech and Royal Prayer in Chronicles* (SBLDS, 93; Atlanta: Scholars Press, 1987), pp. 121-24; Dillard, *2 Chronicles*, pp. 228-29.

40. Examples are numerous, two other typical cases being Abijah's address to Jeroboam and all Israel (13.4-12) and Jehoshaphat's address to the assembly of Judah and Jerusalem (20.6-12).

a clear linking of the dynastic promise with this king above all is required.[41] What could have been easier than to incorporate into the word of 30.6-9 an assurance that Yahweh would remember his promise to David, linking this to the promise of restoration in 30.9? The fact that he has not done so, after having linked the promised restoration to an exhortation to people and cultic personnel to serve Yahweh in his sanctuary (30.8, cf. 29.11), is no less revealing about our author's major concerns than the passages discussed above, with which our present texts are thoroughly in accord.

5. Conclusions

Our investigation has led us to consider three key passages in Chronicles: the concluding section of the work on the reign of Zedekiah (36.11-21), and two closely related sets of text, one from the temple dedication pericope (7.12-22), the other from the account of Hezekiah's reign (29.5-11; 30.6-12). These three passages embody both statements enunciating fundamental theological beliefs of the author and exhortations directed at the work's readers concerning their present and future under Yahweh. Yet while all three are unanimous in their concern for the welfare of people and temple, in their affirmation that the future of the people depends upon their present relationship to Yahweh, focused on the temple and its cult, none indicates that a restored Davidide has any role to play in ensuring the continuation of revival and restoration among the people. Indeed, we saw strong indications to the contrary. In particular, the Chronicler set the 'democratic' nexus of people and temple over against the royalist dyad of dynasty and temple as found in Psalm 132 and happily associated restoration of people and temple with the inauguration of Persian sovereignty, with not the least attempt to temper this by mention of a hoped-for future restoration of the Davidic dynasty. This must mean that when the Chronicler presents to his contemporaries, in the guise of Hezekiah's reign, a model of what faithful adherence to the temple and its cult could be, it is as prototype of the

---

41. In fact none of the lengthy accounts in Chronicles devoted to the four post-Solomonic kings who take a lead in producing revival and restoration—Asa, Jehoshaphat, Hezekiah, and Josiah—ever makes reference to the dynastic promise, or gives any other overt indication that the author looks towards the restoration of just such a Davidic king in the future.

ideal *religious leader*, rather than of an ideal *future Davidide*,[42] that the author depicts Hezekiah.[43]

Now, unless there is considerable incoherence between the thrust of these passages and the thrust of the rest of Chronicles, we must conclude on the one hand that a hope for the future restoration of the Davidic dynasty was not an important item of belief for our author, and clearly not one which he was seeking to commend to his readers. Hence the pressing questions that our analysis of the messianic-cum-royalist approach posed to the text of Chronicles remain unanswered, precisely because they do not even arise, since the major premise from which they derive is not one shared by the text. But on the other hand, as we concluded much earlier in our discussion, the belief that God had promised to David a continuing dynasty was one manifestly held by the Chronicler. Thus the forbearance of God to the dynasty[44] despite the havoc it wreaked on temple and cult is only explicable as a corollary of his undertaking to David—witness Jehoram (21.7).[45] But there was also a limit to that forbearance, as witness Zedekiah (36.11-12). Yet belief in such a promise does not inevitably imply a hope for the future restoration of the dynasty. Sufficient vindication of the divine undertaking to David is given by the Chronicler's own account of the continuance of the

42. A similar conclusion would result from an examination of the accounts of the reigns of Jehoshaphat (cf. especially 2 Chron. 20) and Asa (cf. 2 Chron. 14–15).

43. To this extent at any rate the Chronicler's outlook is 'hierocratic' rather than 'messianic' or 'royalist'. But this certainly need not imply satisfaction with the politico-religious status quo in the Jerusalem community. Cf. further below.

44. Note again that in 21.7 it is precisely a question of forbearance to the *dynasty* (*byt dwyd*) rather than more generally to Judah, as the Kings parallel has it; cf. n. 9 above.

45. Williamson ('Eschatology', pp. 141-54; 'Dynastic Oracle', pp. 316-18) contends with special reference to 1 Chron. 28.7 that for the Chronicler Solomon's perfect obedience to conditions imposed on the dynastic promise to David was both a necessary and a sufficient condition for the perpetuity of an *unconditional* promise to the dynasty. But in that case it is to be expected that the Chronicler would have cited this putative crucial guarantee both here, where the continuation of the dynasty is being justified in the face of a bad dynast, and in the chronistic additions 13.5-8 and 23.3, where its continuation is under threat. In all three texts the appeal is simply to the promise as made to David, with no hint that it was underwritten by Solomon. In any case, it is by no means clear that 1 Chron. 28.7, with its reference to the perdurance of Solomon's kingdom (*whkynwty 't mlkwtw 'd l'wlm*), has reference to a continuing dynasty, any more than does the similar statement of David's rule in 28.4 (*wybḥr...by...lmlk 'l yśr'l l'wlm*). Cf. also n. 26 above.

dynasty through many historical vicissitudes over a long period of time. Moreover, since in all the post-Solomonic history the only invocations of the promise to David are made when dynastic continuity is under some threat, the silence concerning it when finally the dynasty falls victim to its own spiritual waywardness is eloquent indeed.

The implication of this silence is that with the destruction of the pre-exilic kingdom, the kingdom of God among his people now had to assume a different form.[46] Thus there is implicit in the message of the book an openness to the future. But it is a future arising from the possibilities of the present. Chronicles urges its readers to embrace the richness of the possibilities open to the people of God through the divinely appointed temple and its worship. This does not complacently idealize the fourth-century Jerusalem community, but neither does it direct the reader's gaze away from a disappointing present to a glorious future that can only be awaited in hope. Rather it summons the community to move forward from present complacency or discontent to a renewal of faith in God and joy in his worship.[47]

46. A similar concept operates in Chronicles' readiness to portray in terms of figures from a different dispensation, i.e. Moses and Joshua, the monarchs of the Davidic dynasty who for the Chronicler most truly incarnated the kingdom of God, i.e. David and Solomon. On this comparison in general, see Braun, 'Solomon', pp. 586-88; H.G.M. Williamson, 'The Accession of Solomon in the Books of Chronicles', *VT* 26 (1976), pp. 351-61. While 1 Chron. 17.14; 28.5; 29.23; 2 Chron. 9.8; 13.8 strictly refer to Solomon's rule, the implication of 1 Chron. 29.23 especially is that the same can be predicated of David's. Accordingly, this entails the Chronicler's recognition that as the kingdom of God through Moses and Joshua gave way to a different, though significantly analogous, form through David and Solomon, so the kingdom of God through the Davidic dynasty itself had ceded place to that through the temple community of his own day.

47.   I read a paper to the SBL Annual Meeting in 1989 on this 'revivalist' tendency in Chronicles, which I hope to publish in a revised form.

JSOT 59 (1993), pp. 73-92

ON THE RELATIONSHIP OF THE BOOKS OF EZRA AND NEHEMIAH

David Kraemer

Modern study of the book(s) of Ezra and Nehemiah[1] has been dominated by a powerful historicist bent. Being primarily interested in the
history of the period for which these documents are the primary witnesses, scholars of the books have sought to recover the correct
chronological order of the events that they presumably record. On
account of this prejudice, such scholars have assumed that the Ezra–
Nehemiah narrative is seriously confused. Attempts to restore the
'original' order have resulted in various rearrangements of the narrative
and documentary materials. For these purposes, the materials at hand,
whether considered to be contained in one or two books, have been
read as a single historical account.[2]

A necessary corrective to this approach is offered by Brevard
S. Childs. He writes,

> In my judgment, the usual critical move which disregards the present
> form of the tradition and seeks to reconstruct a more historical sequence
> on the basis of literary and historical criteria runs the risk of failing to
> understand the theological concerns which are reflected through the
> canonical process. It seems obvious that an accurate historical report of
> the Persian period according to the canons of modern historical writing is
> not being offered, but that the biblical material has been shaped and
> transmitted toward another end.[3]

1. On the question of whether these are one or two books, see below.
2. An excellent review of the approach described herein—itself an example of
this approach—is H.H. Rowley's essay on Ezra and Nehemiah in *Ignace Goldziher
Memorial Volume* (Part 1; Budapest, 1948), pp. 117-49, repr. in Rowley, *The
Servant of the Lord, and Other Essays on the Old Testament* (London: Lutterworth
Press, 1952), pp. 135-68.
3. B.S. Childs, *Introduction to the Old Testament as Scripture* (Philadelphia:
Fortress Press, 1979), p. 635.

Childs then goes on, all too briefly, to describe his sense of the ideological agendas of this canonical book.[4] In doing so, he makes eminently clear that considerations other than those of the historian give shape to the final literary documents. Following Childs's lead, Tamara Cohn Eskenazi undertakes the only full-length literary study of the canonical book of Ezra–Nehemiah, exhibiting a fine literary sense in her close reading of the text and showing the important contributions that this previously neglected methodological perspective can make.[5]

Eskenazi's method is one that I fully endorse. The caution that we are dealing here with literary formulations and not with self-conscious historical records is one that cannot be repeated too often. Naturally, the recognition of this condition has consequences regarding the way these materials may be approached—highlighting their rhetoric and ideological prejudices and diminishing their value as historical sources. All of this is amply accounted for in Eskenazi's study. But I am of a different mind from Eskenazi in one crucial matter, and this difference leads me to conclusions that diverge significantly from hers or, for that matter, from any yet proposed.

I am speaking of Eskenazi's choice to read Ezra–Nehemiah as a single book rather than as two distinct works. Her reason for doing so is well understood. The ancient canonical traditions (before Origen) apparently all consider Ezra and Nehemiah to be one book. Thus, a canonical approach, following Childs, bids that they be considered together.

But this choice is, in my opinion, an ill-advised one. To begin with, the fact that the ancient believing community received these works as a single book is far from probative when considering their original status as literature. The community may have read them together, at a point subsequent to their formulation, for various reasons, including reasons that approximate those of the modern historians (they were concerned, after all, with these works as a record of holy history). From their canonical status, we learn nothing about the literary condition of these works at their inception.

Moreover, reading Ezra and Nehemiah as one forces Eskenazi to make a jump that I think cannot ultimately be supported. In order to claim a unity for the agendas of the two books, Eskenazi argues that the first major segment of Nehemiah is about the expansion of the 'house of

4.   Following the tradition of the Hebrew canon, Childs treats the books as one.
5.   T.C. Eskenazi, *In an Age of Prose: A Literary Approach to Ezra–Nehemiah* (SBLMS, 36; Atlanta: Scholars Press, 1988).

God'—obviously a major concern in Ezra—to include the city of Jerusalem as a whole.[6] But, unlike in Ezra, where the centrality of the 'house of God' is explicit and pervasive, the house is nowhere mentioned explicitly in the relevant sections of Nehemiah. In fact, on each occasion where Eskenazi notes the house of God in Nehemiah, the explicit text speaks of the city and its walls, giving no hint that these are to be judged as anything other than that. The strongest support of Eskenazi's claim is the expression of opposition by the Temple's opponents, in their correspondence with Artaxerxes, in terms of the city and its walls (Ezra 4.7-24). But the context in which this correspondence is quoted denies the equation that Eskenazi wants to make, speaking of 'the House of God *which is in Jerusalem*' (see, e.g., 5.2 and 6.5, my emphasis), not of the House of God which is Jerusalem. Furthermore, the voice of the letter is that of the opponents—the story's antagonists—so their usage is hardly determinant in the mind of the reader. What is more important, as I see it, is the purpose for which the quoted document is appropriated, and that is clearly the Temple. For the author of Ezra, in fact, the Temple is the center of concern. This same centrality does not extend to Nehemiah.

On the other side, there are many reasons to assume, *prima facie*, that these are distinct works. Most of these have been noted before, and there is no reason to review them all here. Just to mention a few of the most important factors:

1. The book of Nehemiah, in the middle of the canonical whole, bears an introduction that clearly marks what follows as an independent composition.[7]
2. The repetition of the identical list in Ezra 2 and Nehemiah 7 is no problem if the two books are distinct.
3. Similarly, the fact that the discussion of Ezra's activities is dropped between the end of Ezra and Nehemiah 8 is more easily accounted for if these are two works.
4. Important stylistic differences also distinguish the two.[8]

6. See *Age of Prose*, p. 2 and pp. 53-57.
7. See S. Talmon, 'Ezra and Nehemiah (Books and Men)', *IDBSup*, p. 318.
8. Ezra includes narrative and documents in both Hebrew and Aramaic; Nehemiah restricts itself exclusively to Hebrew. Ezra's memoir in Ezra is primarily a first-person account; his activity in Nehemiah is witnessed and recounted in the third person.

5. Not to be underestimated, as well, is the power of the opinion held by some, at least by the time of Origen, that these are two books and not one. Whatever the antiquity of such an opinion, its wisdom has to be weighed seriously.

6. Most importantly, as I will demonstrate in detail below, the two works, when considered independently, exhibit important ideological differences that make it extremely difficult to read them as a single unit.[9]

This last point is, I think, the most important reason for undertaking the sort of reading proposed here. M.A. Thronveit articulates the justification for such an approach this way:

> the safest course would be to take seriously the *a priori* assumption of separate authorship and investigate both works individually from a theological point of view, leaving the question of authorship open until the intent and message of both are better understood.[10]

Thronveit arrives at this position after reviewing the many attempts—ultimately inconclusive, in his judgment—to determine the relationship of the authorships of these works and Chronicles based upon linguistic criteria. His conclusion is that the most promising means of answering the question of authorship is to begin by reading the works independently.

Reading the works as just described, with the overall methodological emphases otherwise recommended by Eskenazi, I conclude that the relationship of the books of Ezra and Nehemiah is, in a general sense, analogous to that of 1 and 2 Maccabees; that is to say, they report an overlapping but not identical historical period, but from significantly

---

9.   I find A. Kapelrud's argument for the unity of the 'Ezra-narrative' on the basis of linguistic criteria to be unconvincing. First, he assumes the unity *a priori*; thus, he is likely to find common post-exilic usages as evidence of unity. Second, Kapelrud admits that Neh. 8 is distinct from the Ezra materials in many important ways; see his review in *The Question of Authorship in the Ezra-Narrative: A Lexical Investigation* (Skrifter utgitt av det Norske Videnkaps-Akademi i Oslo. II. Hist.-Filos. Klasse, 1944, no. 1; Oslo: J. Dybwad, 1944), p. 93. Given the differences, the choice between unity and independence based upon this evidence alone is highly arbitrary. For a good illustration of the difficulty of using lexical characteristics to determine authorship, see S. Japhet, 'The Supposed Common Authorship of Chronicles and Ezra–Nehemiah Investigated Anew', *VT* 18 (1968), pp. 330-71.

10.   M.A. Thronveit, 'Linguistic Analysis and the Question of Authorship in Chronicles, Ezra and Nehemiah', *VT* 32 (1982), p. 215.

different ideological perspectives. The book of Ezra is a priestly book; its concerns are the Temple, the priesthood and Levites, and purity—that is, the cult. The book of Nehemiah, in contrast, is a lay book, sometimes exhibiting antagonism to priestly concerns and supporting, instead, what might be called scribal values.[11] After justifying these claims, following, I will remark upon their consequences for Ezra–Nehemiah scholarship.

My analysis of the books and their respective ideologies begins by reviewing the overall structure of each book, asking how structure carries with it the ideological preferences of its author. Next, I compare and contrast the respective treatments of the figure of Ezra in each book, with a mind to the same concerns. Third, I analyze the treatment of common motifs in the two books, seeing how these treatments support the ideologies previously identified. Finally, I examine the place of Torah in each of these books, showing how variant assumptions regarding the place of Torah in the restoration community reflect the very same biases indicated in the other materials. I will show that, in each of these areas, the different perspectives described above are powerfully confirmed.

Structure and Theme[12]

Ezra devotes its first six chapters to the rebuilding of the Temple. Chapter 1 records the decree of Cyrus confirming the right of the Jews to return to Judea to restore their sanctuary. Chapter 2 is a lengthy list of those returning; the context establishes that the purpose of their return is to rebuild the Temple (v. 68). Chapter 3 records the successful rebuilding of the altar for the purpose of offering sacrifices, the celebration of the Sukkot holiday (marked by the offering of sacrifices), and the celebration of the laying of the foundation of the House of God.

11. I use the term 'scribe' perhaps anachronistically. Various functions are attributed to scribes in ancient Israel (pre- and post-exilic) as well as in neighboring societies; see J.M. Myers's discussion, *Ezra–Nehemiah* (AB, 14; Garden City, NY: Doubleday, 1965), pp. 60-61, and the excellent brief essay by A. Demsky, *EncJud* XIV, cols. 1041-43. My argument, following, is that the accounts of Ezra's responsibilities as a scribe may not reliably be used as evidence for this period because they are in tension with one another. When I speak of 'scribal' ideals below, I anticipate the scribe of the late Second Temple period.

12. A more detailed outline may be found in Myers, *Ezra–Nehemiah*, pp. xxxviii-xli. For a comprehensive analysis of the structure of the books, see Eskenazi, *Age of Prose*, pp. 37-126.

Chapters 4 and 5 narrate the opposition of the local population to the rebuilding effort and the reconfirmation of the right of the community of Jewish returnees to do so. Chapter 6 speaks of the support of the Temple project out of the royal treasuries, the completion of the rebuilding, and the celebration of its rededication—accompanied by sacrifices, the purification of priests and Levites (alone), and the bringing of sacrifice in celebration of the Passover.

Chapter 7 introduces us to Ezra, ascribing to him several roles and purposes. But the bulk of the chapter, the letter of Artaxerxes to Ezra, speaks of the Temple, its sacrifices and its supplies. Ezra himself characterizes the purpose of the king, expressed in the letter, as being 'to beautify the house of the LORD which is in Jerusalem' (v. 27). Chapter 8 first lists the leaders of those going up with Ezra. It then speaks of the recruitment of Levites and Temple servants and of other preparations for going up to the Temple. It ends by describing the first acts undertaken by the returnees upon their arrival—the weighing out of gold and vessels for use in the House of God and the bringing of sacrifices. Finally, chs. 9 and 10 recount the events surrounding the intermarriage crisis; the language of the account is strongly priestly (see below on intermarriage).

Overall, it may be seen, the thematic structure of the book of Ezra is built upon priestly concerns. To be sure, certain small details diverge from this single-mindedness, but they are, when weighed against the whole, entirely insignificant. The Temple and its cult, and the purity of those who serve and worship there, constitute virtually the full range of interests to which the author of this book devotes himself.

The book of Nehemiah poses a striking contrast. Chapters 1–7 describe the rebuilding of the city, of its walls, and of the community that dwells within them, all under the direction of Nehemiah. Chapter 1 shows Nehemiah inquiring into the well-being of the inhabitants of Jerusalem. Concern is expressed for the disrepair of the walls and gates of the city. Nehemiah laments the condition that is reported to him, accounting it as a product of the disobedience of the people. His language is marked strongly by Deuteronomic expressions.[13] In ch. 2, the king empowers Nehemiah to return and oversee repair of the city. Local inhabitants are said to oppose the city's repair. So, by night and in secret, Nehemiah surveys the city's walls and gates. Further acts of

---

13. See, e.g., vv. 5 (Deut. 10.17) and 9 (Deut. 30.4 and 19.29).

opposition are then mentioned. Chapters 3 and 4 describe the repair effort. Notably, upon being rebuilt, the *gates* are sanctified by the High Priest. There follows, in ch. 3, a long list of the assignments of various groups of builders. Priests, Levites and Israelites undertake various assignments, building side by side. The chapters go on by describing further opposition and the establishment by Nehemiah of guards to assure that the repair effort will not be interrupted. Chapter 5 diverges from the foregoing themes, speaking of Nehemiah's enforcement of various aspects of the Torah's social legislation, including the return of lands and the release of debts. Chapter 6 returns directly to the concerns of earlier chapters. Chapter 7, finally, repeats the list of Ezra 2, but with a very different purpose (see below).

In ch. 8, we are again introduced to Ezra. Crucially, the account is now in the third person. Central to Ezra's activities in this chapter is the reading of the Torah scroll in public. The Sukkot holiday is celebrated with the construction of booths—no sacrifice is mentioned. Chapter 9 begins with the separation of Israelites from foreigners. In response to the offense, the people read Torah, confess their sins and prostrate themselves. Following, the people gather to bless God, recounting the history of Israel as a preliminary to the re-establishment of the covenant. This history includes the giving of Torah to Moses at Mt Sinai *for the first time in any such biblical historical review*; the Temple is ignored completely. Chapter 10 tells of the covenanting, listing the parties to that covenant. It then refers to renewed efforts to observe various laws of the Torah, including the Sabbath and the offering of various agricultural gifts to the priests.

Chapter 11 returns us to the project for repopulating Jerusalem—the building of city and community go hand in hand and continue to be central. A lengthy list of 'chiefs of the province' who dwelt at Jerusalem follows. Chapter 12 continues with a list of priests and Levites who 'went up with Zerubbabel'. No precise purpose is described for this 'going up', but, since the chapter continues by describing the celebration of the dedication of the wall of Jerusalem, it is clear that all activities have been directed toward this end. Chapter 13, the final chapter, describes various offenses against Torah by the people and efforts to ameliorate this condition. Notably, Nehemiah discovers various offenses by the High Priest and expels him from the Temple (vv. 4-9).

This book is not so single-minded as is the book of Ezra. Because of its apparent variety, it may be simplest to characterize its concerns by means of negation—unlike Ezra, the book of Nehemiah is not significantly concerned with the Temple and the cult. The first major section of the book is concerned with the viability of the city and the community. The Temple goes virtually unmentioned here—the two minor references (2.8 and 6.10) are entirely by-the-way[14]—and this despite the fact that the Temple itself is apparently not in good repair (see 3.34, 'will they sacrifice?').[15] A similar omission has been noted in the ritual history rehearsed in ch. 9, and here, as elsewhere in the latter part of Nehemiah, the center stage is now occupied by Torah. If the book of Ezra is a priestly book, Nehemiah represents the wedding of the concerns of the governor and the (non-priestly) scribe. Furthermore, as will be spelled out later, this wedding is forged with not a little antipathy toward the priest and his competitive centrality.

The Figure of Ezra

The present apparently confused state of the so-called Ezra memoir is the primary reason that scholars have sought to rearrange the material in these books. But at the root of this alleged confusion is a factor that has been largely ignored by students of these books: the accounts of Ezra in the book of Ezra and in Nehemiah differ radically in their pictures of Ezra and his purported activities. These differences align precisely with the ideological divergence already identified.

In the book of Ezra, we are first introduced to Ezra with a lengthy and detailed pedigree (7.1-5). Though Ezra is characterized as both a priest and a scribe, it is his priestly connections that are important—he is descended from Aaron (v. 5), the original High Priest, from Zadoq (v. 2), the traditional high-priestly line from the time of David, and from Seraiah (v. 1), the last of the High Priests at the time of the destruction. No more illustrious sequence of connections could be imagined! Furthermore, though Ezra is described also as a scribe whose purpose is to teach God's law (v. 10), such an activity is never undertaken by Ezra in the narrative of this book.[16] In fact, when we first hear Ezra's own

14. The former reference is omitted by the LXX.

15. Caution is necessary, however, in making this suggestion because of textual uncertainties. See J. Blenkinsopp, *Ezra–Nehemiah: A Commentary* (OTL; Philadelphia: Westminster Press, 1988), p. 243.

16. Ezra is described as a scribe twice in this chapter (vv. 6 and 11). In v. 6, his skill as a scribe is praised but we have no information defining the scribal task. Verse 11

voice (7.27)—inescapably establishing our impression of who he is and what his concerns are—he praises the king for seeing fit to 'beautify the House of the Lord' and praises God for choosing him to stand at the head of that task. Ezra devotes himself, in the book of Ezra, to the Temple and the cult.

It is the matter of the intermarriages and the reaction to them, consuming the last two chapters of the book, that requires the most detailed attention in the present context. The ninth chapter begins with Ezra's report of his introduction to the offense, spoken of in these words: 'the holy seed has become intermingled with the peoples of the land; and it is the officers and prefects who have taken the lead in this trespass' (v. 2, NJPS translation). The language is the language of the priesthood; trespass (*ma'al*) is a technical term for committing offense with respect to holy things.[17] What is objectionable is that the holy seed (a term with precedent only at Isa. 6.13)[18] is being intermingled with unholy seed. Notably, Deuteronomy's prohibition of intermarriage with the surrounding nations (7.3-4) is supported by no such justification; there the concern is the attraction of idolatry, as befits the apparent context of the Deuteronomic legislation.[19] So the concern voiced here is a new one and may be understood to represent the unique and particular prejudice of the present author.

The chapter continues in the same vein. Ezra responds in horror and remorse to what he has learned. He initiates acts of mourning and

---

somehow associates Ezra's scribal function with the laws of YHWH, but again, what that association might be is not spelled out. In v. 10, Ezra is praised for preparing himself 'to investigate the teaching [Torah] of YHWH, to observe and to teach ordinances and judgments in Israel' (my translation). Though the fact that Ezra is a scribe is not mentioned in this verse, the context strongly intimates that these activities are a function of Ezra's scribal commitments. Nevertheless, as mentioned, Ezra never undertakes to investigate or teach scripture in this book. We are left with the impression that the descriptions are somehow formulaic; they have no immediate association to reality.

17. The term is used especially in Leviticus, Numbers, Ezekiel and Chronicles— that is, in documents that speak from a priestly perspective.

18. Itself a late gloss. See Blenkinsopp, *Ezra–Nehemiah*, p. 176.

19. The description of the people as 'holy' in Deut. 7.6 is not to be equated with the notion of holiness expressed here. There, holiness means to separate from idol worship; 'holy to the Lord' means 'separated [from idolatry] to the Lord'. Here, in Ezra, the holiness of the seed is an essential, priestly holiness, residing in the seed by its very nature.

repentance; the timing of these acts is correlated with the times of sacrifices (vv. 4-5). His prayer describes the sin of the people—the reason for their earlier exile—in general terms, but the context sets the sin clearly as the profanation of holy seed. The land that they have come into and in which they have sinned is described as a land of *niddâ*, a term otherwise found only in priestly contexts.

Chapter 10 continues with the response to the intermarriages. The leaders, with Ezra, undertake a covenant to separate from the foreign women. In the course of the narrative, Ezra's name is given either without qualification (10.1, 5) or with emphasis on his priestly identification (10.10, 16); his actions continue to illustrate his priestly concerns, and the language brought to relate his activities remains priestly as well; 'trespass' is ameliorated through 'separation', each word being repeated several times (see vv. 2, 6, 8, 10, 11 and 16).

So, in the book of Ezra, Ezra is a well-connected priest whose exclusive concern is the strengthening and purification of the cult. His primary activity involves the elimination of intermarriages, an offense that is newly and uniquely described in priestly terms. As befits the emphasis of the book as a whole, Ezra is a man of the priesthood.

Now consider the Ezra of Nehemiah. The portrait of this Ezra, related exclusively in the third person, is restricted primarily to ch. 8 (after this, Ezra recedes from prominence and is nowhere central to the narrative). Again, in the course of the narrative, we discover that Ezra is both a scribe and a priest, but—in contrast with the picture in Ezra—in Nehemiah, Ezra acts everywhere as a scribe and nowhere as a priest. Here, Ezra the scribe, introduced with no pedigree, devotes himself to the reading of Torah in public and the instruction of the people. With the leaders of the people and the priests and Levites, Ezra does not bring sacrifices but studies Torah (vv. 13-18). Learning about the Sukkot holiday, they respond by constructing booths; nowhere is sacrifice mentioned, and this despite the fact that, in the Priestly law, Sukkot is the holiday that is accompanied by the most sacrifices (by far—see Num. 29.12-38). Rather, instead of offering sacrifices day by day, they celebrate by reading Torah day by day (Neh. 8.18). Supporting the thrust of what is recounted here is the weight of the appositives that accompany Ezra's name: on only one occasion (8.2) is Ezra described simply as a priest; on two occasions (8.9 and 12.26) Ezra is both a priest and a scribe; in all other instances, five in all (8.1, 4, 5, 13; 12.37), Ezra is spoken of as being a scribe alone. In sum, the narrative exposition and the linguistic signals combine to make a single, unmistakable point.

Thus, the Ezra remembered in Ezra is not the Ezra known in Nehemiah. In Ezra, Ezra is a priest, a man concerned with the cult and its purity, while in Nehemiah he is a scribe, a man of the book, who is entirely unconcerned with the Temple or sacrifices. These are two different Ezras, the one bearing little relationship to the other. The disparate portraits do, however, bear powerful relationship with the ideological bents of the books in which they appear.

Motifs

The differences in these books in the treatment of various common motifs or details align precisely with the prejudices that I have identified. I analyze these variant treatments in no particular order.

Crying

On several occasions in these books the people, or some segment of the people, are moved to tears. This occurs twice in Ezra, first when the elders who remember the first Temple see its paltry replacement (3.12), and second in response to the recognition of the intermarriage offense (10.1), which, as we have seen, is a priestly concern in this context. In Nehemiah (8.9), they cry following the public reading of the Torah, apparently for fear of not having fulfilled its precepts. People cry in each book over the primary ideological concern of the book, as identified above.

Sukkot

Sukkot is observed in both books. In Ezra (3.4) it is a holiday of sacrifices; booths are not even mentioned. In Nehemiah it is a holiday of booths and of the reading of Torah; sacrifices are not even mentioned in this connection.

Opposition

Both books report that elements of the local population opposed the efforts of the returning community. In Ezra (chs. 4–5), this opposition is directed exclusively against the effort to rebuild the Temple; in Nehemiah (2.10-20; 3.33-38; 4; 6) it is directed against the effort to rebuild the wall and gates of the city.

Sources

The centrality of various kinds of sources (lists, letters, documents), particularly in Ezra but also in Nehemiah, has often been noted. What has not been noted is the different purposes to which these sources are put. A few examples will suffice to illustrate this difference.

I have already alluded to the different purpose for the quotation of the much-discussed list of returnees at Ezra 2 and Nehemiah 7. The list in Ezra is introduced simply by identifying those included as the ones who returned. But it is followed by speaking of those who came to the House of the LORD in Jerusalem and volunteered to support the rebuilding project (vv. 68-69); the return leads to rebuilding. In contrast, in Nehemiah the list is framed in such a way as to make clear that return leads to rebuilding and repopulation of the city (see 7.4-5 and 69-71), where 'the work' for which donations are made is, given the context, clearly the rebuilding and repopulation effort. Note that even the priests, along with the Levites and others, make donations—they give of their uniquely priestly wealth. Obviously, then, the donations are not directed to the priesthood itself.

In Ezra, other sources similarly address the priestly concerns. Thus, the list at the end of ch. 1 is a list of the vessels of the House of the Lord. The correspondence preserved in chs. 4–5 concerns the right of the returnees to rebuild the Temple. Cyrus's decree, at the beginning of ch. 6, affirms that right and describes the dimensions of the House to be built (!). And so forth.

The contrast in Nehemiah is unmistakable. The list in ch. 3 records those who together built the walls and gates of the city. The list in ch. 7, as we have seen, is also directed toward rebuilding and repopulation. The covenantal history, in ch. 9, is concerned with Torah and its observance—the Temple is completely ignored. The list at the beginning of ch. 10 records those who affirm this very same covenant. The list in ch. 11 reflects the concern for repopulating the city. Again, whatever the sources that might have been available to the authors of these two books, they employ these sources consistently to serve their different purposes.

Intermarriage

We have already seen that the objection to intermarriage in Ezra is framed in terms of priestly definitions. In Nehemiah, the matter is somewhat more complex, but the characteristic differences do again emerge.

We first read of the separation from foreigners in Nehemiah at the beginning of ch. 9. We are not told what motivates the separation, but it is notable, at least, that 'the seed' that separates here is not 'the holy seed', as in Ezra, but simply 'the seed of Israel' (v. 2). (In Nehemiah it is *the city* that is holy rather than the seed; see 11.1.) When we return to discussion of the separation, at 10.29-31, the motivation is added: they separate 'to the Torah of God...to walk in the Torah of God which was given by the hand of Moses, the servant of God...' Unlike in Ezra, where the separation is only 'from', as an act to eliminate the pollution of the holy seed, here the separation has a positive purpose—to unite with the Torah of God. Notably, this affirmative motivation has neither a parallel in Ezra nor a precedent in Deuteronomy, where the concern is separation from idol worship (conceived and expressed as a negation).

The final mention of separation from foreigners in Nehemiah (13.1-3) makes explicit reference to Deut. 23.4-5. What is crucial here is that, aside from the fact that the concern is not priestly—it rests on historical causes—the motivation to separate is described as emerging from a reading of Torah. Again, Torah is central. The scribe has superseded the priest.

Covenant
Covenants are undertaken in both Ezra (10.2-8) and Nehemiah (chs. 9–10).[20] In Ezra, the covenant has but one purpose—to purify the seed of Israel by expelling the foreign women and their offspring (10.3).[21] In Nehemiah, by contrast, the covenant is conceived far more generally. The blessing that introduces the covenant places the giving of Torah and its observance at the center of its history. At the same time, the only major element of Israelite history that is conspicuously absent from the blessing is the building of the Temple of Solomon.

Sin and Punishment
Both books offer explanations of recent travails of Israel, typically understanding them as punishments for sin. Both books articulate this ideology in general terms (Ezra 9.6-7; Neh. 1.6-7; 9.26, 28-29, 34) and then propose specific transgressions that are understood to lie at the root of the attendant punishment. In Ezra, the specification focuses on the intermarriage and that alone. This is evident in the shift from the general

20. The term used in Neh. 10 is not $b^e r\hat{\imath}t$ but $^{'a}m\bar{a}n\hat{a}$. There is no question that the two terms are synonymous, as suggested by the verb, krt, used for undertaking such a commitment—this is the common biblical term for entering a covenant; see Gen. 15.18; 21.27, 32; 26.28; etc.

21. I understand the statement, 'and do according to the teaching [Torah]', to qualify what is specified earlier in the verse; that is to say, 'doing the Torah' is here equated with expelling the foreign wives and children.

to the specific in 9.10-12 and 9.14. By contrast, the only specification in Nehemiah (13.18) offers Sabbath transgression as the sin at the root of recent disasters. But the general description in ch. 1 (v. 7) lists several categories of laws that have been transgressed (*miṣwôt, huqqîm, mišpāṭîm*), suggesting that, whatever the specifics may be, they extend well beyond any individual transgression or category of transgressions. Furthermore, it is clear that sin is conceived in Deuteronomic terms (see 1.6-9; 9.28). In Nehemiah, neither the language nor the conception is priestly.

Priests, Governors, and Scribes
Though there are priests, governors, and scribes in both books, they have different functions in each. In Ezra, not only priests but also governors and scribes (Ezra) serve priestly purposes (the rebuilding of the Temple, the offering of sacrifice, the elimination of intermarriages in terms described above). In contrast, in Nehemiah, priests serve the purposes of the governor (the rebuilding of the city and reconstitution of the community) and the scribe (reading and teaching the Torah in public; see below).

Torah

The centrality of Torah to the Ezra traditions has been widely discussed. What has not been recognized is (1) the fact that this centrality is true only in the book of Nehemiah, and (2) that the visions of Torah in Ezra and Nehemiah differ radically from one another. The difference parallels, and perhaps lies at the foundation of, the characteristic ideological differences that we have earlier identified.

In Ezra, the Torah document—when referred to explicitly—acts exclusively as justification of priestly laws and then only by assertion. There is no evidence, anywhere in this book, that the Torah is actually *read* in public, let alone studied, and there is no indication, at places where explicit reference is made to a written law, that that law is constituted of anything but priestly matters. So, at 3.2, they build the altar and offer sacrifices on it 'as written in the Torah of Moses'. In v. 4 of the same chapter, the Sukkot festival is celebrated 'as written', but what is written is, apparently, only the obligation to bring sacrifices. Later on, the priests and Levites are appointed to their proper place in the divine worship 'according to the writing of the book of Moses' (6.18). This is the sum total of explicit references to a written Torah in the book of Ezra.

Now, consider the place of the book of the Torah in Nehemiah. Here the Torah is something that is read aloud in public (ch. 8). The text goes to extraordinary lengths to emphasize the public nature of the reading— mention of the presence of 'the whole people' (*kol hā'ām*) is repeated no fewer than nine times (vv. 3, 5, 6, 9, 12, 13; this construction does *not* appear in Ezra). In fact, in Nehemiah, such reading of Torah is *the* public ritual; it has replaced sacrifices almost entirely. Its replacement of sacrifice is likewise evident at the beginning of ch. 9 where the reading of Torah constitutes part of the ceremony of atonement for having married foreigners (v. 3). No more do sacrifices effect atonement; confession, prostration and the reading of Torah do.

Furthermore, the Torah is not merely read here—it is interpreted and explained (8.8). Such reading and interpreting of the Torah leads to discovery: by reading the Torah, the people discover that they are to celebrate Sukkot by constructing booths (8.14-17; crucially, they discover nothing here about sacrifices). They also discover that they are to separate themselves from foreign women (13.1). Torah, in this book, is an open, public document that is meant to be read and learned, discovered and observed.[22] To be sure, the Torah is sometimes alluded to, as justification, in the manner of Ezra (see Neh. 10.35 and 37). But this is not the approach that predominates. Rather, it is a public, variegated Torah (its laws are both priestly and non-priestly) that characterizes Nehemiah—precisely the sort that would come to characterize the scribal office in later Israel; perhaps what we see here is the first hint of such a development.

The difference between priestly and scribal law requires further elaboration. In the ancient world, priesthoods were guardians of sacred traditions. The traditions that they guarded were, in particular, the secrets of the cult and the performance of its rituals. Such knowledge enabled the priests to conduct their art correctly. Of course, it was this priestly art for which the people depended on the priests—it was the source of priestly power. The sacred knowledge, standing at the foundation of their power, was jealously guarded by the priests.[23]

22. A similar characterization is employed by Eskenazi, *Age of Prose*, p. 191. She does not, however, distinguish between the Torah ('book', 'text') seen in Ezra and that in Nehemiah.

23. See E.O. James, *The Nature and Function of Priesthood* (New York: Barnes & Noble, 1955), pp. 208, 223-24; and L. Sabourin, *Priesthood: A Comparative Study* (Leiden: Brill, 1973), p. 6.

In consideration of this relation between priesthoods and their laws, the image of Torah we find in Ezra—with its priestly inclinations—is fully to be expected. Again, in Ezra, the Torah is a book that describes the laws of the sacrificial cult. It is guarded, not publicized, and it is alluded to only as authoritative justification of laws that pertain to the priest. This Torah is revealed only to the extent that the priests require. If it supports their center of power, well and good. Otherwise, there is no need to share its content.[24]

The scribe, in contrast, has no essential investment in jealously protecting the law. On the contrary, his craft is devoted to the copying and promulgation of the law. This may well explain why scribes in Israel would later (at least) conclude that sacred power resides in the book itself and with those who devote themselves to it. Of course, this power is not restricted to a priesthood; thus, neither should the law be. In Nehemiah, we see this ideology in its nascent form—the Torah is brought out into the open and made central to the new ritual. It is available to all and there is no limit on what one might discover therein, beyond the actual substance of the document itself. And, given the alternatives made available through interpretation—clearly a part of the scribal project as described here—even this may not be a limit.[25]

Opposition to the Centrality of the Priesthood in Nehemiah

Another element of the different views of Torah in the books at hand needs to be emphasized. I am speaking of the fact that, if the sacred law,

24. It may be wondered whether there is anything beyond priestly law (including laws of particular interest to the priests outside of P) in the Torah book of Ezra. Perhaps the debate that lies at the heart of the many differences that I have outlined is the very identity of the 'Torah of Moses', with the author of Ezra supporting a circumscribed, priestly identity and the author of Nehemiah arguing for a much broader Torah—essentially the document that we know. In any case, it seems to me to be more productive to explore the identity of the Torah as explicitly referred to—in Ezra and *independently* in Nehemiah—than to try to divine the identity of the Torah that may or may not lie at the foundation of individual laws as described in these later books. This latter approach is hopelessly mired in confusion and imprecision. An excellent review of the problem may be found in C. Houtman, 'Ezra and the Law: Observations on the Supposed Relation between Ezra and the Pentateuch', in A.S. Van der Woude (ed.), *Remembering the Way...*(OTS, 21; Leiden: Brill, 1981), pp. 91-115.

25. See M. Fishbane, *Biblical Interpretation in Ancient Israel* (Oxford: Clarendon Press, 1985), pp. 110-11.

properly guarded, is at the source of priestly power, then the scribal approach to Torah, which seeks to disseminate it and render it public, undermines this source of priestly power. This is but one of several pieces of evidence in Nehemiah of its opposition to the centrality of the priesthood.

The most obvious evidence for the book of Nehemiah's undermining of priestly centrality is its almost complete neglect of the Temple and sacrifice, as I have noted in detail above. Related to this is the obvious displacement of sacrifice or Temple with Torah, in a way that may be understood as 'granting sanctity to the Torah, not to the Temple'.[26] This displacement of sanctity, noted by Eskenazi, typifies much of the approach in Nehemiah.

Eskenazi touches on several of these displacements. In connection with Neh. 3.1, she notes the fact that the gates of the city are being sanctified—an act that one would more expect in connection with the House of God.[27] Of course, such sanctification, directed at a non-priestly property, undermines the centrality of the Temple as such. The same is true in connection with the purification of all the people at Neh. 12.30 (and cf. Ezra 6.20). On this matter, Eskenazi comments, 'The purification of all the people...demonstrates that they are brought into the same ritual status as priests and Levites...This amplifies the point made by the Israelite pedigrees: the sanctity of the people, not merely of clergy, matters'.[28] In just this way does the author effectively undermine the centrality of the priesthood.

To these points we may add the following: in ch. 3, the priests, Levites and Israelites are described as engaging in the construction of the city, side by side. Thus does the author claim that this construction is what is truly important, so important that even the priests and Levites must serve this end. Moreover, he shows that, for what really matters, the priests and Levites are in no way superior to the Israelites as a whole. Particularly striking in its statement of this same opposition to the priesthood is the recounting of the cultic abuses of the High Priest, at 13.4-9, and of Nehemiah's actual expulsion of the High Priest from his chamber in the Temple. Morton Smith comments on this event:

26. Eskenazi, *Age of Prose*, p. 106.
27. Eskenazi, *Age of Prose*, p. 84.
28. Eskenazi, *Age of Prose*, pp. 117-18.

> By all traditions of ancient religion the high priest was the final authority
> on cult law, especially on purity law, and above all on purity law as it
> applied to his own temple. Yet here is Nehemiah, not a priest at all...not
> only declaring unclean and forbidden what the high priest has declared
> clean and permitted, but also overriding the high priest's ruling and
> cleansing the Temple of the pollution which he said the high priest has
> introduced into it.[29]

More explicit opposition to the priesthood, and undermining of its
authority, could hardly be imagined. The same scenario repeats itself at
the end of this last chapter, where it is Nehemiah the layman who
purifies the priests of their pollution from foreigners. What, from the
priestly perspective, could be more humiliating?

Conclusions

We have seen that Ezra is a book that speaks for a priestly authorship. It
believes that post-exilic sacred history leads to the rebuilding of the
Temple and the rehabilitation of the cult. Sin, in its view, is the pollution
of the cult, and atonement, therefore, can be achieved only by the
removal of that pollution. As is to be expected, the priests are its main
actors, and its great hero, Ezra, is the priest who accomplishes the necessary purification.

   The book of Nehemiah contends that the realm of the sacred far
exceeds the limits of the cult. Not only is the Temple holy; so too is the
city as a whole. Not only is the priesthood holy, but so too is Israel at
large. Since the city and the laity are central to this authorship's conception of the sacred, sacred history, in this book, leads to rebuilding of the
city; the Temple, though possibly in disrepair, is ignored. And, as the city
replaces the Temple, so the Torah replaces sacrifices and scribes replace
priests. In this context, sin is an offense against the Torah, more generally conceived, and the hero, again Ezra, is the one who teaches Torah
and thus brings the people back to its observance. By the same token,
Nehemiah, the other great hero, is the one who assures the viability of
the community as a whole, who oversees the covenanting that is centered on Torah, and who takes control of the priesthood that has itself
polluted the sacred precincts.

---

   29. *Palestinian Parties and Politics That Shaped the Old Testament* (London:
SCM Press, 1987; New York: Columbia University Press, 1st edn, 1971), p. 101.

The fact that these characterizations do not account for all of the details of these books should not be taken as a challenge to their basic soundness. Theoretically, these documents could have been composed either by authors who witnessed the same events or by authors who had access to a common record. There can be no surprise, therefore, that their accounts sometimes overlap. Presumably, Ezra was both a priest and a scribe; foreign women were expelled by the community; the Temple did operate and sacrifices were offered there. But what is more important is the undeniable differences in the use of these materials that resulted from the divergent ideologies of the authors. They did not fully censor out what did not support their individual pictures. They did, however, shape it with a stamp that was so powerful as to leave their prejudices in little doubt.

These conclusions have important consequences for those who would want to employ these books as evidence for the period that they purportedly describe. Generally speaking, Ezra and Nehemiah are two competing, perhaps even contradictory (but *not* complementary) accounts of the same history. For the most part, therefore, they constitute poor sources for traditional histories. They are prejudiced, ideologically motivated witnesses—hardly the sort whose testimony a critical historian should gullibly repeat. Only where their overlap is significant, such as in those few areas listed in the previous paragraph, is there room for greater confidence. But these areas are few, and there is very little, therefore, that can be said without hesitation.

Still, there is undoubtedly in these books an ideological history to be told. Recorded in them we see the beginnings of a debate that would, in fact, have major consequences in the history of Judaism for the next five hundred years. The question that these authors are debating is that of the locus of the sacred. Is religious power in Israel to be found in the priesthood and the cult or in the Book and those who disseminate it? For the next many hundreds of years the view represented by the author of the book of Ezra would predominate, at least among the parties who had recognized political power. But the alternative supported by the author of the book of Nehemiah would never disappear and, over the long term, it was this view—the vision of the lay teacher of Torah—that would emerge triumphant.[30]

---

30. I am grateful to S. Garfinkel and, especially, to T. Eskenazi for their generous critiques and comments which helped me to refine many points in my argument.

JSOT 56 (1992), pp. 41-68

NEHEMIAH AS CULTURAL REVITALIZATION:
AN ANTHROPOLOGICAL PERSPECTIVE*

Kenneth D. Tollefson and H.G.M. Williamson

1. *Introduction*

The book of Nehemiah includes material of considerable literary diversity, and few, if any, would deny that this is traceable to the use of various sources by the work's eventual compiler(s). With that, however, the scholarly consensus ends, for there is the widest possible divergence of opinion both about the nature and extent of some of the sources used, and, more especially, about the question whether sense (literary, theological or historical) can be made of the finished product. Of course, a final answer to these difficulties cannot be reached without consideration of the book of Ezra as well, for the Masoretes were certainly right in their preservation of the ancient tradition that Ezra and Nehemiah are in reality both parts of a single work. Nevertheless, Neh. 1.1 clearly marks the start of a major new section within the work, so that it is reasonable as a preliminary step to confine ourselves here to the book of Nehemiah alone.

At first sight, the easiest source to isolate is the first-person account of Nehemiah, usually known as the Nehemiah Memoir (NM). Even here, however, differences of opinion rise to the surface when a detailed delineation is attempted. Many scholars maintain that the prayer in 1.5-11 was added only by a later editor, generally identified as the Chronicler

*   We wish to thank E.E. Lemcio of Seattle Pacific University for bringing us together for this project. While we have both worked over all the material together, Williamson provided the initial draft of sections 1 and 4, Tollefson of sections 2 and 3. Section 3 is the one to have been most extensively rewritten, and so comes closest to genuine joint authorship. We are grateful to the editors of *JSOT* for their many suggestions on how to improve an earlier draft of this article.

(e.g. Kellermann 1967: 9-11; bibliographical documentation has largely been omitted from this introductory survey, since its purpose is not a history of research but a *mise en scène* for what follows; cf. Kellermann 1967, Williamson 1985 or Blenkinsopp 1989 for fuller references). Chapter 3 was certainly not composed by Nehemiah, since it is not written in the first person and because it presupposes the completion of the work (contrast 6.1 with, e.g., 3.1, 3, 6), but opinions differ as to whether Nehemiah included it in his account or whether it has been added later. The same disagreement exists with regard to the list in 7.6-72. Some would still maintain that 11.1-2 is a rewritten version of the NM account of the repopulation of the city (cf. 7.4-5), though most now (rightly) follow Kellermann (1967: 43) in seeing a separate account here. Neh. 12.27-43 includes material from the NM, but has uncharacteristically been expanded with other material, while 13.4-31, though generally ascribed to Nehemiah, is sometimes regarded more as a supplement than as part of the NM proper (e.g. Ackroyd 1970: 28-29).

The remaining material in Nehemiah is even more fiercely disputed. Nehemiah 8–10 could have been derived in its entirety from the Ezra Memoir, or could be a compilation of three originally discrete sources (one of which might have been the EM), or it might be in whole or in part the work of the final compiler, whether or not the Chronicler. If 11.1-2 is not from the NM, as noted above, then the same conclusion will hold for the various lists that follow in 11.3–12.26, but their date, and how they fit into the overall shape of the work, is uncertain, and so on.

In view of what follows later, we wish nevertheless to draw attention to one suggestion that has been independently advanced by Williamson (1985: xxxii-xxxiii):

> When these passages are…considered together, it will be seen that they share a number of features in common, principally their stress on the wholehearted participation in various activities and reforms by all the people under priestly leadership. Moreover, these activities are all paralleled in the NM, but Nehemiah himself does not feature in any of them.

Whether or not this points to a collection of documents that were housed in the temple archives, the observation of an alternative record that focuses on the participation of the community rather than on the personality of Nehemiah is noteworthy. Why the compiler has switched from the one to the other at the points that he does, however, has not yet been fully explained.

Matters can hardly be said to improve when we move on to ask how scholars have responded to this diversity of material by way of a composition history. Among the major solutions to have been suggested are the following.

(a) The work of the Chronicler concluded with something akin to what is now found in the apocryphal book of 1 Esdras (i.e. Ezra 1–10 + Neh. 8), with the NM being added subsequently and parts of the concluding chapters being yet later additions, stretching down to the Maccabean period (e.g. Mowinckel 1964a: 1-61). (b) The book in its present order is largely the conclusion of the Chronicler's work, but it has been expanded later by the addition of many of the lists and some other material in the second half (e.g. Noth 1943: 126-31 [ET 1987: 46-50]; Kellermann 1967: 73). (c) The book represents the original ending of the Chronicler's work, but the present order (especially of Neh. 8–10) is the result of erroneous scribal transpositions in the course of transmission (e.g. Torrey 1896: 29-34; 1910: 252-84; Rudolph 1949). (d) The present order was intended from the start, either (1) by the Chronicler, for theological reasons (e.g. Clines 1984: 11-12), or (2) because it represents the correct historical order of events, so that no further explanation is needed (e.g. Kidner 1979; Fensham 1982), or (3) because though it has nothing to do with the Chronicler it makes good theological (e.g. Williamson 1985: 275-76) or literary (Eskenazi 1988) sense.

The purpose of this brief review, the outlines of which will be familiar to any who have worked intensively on the book of Nehemiah, has only been to suggest that no fully satisfying proposal for the present shaping of the material has yet been advanced with regard to either its arrangement or its generation. Even where descriptive readings have been undertaken (e.g. Childs 1979: 624-38; Williamson 1985: xlviii-lii; Eskenazi 1988, but contrast Clines 1989), it is difficult to avoid the impression that commentators are struggling to make sense of what happens to be there rather than fully understanding *why* it is there. This is especially marked with regard to the last chapter, which seems to peter out unsatisfactorily ('subordinated...and not given an independent significance', Childs 1979: 633; 'a complicated and not very satisfactory editorial arrangement of the material', Blenkinsopp 1989: 353; 'trails like an afterthought', Eskenazi 1988: 123), but it applies too to a certain extent to Nehemiah 8–10, even though many continue to promote these chapters as the climax of the work as a whole.

In view of these uncertainties, a fresh angle of approach to this material is demanded, one which may enable scholars to set these familiar problems within a new context from which to analyse the narrative. It has already been pointed out (Williamson 1987a: 191, 199) that a socio-logical approach to this material is in its infancy, and that it needs to be developed in conjunction with, and not as an alternative to, more traditional literary-critical methods. The same remarks could have been made with regard to the closely related area of socio-cultural anthropology. The Nehemiah story is of interest to anthropology because it contains excellent data for the study of the effects of foreign domination, planned change and subsequent cultural revitalization. The Persian empire demonstrated remarkable ability in governing the many countries it conquered. It achieved this through the decentralization of its administration and the development of local communities. The Nehemiah material provides a description of the effectiveness of one Persian government official in administering one such project. Anthropologists have observed that the successful completion of such projects of planned change frequently result in what are known as revitalization movements.

Internal evidence suggests that the general organization of the Nehemiah story is remarkably similar to the sequence of events that occur in this kind of social movement. This article seeks to apply the Wallace model of cultural revitalization to the Nehemiah story. Following an explanation of this model, we shall outline the biblical text as it stands in terms of the model, with only a minimum of comment on its relation to the literary issues just raised. In particular, for clarity's sake, no attempt will be made at this stage of the investigation to follow through the consequences of possible rearrangements of the text, nor to discuss the relationship of the text to the possible course of events that may lie behind it. That will be reserved rather for the concluding section, where some preliminary remarks will be offered about the integration of the anthropological and the literary/historical approaches in view of the problems alluded to in this introduction.

2. A Working Model of Cultural Revitalization

Cultural revitalization movements tend to reverse the processes of disorganization and entropy that eventually plague all societies. Human societies survive by means of complex systems of culture that include values, beliefs and sentiments. Successful cultures adapt to physical environments through long-term technoeconomic strategies. For the purpose of studying such adaptation, culture can be conveniently divided into technological, social and ideological subsystems. Changes may occur in all three areas simultaneously or at differential rates. Irregular rates of change may disturb the tenuous cultural equilibrium among the various subsystems and contribute to general cultural disharmony and dissatisfaction with existing practices. When this occurs, some creative individual will frequently design and advocate an alternative system, and the revitalization process is set in motion.

The Concept of Revitalization
The cultural revitalization process emerges as cultural discontent increases in an attempt to create a more meaningful ethos. One anthropologist identified some 6000 examples of this type of cultural revision in Africa (Barrett 1968). Thousands of additional examples can be cited from other areas of the world (Hiebert 1976: 388). This kind of cultural reconstruction, which may be as old as the human race and as widely distributed, is collectively known to anthropologists as cultural revitalization (Cohn 1969: 2).

According to Wallace (1956: 265), a revitalization movement is a 'deliberate, organized, conscious effort by members of a society to construct a more satisfying culture'. Revitalization movements emerge out of general discontent with existing values, beliefs and symbols of identity. Through the process of cultural revitalization, a society may seek to revise and reconstruct conflicting values, cultural distortions and archaic beliefs to form a new cultural synthesis or *Gestalt* in an effort to restore cultural vitality to their ethos.

The process begins when social dissatisfaction emerges in a society as individuals begin perceiving their culture in untraditional ways. While at any given time no two individuals may share exactly the same 'mazeway' (defined by Wallace 1956: 266 as the 'nature, society, culture, personality, and body image, as seen by one person'), still they are sufficiently similar to permit the members of society to share in a common mazeway. When the individual's mazeway no longer holds to past perceptions, then the level of stress may rapidly increase. The individual is thus caught between the increasing stress of traditional forms and present realities. In revitalization movements, the group seeks to reduce this dissonance by creating a more tenable cultural synthesis.

All cultures are constantly changing; changing symbols produce stress and distortion. Therefore, cultures must modify and adapt to survive. Whitehead (Bennis and Slater 1968: 70) notes that 'the art of free society consists in the maintenance of the symbolic code, and secondly, in the fearlessness of revision... Those societies which cannot continue reverence to the symbols with freedom of revision must ultimately decay.' Thus cultural revitalization is no social luxury; it is an absolute necessity.

The Process of Revitalization

Wallace (1956: 270-75) identifies five general stages relating to revitalization movements: (1) Period of Steady State; (2) Period of Individual Stress; (3) Period of Cultural Distortion; (4) Period of Revitalization; and (5) Period of a New Steady State. The most crucial factor in reversing cultural deterioration is the revitalization stage in which occur six significant phases: mazeway reformulation, communication, organization, adaptation, cultural transformation and routinization.

During the 'steady state' stage, social interaction is characterized by general uniformity of cultural beliefs and practices. Members subscribe to a common system of values; individual needs and group concerns are satisfactorily resolved; and the socio-political system relates favourably to the ideological system.

As increasing changes occur in one or more of the subsystems, gradual feelings of dissatisfaction and stress develop. For example, major changes in technology may cause significant changes to occur in the social or ideological spheres. If traditional means for reducing this increasing level of stress prove ineffective, then a second stage characterized by rising 'individual stress' emerges. Increased levels of stress may, in turn, contribute to the rise of a third stage, 'cultural distortion'.

During the cultural distortion stage, stress at the individual level becomes chronic and the mazeway may become disorganized, culminating in social disillusionment and apathy. If unchecked, this cultural deterioration process may result in decreased birth rates, increased death rates, low morale and persistent factionalism (Wallace 1956: 270). Frequently during such periods, some person or (more rarely) group will marshal existing cultural resources to produce a new creative cultural synthesis to reverse this deterioration process and avoid cultural extinction.

This formulation of a new cultural synthesis comprises the fourth stage, 'cultural revitalization'. Revitalization movements may be secular or religious, depending upon the direction taken by the leader or prophet in organizing the new vision and upon the selection of cultural symbols and values. Revitalization is usually the result of an abrupt and dramatic moment of personal inspiration or revelation rather than the result of a group discussion or period of long deliberation. Wallace (1956: 270) refers to this first phase of the revitalization stage as 'mazeway reformulation'.

Revitalization movements are usually accompanied by visions or dreams in which the individual's and society's troubles are attributed to the violation of certain rules. The vision or inspiration includes promises of social revitalization if certain rules are followed and rituals are practised. These visions and inspirations are usually expressed in terms of millennial aspirations, feelings of guilt and anxiety, and utopian desires. Once the new vision is fully formed in the mind of the prophet, he or she feels compelled to share it with others. Prophets usually maintain a strong sense of personal identity and a conviction of what it will take to lead a 'sick' and stressful society to a new level of vitality (Wallace 1956: 270).

In the second or 'communication' phase, the visionary enthusiastically shares the vision with others who, in the case of religious revitalization movements, are usually promised two benefits for compliance: supernatural protection and material benefits. Communication may be made by the group or by individuals on the one side, and on the other it may either be shared with the whole society or be geared to a specific segment. Disciples recruited to the growing movement are charged with the task of sharing the vision with others.

In the third phase, the new converts are organized into an effective political machine for implementing the vision. Wallace (1956: 273) suggests three levels of personnel in the new organization: the prophet, the disciples and the followers. Revitalization movements become increasingly political during this phase, while the followers frequently experience a revitalizing experience similar to the prophet.

Revitalization movements usually encounter resistance from powerful internal groups or from interested foreign parties, causing the movement to respond with a fourth phase, 'adaptation'. The movement may be forced to modify some of its original vision; it may be forced to resort to political force, or to diplomatic manoeuvring. In the process, the new vision becomes more acceptable to the general public and better suited to the socio-economic environment. Hostilities during this period may erupt into physical conflict.

The fifth phase in the revitalization stage is 'cultural transformation', in which the group as a whole accepts the prophet's vision as a social mandate to modify existing beliefs, to accept new practices and to instigate new programmes. These new programmes may be more or less realistic, more or less adaptive and more or less well conceived. Some may even fail. However, many programmes do become viable movements and in the process contribute to substantial and significant social and cultural changes that reverse the effects of inertia and entropy, so enabling societies to survive.

If the movement successfully comes to terms with the opposition, with the challenge of decreasing the level of individual and social stress, and with finding a realistic techno-environmental adaptation, a sixth phase will follow, 'routinization'. In this phase, the new elements of the vision become integrated into the daily life of the people. That is, they become part of the economic, social, political and religious life of the community. Although these six phases tend to be developmental and sequential, they may also overlap.

A successful revitalization experience will form the basis for the emergence of a 'new steady state stage'. This is not a return to a previous state or former status quo, but to a new kind of cultural configuration—a new cultural mazeway. It represents a new stage of cultural adaptation and integration that initiates another cycle of the cultural revitalization process.

Revitalization movements may take one of two forms: nativistic or importation (Hiebert 1976: 388-90). Nativistic movements seek to expel all that is foreign in the local culture and to revive that which is relevant in the traditional culture. Importation movements seek to integrate that which is relevant from both traditional and foreign sources. Colonialism and urbanization contribute to the impetus for revitalization movements by causing domination and suppression of subordinate groups.

Linton (1943: 230) notes that while all groups seek to perpetuate their own culture, this effort becomes intensified when another society threatens their existence. Bruner (1974: 258) suggests that subordinate groups must assert their ethnicity when participating in a dominant society or else become absorbed by the more powerful group.

When the cultural revitalization model is applied to the Nehemiah material, there seems to be a remarkable similarity between the six phases within the revitalization stage and the sequence of events within the Nehemiah story.

3. *Cultural Revitalization in the Nehemiah Material*

The value of any model, from a social science perspective, is relative to its ability to predict human behaviour. Part of the Wallace model of cultural revitalization seems to describe the general behaviour and sequence of events as given in the Nehemiah narrative. The present study argues that this similarity between the model and the shape of the narrative in Nehemiah is more than coincidence.

Data for the first three stages of the revitalization model may be found in the historical and prophetic literature of the Old Testament and may be regarded as presupposed in the situation described at the start of the book (Tollefson 1987: 36-37). The compiler of the Nehemiah story therefore starts his narrative at the beginning of what an anthropologist would refer to as the fourth stage of the revitalization process. That is, the Nehemiah narrative follows the same general sequence of events that are described in the six phases of the fourth stage ('period of cultural revitalization') in the Wallace model of the revitalization process. It is confusing that Wallace's terminology leads him to write of a period of cultural revitalization as one stage in the overall revitalization process. This stage is clearly central to the whole process, however, and it is to this particular stage that the following analysis is confined.

Mazeway Reformulation Phase (Nehemiah 1.1-10)
The Nehemiah story begins with the presentation of the Jerusalem predicament: economic exploitation, community deterioration, cultural distortion and social disillusionment. In Myers's words (1965: 91), the people were 'in dire straits and in disgrace'. The city lay in ruins, their economy was depressed, their security in shambles. The problem was succinctly stated as 'a broken wall and burned gates' (Neh. 1.3).

The Jerusalem predicament was reported to Nehemiah. The effect was dramatic. The depth of Nehemiah's anguish is revealed in his own words, 'I wept...mourned...fasted and prayed' (1.4). The content of his prayer (1.5-11) indicates that the problem of the broken wall was more than political; it was also moral, envisaging a restored community living under a restored Law (1.9; cf. Deut. 28.52). We have already noted that many scholars doubt that this prayer was an original part of the Nehemiah Memoir. In the present context, however, it plays the vital role of setting out Nehemiah's 'top value' (overriding objective) in the prophetic vision, and the continuation of the story then sets out in detail his strategy for attaining it. In other words, the Nehemiah story presents both the problem and its solution, and it proceeds from symptoms to causes, from physical community to spiritual community. The solution grows out of the vision of Nehemiah for a restored wall and Law, symbolic of a restored political and religious community. Nehemiah's vision, which seems to be the consuming passion and ultimate objective of the story, simultaneously undermined his old ethos (mazeway) and exposed him to a new level of religious awareness.

The Communication Phase (Nehemiah 1.11–2.20)
Any significant plan must be shared with some community in order to become effective. Nehemiah shared his plan first with the king, in an effort to obtain building material along with a building permit; and he shared it second with the people, in an effort to acquire their support and labour.

Proper timing in communication is imperative. Nehemiah appears to have waited four months before he revealed his feelings to the king (2.1; for a discussion of the chronological problems of this verse in comparison with 1.1, cf. Williamson 1985: 169-70). We may guess that he needed time to develop a plan for his construction project and an appropriate political climate in which to share it with the king. In other words, he took time to translate his vision into a workable plan.

Moreover, he also needed a favourable political climate for making known his proposed plan to refortify what had only recently been described to the king as a 'rebellious city' (Ezra 4.12). On that occasion, Artaxerxes had ordered that building work on the walls of Jerusalem should be halted (Ezra 4.21). The ever-present threat of unrest in the western part of the empire, however, necessitated a high level of internal security in this region. Nehemiah may have been taking advantage of this situation when in his presentation to the king he tactfully affirmed his inferior status, his loyalty and his willingness to abide by the king's decision.

In contrast with his caution in approaching the king, Nehemiah moved swiftly on his arrival in Jerusalem to communicate his plan to the people whom it most directly concerned. In doing so, he focused on the tragedy and disgrace of the current situation (Neh. 2.17), and then turned the minds of the people to the divine mandate to rebuild the city, citing the king's willingness to supply the building permit along with the needed material resources (2.18). The response of the people was positive and the project was begun.

A significant factor in the communication phase was Nehemiah's ability and willingness to identify with the local people in their present predicament: 'You see the trouble we are in...let us build...that we may no longer suffer disgrace' (2.17). Nehemiah carefully defined the project in terms of a common cause in which leader and people would struggle together.

The Organizational Phase (Nehemiah 3.1-32)
Although Nehemiah 3 was almost certainly not originally compiled by Nehemiah, it is probable that he himself incorporated it into his Memoir (see Williamson 1985: 200-202). Even if not, it is certainly appropriately positioned in terms of the revitalization model here being applied. It portrays a Nehemiah who displayed an open style of leadership and made use of indigenous organizations whenever possible. He delegated authority to fit the task, he incorporated local loyalty groups, and he appealed to self-interest to accomplish the assignments.

We are told that Nehemiah divided his labour force into some forty local units and assigned each crew one or more sections on the wall. Some were to repair the wall near their home, shop or place of employment, which appealed to their enlightened self-interest to motivate them to protect that which was important to them. Nehemiah's evident concern for people and skill in organizing groups is revealed in the way in which leaders and groups are listed along with the section(s) each unit completed. While most political leaders tend to record the significance of their accomplishments, here it is the work of the people that is highlighted. Nehemiah's attitude toward his followers may have helped to gain their loyalty later in the story when he needed their support (Neh. 6).

In all this, it is worth observing that the shift from Nehemiah's first-person account is appropriate, from a literary point of view, to the contents of the chapter as just analysed. As we shall see more fully later on, the use of an alternative account to that of Nehemiah himself matches the movement from individual vision to community appropriation which is a central feature of the revitalization model. In view of the extensive reflection of this movement in literary terms later in the book, its first appearance here in what is, from the point of view of content, so suitable a context may not be without significance.

Adaptation to the Project (Nehemiah 3.33 [English 4.1]–7.4)
Revitalization movements call forth revolutionary organizations and so will normally encounter some resistance from powerful internal parties or from opportunistic foreign elements. Opposition in the Nehemiah story occurred in three forms: foreign military threat against the city (3.33[4.1]–4.17[23]), factionalism among competing social classes within

the city (ch. 5), and foreign diplomatic pressure against the leadership (ch. 6). Although the foreign opposition is portrayed as coming from all points of the compass (4.1[7]), the moving spirit behind it was undoubtedly Sanballat of Samaria, with whom Tobiah worked closely, possibly as a junior colleague who had close personal ties within Jerusalem itself (cf. Kellermann 1967: 167-70; Williamson 1985: 183-84).

The Jerusalem restoration project threatened both the economic and political hegemony of Samaria as well as the military stability of the surrounding region. In a series of swift and decisive actions, the leaders in Samaria are described as rapidly escalating the level of opposition from sabre-rattling speeches to the threat of an all-out military attack.

Sanballat and his associates adopted various tactics to stop the project. First, they jeered at the paucity of workers and the magnitude of the project (3.33-35[4.1-3]). Secondly, they formed a joint military campaign and moved against the city of Jerusalem (4.1-2[7-8]). Thirdly, they plotted to infiltrate the city and to initiate a sudden attack from within the half-completed walls (4.5[11]). And fourthly, they attempted to influence the rural people to discontinue their support for the project, by focusing on the quantity of rubble (3.34-35[4.2-3]), by intimidating them with surrounding armies, and by threatening the people with physical harm (4.5-6[11-12]; for discussion of the text of this passage, cf. Williamson 1985: 221-22).

Weeks of arduous labour on the wall took their toll on the energy and resources of the community and appear to have brought to a head a situation that must have been developing over a considerable period of time. Food was scarce, prices were high and taxes were oppressive. Some of the poor were forced to mortgage their homes, others even to sell their children into slavery, in order to obtain money to buy food. Frustrated and angry, the workers took their complaints to Nehemiah (5.1-13). The situation was perceived by them as a simple case of class conflict in which wealthy landowners were exploiting deprived peasants.

All-out class warfare would have debilitated the community still further, and thus would have played into the hands of the enemy. In this story, therefore, Nehemiah sought to preserve the community through his vision of a restored 'covenant of brotherhood' in which the well-to-do lend money and materials, interest free, to the poor, in order to help them through their difficult times. As Blenkinsopp has written (1989: 258),

In both the so-called Covenant Code and Deuteronomic Law procedures
permissible in themselves are excluded in the case of the poor, and one of
these is forcible seizure of pledges against defaulting (Exod. 22.24 [25];
Deut. 24.10-11). The same solicitude for the poor fellow Israelite is
expressed in the Holiness Code, which requires support of the poor, as an
obligation not as charity, and states explicitly that the insolvent 'brother'
who sells himself must not be treated as a slave (Lev. 25.35-39).

When the military alliance failed to achieve its objective, Sanballat vented
his anger on Nehemiah personally. Astute politicians have long been
suspicious of the powerful stranger who enters a province, 'for strangers
are never called in except by those who are ambitious and discontent'
(Machiavelli 1963: 7). When Sanballat proved to be incapable of stopping
the construction project, he, with the increasing support and perhaps
even initiative of Tobiah, sought to destroy, or at least undermine, the
political career of Nehemiah (1) through an assassination plot (6.1-3),
(2) through a false charge against Nehemiah of planning to have himself
made king (6.5-7), (3) through an innocent-looking plan publicly to disgrace the man by scaring him into retreating into the temple where, as a
layman, he did not belong (6.10; cf. Num. 18.7; Bowman 1954: 96;
Myers 1965: 139), a plan that may have been intended to drive a wedge
between him and the priesthood, and (4) through a 'fifth column' of
Samarian sympathizers who shared information freely with the enemies
of the Jerusalem community (6.17-19).

   Niehoff (1966: 31) suggests that in societies generally 'the single most
important characteristic of the local society is its leadership'. It is not
surprising, then, that the opposition attacked Nehemiah so vigorously.
The success of the construction project at Jerusalem was largely
attributable to the effectiveness of Nehemiah in motivating the workers
and earning their respect and loyalty. Moreover, as governor, Nehemiah
was entitled to the customary salary, which came out of the local tax
levy. Former governors had readily accepted it, and, along with their
officials, had grown wealthy while in office. Nehemiah, however, made
clear that he was conscious of the heavy burden that the people were
already having to bear (5.18), and he insisted that despite the considerable expenses of his office he would refuse to claim his entitlement
(5.14-19). The quality of his leadership helps to explain the support of
the people and the effectiveness of the project.

   Once the perimeter of the city was secure, Nehemiah turned his
attention to strengthening community organization. He appointed his
brother and another faithful follower to have charge over the city (7.2),

he enlarged the duties of the loyal temple personnel to include the patrol of the city gates, and he enlisted the services of a number of the citizens to guard the wall (7.3). In the continuing process of organizing the community, Nehemiah demonstrated considerable ability both to acquire and to share power. Moreover, he is portrayed as exhibiting prowess in noting problems and waiting for the appropriate time to address them. For example, in the current sequence of the text (which is our only concern at present), it is implied that a resolution of the urban population problem (7.4) was delayed until the necessary level of community commitment had been achieved (cf. 11.1).

The Cultural Transformation Phase (Nehemiah 7.5–10.39)
Most community development projects are terminated at this juncture: the wall was completed, the gates were hung, and the new administrators were appointed. Indeed, if the resumption of Nehemiah's first-person account with the dedication of the wall in 12.27-43 is anything to go by, it is not impossible that his original Memoir presented the course of events in just this way. The text which we have, however, closely follows our suggested model, for the basic problem in the Jerusalem community remained unresolved. The community was estranged from its cultural heritage and spiritual roots. Royce (1982: 7) says that no community can ignore its cultural heritage and survive with 'a distinctive identity'. Bennett and Trumin (1964: 19) assert that the major task of any society is to provide its members with 'meaning and motivation...a sense of the worthwhileness of the whole human venture'. Until the Jerusalem community experienced cultural renewal, they would continue to lack a cause and a ground for commitment.

In the Nehemiah story, the author resorts to the reuse of an older list with genealogical intent (7.5) to move beyond the physical wall to the issue of the spiritual Law. Genealogies link people to their lands, their ancestors, their cultures and their gods. Genealogies are more than sterile lists of progeny; they are cognitive maps of reality. Lichtman (1978: 11) explains that in order for any people to understand themselves they need to catch a vision of their past. The compiler of the Nehemiah account used what may originally have been a census list to serve this genealogical function (7.5) in order to stress the historical continuity of the people with their land and culture and to stress their ethnic distinctions from the bordering non-Jewish states (Kidner 1979: 21-22).

Neh. 7.6 recalls that each had returned to 'his city', implying that even though the old land tenure system had been disrupted by the exile, it was still viable. Since this traditional land system was now under review, the charts of the first return were used to trace descent. Genealogies could also be used to determine the bona fide members of the community. The Nehemiah material seems to use the genealogical charts to define the ethnic boundaries of the community (cf. 7.64). The compiler is beginning to define this revitalization movement as a nativistic one in which the traditional would be retained and the foreign would be eliminated.

At this point in the narrative, we reach a section often regarded as an editorial insertion (chs. 8–10). From an anthropological perspective, however, it makes good sense. In the first place, anthropologists have observed that revitalization movements are a common consequence of projects of change (Goodenough 1966: 304). Frequently, the agents of that change, who assist people with their development and who show a genuine empathy with them, are asked by such local groups to help them find a more meaningful way to live.

Secondly, and more significantly, the rest of the Nehemiah material (chs. 11–13) presupposes the kind of group activities included in this section. That is, it tells us when and how the people changed their ethos and became committed to the radical types of changes described in the next section. In other words, *it supplies the 'cultural transformation phase' that occurs in all such revitalization movements.*

It is difficult to explain the rest of the socio-cultural changes in this story without this type of activity. The initial work reported in Ezra 7–10 and the building of the wall by Nehemiah (Neh. 1–6) seem to receive their significance only in the light of the religious reordering of the community of faith in Nehemiah 8–10.

In these chapters, the people experience a radical change in their ethos, much as Nehemiah had done in 1.4-10. The prior experience of the 'prophet' at this point becomes the experience of the people. Within these three chapters the people work their way through some critical problems and eventually institute a revised set of values and symbols. In Lewin's terms, they unfreeze their present ethos in Nehemiah 8, they are prodded to move towards a new ethos in Nehemiah 9, and they commit themselves to that new ethos in Nehemiah 10.

The process of cultural revitalization begins with the reading of the Law of Moses along with a running commentary provided by the Levites. It culminates in an intensely personal experience for the people—'they wept' (8.9). Like Nehemiah (1.4), the people seem to confront and to re-evaluate their present lifestyle in the light of the Law (see above on 'mazeway reformulation phase'). By way of his stress on the people's mourning and weeping (8.9-11), the compiler takes special pains to point out that what happened to Nehemiah at the beginning of the story (1.4) was now happening to the people. This parallel experience seems to be vital to the story because the vision now belongs to the people and motivates them to action.

Here again, therefore, as we noted briefly in the case of Nehemiah 3 above, the change in literary form from first- to third-person account is appropriate to the point reached in the revitalization process. To whatever extent the compiler was acting under the constraint of the nature of the sources at his disposal, it is contextually satisfying that attention should at this point be deflected away from Nehemiah himself as the people are pictured appropriating his personal vision for a second time at the community level.

To the people's reaction to the reading of the Law, the leaders responded by reviving the old ceremonies of the covenant. The obvious place to begin was with their ceremonial calendar. Since they were in the seventh month, they decided to observe the feast of booths. The ceremonies and symbols of this festival took the people back to their cultural roots—the exodus and the reception of the Law at Sinai.

Celebrations and ceremonies enable people, in the form of play, to extend the frontiers of their thinking. Rituals commemorate those things that make us 'distinctive and worthy in our own eyes' (Cox 1969: 8). They reduce the incomprehensible world, in which we are born and die alone, into a complex web of people, symbols and activities that 'bind us to one another' (Myerhoff 1982: 112). Religious celebrations go to the very foundations of group values and understandings, and in the process weave those cultural distinctives into the 'private psyche' of our minds, replacing external controls with internal motivation. They help to 'link' a person to his or her story (Cox 1969: 14). The feast of booths gave the people an alternative to their present existence and renewed a sense of continuity with the past.

There is a change of atmosphere, however, between the joyous celebration of Nehemiah 8 and the sombre gathering of an assembly for confession in ch. 9. The reading of the Law not only revealed the source of their new-found joy, but also pointed up the need for radical change in their present ethos. Three specific problem areas that come to the surface in the following chapter (ch. 10) are the presence of foreign wives, the lack of Sabbath observance and inadequate support for the temple.

In Nehemiah 9, three recognizable methods used for motivating group change are apparent: staging a public demonstration to rally the people (9.1-3), increasing the magnitude of cultural dissonance to an intolerable level (9.6-35), and rubbing raw public sores of discontent (9.36-37). First there was a public demonstration led by a number of the Levites but involving the people as a whole. This was followed by a reading of the Law and a general confession of sins (9.1-5).

Secondly, a public prayer was used to increase the intensity of the cultural dissonance by drawing attention to the inconsistencies that existed between beliefs and circumstances (which in the theology of the prayer are linked with behaviour). Individuals habitually strive for consistency in their lives. Psychological tests demonstrate the extent to which an individual's opinions and attitudes 'tend to exist in clusters that are internally consistent' (Festinger 1957: 1). Social scientists use the term 'dissonance' to refer to those inconsistencies in which actions or circumstances do not logically follow or grow out of stated beliefs.

Dissonance is stressful. The greater the magnitude of dissonance, the greater the pressure to reduce it (Festinger 1957: 18). Through the prayer of ch. 9, the compiler deliberately and skilfully increases the level of dissonance by focusing public attention on the incongruity between their historic beliefs and their present social situation (9.6-35).

The prayer reviews the fundamentals of their faith and history, including creation, the call of Abraham, the Egyptian captivity, the wilderness wanderings, the conquest of Canaan and the Babylonian occupation. It focuses upon the discrepancies between the people's beliefs, the past behaviour of the nation and the present circumstances, with the basic inconsistencies being described, applied and intensified (cf. Williamson 1988). By the end of the prayer, the level of dissonance is so intense and the esteem of the people so deflated that they are ready to act to heal their psychic wounds.

Thirdly, the prayer rubs raw specific social sores of discontent. It reminds the people that their national life is in a state of economic bankruptcy, that they are slaves in their own land, and that their labour, crops and cattle are being claimed in taxes by foreigners (9.36-37). Schaller (1972: 89) observes that 'without discontent with the present situation there can be no planned, internally motivated and directed intentional change'. Change is threatening. Consequently, the leaders in the story prod the people to keep them moving toward their objective.

However, the prayer also holds out hope to the people in the midst of their affliction by emphasizing God's mercy, patience, longsuffering and forgiveness (9.31). Repentance and prayer have changed the history of their people in the past and can do so again in the present. To Cox (1969: 148), repentance acknowledges that 'the future is not just a continuation of the past. The unexpected and unprecedented can happen. [People]...are not fated by tragic flaws, but free to start over. Penitence simply means starting out in a new direction.'

The prodding is portrayed as successful, for the next thing reported in the story is that the people indicate their willingness to commit themselves on oath to keep the Law in general (10.30[29]), and specifically to marry only within their covenant community, to keep the Sabbath, to rectify certain socio-economic abuses, and to support the services of the temple and its personnel (10.31-40[30-39]). These stipulations are demanding and costly, since the temple services required a considerable expenditure of funds (Myers 1965: 178-80).

Royce (1982: 7) warns that 'no ethnic group can maintain a believable (viable) identity without signs, symbols, and underlying values that point to a distinctive identity'. The public affirmation of the Law is said to have been witnessed by each segment of the community, priests, Levites and political leaders (9.38). (For discussion of the compiler's intention to provide 'a comprehensive list of nearly all the families and individuals whom he regarded as being of good standing within the community', cf. Williamson 1985: 325-30.) The signing was accompanied by the usual sanctions of oaths and curses, adding a measure of solemnity to their action.

The Routinization Phase (Nehemiah 11.1–13.31)
The renewed commitment to the covenant was accompanied by an increased sense of community, of ethnic identity and of self-sacrifice for the common good. Consequently, it was possible to put into effect such innovative programmes as a repopulation of the city, a survey of rural leadership, a review of a politically divided priesthood, a dedication of the wall and a commitment to increase temple support.

Once again, the material included in the first part of this section (11.1–12.26) is not drawn from Nehemiah's first-person account but, in all probability, from alternative records which, if the priestly concerns that find expression here are to be taken seriously, may have been available to the compiler from the temple archives (cf. Williamson 1985: xxxii-xxxiii and 341-66; 1987b: 26-29). The separate literary origins of the accounts

of the repopulation of the city in particular (7.4-5; 11.1-2) are indicative
of the assimilation of Nehemiah's vision by the community.

The insecurity of the 'broken wall community' had contributed to low
population density and to inadequate support for the temple. Broadly
speaking, the leaders had been living in the city and the people in the
countryside. But the people now had a new cause and a new commitment to the Law, and so willingly accepted the application of the principle of the tithe to the relocation programme to repopulate the city of
Jerusalem (11.1-2).

Furthermore, the story seeks to define the membership of the priesthood through a genealogical review (12.1-26). The impression is given
elsewhere in the book, especially at 13.4-9 and 28-30, that at this time
some, at least, of the priests were sympathetic to foreign governments
and foreign marriages. The book of Malachi, which many date to this
period or shortly before, is also sharply critical of their stewardship of
the temple and its services. There is thus a clear recognition that they
were out of step with the ethos of the reform movement which, as we
have seen, had by this stage attracted the backing of the bulk of the
population. The genealogical review is thus presented as wisely reserved
until the point at which maximum political leverage could be mobilized,
and it functions to draw the priesthood into the programme of a nativistic revitalization movement.

Following these preparatory measures, it was time for the community
to come together in a new sense of unity to celebrate the completion of
the wall (Neh. 12.27-43). The story as it stands seems again to project a
sense of timing in these administrative decisions (Myers 1965: 202). This
is revealed in the delay of the dedication until the community had
resolved its problems and could join together in a common cause. It is
also underlined on the literary level by the fact that here, apparently for
the only time in the book, Nehemiah's first-person account and an alternative report of the same event have been intertwined rather than being
juxtaposed (for the details, cf. Williamson 1985: 369-71).

With the problems of the settlement of Jerusalem and the review of
the priesthood resolved and the celebration concluded, attention switches
to the mundane affairs of the daily routine. Neh. 12.44-47 presents a picture in which the institutional changes have been completed and the
funding of the temple services has been secured. The leaders were collecting tithes and offerings, the temple assistants had been properly
purified, the scheduled sacrifices were being made, and the temple

personnel were receiving their ascribed supplies. The implication of 13.6 is that at this point Nehemiah's mission in Jerusalem was accomplished and that he returned to Persia.

The story might have ended here, but many times a change toward a 'higher level of group performance is...short lived; [because] after "a shot in the arm", group life soon returns to the previous level' (Lewin 1947: 34). Problems soon surfaced in Jerusalem, as they do in all projects of planned change, and so Nehemiah took it upon himself to return to resolve them (13.4-31).

Read as a conclusion to the routinization phase of the revitalization model, Nehemiah 13 suggests that Nehemiah's authority, consolidated in Nehemiah 10, enabled him to move swiftly and effectively in addressing the lingering problems. He appears to act quite specifically on the basis of the various clauses of the people's pledged undertakings. First, he expelled Tobiah, a foreigner, from the temple (13.4-9); secondly, he restored the support of the temple and its workers (13.10-13); thirdly, he reinforced Sabbath observance (13.15-22); and fourthly, he addressed the problem of mixed marriages (13.23-28). The success of any revitalization movement is relative to its ability to institutionalize change into the cultural patterns of the people (see the similar conclusion of Eskenazi [1988: 122-26], though expressed in the very different terms of a purely literary analysis). The story ends at this point with the implication that a new steady state has emerged and ushered in a new cycle in the revitalization process.

4. *Concluding Reflections*

The general sequence of events in the Nehemiah story corresponds well with the numerous revitalization movements from other parts of the world as categorized by the Wallace model. In biblical studies, comparisons of this sort often stop at this point, tacitly leaving the reader with the impression that they have somehow bypassed or even superseded the results of more familiar historical-critical inquiry. In view of the clear evidence for the use of diverse sources by the compiler of the Nehemiah story as outlined in our introduction, however, this seems to be a promising case for genuinely interdisciplinary reflection.

In our analysis of the book of Nehemiah in the light of the Wallace model, we have deliberately taken the text at face value and in its present sequence. This at once raises the question of the level of reality to which the model applies. There are three main possibilities that could theoretically be considered, and readers may be drawn to adopt one or another on the basis of a wide range of broader considerations that cannot all be addressed here.

First, it could be held that we are dealing throughout with historical reality. That is to say, the book of Nehemiah accurately portrays both the events that took place in Nehemiah's time and the order in which they occurred. In that case, the text will conform to the model for the simple reason that that is what actually happened. The fact that it is preserved in a biblical narrative rather than in the notebook of an anthropological field-worker observing a society in the process of cultural change is neither here nor there.

At the other extreme, it would be possible to maintain that the book of Nehemiah is a work of fiction, either bearing no particular relation to historical reality whatsoever, or having a relationship to history so distorted by its literary form or by the tendentious and one-sided nature of its presentation through the eyes of Nehemiah that a reconstruction of events in Jerusalem at the time in question is beyond reach. In that case, we should have to conclude that the model can do no more than aid our appreciation of the literary formulation of the work. Whether consciously or unconsciously, the author conformed his narrative to a process which, as has been noted, is widely attested in many types of society at a time of change—a process that we may therefore presume would also have been familiar to him or that he instinctively followed without fully realizing what he was doing.

It is unlikely, however, that either of these two positions will appeal as they stand to the majority of scholars. When all due allowance has been made for the fact that the NM is very much one man's view of the situation (for a forceful demonstration of which, cf. Clines 1990: 124-64), most still wish to maintain that it is nevertheless one among several possible portrayals of what actually happened. Similarly, the evidence for the use of sources in other parts of the book suggests, at the least, that the description is unlikely to be solely the fictitious creation of a literary artist. At the same time, however, it must also be recognized that the combination of those sources leaves open the possibility that the sequence of events may not now be accurately reflected, and that at the stage of composition considerations other than the narrowly historical are likely to have been operative. Of course, the highly selective nature of all the material at our disposal needs to be borne in mind throughout.

Even after conceding that in the interests of clarity and brevity these positions have been sketched in black and white terms, we believe that many readers will recognize here the problem of how to hold together the apparently conflicting results of two different approaches to the text. At the risk of being accused of 'wanting to have our cake and eat it', we remain unwilling to evade the problem by adopting either of the two extreme positions mentioned above. A third approach at least deserves to be explored, one that seeks to do justice to the element of truth in both of the other positions. The following remarks are offered not in the confidence that all the problems have been solved, but rather by way of stimulus and invitation to others to engage with the difficulties that our proposed model raises when laid alongside the results of more familiar literary and historical criticism.

First, to start with a relatively simple observation, it may be suggested that the model outlined above helps us towards a better understanding of the choice of an alternative account from that of Nehemiah for much of the second half of the book. That the compiler was faced with a genuine choice in this regard seems to be certain from the accounts of the repopulation of the city. At 7.4-5 (or at 7.72[73] if the list formed an original part of the NM), Nehemiah's account of this incident is broken off short, but when the narrative resumes at 11.1 it is on the basis either of another source (the most probable explanation in our view), or on the basis of a rewritten version of Nehemiah's account, or else it is his own free composition. Whichever way, he has deliberately chosen not to resume the NM as it stood, even though for other reasons he did precisely that towards the end of ch. 12 and in ch. 13. The dilemma that commentators face here is typified by Blenkinsopp: 'We assume that Nehemiah did have an account of this event, surely one of the more important of his administration, but that for some reason it has been replaced by another' (1989: 323).

The revitalization model enables us to move beyond observation towards explanation of the compiler's choice. (It should be noted that Eskenazi [1988: 95-126] also makes a virtue out of the same situation in the context of her literary approach to Ezra–Nehemiah. Naturally, her approach and ours are in no way mutually exclusive.) As we noted above with regard to ch. 8, 'this parallel experience seems to be vital to the story because the vision now belongs to the people and motivates them to action'. Thus the change in literary form fits with the revitalization model. Beyond that, however, it is possible that the latter has actually played a part in determining the compiler's choice, and hence the form of the literature, in the first place. Admittedly, this leaves us with the apparent conundrum of combining literary form with historical reality, but is it too imaginative to suppose that the compiler may have consciously or intuitively perceived the historical significance in this shift of focus from individual to community and so successfully managed to reflect it in his literary presentation?

A similar conclusion can be drawn with regard to the account of the dedication of the wall in 12.27-43. From a literary point of view, this paragraph is unique in the book of Nehemiah in that it combines the NM with an alternative account of the same event. Elsewhere in the NM, Mowinckel (1964b: 13-42) and others have suggested the possibility of extensive glossing, but even if that possibility were allowed, it would still not come close to the compiler's procedure in this paragraph. If, however, the account is to be viewed not only as a celebration of Nehemiah's personal triumph (in which case it might have been expected earlier in the book), but also as a climax to the revitalization of the community that he had initiated, then the combination is both effective and explicable.

Secondly, we have already noted that the model goes a long way towards explaining what is going on in ch. 13. Far from being an awkwardly attached appendix that we should not miss if it were absent, it functions as part of the routinization of the cultural transformation attested in ch. 10. Here, however, we run up against the problem of how to relate a reading of the book on the basis of the model with the results of historical criticism. For those who assume that the sources used in the book rest on generally sound historical memory, it has seemed to many that the events of ch. 13 preceded those of ch. 10 (following Bertholet 1902: 76). The abuses that Nehemiah deals with are closely related to the clauses of the pledge in 10.31-40(30-39). On the basis of this observation, many scholars have concluded that it is more probable (1) that Nehemiah exposed these abuses and the community entered into an agreement that they would not happen again, than (2) that after the community had agreed to an arbitrary list of stipulations precisely these same points were later abused. Of course, there is room for difference of opinion here; taking human fickleness, as exemplified by Nehemiah 9, into account, it is possible to argue that the terms of the pledge in ch. 10 explain and justify the strength of Nehemiah's reactions in ch. 13. However, since it is the majority view outlined just above that seems to raise the greater problem for an interdisciplinary approach, let us follow through its implications a little further.

On the one hand, assuming that ch. 13 originally belonged to the NM, it would be hazardous to speculate about its function in its original setting, since, as we have seen, the NM has not been preserved in its entirety. It does not seem unlikely, however, that for personal reasons Nehemiah emphasized his own role at the expense of underplaying the degree of community involvement that revitalization demands if it is to be successful. Thus, although the compiler may have altered the chronological order of certain specific events, his presentation may yet portray the social process taken as a whole more faithfully than any one of the sources at his disposal in isolation.

On the other hand, it would be a mistake to conclude from these observations that routinization did not in actual fact take place. Because the materials of chs. 10 and 13 are so closely related, the compiler opted for his present ordering of the material as the most forceful means for giving it literary expression. But his summary in 12.44–13.3 already shows that the process was in any case taking place 'on the ground', while his chronological notices ('on that day', 12.44; 'on that day', 13.1; 'before this', 13.4; 'in those days', 13.15; 'also in those days', 13.23) alert the reader that his concerns are more thematic than sequential. In other words, he makes clear that his use of 13.4-31 in its present *literary* setting is a device for emphasizing the socio-historical *actuality* of what has already been stated more briefly in 12.44–13.3.

Thirdly, what does our reading contribute to an unravelling of the problems of Nehemiah 8–10? Here again, it may be helpful to distinguish between history as a series of events and the form in which the historian chooses to give expression to it. As we noted earlier, 'the value of any model, from a social science perspective, is relative to its ability to predict human behaviour'. The Wallace model of cultural revitalization 'predicts' the presence of a cultural transformation phase, and at the right point Nehemiah 8–10 describes one. At the simplest level, therefore, our reading strongly supports those who believe that the positioning of these chapters is not merely the result of scribal error in the course of transmission.

Beyond that, however, the issue is complicated by two factors. First, because the compiler has handled the sources selectively (it is, as we have seen, at precisely this point that the NM is broken off), we remain in the dark about many events of which the compiler may have known (let alone those which remained totally unrecorded). And secondly, we must remember that the account is not only concerned with Nehemiah, but with Ezra as well. For purposes that range wider than the book of Nehemiah alone, therefore, it is entirely understandable that the compiler should have chosen to include part of the Ezra material at this point. As many commentators have pointed out, it is likely that the compiler wished to present the work of the two reformers as contributing jointly to the restoration of the Judaean community. This section achieves that aim by delaying to this point the presentation of the Law, with the result that the seemingly more political work of Nehemiah now becomes more integrated into the reconstitution of the covenant community. In other words, there were two very different 'prophets', but their work is brought together and dovetailed in the cultural transformation stage. For all that we know, therefore, the cultural transformation phase may historically have taken a different form that may or may not have been recorded in one of the sources available to the compiler; it is clearly idle to speculate about what by definition we cannot know. But once again it is reasonable to hold that the compiler has accurately reflected the broad outline of the social processes that were at work while at the same time selecting to this end materials that served some other more conscious purposes. Here too there is no suggestion that these few brief remarks can solve the complicated problems raised by these chapters. We hope, at least, that they may serve to clarify the issues at stake in an interdisciplinary study that refuses to adopt the overly simplistic solutions of either an exclusively literary or a narrowly historical approach.

BIBLIOGRAPHY

Ackroyd, P.R.
    1970   *The Age of the Chronicler* (Auckland: Colloquium).
Barrett, D.B.
    1968   *Schism and Renewal in Africa: An Analysis of Six Thousand Contemporary Religious Movements* (London: Oxford University Press).
Bennett, J.W., and M. Trumin
    1964   'Some Cultural Imperatives', in P. Hammond (ed.), *Cultural and Social Anthropology* (New York: Macmillan): 9-21.
Bennis, W., and P.E. Slater
    1968   *The Contemporary Society* (New York: Harper & Row).
Bertholet, A.
    1902   *Die Bücher Esra und Nehemia* (Tübingen: Mohr [Paul Siebeck]).

Blenkinsopp, J.
1989   *Ezra–Nehemiah: A Commentary* (London: SCM Press).
Bowman, R.A.
1954   'Introduction and Exegesis to the Book of Ezra and the Book of Nehemiah', *IB* 3: 551-819.
Bruner, E.M.
1974   'The Expression of Ethnicity in Indonesia', in A. Cohn (ed.), *Urban Ethnicity* (New York: Tavistock).
Childs, B.S.
1979   *Introduction to the Old Testament as Scripture* (London: SCM Press).
Clines, D.J.A.
1984   *Ezra, Nehemiah and Esther* (Grand Rapids: Eerdmans).
1989   'The Force of the Text', in J.C. Exum (ed.), *Signs and Wonders: Biblical Texts in Literary Focus* (Atlanta: Scholars Press): 199-215.
1990   'The Nehemiah Memoir: The Perils of Autobiography', in *What Does Eve Do to Help? And Other Readerly Questions to the Old Testament* (JSOTSup, 94; Sheffield: JSOT Press): 124-64.
Cohn, A.
1969   *Custom and Politics in Urban Africa* (Berkeley: University of California Press).
Cox, H.
1969   *The Feast of Fools* (Cambridge, MA: Harvard University Press).
Eskenazi, T.C.
1988   *In an Age of Prose: A Literary Approach to Ezra–Nehemiah* (Atlanta: Scholars Press).
Fensham, F.C.
1982   *The Books of Ezra and Nehemiah* (Grand Rapids: Eerdmans).
Festinger, L.
1957   *A Theory of Cognitive Dissonance* (Stanford: Stanford University Press).
Goodenough, W.H.
1966   *Cooperation in Change: An Anthropological Approach to Community Development* (New York: John Wiley & Sons).
Hiebert, P.
1976   *Cultural Anthropology* (Philadelphia: J.B. Lippincott).
Kellermann, U.
1967   *Nehemia: Quellen, Überlieferung und Geschichte* (BZAW, 102; Berlin: Töpelmann).
Kidner, F.D.
1979   *Ezra and Nehemiah* (Leicester: Inter-Varsity Press).
Lewin, K.
1947   'Frontiers in Group Dynamics', *Human Relations* 1: 5-41.
Lichtman, A.J.
1978   *Your Family History* (New York: Vintage Books).
Linton, R.
1943   'Nativistic Movements', *American Anthropologist* 45: 230-40.
Machiavelli, N.
1963   *The Prince* (ed. L. Crocker; New York: Washington Square Press) (Original Italian, 1513).

Mowinckel, S.
1964a   *Studien zu dem Buche Ezra–Nehemia*. I. *Die nachchronistische Redak-
             tion des Buches: Die Listen* (Oslo: Universitetsforlaget).
1964b   *Studien zu dem Buche Ezra–Nehemia*. II. *Die Nehemia-Denkschrift*
             (Oslo: Universitetsforlaget).
Myerhoff, B.
1982   'Rites of Passage: Process and Paradox', in V. Turner (ed.),
             Celebration (Washington, DC: Smithsonian Institution Press): 109-35.
Myers, J.M.
1965   *Ezra–Nehemiah* (AB, 14; Garden City, NY: Doubleday).
Niehoff, A.
1966   *A Casebook of Social Change* (Chicago: Aldine).
Noth, M.
1943   *Überlieferungsgeschichtliche Studien* (Halle: Max Niemeyer) (= ET,
             The Chronicler's History [JSOTSup, 50; Sheffield: JSOT Press,
             1987]).
Royce, A.P.
1982   *Ethnic Identity: Strategies of Diversity* (Bloomington: Indiana
             University Press).
Rudolph, W.
1949   *Esra und Nehemia samt 3. Esra* (Tübingen: Mohr [Paul Siebeck]).
Schaller, L.E.
1972   *The Agent of Change* (Nashville: Abingdon Press).
Tollefson, K.D.
1987   'The Nehemiah Model for Christian Missions', *Missiology* 15: 31-55.
Torrey, C.C.
1896   *The Composition and Historical Value of Ezra–Nehemiah* (BZAW, 2;
             Giessen: J. Ricker).
1910   *Ezra Studies* (Chicago: Chicago University Press).
Wallace, A.F.C.
1956   'Revitalization Movements', *American Anthropologist* 58: 264-81.
Williamson, H.G.M.
1985   *Ezra, Nehemiah* (Waco, TX: Word Books).
1987a   'Post-Exilic Historiography', in R.E. Friedman and H.G.M.
             Williamson (eds.), *The Future of Biblical Studies: The Hebrew
             Scriptures* (Atlanta: Scholars Press): 189-207.
1987b   *Ezra and Nehemia* (OTG; Sheffield: JSOT Press).
1988   'Structure and Historiography in Nehemiah 9', in D. Assaf (ed.),
             *Proceedings of the Ninth World Congress of Jewish Studies, Panel
             Sessions: Bible Studies and Ancient Near East* (Jerusalem: Magnes):
             117-31.

JSOT 54 (1992), pp. 25-43

OUT FROM THE SHADOWS:
BIBLICAL WOMEN IN THE POST-EXILIC ERA

Tamara C. Eskenazi

This paper has three related goals: first and foremost, to recover material concerning women for the purpose of shared communal inquiry; secondly, to begin to challenge the claim that the post-exilic era marks a decline in women's status; and, thirdly, to suggest a context for under-standing the opposition to foreign women in Ezra 9–10 and to draw from it implications concerning women's roles and rights.[1] The paper confines itself to only one of the different tasks of a feminist historiography of religion: the recovery of women's stories and traditions.[2] As the title indicates, my purpose is to bring biblical women of the post-exilic era out from the shadows.

The post-exilic or Persian period (sixth to fourth century BCE) was a pivotal era, a time of restructuring Jewish life in the aftermath of military, economic and religious devastation. Recognizing the importance of the era we ask: Where are the women? At first glance they seem absent. The long list of returnees often identifies the groups by referring to them as 'sons' (e.g. בני פרעש, lit. 'sons of Parosh', Ezra 2.3). The term אבות

---

1. An abbreviated version of this paper was presented at the Annual Meeting of the Society of Biblical Literature (New Orleans, November 1990). The paper is in indirect conversation with H.C. Washington, 'The "Strange Woman" of Proverbs 1–9 and Post-Exilic Judean Society', also presented at that meeting. I thank Professor Washington for making a copy of his paper available to me. My own study supports some of his conclusions by approaching the issues from another set of concerns and texts.

2. See, e.g., J. Plaskow, *Standing again at Sinai* (San Francisco: Harper & Row, 1990), esp. pp. 25-60. Plaskow identifies three necessary tasks: recovery, analysis and reconstruction (or reshaping of memory).

(lit. 'fathers', 'patriarchs') is a prominent word for community, replacing
מִשְׁפָּחָה (lit. 'family') or שֵׁבֶט (lit. 'tribe/clan') of the pre-exilic era. It is
perhaps such terminology that has encouraged some scholars to suggest
that this era is responsible for an entrenchment of patriarchy, after a presumably more egalitarian pre-exilic period. Thus, S. Terrien concludes
that 'the religious functions of men and women differed markedly
before and after the exile in Babylon (sixth century BC). Ancient Israel
ascribed to women a religious status that was displaced and lowered in
nascent Judaism.'[3] By 'nascent Judaism' Terrien refers to the community and literature developed during the Babylonian exile in the sixth
century BCE and shortly after.[4] He concludes, 'In the old days, woman
worshiped on a footing of equality with man. After the exile, woman
was relegated to the status of second-class religionist. It was only
through man that she had access to the holy.'[5]

Terrien's conclusion echoes the opinions of others who have considered ancient Israel superior to early Judaism, only this time superiority is
claimed on the basis of gender issues. But Bernadette Brooten[6] and
Carol Meyers[7] have taught us to look more closely at available sources
and ask new questions. Brooten identifies the presence of women in
leadership roles in Judaism during the Graeco-Roman period. She shows
how inscriptions contrast with and contest the evidence of the Mishnah.
Meyers, on the other hand, illustrates ways in which we can recover a
more plausible understanding of the reality of ancient Israelite women's
lives (as distinct from biblical representations of women) through a critical re-reading of the text and by using insights from the social sciences. I
draw upon their work as I examine an era chronologically situated

3. *Till the Heart Sings: A Biblical Theology of Manhood and Womanhood*
(Philadelphia: Fortress Press, 1985), esp. p. 4. See also E. Gerstenberger, *Jahwe—
ein patriarchaler Gott? Traditionelles Gottesbild und feministische Theologie*
(Stuttgart: Kohlhammer, 1988).

4. *Till the Heart Sings*, p. 71.

5. *Till the Heart Sings*, pp. 85-86. For a critique of several of Terrien's conclu-
sions, see M.I. Gruber, 'Women in the Cult according to the Priestly Code', in
J. Neusner, B.A. Levine and E.S. Frerichs (eds.), *Judaic Perspectives on Ancient
Israel* (Philadelphia: Fortress Press, 1987), pp. 35-48.

6. See her book, *Women Leaders in the Ancient Jewish Synagogue:
Inscriptional Evidence and Background Issues* (BJS, 36; Chico, CA: Scholars
Press, 1982).

7. *Discovering Eve: Ancient Israelite Women in Context* (Oxford: Oxford
University Press, 1988).

between the two that they explore. Like them, I argue that much more can be said about the roles and powers of ancient Jewish women than has been acknowledged hitherto.

With these observations as background, let us look at some post-exilic texts and ask our question: 'Where are the women, and what are they doing?' When we look closely we discover that hidden in the shadows stand several interesting Jewish women of the post-exilic period, some even more visible at times than their pre-exilic sisters. This paper focuses on two sources for the recovery of these women: the archives from the Jewish community in Elephantine, Egypt, and the book of Ezra–Nehemiah.

The Evidence of Elephantine

The prominence of women in the Elephantine documents has been recognized long ago. Several critical editions of the material have been available to scholars for some time.[8] About 25 years ago B. Porten had already highlighted the roles and lives of women in his book, *Archives from Elephantine*. As we come to ask new questions about women, Porten's pioneering work and the clarity with which the documents themselves speak about women prove to be exciting sources for fresh inquiry. I will sum up and illustrate some of the things that such an inquiry discloses.

The Jewish community in Elephantine consisted of Jewish mercenaries and some merchants who had settled there before the Persian conquest of Egypt in 525 BCE. The Jewish colony survived until about 400 BCE, when Egypt revolted against the Persians. Dozens of original contracts, family archives, letters and ostraca written during this period have been discovered in Elephantine since the nineteenth century. The Elephantine documents include the oldest Jewish papyri in existence, many of them

---

8.   A.E. Cowley, *Aramaic Papyri of the Fifth Century BC* (Oxford: Clarendon Press, 1923); G.R. Driver, *Aramaic Documents of the Fifth Century BC* (Oxford: Clarendon Press, rev. edn, 1965 [1954]); E.G. Kraeling, *The Brooklyn Museum Aramaic Papyri: New Documents of the Fifth Century BC from the Jewish Colony at Elephantine* (New Haven: Yale University Press, 1953); B. Porten, *Archives from Elephantine: The Life of an Ancient Jewish Military Colony* (Berkeley: University of California Press, 1968); B. Porten and A.L. Yardeni, *Textbook of Aramaic Documents from Ancient Egypt* (2 vols.; Winona Lake, IN: Eisenbrauns, 1986, 1989). In this essay, C refers to Cowley and K to Kraeling.

in good condition. Like the Qumran Scrolls, these primary documents
are significant for reconstructing the reality of an otherwise scarcely
known Jewish group, this time in the sixth–fourth century BCE. Like the
Scrolls, these documents challenge common perceptions about the
Judaism of that time and present an alternative. Much attention had been
lavished on the religious practices of the community. In particular,
Jewish worship in a temple to Yahu at Elephantine has been of interest,
as have the references to goddesses such as Anath (C 22.125). This
paper, however, is limited to sketching some important facts about the
lives of three women: Mibtahiah, Tapmut and Yehoishma.

The archives of Mibtahiah daughter of Mahseiah are fascinating. They
reveal a thrice married woman able to buy and sell property, inherit,
divorce and lend money. Cowley refers to her as the 'notorious'
Mibtahiah,[9] but we may think otherwise. Mibtahiah's story emerges
from a series of contracts involving property that her father bequeathed
to her. When Mibtahiah first marries a Jewish man, her father secures
her rights to property. A contract grants a portion of a house to
Mibtahiah (C 8, 460 BCE). The future husband has no entitlement to the
house (C 9); he may dwell there with her, but the property is hers.[10]
This husband, who bears a Jewish name, disappears from the records,
presumably because he died. Next Mibtahiah apparently marries an
Egyptian architect and later divorces him.[11] Their marriage and divorce
documents have not survived, but C 14 preserves the record of their
amicable division of property in which arrangements are made to everyone's satisfaction (it appears that Mibtahiah was also this husband's
business partner).

Shortly after, Mibtahiah marries another Egyptian architect. The marriage contract for this union (C 15, 441 BCE) is virtually complete, and it
is very interesting for several reasons. It indicates that Mibtahiah brings
much property to the marriage. It carefully spells out in detail what this
property is, and it stipulates what may happen to the property and
goods in the future. The contract shows that Mibtahiah's belongings
remain hers, regardless of marriage. It also contains stipulations to protect

---

9. *Aramaic Papyri*, p. 177.

10. In case of divorce, the contract, given to the husband, specifies: 'half of the
house *shall be* hers to take, and as to the *other* half you have power over it in return
for the improvements which you have made in this house' (C 9.10-12).

11. A property settlement is agreed upon (C 14, about 441 BCE).

both partners, allowing either to initiate a divorce.[12] There are, in
addition, provisions in case of abuse. In the course of time, two children
are born to this couple; they receive Hebrew names and the husband's
name changes from an Egyptian to a Hebrew one, suggesting that he
has become a member of her community, i.e., he has been integrated
into the Jewish community.[13]

A different story is that of Tamut or Tapmut, a woman, probably
Egyptian, who is one man's slave but another (free) man's wife. While
still a slave, Tamut marries a Jew named Anani son of Azariah. A series
of documents and contracts help us trace the fortunes of this woman
and her daughter.[14] Her marriage is recorded in a contract known as
K 2 (449 BCE), which is noteworthy for several reasons. First, Anani
ben Azariah is described as a לחן of Yahu the god who is in Yeb the
fortress' (K 2.2). The term לחן occurs several times in Elephantine documents, and, although its meaning is unclear, it has been understood to
refer to some kind of official in the temple.[15] Second, like other
Elephantine marriage contracts, this one indicates that either partner can
divorce the other, with financial burden falling on the one who initiates
divorce:

> If tomorrow or another day Anani rises up on account of her [?] and says,
> 'I divorce Tamut my wife', the divorce money is on his head. He shall
> give to Tamut in silver 7 shekels, 2 R., and all that she brought in in her
> hand she shall take out, from straw to thread. If tomorrow or another day,
> Tamut rises up and says, 'I divorce my husband Anani', a like sum shall

12. Mibtahiah can divorce Ashor (C 15.22ff.) and he can divorce her (C 15.27).
Stipulations are made also concerning abuse (C 15.29).

13. See C 18 and Cowley's comments and interpretation (*Aramaic Papyri*,
p. 84). It is noteworthy that such marriage was possible and unhindered by Persian
authorities. K.G. Hoglund, in his dissertation, 'Achaemenid Imperial Administration
in Syria–Palestine and the Missions of Ezra and Nehemiah' (PhD dissertation, Duke
University, 1989), claims, among other things, that Persian authorities required or
preferred ethnic purity. The Elephantine documents clearly challenge this part of
Hoglund's otherwise compelling thesis.

14. Most of these documents are included in Kraeling, *Brooklyn Museum
Aramaic Papyri*.

15. See Kraeling, *Brooklyn Museum Aramaic Papyri*, pp. 140, 144-45. But see
also Dan. 5.23. For a discussion of the term, see S.A. Kaufman, *The Akkadian
Influences on Aramaic* (The Oriental Institute of the University of Chicago,
Assyriological Studies, 19; Chicago: University of Chicago Press, 1974), p. 66
n. 176. I thank Donald R. Vance for this reference.

be on her head. She shall give to Anani in silver 7 shekels, 2 R., and all which she brought in in her hand she shall take out, from straw to thread (K 2.7-10).

According to this agreement, the surviving spouse also gains control over the property when the other dies. This contract shows that although Tapmut is still a slave, she is also a lawful wife and as such has property and legal rights.

Another document (K 4, Oct. 30, 434 BCE) tells us that Anani, who had purchased a house (K 3, Sept. 14, 437 BCE), gives Tapmut half of it. After her death, her portion is to go to the children of Tapmut and Anani, a son named Pilti and a daughter Yehoishma. Anani's portion likewise goes to these children when he dies.[16] It is clear in this document that both son and daughter inherit.

Approximately ten years later (K 5, June 12, 427 BCE), Tapmut and her children are released from slave status by their master.[17] A few years later, Anani gives Tapmut's daughter Yehoishma, here identified as his daughter (whether biologically or legally is not specified), a house or part of a house (K 6, July 11, 420 BCE). Later that year Yehoishma marries. Her very extensive marriage contract (K 7, Oct. 2, 420 BCE)[18] discloses a great deal about Yehoishma and her status.[19] From the list of items in the contract, we discover that Yehoishma, a former slave and the daughter of a former slave, is quite wealthy. Much property and many movable possessions are hers and will remain with her if either she or the groom divorces the other. As in K 2, either party may initiate divorce and pay the equivalent of 'divorce proceedings' costs. Other stipulations in the contract are also reciprocal. The recurrence of such

16. All other relatives are excluded. Those excluded from claim to Tapmut's rights are: son, daughter, brother or sister of Anani (4.13); and those excluded from rights over the children's property at the death of Anani or Tapmut are: 'mother, father, brother, sister or another person' (4.19-20).

17. Although she is expected to look after her master, as a daughter or son would (K 5.11).

18. This contract is 'the most elaborate of the known Aramaic marriage documents' (Kraeling, *Brooklyn Museum Aramaic Papyri*, p. 201). The contract has 44 lines.

19. Here Ananiah son of Haggai asks for the bride in marriage. The one who gives her away is her so-called brother, son of her former owner (not Pilti her brother and son of her mother, nor Anani son of Azariah, her probable biological father and husband of her mother).

features indicates that K 2 is not unique but rather typical for Elephantine.

One other document among the remaining contracts, K 12 (Dec. 12, 402 or 401 BCE), deserves our attention. This is a document given (i.e. dictated) by *both* Anani and his wife Tapmut to their son-in-law (husband of Yehoishma) in the course of the sale of yet another house. What is fascinating for our purpose is the fact that Tapmut, an ex-slave, now sells property with her husband. Moreover, Tapmut, whose husband had been identified as a לחן of the temple of Yahu, is herself now identified as a לחנה of the temple of Yahu. In other words, although born an Egyptian and raised as a slave, she now has an official temple role.[20]

These documents from Elephantine begin to sketch legal and social roles for women that we do not normally ascribe to biblical or post-exilic communities. They show women in the Jewish community who are able to rise from slavery to a position in the temple, to divorce their husbands, hold property, buy and sell. The documents also confirm the fact that daughters inherit even when there is a son. Consequently, these documents compel us to revise some typical assumptions about women's roles in the post-exilic era.

The Evidence of Ezra–Nehemiah

Since the Elephantine documents come from Egypt, it may be claimed that the practices they disclose are uniquely Egyptian, not Jewish, and therefore say little about Judaism at the time, if by Judaism we mean the traditions preserved in the Bible and its communities. One must therefore ask: are these roles and rights similar to those in Judah? I contend that there was continuity during this Persian period between the practices in one Jewish community and another when both were under the same Persian imperial government, and communication was relatively easy and contacts were frequent. Furthermore, there are reasons to suppose that the marriage documents from Elephantine reflect

---

20. For a discussion of the meaning of the term, see Kaufman, *Akkadian Influences on Aramaic*, p. 66, and Kraeling's comment on K 12.2 (Kraeling, *Brooklyn Museum Aramaic Papyri*, p. 274). One cannot claim that Tapmut is an official in her own right. More likely she receives the title because she is the wife of an official. This, however, does not diminish the significance of the position and the title.

Mesopotamian rather than distinctly Egyptian customs, in which case similar influences could be supposed for Judah. E. Lipiński shows some important affinities between Elephantine marriage contracts and Mesopotamian ones. In particular, the provisions that enable a woman to initiate divorce appear in both Elephantine and Western Asiatic documents in contrast with earlier Egyptian marriage contracts. 'Thus the equal capacity of the spouses in Elephantine, at least as far as the dissolution of the marriage is concerned, is not due, in all likelihood, to the Egyptian environment, as some authors have surmised, but belongs to a genuine Semitic tradition.'[21] According to Lipiński, the fact that divorce on the wife's initiative first appears in Egypt in Persian times 'is best explained as the result of the Semitic influence'.[22] When we bear in mind that the decisive Jewish community in Judah had come from Babylonia, the influence of Mesopotamia upon its marriage practices becomes all the more probable. References to women in Ezra–Nehemiah indirectly support the view that wives in Judah had some similar rights.

As already noted, the use of the term אבות, 'fathers', sets a tone. It could be taken in at least two ways. The emphasis on 'fathers' could lead us to conclude that we are encountering 'patriarchy' and hence a system possibly inherently oppressive to women.[23] But we could instead understand 'fathers' to denote 'families', or 'ancestral houses' (as indeed many translators render the term),[24] signalling the resurgence of the family, or household, as the fundamental socio-economic and political unit. Scholars have argued that the various social and economic conditions during the period of the monarchy will have undermined the authority and economic role of the family unit.[25] C.V. Camp, who sums up the evolving roles of the family, observes that the post-exilic family was re-invested with authority and meaning that it had lost during the

21. 'The Wife's Right to Divorce in the Light of an Ancient Near Eastern Tradition', *Jewish Law Annual* 4 (1981), pp. 9-27 (20, 21).

22. 'The Wife's Right', p. 23. For a different view about the relation between marriage agreements from Babylonia and Egyptian practices, see M.T. Roth, *Babylonian Marriage Agreements 7th–6th Centuries BC* (AOAT, 222; Neukirchen–Vluyn: Neukirchener Verlag, 1989), esp. p. 14 n. 60.

23. But see Meyers, *Discovering Eve*, pp. 24-46.

24. See, e.g., J. Blenkinsopp, *Ezra–Nehemiah: A Commentary* (OTL; Philadelphia: Westminster Press, 1988), p. 76, translating Ezra 1.5.

25. See C.V. Camp, *Wisdom and the Feminine in the Book of Proverbs* (Bible and Literature Series, 11; Sheffield: Almond Press, 1985), pp. 244-46, for a convenient summary of pertinent changes during the monarchy.

monarchic period. In kingless Judah, the family once again 'not only functions as the primary unit of production of this period but also re-emerges as one locus of community-wide authority...'[26]

According to Meyers, socio-economic realities in pre-monarchic Israel dictated a certain practical egalitarianism between women and men in light of shared economic responsibilities. I suggest that conditions similar to pre-monarchic Israel recur in the post-exilic era. If, as Meyers holds, the emphasis on family in pre-monarchic Israel meant more equitable distribution of power for women, then the re-emergence of the family as the significant socio-economic unit in the post-exilic era likewise leads to greater power for women than was available during the monarchy. Other important conditions that Meyers identifies as conducive to gender parity in pre-monarchic Israel also recur in the post-exilic era and can therefore be supposed to generate similar dynamics. Once again, pioneer-life conditions characterize Judahite reality, and once again, the population is primarily rural (note the need to settle Jerusalem by casting lots and seeking volunteers; Neh. 11.1-2). Once again, the community experiences an era when internal boundaries are in flux.[27] If Meyers's thesis correctly describes pre-monarchic Israel, I suggest that it also supports a measure of egalitarianism in post-exilic Judah.[28]

The particular importance of women's roles in the post-exilic period had already been recognized by A. Causse, writing in 1929 and 1937.[29] As R.J. Coggins points out, Causse's conclusions sharply contrast with works such as Terrien's in that Causse identifies 'an increasingly important role for women' in the post-exilic period.[30]

26. *Wisdom and the Feminine*, p. 246. Camp devotes a whole chapter to 'The Ethos and World View of Post-Exilic Israel' (pp. 233-54).

27. See D.L. Smith, *Religion of the Landless: The Social Context of the Babylonian Exile* (Bloomington, IN: Meyer Stone Books, 1988). See also R.R. Wilson, 'Family', in P. Achtemeier (ed.), *Harper's Bible Dictionary* (San Francisco: Harper & Row, 1985), pp. 302-303.

28. To some extent, the force of my assertions in this essay depends on the solidity of Meyers's findings for pre-monarchic Israel. In another sense, however, my assertions depend on hints in the biblical texts for this period combined with the evidence of Elephantine.

29. *Les disperses d'Israël: Les origines de la Diaspora et son rôle dans la formation de Judaïsme* (Paris: Alcan, 1929), and *Du groupe ethnique à la communauté religieuse: Le problème sociologique de la religion d'Israël* (Paris: Alcan, 1937).

30. R.J. Coggins, 'The Origins of Jewish Diaspora', in R.E. Clements (ed.), *The World of Ancient Israel* (Cambridge: Cambridge University Press, 1989), p. 170.

Let us turn to Ezra–Nehemiah in order to examine what roles women have. As noted above, at first glance women seem all but absent from Ezra–Nehemiah, except as a problem when they are foreign. As such, their very presence is a problem for which absence is a solution. The most important example of this is Ezra 9–10. In these chapters Ezra is shocked by discovering that religious and other leaders have married women from 'the peoples of the lands' (Ezra 9.1-2).[31] He interprets this development as a dreadful violation of God's commandments, and he inspires the community to take steps against these marriages (Ezra 10).

The language of the opposition to these marriages is religious and ethnic, claiming that such marriages encroach on the holiness of the community and compromise the separation thought necessary for the maintenance of holiness. But recent studies have suggested a more economic and political basis for the opposition to mixed marriages. J.P. Weinberg, in particular, depicts the post-exilic community as a 'civic temple community' (*Bürger-Tempel-Gemeinde*),[32] and K.G. Hoglund

Coggins says that, in *Du groupe ethnique à la communauté religieuse*, 'Causse explored such issues as the effect of the exile on the family and the particular roles of individual members of the family, with an increasingly important role for women (this is in sharp contrast to some other more recent studies which have seen this as a time of increased patriarchalisation: Terrien, 1986, pp. 71-86)' ('Origins', p. 170).

31. The text states: 'After these things had been done, the officials approached me and said, "The people of Israel and the priests and the Levites have not separated themselves from the peoples of the lands whose abominations are like those of the Canaanites, the Hittites, the Perizzites, the Jebusites, the Ammonites, the Moabites, the Egyptians, and the Amorites. For they have taken some of their daughters to be wives for themselves and for their sons; so that the seed of holiness has mixed itself with the peoples of the lands. And in this faithlessness the hand of the officials and chief men has been foremost"' (Ezra 9.1-2). It is important to realize that the prohibitions against mixed marriages pertain to both men and women, according to Ezra's 'confession' (Ezra 10.12). The fact that the problem here is confined to foreign wives, not husbands, suggests that it is the men, thus far, who are the culprits. The patterns of intermarriage and the differences in such patterns between women and men are worth pursuing through the use of sociological models for analogous situations. See Smith, *Religion of the Landless*, for a helpful use of contemporary sociological models for an analysis of the postexilic era. See also T.C. Eskenazi and E.P. Judd, 'Marriage to a Stranger in Ezra 9–10', in T.C. Eskenazi and K.H. Richards (eds.), *Second Temple Studies*. II. *Temple and Community* (JSOTSup, 175; Sheffield: JSOT Press, 1994).

32. See, e.g., 'Die Agrarverhältnisse in der Bürger-Tempel-Gemeinde der

uses such an understanding of the post-exilic community to explain the specific economic and political grounds for opposition to mixed marriages.[33] These and other scholars suggest that concern with ethnic purity and objections to intermarriage are the products of the socioeconomic issues of the era. Thus Hoglund writes concerning Ezra 9–10,

> One dimension of marriage is as a means of transferring property and social status from one group to another. By circumscribing the options available in marriage through prohibition of marriage outside the group, all property, kinship-related rights and status remain within a closed group.[34]

Accordingly, ethnic purity may be an excuse for a more pragmatic economic and social concern about loss of inherited land. This explanation for the opposition to mixed marriages is appealing. Its strongest support comes, in my opinion, not from the sociological or linguistic analyses, but from Elephantine documents such as the ones we have discussed. *The fear of mixed marriages with their concomitant loss of property to the community makes most sense when women can, in fact, inherit.* Such loss would not be possible when women did not have legal rights to their husbands' or fathers' land. The Elephantine contracts thus help us understand the danger to the land and to the socio-economic life of the Judean community. The perceived socio-economic danger from foreign wives in Judah thereby implies that these women had similar rights to those held by women in Elephantine.

In reflecting on the subject of foreign wives, it is important to remember that an opposition to foreign women, so easy to criticize from a distance, is at the same time an affirmation of women who belong to the group. Although foreign women in Ezra 9–10 do not seem to have been given an opportunity to fight against divorce, it is the case that Ezra–Nehemiah considers foreign husbands as abhorrent as foreign wives. Consequently, the Judahites solemnly pledge not only to keep their sons from marrying outside the group but likewise to prevent their

Achämenidenzeit', *Acta Antiqua Academiae Scientiarum Hungaricae* 22 (1974), pp. 473-85.

33. See Hoglund, 'Achaemenid Imperial Administration', esp. pp. 380-453. See also Washington, 'The "Strange Woman" of Proverbs 1–9 and Post-Exilic Judean Society'.

34. Hoglund, 'Achaemenid Imperial Administration', pp. 436-37.

daughters from doing so. The intermarriage prohibitions of Ezra–Nehemiah are consistently symmetrical.[35] Rather than being simply a misogynous act, this dismissal of foreign wives is an opposition to some women in favor of others.

Let us now look at some women who are hidden in Ezra–Nehemiah. We turn first to the lists of returnees in Ezra 2 and its parallel in Nehemiah 7. The returnees are listed according to ancestors' names, place of origin or, occasionally, occupation; the names of family 'heads' are generally masculine. One group in particular is of special interest. Ezra 2.55 mentions the descendants of *hassōperet* (*sôperet* in Neh. 7.57; cf. 1 Esdr. 5.33). The word literally means 'the female scribe'. Translators or commentators, however, tend to say that this name denotes either a profession that had become a proper name,[36] or 'the guild or office of scribes'.[37]

Unfortunately, scholars regularly ignore some of the implications of this feminine form. They do not read here a reference to a female. The rationale for bypassing a reference to a woman is derived from the one example in Eccl. 1.1 where a seemingly feminine noun (*qōhelet*) refers to a masculine subject; it overlooks, alas, the numerous other occurrences of such feminine nouns that are recognized as references to females (for example, the word 'herald', *mᵉbaśśeret*, in Isa. 40.9, referring to a female herald, not simply to any professional announcer who is a member of a guild). Overruling the obvious meaning of the word seems to depend on the prior assumption that the term in Ezra–Nehemiah could not refer to a female scribe because such guilds were not likely to have existed in ancient Judah. Recognizing that conclusions from names are always tenuous, I nevertheless propose that we indeed consider the possibility that this family owes its origin to a female scribe. The presence of female scribes in the ancient Near East has been documented.[38] Furthermore, Ezra–Nehemiah itself indicates that a clan may

---

35. E.g., 'We will not give our daughters to the peoples of the land or take their daughters for our sons' (Neh. 10.30).

36. H.G.M. Williamson, *Ezra, Nehemiah* (WBC, 16; Waco, TX: Word Books, 1985), p. 27.

37. F.C. Fensham, *The Books of Ezra and Nehemiah* (NICOT; Grand Rapids, MI: Eerdmans, 1982), p. 55.

38. S. Meier, 'Women and Communication in the Ancient Near East' (unpublished paper, presented at the 1988 International Meeting of the SBL, Sheffield), illustrates the presence and functions of female scribes.

take the name of its matriarch (see below). Similar developments, I suggest, may account for this reference to a female scribe.[39]

When commentators ignore or dismiss the feminine aspect of the term, not so much on linguistic grounds as on the basis of presuppositions that mandate exclusion of women, they—translators and commentators, not the biblical text—efface women's presence. I have found only one who entertains the possibility of an actual female scribe: the Jewish mediaeval commentator who appears in *Miqra'ot Gedolot* for Ezra–Nehemiah as Abraham Ibn Ezra[40] proposes that the term could be translated as 'female scribe' (he writes concerning *hassōperet*, יתכן שהוא שם תואר לאשה או פועלת, 'It is possible that this is a title for a woman or a female worker').

Equally intriguing is the episode alluded to above, concerning a clan clearly named after the matriarch's family. According to Ezra 2.61 (Neh. 7.63 and 1 Esdr. 5.38), the Barzillai clan is named after the wife's family because the man has taken her name. Thus we read, 'the descendants of Barzillai (who had taken a wife from the daughters of Barzillai the Gileadite, and was called by their name)' (Ezra 2.61). Such appropriating of a wife's family name, which most likely indicates that the person also received a share of the wife's inheritance,[41] is rarely attested in the Bible. It therefore provides an important example of a deviation

---

39. Admittedly, one could argue that even if my assumption is correct that the reference is to a female scribe, the clan head would have been pre-exilic and therefore the text says little about post-exilic Judah (I am indebted to Donald R. Vance for this critique). The term, however, appears in two post-exilic lists (Ezra 2.55 and Neh. 7.57). Of the two, Ezra 2 is generally considered the later (see, e.g., H.G.M. Williamson, 'The Composition of Ezra i–vi', *JTS* NS 34 [1983], pp. 1-30). It is therefore noteworthy and significant that whereas Neh. 7.57 has *sôperet*, which could be either a name or a title, the later list in Ezra 2.55 has *hassōperet*, using the definite article and thereby eliminating the option of reading the word as a name. The fact that post-exilic scribes or transcribers apparently read *sôperet* as a title, not a name, indicates that the notion of a female scribe was a meaningful one in the post-exilic community.

40. Although the commentary on Ezra–Nehemiah in *Miqra'ot Gedolot* is attributed to Ibn Ezra, the actual commentator may be Moses Kimḥi (I thank Sara Japhet for this information).

41. Williamson writes, 'The difficulty in Barzillai's case was presumably that he had taken the name of his wife, who was not of a priestly family. He may have done this in order to become the family's heir. Kidner suggests that this "could have been regarded as a renunciation of his priesthood since priests were forbidden an inheritance in the land (Num 18.20)"' (*Ezra, Nehemiah*, p. 37).

from the more common pattern where the woman is incorporated into her husband's family by taking his name.

It is interesting to note another reference to women in the list. Having stated that 42,360 people had returned, the list mentions that there were, in addition, male and female servants and male and female singers (Ezra 2.65 // Neh. 7.67). It is tempting to link the female singers with the Temple cult, but their place in the list (between servants and animals) suggests that they more likely held a position of entertainers without much status.

Another interesting name appears in yet another list. According to Ezra 8.10, the descendants of Shelomith go up with Ezra. Like some other post-exilic names, Shelomith can be masculine or feminine.[42] The Greek versions of Ezra add a name (Bani) here, rendering the sentence in a way that excludes reading Shelomith as a woman's name: 'from the descendants of Bani, Shelomith son of Josiphiah...' The Hebrew text, however, leaves the sex of the person unspecified. This sentence in the MT states: 'From the descendants of Shelomith: the son of Josiphiah, and with him one hundred sixty men'. According to 1 Chron. 3.19, Shelomith is a daughter of Zerubbabel, the last-known descendant of David to possess any political power (see his role in the return in Ezra 1–6). A seal bearing an inscription 'to Shelomith, the maidservant of Elnathan' was discovered in 1975. E. Meyers identifies the seal with Shelomith, daughter of Zerubbabel, and argues that the seal offers a significant postscript to the fate of the Davidic house. He suggests that Elnathan, a governor of Judah (approximately 510–490 BCE), may have attached himself to the Davidic line by marrying Shelomith.[43] It is possible that Ezra 8.10 refers to descendants of the famed princess.

No one links Shelomith of the seal—or the one in 1 Chron. 3.19—with the Shelomith in Ezra 8.10. Instead, translations and commentaries typically erase Shelomith's presence by revocalizing the name and following the LXX, usually citing M. Noth as a source of authority. The reasons for choosing the LXX for Ezra 8.10 go back to M. Noth who considers שלמית a man's name and a corruption of שלמות.[44] The implicit

42. See J.J. Slotki: 'Only here is it used as a man's name; elsewhere it is borne by a woman (Salome)' (*Daniel, Ezra and Nehemiah* [London: Soncino, 1951], p. 157).

43. 'The Shelomith Seal and Aspects of the Judean Restoration: Some Additional Reconsiderations', *Eretz Israel* 17 (1985), pp. 33-38.

44. *Die israelitischen Personennamen im Rahmen der gemeinsemitischen*

rationale is clear. A clan's head is masculine, but this biblical text has a woman's name; it must be a mistake, hence the name must be changed. The logic is of course circular, though perfectly understandable in light of the presuppositions that have governed our reading of the post-exilic era.[45] Unfortunately, most recent commentaries reiterate Noth's view without exploring further the implications of the given MT text.[46]

Another interesting reference to women occurs in a list of those who built Jerusalem's walls. Neh. 3.12 reads:...ועל ידו החזיק שלום הוא ובנותיו, 'Next to him...Shallum repaired—he and his daughters' (JPS). The translations and commentaries are at times amusing, often irritating. The Jerusalem Bible emends the text, saying that the building was done by 'Shallum...by him and his sons'.[47] Batten is particularly amusing. He writes,

> 'Daughter' is a regular term for the hamlets which grow up about a city and which are dependent upon it, 11^{25-31}. Ryle prefers a literal interpretation that Shallum's daughters aided him in the work. But as women in the East were quite sure to have a large share in such work as this, their special mention here is unnecessary. Against the other view it may be urged that a solitary mention of hamlets is inexplicable. Berth[olet] says it would be easiest to reject the words but that such a course is arbitrary. *The meaning is really unknown.*[48]

Suddenly the meaning of 'he and his daughters' is unknown. It is most intriguing that a fairly clear statement should create such confusion, a confusion bred solely by a refusal to recognize the role of women in the building of the city walls. Fortunately, modern commentators fare better,

---

Namengebung (Stuttgart, 1928), p. 165 n. 6. See also A.H.J. Gunneweg: 'Since this can only be a man's name, it is to be corrected' (*Esra* [KAT; Gütersloh: Gerd Mohn, 1985], p. 145 n. 10b).

45. It is the case that Shelomith can be both masculine and feminine. It is masculine in 1 Chron. 26.28 and possibly in 2 Chron. 11.20. Shelomoth appears in the *kethib* of 1 Chron. 23.9; 26.25 and 26, but is altered to Shelomith in the *qere*. Nevertheless, the fact that Ezra 8.10 refers to a clan name that elsewhere in this era refers to a woman has not been brought to the attention of the readers, let alone argued one way or the other.

46. See, e.g., Blenkinsopp, *Ezra–Nehemiah*, p. 159.

47. Shallum is 'ruler of half the district of Jerusalem' (Neh. 3.12), which suggests that he belongs to a prominent family.

48. L.W. Batten, *A Critical and Exegetical Commentary on the Books of Ezra and Nehemiah* (ICC; New York: Charles Scribner's Sons, 1913), pp. 213-14 (emphasis added).

both as translators and interpreters. Williamson and Brockington resist emendation and suppose a reference to women. They conclude, on the basis of Num. 36.8, that, if Shallum had no sons, 'it would be natural for the daughters to help on an occasion like this, since they would inherit his name and property'.[49] On the basis of the Elephantine documents, we may add that daughters could inherit even when there were sons.[50]

The lists that have been examined thus far are among the most important ones in Ezra–Nehemiah,[51] referring to key events: the return from exile, and the building of the city's walls. If my readings are correct, then a woman makes an appearance in each of these events. These appearances are significant even if mere tokens.[52] Obviously, they do not establish gender balance but they nevertheless reflect women's presence in symbolic and practical ways.

Women have other roles in Ezra–Nehemiah. The prophet Noadiah (Neh. 6.14)[53] is an example. She appears as an opponent of Nehemiah. Since Nehemiah attacks many a leader who disagrees with his policies, little can be concluded about Noadiah's message. All we can determine is her prominence. After a confrontation with another prophet, Nehemiah calls for vengeance: 'Remember Tobiah and Sanballat, O my God, according to the things that they did, and also the prophet Noadiah and the rest of the prophets who wanted to make me afraid' (Neh. 6.14). We have no further information about Noadiah. The other named opponents are well known: Tobiah was an Ammonite official who has hampered Nehemiah all along; Sanballat was the governor of Samaria. The mention of this otherwise mysterious prophet together with them suggests that

49. Brockington, cited by Williamson, *Ezra, Nehemiah*, p. 207. Williamson writes, 'The reference to participation by Shallum's daughters is interesting. The temptation to emend to "sons" should be resisted... Nor can we interpret this as a reference to the (daughter) villages of Jerusalem, since the suffix "his" is masculine. If Shallum had no sons, "it would be natural for the daughters to help on an occasion like this, since they would inherit his name and property" (Brockington, with reference to Num 36.8)' (*Ezra, Nehemiah*, p. 207).

50. Thus Yehoishma daughter of Anani inherits even though she has a brother Pilti.

51. On the significance of lists, see T.C. Eskenazi, 'The Lists of Ezra–Nehemiah and the Integrity of the Book', *JBL* (1988) pp. 641-56.

52. Much as it is significant that one of the judges in the book of Judges is a woman.

53. Like Shelomith, the name Noadiah can be masculine and feminine. It is masculine in Ezra 8.33.

her status may be comparable, and that she, like them, was a prominent person. The reference to Noadiah the prophet further indicates that the prophetic office was open to a woman in the post-exilic period.[54]

Let me close with attention to women's presence at the climax of the restoration, namely at the public reading of the Torah. The climactic scene begins as follows:

> And Ezra the priest brought the Torah before the assembly (קהל), both men *and women* and all who could hear with understanding, on the first day of the seventh month. And he read from it facing the square before the Water Gate from early morning until midday, in the presence of the men *and the women* and those who could understand; and the ears of all the people were attentive to the book of the Torah (Neh. 8.2-4, emphasis added).

Later generations considered this gathering as a second giving of Torah, analogous to the Sinai event. *Qāhāl*, after all, refers not to a mere aggregate of people, but to a congregation constituted for official holy purposes.[55] But whereas there are doubts about the role and presence of women at Sinai, given the androcentric message 'do not go near a woman' (Exod. 19.15), which implies that only men were addressed, no such doubt belongs to this event. Here women's presence is explicitly and emphatically recognized (note the repetition), indicating religious egalitarianism, at least on this level of participation.

Conclusions

We have begun with two pictures, each one drawn from a separate community, and each based on different types of sources. I suggest that we link them. I have tried to bring the women of Elephantine to the fore as persons who have rights and roles that our biblical texts do not explicitly describe. I have also examined the overlooked presences of women in Ezra–Nehemiah. Without more documents from Judah, it is impossible to know for sure whether the Jewish women of Judah had privileges and obligations similar to those of their sisters in Elephantine. The evidence suggests that they probably did. The tension concerning foreign women is one such indication; the mention of women in key

---

54. Only four named women are called 'prophet' in the Hebrew Bible. The other three, Miriam, Deborah and Huldah, are pre-exilic.

55. See Deut. 31.9-13.

passages is another.[56] The pioneer conditions of the return and the new emphasis on the family add yet another piece of evidence. But even if one does not wholly accept an analogy between Jerusalem and Elephantine, one conclusion is nevertheless inevitable: whatever their precise role, the Jewish women in the post-exilic era have not been effaced from history. Their importance is attested in extant literature, some of their names and also some evidence about their significance have been preserved. It has been my intention to make them more visible. Recognized, these women can help us reconstruct the world of our mothers with greater precision and enhance our understanding of the roots of our cultural and religious traditions.[57]

56. E.g., the reference to *hassōperet/sôperet* and the Barzillai clan likewise contribute to this view.

57. Versions of this paper had been discussed in two settings: the Joint PhD Colloquium at Iliff School of Theology/Denver University in Denver, and the Jewish Feminist Critique Group in Los Angeles. I thank the participants for their rigorous critique and helpful suggestions. In particular, I thank Donald R. Vance (Iliff/Denver University), Miriyam Glazer (University of Judaism) and William Cutter (Hebrew Union College), who, as respondents, contributed stimulating insights to the work in progress.

INDEXES

INDEX OF REFERENCES

OLD TESTAMENT

INDEX OF AUTHORS